KU-452-308

Spectrum Guide to
TANZANIA

Camerapix Publishers International
NAIROBI

Spectrum Guide to Tanzania

Revised edition 1998

© 1992 Camerapix

First published 1992 by
Camerapix Publishers International
PO Box 45048
Nairobi, Kenya

ISBN 1 874041 69 5

This book was designed and produced by
Camerapix Publishers International
PO Box 45048
Nairobi, Kenya
Fax: (254-2) 448926/7
Tel: (254-2) 448923/4/5

E-mail: info@camerapix.com

The **Spectrum Guide** series provides a comprehensive and detailed description of each country covered, together with all the essential data that tourists, business visitors, or potential investors are likely to require.

Spectrum Guides in print:
African Wildlife Safaris
Eritrea
Ethiopia
India
Jordan
Kenya
Maldives
Mauritius
Namibia
Nepal
Pakistan
Seychelles
South Africa
Uganda
United Arab Emirates
Zambia
Zimbabwe

All rights reserved. No part of this publication may be reproduced, stored in a retrieval system, or transmitted in any form, or by any means, electronic, mechanical, photocopying, recording, or otherwise, without permission in writing from Camerapix Publishers International.

Printed in Hong Kong / China

Publisher and Chief Executive:
The Late Mohamed Amin
Project Director: Rukhsana Haq
Production Editor: Jan Hemsing
Picture Editor: Duncan Willetts
Editors: Catie Lott and Bob Smith
Associate Editor: Roger Barnard
Editorial Assistant: Rachel Musyimi
Photographic Research: Abdul Rehman
Design: Craiq Dodd
Graphics and Typography: Lilly Macharia

Editorial Board

This updated edition of *Spectrum Guide to Tanzania* is one of the latest in the acclaimed series of high-quality, colourfully illustrated international *Spectrum Guides* to exotic and exciting countries, cultures, flora and fauna.

Home to Africa's highest mountain, its deepest lake and one of the last great animal migrations, Tanzania is a country that constantly invites superlatives.

This spectacular tourist destination appears in living colour thanks to the photographic work of *Spectrum Guide* Publisher and Chief Executive The Late **Mohamed Amin** and his colleague, **Duncan Willetts,** who is equally renowned for his superb photography. Tanzania, with its mountains, forests, lakes, rivers and game-filled savannah plains, has long been one of their favourite countries.

The person responsible for the complex liasion and logistics was *Spectrum Guides* Project Director **Rukhsana Haq.**

Working closely together, Editors **Catie Lott** and **Bob Smith** laboured long and hard to produce a fascinating, in-depth and readable guide book.

Calling upon his extensive knowledge of the country, Englishman **John Barraclough** waxed poetically upon the history of the country as well as its many special features. Additional input also came from a number of Tanzanian experts, including long-time residents **Graham Mercer** and **David Bygott; Barry Whittemore,** whose expertise on Tanzanian bird life proved invaluable; **Ed Wilson**, of the World Wildlife Fund in Eastern Africa; **Sam Kasulwa,** of the Tanzania National Parks staff; and **Ian Parker,** a noted naturalist who has worked in the field of African wildlife for nearly half a century.

Jennifer Trenholm coordinated the preparation of manuscripts for typesetting, with the help of Editorial Assistant Kenyan **Rachel Musyimi. Craig Dodd,** one of Europe's leading graphic designers, was responsible for the book's design, with responsibility for the latest revised edition in the hands of **Lilly Macharia.** Production Editor **Jan Hemsing** organized and compiled voluminous details and kept it on line while Kenyan **Abdul Rehman** oversaw photographic research.

Top: Aerial splendour of the yellow-billed stork.
Above: Coconuts gathered by this young Tanzanian proliferate throughout the coast.

TABLE OF CONTENTS

Half-title: *Panthera leo*, largest of Africa's big cats, is a familiar resident of the Serengeti.

Title page: Once common throughout Africa, the elephant now roams less than one-fifth of the continent. Overleaf: Zebra and flamingo share the alkaline waters of Lake Magadi on the Ngorongoro Crater floor. Following pages: Looking out over the Ngorongoro Crater.

Pages 12-13: Reusch Crater and its inner ash pit lie atop Kilimanjaro, the highest point in Africa.

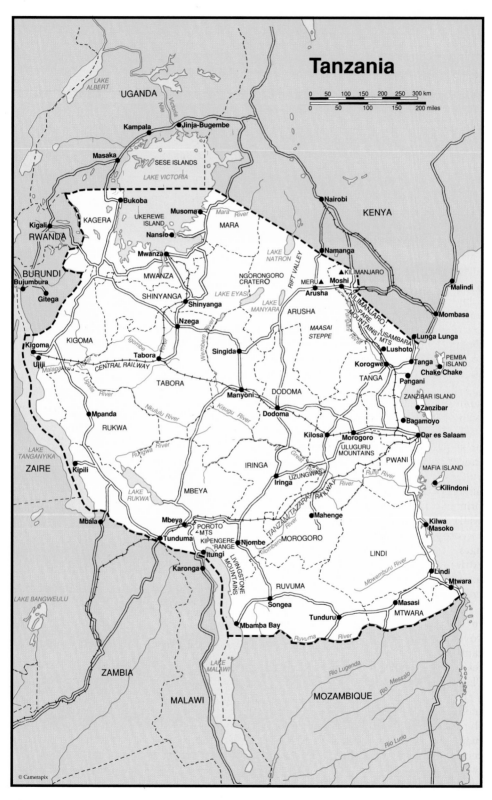

Tanzania

The Tanzania Experience

Think of the "African experience" and a kaleidoscope of images springs to mind; herds of zebra, wildebeest and gazelle stretching to the horizon under pearly dawn skies; a cheetah stalking through dry grass; a warrior striding into the sunset; white beaches backed by coconut palms swaying in the breeze off a warm sea; a snow-capped mountain rising out of the red dust of the plains.

All these images reflect the beauty of not simply a great continent, but just one country — Tanzania.

Basking south of the Equator over an area half the size of Western Europe, Tanzania is a land of boundless fascination and diversity. From the vast lakes of the interior to the blue waters of the Indian Ocean, and from the northern mountains to the southern Ruvuma River, the country is a mosaic of tropical forest, savannah grassland and shimmering lakes containing some of the largest and most beautiful wilderness areas in the world.

But Tanzania is much more than a set of stereotyped Hollywood images. It is a modern, progressive state with a rich cultural and historical heritage that began almost four million years ago when our primitive ancestors first left the forest and walked upright onto the plains.

Formed by massive earth upheavals of ages past, when the Rift Valley split East Africa from Mozambique to Ethiopia, the area was already home to an ape-like creature that stood on two legs.

This ancient traveller left his footprints in Laetoli, northern Tanzania, to be discovered in 1979 by Mary Leakey, of the famous husband and wife archaeological team. The fossils proved to be the oldest "hominid" tracks so far unearthed.

During excavations twenty years earlier more evidence was discovered to support the view that Tanzania is the cradle of mankind. At nearby Olduvai Gorge, fossil remains of *Homo habilis*, or "Handy Man", were dated by Dr Louis Leakey as 1.75 million years old. He believed that *habilis* had the physical attributes and intelligence to make tools and, as such, was a possible direct ancestor of modern man.

This early relative eventually migrated from East Africa, its descendants returning centuries later from Asia, India, Europe and other parts of the continent as traders, warriors, farmers, craftsmen and explorers. Throughout the ages they intermingled, melding the people, their history, language, customs and culture into contemporary Tanzania.

Today Tanzania is united in independence; a people proud of their past with a vision of the future . . . and a land still waiting to be discovered by those who dream of seeing the legendary animals of the Serengeti or the famous snows of Kilimanjaro.

Welcome.

Above: Young Maasai girl who has undergone the circumcision ritual.

Travel Brief and Social Advisory

Some do's and don'ts to make your visit more enjoyable.

Getting around

By road

The main overland routes to Tanzania are from Kenya's capital city of Nairobi to Arusha via the border town of Namanga, and to the coastal ports of Dar es Salaam or Tanga from the busy Kenya port of Mombasa via the border point of Lunga Lunga. Travel from Malawi is possible over the Songwe Bridge between Karonga and Mbeya along the shore of Lake Malawi. From Uganda there is a road linking Bukoba to Masaka and Kampala. The TANZAM/TAZARA railway is the most popular form of transport from Zambia, although it is also possible to drive. The 'Tanzam Highway' from the Zambian border to Dar es Salaam is excellent along much of its length. From Morogoro or Dar es Salaam, the Chalinze to Moshi road is also excellent except for a short distant between Korogwe and Mombo.

Often the amount of fuel travellers can purchase at official prices is limited. If you buy petrol on the black market, expect to pay more than the going pump rate. Assuming you have enough petrol, prepare yourself for a bouncing, roller-coaster ride, for the roads are in a constant state of disrepair. Slow and easy are the watch words when touring Tanzania.

Along with the huge craters that can swallow up small cars, other hazards include unpredictable cyclists, careless pedestrians, cattle, goats, sheep, donkeys, unannounced road work, and just plain old bad drivers. Risky options to driving one's own vehicle are buses or *matatus* (a flag-me-down form of workers' taxi). In either case, break-downs are frequent and accidents commonplace.

Regular bus shuttle services operate Nairobi-Arusha-Moshi and Moshi-Arusha-Nairobi.

Several towns (Arusha and Moshi, for example) have central bus stations. Others (Dar especially) have no central depot and buses leave from various points, so ask if you're unsure. Don't allow your luggage to be placed on top of a bus, for your bag may be noticeably lighter by the time you reach your destination . . . or missing altogether.

By air

Dar es Salaam is a popular gateway to East Africa, with a steady stream of international flights. Airlines linking Dar and Kilimanjaro International Airport to the rest of the world include Aeroflot, Air France, Air India, Air Malawi, Air Tanzania, Air Zimbabwe, Alliance Airways, British Airways, Egypt Air, Ethiopian Airlines, Gulf Air, Kenya Airways, KLM, New ACS, Royal Swazi and Swissair.

International tickets must be paid for in hard currency, even when you have bank receipts to prove that the money was exchanged legally. Air Tanzania (whose planes can be identified by the giraffe on their tails) services domestic routes.

Small jets are used between the main airports — Dar, Kilimanjaro, Mwanza, and Zanzibar — while lighter aircraft service the more remote strips — Bukoba, Dodoma, Iringa, Kigoma, Kilwa, Pemba, Shinyanga, Songea, Tabora and Tanga.

By boat

It is possible to reach Tanzania via neighbouring Burundi and Zambia aboard the historic MV *Liemba*, the main ferry plying the waters of Lake Tanganyika. There is no longer a ferry service between Tanzania and the Congo, but cargo boats regularly make the trip and, with a bit of negotiating, it is possible to hitch a ride for a reasonable price. From Kenya you can cross Lake Victoria by ferry from Kisumu to either Mwanza or Musoma.

Opposite: Welcoming faces of Tanzania.

Above: Dar es Salaam's modern railway station.

By train

Most of Tanzania's major towns are connected by rail with the exception of Bagamoyo and Kilwa. It is also possible to travel from Zambia to Dar on the TANZAM (Great Uhuru) Railway. Built by the Chinese in 1960, this railway route passes through some of the most remote — yet spectacular — country in Africa, including part of the vast Selous Game Reserve.

There are three classes on the Tanzania trains and only first class is recommended for long-distance journeys. Fuel shortages and breakdowns make schedules erratic.

The people

The 1996 population of Tanzania was estimated at twenty-eight million. Africans make up the majority of the mainland population with more than 120 tribes. No tribe exceeds more than ten per cent of the population, with the Sukuma being the largest. Other major tribes include the Nyamwezi, Ha, Makonde, Gogo, Haya and Chagga. The Arab influence on Zanzibar

and Pemba islands is reflected in the people who are a mix of Shirazis (from Persia), Arabs and Comorans (from the Comoro Islands).

Safety

Tanzania is one of the poorest countries in the world, so it is unwise to make an ostentatious display of wealth. Rather than invite temptation, leave family treasures at home. Dar es Salaam is as safe as most capital cities in Africa, but apply common sense. Muggings do take place after dark and bag- and watch-snatching can occur during the day. Safeguard money, passports, traveller's cheques and airline tickets. Do not leave personal documents in your hotel room. Most hotels and lodges have safes, but always obtain a receipt.

Clothes

Tanzania has no winter, and lightweight clothing is worn all the year-round. For women, cotton slacks and a blouse on safari along with a lightweight casual dress for evenings is ideal. For men, cotton sport

18

Above: Descending a steep and twisty murram road into the Great Rift Valley.

shirts and trousers or safari suits during the day and a jacket for evenings. Mornings are hot and a wide-brimmed hat and sunglasses are a must. Northern Tanzania and the highlands can be cool in the evening, so take a cardigan or jacket. For footwear, choose comfort before style. Pavements are uneven and dusty in the cities and towns, and nonexistent in the bush. It is considered insulting by local tradition to dress scantily or improperly.

Laundry

Laundry services are available at large hotels and resorts. Low-budget travellers must be prepared to wash by hand as laundry services are nonexistent outside major towns. Consider packing drip-dry clothing.

Health

A yellow fever certificate is mandatory if you are arriving from an infected area. Vaccinations for cholera, tetanus, yellow fever, hepatitis, TAB and polio are strongly advised. Malaria is endemic in all lowland areas and particularly virulent. It is not only extremely debilitating but potentially deadly. Take a prophylactic starting two weeks before your arrival. Consult a doctor for the most suitable type. If you suffer any kind of fever on your return, seek treatment *immediately* and tell your doctor where you have travelled. Do not drink the local water. Stick to bottled or sterilized liquids and avoid iced drinks. Bilharzia (minute flatworms carried by freshwater snails) is endemic in many lakes and rivers in Africa. Resist the temptation to swim or wash in them. The disease is painful and causes cumulative liver damage. Lake Victoria is heavily infested. Medical insurance is strongly advised.

What to take

Carry enough prescribed drugs for your trip. Pharmaceuticals are expensive and often unavailable. It is a good idea to carry a spare pair of glasses or solution for contact lens wearers.

19

Photography

Carry enough photographic equipment and film with you as very little is available outside Dar es Salaam, Arusha and Zanzibar. What can be found in the major towns is limited (slide film is virtually unavailable) and expensive. Check at large hotels if you're desperate. A word of caution; don't take photographs of anything associated with the government or the military. At best your film may be confiscated. At worst you could end up in the nearest jail. If you wish to photograph an individual, always ask permission.

When to go

The best seasons for photographic safaris in northern Tanzania are between November and March, and June and October. In the south, central and western areas of Tanzania, the months between June and November are more suitable. A visit to either the Selous or Rungwa Reserve is best planned between July and November. Tourists willing to brave 'off season' are rewarded with greener parks at their best for photography, special hotel and lodge rates, and fewer visitors.

On safari

You'll enjoy Tanzania all the more if you plan your itinerary carefully, allowing adequate sight-seeing in each place. It may mean limiting the parks and reserves on your list, but it also means cutting down the number of jolting kilometres you travel each day.

Remember, the animals are wild! Do not feed them or make excessive noise to attract their attention. Keep to designated trails and never leave your vehicle except at recognized areas. Close all windows and zippers when leaving your room or tent. Many visitors chart the success of their safari by how many animals they sight in the shortest possible time. But try reading up on wildlife before your visit so you can identify not only the 'big five' but also the smaller animals and birds. Tell your guide

that you are in no hurry. The slower you drive the more you see. Keep your camera loaded and ready for action. The best time to view wildlife is early morning or late afternoon.

Money on safari

A good supply of traveller's cheques is essential. In remote parts, a supply of cash is also advisable as banks (if there are any) may only be an agency operating once or twice a week.

On the beaten track

Take enough Tanzanian shillings to cover running expenses as well as extra for emergencies. The rest should be in traveller's cheques. Most hotels require payment in hard currency and independent travellers should be aware of 'hidden extras' (such as service fees and sales tax) that may be added to the bill. Make sure you are aware of all the charges before accepting accommodation. Unless you're camping or staying in low-budget establishments, an abundance of Tanzanian money is probably unnecessary. Before you change cheques to buy souvenirs and gifts, shop around for the best exchange rate. Hotels tend to charge a hefty commission. Credit cards can be invaluable for settling bills at major hotels or lodges.

Off the beaten track

Currency exchange outside major towns, and particularly on the northern game circuit, can involve problems when it comes to large denomination notes. Never rely on changing traveller's cheques except at an overnight stop. Even then hotel staff may not know the current exchange rate and may be reluctant to take your word. Carry small denomination notes and packets of cigarettes for the 'helpers' who suddenly appear when your vehicle has a flat tyre or you become bogged down in the mud. Local muscle power can be a blessing when the alternative could mean being stranded for hours or even days.

Opposite: Chapel of the Catholic Mission in Bagamoyo, terminus for the great caravans from the interior and the starting point for early explorers.

Where to stay

Tanzania offers a wide range of accommodation, from interesting, well-sited, recently constructed hotels like the luxury Sheraton Dar es Salaam, game lodges to hostels for the intrepid young. Back-packers should be prepared to carry their own bedding, food, crockery, cutlery and cooking utensils. See Listings for 'Accommodation'.

Camping

Camping in the bush is the ultimate way to enjoy Africa. But high fees make this prohibitive for the budget visitor.

Camping fees in the national parks and park entry fees per person and per vehicle increase with monotonous regularity. It has become a way of life and not only in Africa. The rates for vehicles registered outside the country are considerably higher than for Tanzanian-registered vehicles. All fees must be paid in foreign currency and are subject to change. Four-wheel drive vehicles are strongly recommended.

Up-to-date prices for accommodation and park entry can be obtained from tour operators or the National Park Headquarters, PO Box 3134, Arusha, Tanzania.

Pitch camp well before sundown, if possible on level ground with short grass and plenty of shade. Thorn trees provide cover but the thick carpet of thorns beneath them can make sleeping uncomfortable.

Avoid dried-up river beds: sudden storms create flash floods that could sweep you away — vehicle and all. Do not camp across or next to game trails. Animals can be curious as well as dangerous. Ensure adequate control of camp fires. If stones are available, place them around the fireplace and make sure all dry grass and leaves are cleared. Your camping list should include: tents with sewn-in groundsheets and mosquito-net windows, sleeping bags, folding chairs and table, pots and pans, airtight containers for bread and biscuits, salt and sugar, at least one axe for clearing camping sites and chopping wood, a bowl for washing, a kettle for tea and coffee, a gas lamp, flashlight, candles, matches, spade (preferably the folding variety), lots of water, plates, mugs, knives, forks, spoons, food, insect repellent, and a pair of binoculars.

National Anthem

1. Mungu ibariki Afrika
Wabariki viongozi wake
Hekima, umoja, na amani
Hizi ni ngao zetu
Afrika na watu wake.

Chorus: Ibariki Afrika
Ibariki Afrika
Tubariki watoto wa Afrika.

2. Mungu ibariki Tanzania
Dumisha uhuru na umoja
Wake kwa waume na watoto
Mungu ibariki
Tanzania na watu wake.

Chorus: Ibariki Tanzania
Ibariki Tanzania
Tubariki watoto wa Tanzania.

English Translation

1. God bless Africa
Bless its leaders
Let wisdom, unity,
and peace be the shield of
Africa and its people.

Chorus: Bless Africa
Bless Africa
Bless the children of Africa.

2. God bless Tanzania
Grant eternal freedom and unity
to its sons and daughters
God bless Tanzania and its people.

Chorus: Bless Tanzania
Bless Tanzania
Bless the children of Tanzania.

Opposite: With a little help from their friends, two fishermen haul their *ngalawa* to shore at low tide.

PART ONE: HISTORY, GEOGRAPHY, AND PEOPLE

Above: Zanzibar was the starting point for many explorers, as this house plaque indicates. Fresh produce, supplies, and labour were easily procured from the island.

Opposite: One of 560 carved Islamic doors found on Zanzibar. Their cultural and historical importance is now recognized and many are being restored.

Land of Lakes and Mountains

An East African leviathan girded by Equatorial splendour, Tanzania warms its eastern borders in the pellucid waters of the Indian Ocean. Off its white sandy beaches and mangrove swamps lie the balmy islands of Pemba, Mafia and Zanzibar.

Inland the country is largely bounded by natural frontiers — Lake Tanganyika, Africa's deepest lake, to the west; Lake Malawi in the south-west; the Ruvuma River forms the southern border with Mozambique; Lake Victoria, the world's second-largest lake, borders the north; and volcanic Mount Kilimanjaro, Mount Meru and Mount Longido in the north-east separate Tanzania from Kenya.

These 945,087 square kilometres (364,898 square miles) are dotted with permanent and seasonal lakes and rivers, including the Great Ruaha, the Rufiji, and tributaries of the Nile, which give the country more surface water than any other in Africa.

Tanzania includes the highest and lowest points on the continent: snow-capped Kilimanjaro at 5,896 metres (19,340 feet), and the bottom of Lake Tanganyika, 358 metres (1,174 feet) below sea-level.

It is home to one of the world's last great herds of plains game roaming some of the wildest and least spoilt natural areas, including three World Heritage Sites — Serengeti National Park, Ngorongoro Crater and Selous, the largest game reserve in Africa. Nearly a quarter of all Africa's game is found on the savannahs of Tanzania and one-quarter of the country is made of protected areas; in short, a land made for safari.

Savannah is perhaps the quintessential African landscape, but Tanzania has much more. Mountain ranges, woodland and forest, marsh and swamp, rivers and lakes, mangroves and coral reefs.

Only a very small proportion of this varied terrain is cultivated, by a ninety-three per cent rural population concentrated in the fertile northern highlands around Kilimanjaro, the shores of Lake Malawi, and south of Lake Victoria. From the fertile coastal zone the plain rises up to the Maasai Steppe, an area encompassing 51,800 square kilometres (20,000 square miles) of open grassland supporting three million head of game in the Serengeti alone. Semi-arid, the steppe is an undulating carpet of red oat grass in the rainy season, broken only by the eroded stumps of old, hard basement rocks called inselbergs, or *kopjes.*

The eastern arm of the Rift Valley — which has done so much to form the topography of the land — is about 100 kilometres (62 miles) wide here, dividing the northern steppe from the vast Central Plateau that lies at 1,200 metres (4,000 feet). The Kiswahili name for this semi-arid interior, where only 500 millimetres (20 inches) of undependable rain falls each year, is *nyika*, meaning dry or wasteland, hence the old British name for the country, Tanganyika.

Most of the country enjoys a single rainy season from December to May, although the north and the coastal strip have two rainy periods — one in October and November, the other in April and May.

Roughly encircling the interior is a broken curve of ancient crystalline hills. They rise below Kilimanjaro as the North and South Pare Mountains and the Usambaras, then swing south-west through the Ulugurus and the Udzungwas to finish as the Southern Highlands around the town of Mbeya near Lake Malawi.

These mountains preserve isolated remnants of the Equatorial forest that once stretched in an unbroken belt from West to East Africa. Now they are islands of endemic species, home to animals and plants found nowhere else in the world.

Tanzania's predominant vegetation is tsetse-fly infested miombo woodland; a belt of grassland with fairly thick *Brachystegia* tree cover that reaches from the western

Opposite: Coconut trees are an essential component of coastal life. Every part of the tree is used — the palm frond, the timber, and the creamy fruit.

shores of Lake Victoria to Mozambique. Occasionally this zone of scattered low trees is pocked with smooth granite inselbergs, providing some visual relief in an otherwise monotonous landscape.

Towards Lake Rukwa, in the south, the miombo gives way to more varied vegetation and around Ruaha, Tanzania's second-largest national park, the undulating plateau cut by the Ruaha River supports a bushland of commiphora, acacia and giant baobabs.

Population

Spread across this vast topographical tapestry are twenty-eight million people made up of more than 120 loosely defined 'tribes'. They range from the few hundred Hadzabe, ancient nomadic hunters who live near Lake Eyasi in the north, to the million-strong Sukuma of southern Lake Victoria.

The Hadzabe (Kindiga) speak a Khoisan, or 'click' language similar to the Bushmen of the Kalahari Desert. They are thought by some to be direct descendants of the Stone Age hunter-gatherers who built burial mounds in the Ngorongoro Crater.

Some of these cultural groups can trace an ancestry to prehistoric times; others are merely immigrants of the last 100 years.

It is Tanzania's geography that dictates its demographic map. Poor soil throughout much of the country means that the population is unevenly distributed. South of the Central Line stretching from Kigoma to Dar es Salaam, large areas remain completely uninhabited.

The major centres of population are on the coast — Dar es Salaam is the largest city with two million inhabitants — the shores of Lake Victoria, and on the fertile soils of the northern mountains around Arusha and Moshi.

Tanzania, like many other third-world countries, is experiencing increased urbanization as country folk migrate to the city and the towns.

But movement within and across borders is not a new phenomenon. Migration into and colonization of East Africa has occurred for centuries.

Tanzania has seen Nilotic wanderers — such as the Maasai — and Hamitics from Southern Arabia, Phoenicians, Persians, Omani Arabs, Chinese, Portuguese, Dutch, Germans and the British all make their mark as invaders, traders and travellers.

The first wave of migrants were the Bantu. In the first millennium they came from southern and western Africa, absorbing the resident hunter-gatherers and introducing their skills as ironworkers and potters. In doing so they encouraged settled communities such as Engaruka north of Lake Manyara, which today retains impressive examples of early irrigation schemes.

Ninety-five per cent of Tanzania's Africans derive from this Bantu stock, thought to be an amalgam of Hamitic and Negroid people.

This new blood and its intermingling with indigenous people created a melting pot of languages and cultures that is one of the richest and most varied on the continent. Today the vast majority of Tanzanians speak one or more of the hundreds of dialects that the Bantu language generated as it spread throughout the region.

And it was out of Bantu, with later Arabic contributions, that Kiswahili evolved, the national language and the lingua franca of East Africa. Today fifty million people speak it, from Somalia to Mozambique, Madagascar to the Congo (Zaire).

The Arabs also made another significant contribution to the development of Tanzania. On the coast they built a flourishing Islamic civilization and intermarried freely with the coastal tribes, producing the distinctive Swahili culture and people found on Zanzibar. Beginning around AD 700, Islam spread from the coast to the interior and now Muslims account for one-third of the population.

Even more numerous are the Christians, a result of the nineteenth-century arrival of missionaries from Europe. Despite their evangelical efforts to 'save the Godless', most Tanzanians retain a strong belief in natural spirits, and magic is still an important influence on people's everyday lives.

History: From the Cradle to Independence

An innocuous signpost on the dusty road from Ngorongoro Crater to the Serengeti directs visitors down a track leading, five kilometres (three miles) later, to a dry, undistinguished canyon. Yet it was there, in 1959, that the discoveries of Mary Leakey made world headlines.

Olduvai Gorge is a fifty-kilometre-long (31-mile) natural trench hewn out of the Serengeti Plain, containing walls of exposed fossil-bearing strata dating from almost two million years ago. Its fossils and their manner of preservation make it an ideal site to investigate the ultimate conundrum — the origin of man. One key question for anthropologists remains: at what point did hominids — man's antecedents — diverge from the pongids, or true apes?

There is general agreement that this fork in the evolutionary tree occurred sometime during the last half of the Miocene epoch (24-25 million years ago). Towards the end of this era and the start of the Pleistocene period the world experienced dramatic climatic change.

In tropical Africa temperatures dropped and it became drier. Vast areas of jungle retreated to leave a new type of vegetation cover — savannah. Animals, including apes, were forced out of the shrinking forest into this new environment, triggering major evolutionary changes. Some animals became extinct while other species were created. Many new types of antelope began to appear in the fossil record for the first time.

In 1931 Louis Leakey, the son of a British missionary family working in Kenya, began looking for evidence of the hominid-pongid split at Olduvai with his wife Mary.

Over the years the Leakeys uncovered a large collection of primitive pebble tools, but hominid fossils of any importance remained stubbornly hidden. The couple had to wait until 1959 before their major breakthrough.

Out walking one morning while Louis recovered from fever, Mary spotted two huge teeth and a fragment of skull in a small gully. Crying, 'I've got him! I've got him', she ran back to the tents with the news.

From the 400 fossil bone fragments picked out of the site using dental tools and camel hair brushes, the skull of an adult male hominid was reconstructed. (See 'A Return to Man's Beginning', Part Two.)

It was given the name *Zinjanthropus* — Nutcracker Man — due to its massive teeth and cheekbones. Aged 1.8 million years old, it was later renamed *Australopithecus boisei*, and is now in the National Museum at Dar es Salaam. *Australopithecus boisei* was crucially important. But later discoveries overshadowed it.

Perhaps the most controversial was the collection of bones Louis Leakey named *Homo habilis* — Handy Man. Living between 1.8 and 1.6 million years ago, Handy Man's large cranial capacity and well-developed hands suggest he was a maker of tools — and therefore an entirely new genus. *Homo habilis* became a focal point of Leakey's long-standing and widely challenged argument that the genus *Homo*, which gave rise to modern man, existed alongside *Australopithecus*, but was not a direct descendant.

According to his theory *Australopithecus* represents a dead-end branch in the tree of human evolution, with *habilis* surviving and going on to become *Homo erectus*, and eventually *Homo sapiens*.

Evidence of an even earlier biped was discovered in 1976 by Mary Leakey at Laetoli, near Olduvai. In the soft volcanic ash thrown out by nearby Sadiman Volcano, and now turned to stone, she found a parallel trail of footprints — the tracks of two hominids walking together, preserved for 3.7 million years. Both sets of fossils seemed to vindicate Louis Leakey's theory, though evidence unearthed by other experts was periodically to challenge his ideas.

Above: Years of weathering have fashioned these natural pillars near the Isimila ruins, one of the most important Stone Age sites in Africa.

Leakey died in 1972 but his theories concerning the origin of man continue to fuel anthropological debate, and his views were still championed by Mary until her death in December 1996 and by their son Richard.

Hunters, migrants, and traders

Excluding the Olduvai Gorge site, the majority of interior Tanzania's prehistory remains shrouded in the mists of antiquity. The absence of written records or significant archaeological artefacts is a serious barrier to investigation.

Evidence such as the world's finest examples of hand axes from Isimila, the Ngorongoro burial cairns and the rock paintings at Kondoa, however, suggest that late Stone Age society was well developed.

By about 1,000 BC Cushitic-speaking tribes from the north-east had introduced agriculture to the sparsely populated groups of indigenous hunter-gatherers. These new arrivals, like the Iraqw, quickly gave way to Bantu migrants from the south

and west, and successive waves of Nilotic people from the far north; most recently the Maasai. At the end of the seventeenth century the Maasai reached Dodoma in central Tanzania from their traditional homelands around Lake Turkana in Kenya. Their warlike reputation preceded them and the Bantu tribes put up little resistance against the tall men in ochre who came to graze their precious cattle throughout northern Tanzania.

Only the Gogo, to the west of the Rift Valley, and the Hehe in the south, prevented these areas from also becoming Maasai grazing lands. Concentrated now around Tanzania's game parks in the north, Maasai territory is greatly reduced. The northern clans in particular, however, remain largely untouched by modern influence, living a traditionally fierce and independent existence.

Azania

The first written reference to Tanzania comes from a second-century Greek guide-

Above: Axe head discovered at Isimila.

book, *Periplus of the Erythraean Sea*, which mentions a trading town called Rhapta on the coast of Azania. Historians record that 'men of piratical habit, very great stature, and under chiefs in each place', bartered with Arabs, exchanging ivory, rhino horn, tortoiseshell, and coconut oil for metal axes, knives, spears, glassware, wheat, and cloth.

In his *Geography*, the standard textbook on the subject from the second to the fifteenth century, the Greek astronomer Ptolemy confirms that these people, the Zenj, were tall and dark and commented on their fierce spirit. The Zenj are immortalized in the name Zanzibar.

Although there was trade between the various tribal states on the coast more than 2,000 years ago and maritime Arabs plied the Indian Ocean, settlers did not arrive until the eighth century.

Zanzibar, Pemba, and Kilwa were colonized beginning around AD 700 with the arrival of Arab settlers. It was their penetration of the country's interior, however, which brought Tanzania to the attention of the rest of the world and which had a profound influence on its subsequent history. The Arabs quickly drove trading routes into the harsh hinterland in their quest for ivory and gold. Along the way they established depots at Tabora on the central plain and at Ujiji on the shores of Lake Tanganyika.

Around AD 1200 the Arab traders were joined by the Shirazi. These new arrivals, descended from the inhabitants of Shiraz in Persia, had spent time in Oman before sailing down the coast to Zanzibar. They intermarried with the local tribes and gave birth to a new people and culture — Swahili.

Between the arrival of the Shirazi and the influx of the Portuguese at the end of the fifteenth century, the Swahili culture enjoyed a golden age. It attained a degree of civilization unmatched by most of the medieval world. Islamic architecture outshone any in sub-Sahara Africa.

Built on the foundation of a flourishing economy, this small stretch of East African coast quickly became the pre-eminent economic centre.

By the thirteenth century, Sofala, a port south of the Zambezi and the capital of the gold, copper, and ivory trade, had relinquished its position to Kilwa. Vasco da Gama, the Portuguese explorer, was the first European to see the town. In 1498 he noted that 'the city is large and is of good buildings of stone and mortar with terraces . . . there may be 12,000 inhabitants.'

Da Gama heralded a spate of maritime rivalry between the Arabs and the Portuguese. The Europeans eventually ruled the coast, albeit briefly, and only after 200 years of fighting and plundering was the curtain drawn on the golden age of the Swahili.

Piracy and pillage

In 1505 a flotilla of twenty-three ships sailed from Portugal with one objective — to seize the Indian Ocean trade.

Under Francisco de Almeida diplomacy was briefly attempted to coerce the coastal city states into relinquishing control of their economy. It failed, as did a campaign

Above: Ancient Kaole ruins; remnants of the once-prosperous coastal town founded before the thirteenth century by the Shirazi.

of divide and rule. In frustration the Portuguese turned to aggression.

Zanzibar and Kilwa were sacked and smaller centres plundered. Internal trade links were disrupted as the Portuguese marched inland along the Zambezi River, establishing forts at Sena and Tete in Mozambique. A system of land settlement, called *prazero*, was introduced, offering free land in East Africa to convicts from Portugal. As a result, the southern slave and gold trades both came under Portuguese control, and the system made a significant contribution to the foundation of Portuguese Mozambique. Essentially the Portuguese came as soldiers, not settlers. Their mercantile ambitions lay elsewhere — in the Middle East and India. For them the coastal towns were convenient ports of call on their journey east.

Reviled for their brutality and called *afriti* (devils) by the locals, the Portuguese were eventually driven out by the Omani Arabs in the late seventeenth century, concluding 200 years of rule with a final defeat at Fort Jesus, Mombasa, in 1698. The Portuguese legacy amounted to a few additions to the Swahili vocabulary — and the tradition of bullfighting on the island of Pemba. (See 'Pemba: Clove Capital of the World', Part Two.)

Slavery

The Omanis, however, failed to capitalize on their victory and the coast enjoyed uneasy independence. But with the medieval trade routes in tatters after years of Portuguese mismanagement and exploitation, the lands between the coast and Lake Tanganyika were ripe for redevelopment. In 1840 Sultan Sayyid Said moved his government from Oman to Zanzibar. And so began a new and more sinister chapter in the history of the area.

Actively encouraged by the British, he annexed several coastal towns and developed Arab caravan routes west as far as the Congo and north to Uganda. Sayyid Said's caravans set out from the coast with guides and porters from the Nyamwezi

Above: Root of evil: Infamous tree at Zanzibar market under which slaves were sold.

tribe of central Tanzania, and began a gradual takeover of trade routes, in time even refusing to pay *hongo*, the traditional levy to local chiefs. Now a renewable, profitable commodity lay behind the Arab and Swahili traders' ventures — slaves.

Throughout the eighteenth century demand grew as the sugar plantations of the West Indies and Brazil clamoured for a steady supply of labour; the French colonies of Madagascar, Réunion, and Mauritius wanted plantation workers; the Middle East required concubines, eunuchs and servants.

By the middle of the nineteenth century slavers were operating inland as far as Lake Tanganyika. They preferred to trade for captives rather than use force and local ruling chiefs cooperated. Whole families were sold into bondage for a bolt of cloth.

The slaves were then marched back to Bagamoyo and shipped to Zanzibar, where they found themselves working the clove plantations or placed on a slave ship bound for the French colonies, Persia, India or Arabia.

Tanzania suffered more heavily at the hands of the slave-traders than any other East African country. The shores of Lake Malawi were particularly hard hit. In 1811 Captain Thomas Smollet of the British research ship *Ternate*, described the sale of slaves on Zanzibar: 'The show commences at four o'clock in the afternoon. The slaves, set off to best advantage by having their skins cleaned and burnished with cocoa-nut oil, their faces painted with red and white stripes . . . are ranged in a line, commencing with the youngest, and increasing to the rear according to their size and age. At the head of this file, which is composed of all sexes and ages from six to sixty, walks the person who owns them . . . . When any of them strikes a spectator's fancy the line immediately stops, and a process of examination ensues, which, for minuteness, is unequalled in any cattle market in Europe. . . .

'The slave is then made to walk or run a little way, to show there is no defect about the feet; and after which, if price be agreed to . . . they are delivered over to their future master.'

Above: The seaside ruins of Fort Gareza at Kilwa.

Despite an 1830s ban on slavery throughout the British Empire, and the Sultan's subsequent ban in 1845 on the export of slaves from Zanzibar, the Arab's lucrative 2,000-year-old trade showed few signs of stopping. Their dhows still ran the British and French blockade — only one in four needed to get through to show a profit.

When the British explorers Burton and Speke came to the island in 1857 to begin their search for the source of the Nile, adult males were bringing up to £5 and females slightly more. But conditions in which the slaves were held and transported had deteriorated. According to Burton the space between decks of the dhows was reduced to forty-six centimetres (18 inches), and five men were crammed into a space once meant for two. On the island plantations thirty per cent of the captives died of disease or malnutrition.

Livingstone was horrified: 'The sights I have seen on this journey made my blood run cold, and I am not sentimental.' But despite Livingstone's influence and direct efforts, the slave trade continued to flourish. Near the end of Said's rule 50,000 Africans were bought and sold in Zanzibar's slave market each year. From the late eighteenth to the late nineteenth century more than a million survived the journey to the coast.

Combined with the sale of cloves introduced from the Moluccas in 1818, Zanzibar grew rich and powerful. By the middle of the nineteenth century it was the most important town on the coast of East Africa. (See 'The Life of Spice', Part Two.)

But the voices of protest mounted, particularly in Britain, and in 1873 Sayyid Said's successor, Sultan Sayyid Barghash, was compelled to close the market on Zanzibar. Yet the traffic continued in different guises. Under one, slaves were 'hired' as porters and their wages withheld. Another ruse allowed French and American traders to deal in slaves as contracted labour. What was needed was joint action by the major powers and, in 1885, the Berlin Conference abolished slavery — on paper. Africa was viewed by the empire-builders — Britain, Germany

Above: Tribute to the historic meeting between Stanley and Livingstone on the shores of Lake Tanganyika.

and France — as a continent of almost unlimited potential for exploitation, and in the rush to colonize, any concerted effort to outlaw slavery was forgotten. It was not until 1922 that the last traces of human bondage were eradicated.

The Dark Continent

The 'Dark Continent', land of exotic legend, has held a lure of fame and fortune for travellers throughout the ages. As early as the second century AD, Ptolemy had drawn a map of Africa based on the reports of adventurous sailors. His cartographical attempt shows the continent stretching down through the southern oceans to join Antarctica, with the Nile flowing out of two inland seas far below the Equator near a range of mountains labelled *Lunae Montes*, the Mountains of the Moon.

For almost 1,700 years Ptolemy's map remained the standard work, until the remote, cloud-shrouded range was reached by the white man in his obsessive search for the source of the Nile. In the centuries between, the African interior remained as mysterious as ever, yielding only tantalizing nuggets of what might be. Although trade with the Spanish, French, Dutch, Danes, Swedes, Prussians and especially the British soared during the heyday of slaves, gold and ivory, paradoxically Africa itself remained an almost completely closed book.

Why? The Arab and African suppliers kept their best slave-raiding areas secret while Westerners were happy to pick up their cargoes from the coast without heading into the inhospitable interior. Ptolemy's map still retained its speculative flavour.

In 1788 the Africa Association was founded in London. In accordance with the spirit of the Enlightenment, its members believed that 'so long as men continued ignorant of so large a portion of the globe, that ignorance must be considered as a degree of reproach on the present age'.

Their interest in Africa was not solely academic, however, and a founding member wrote of Timbuktu: 'Gold is there so plentiful as to adorn even slaves. . . . If we could get our manufacturers into that country we should soon have gold enough.' Implicit also was the aim of saving the African from godlessness; civilizing nations 'hitherto consigned to hopeless barbarism and uniform contempt'.

So, with the motives of curiosity, commerce and civilization, the Africa Association set out to bring light to the darkness.

Men with missions
In 1846, although not involved with the Association, but no doubt approving of its civilizing aims, two German missionaries, Johann Krapf and Johannes Rebmann, were unsuccessfully attempting to convert the Wanika tribe of the East African coast to Christianity. Plagued by fever and frustrated by the intractable locals, the two men decided the hinterland might be more amenable.

Armed with his Bible and an umbrella, Rebmann left first on 14 October 1847. Seven months later, after encountering giraffe, zebra, rhino, buffalo and elephant, he saw the summit of a mountain 'covered with a dazzling white cloud'. His guide simply said, 'baridi', meaning cold in Swahili, and Rebmann felt certain he was the first white man to see the snows of Kilimanjaro. (See 'Mount Kilimanjaro: Roof of Africa', Part Two.)

Rebmann was equally taken with the land of the Chagga, 'lovely country, bursting with plenteousness' that surrounded the mountain, but he eventually left the area to continue his fruitless search for promising mission sites.

When news of his 'discovery' reached Europe it was met with scorn, not least by Desborough Cooley, a British geographer who had earlier claimed that 'Kirimanjara' was cloaked in red carnelian. Arguments over the importance of Kilimanjaro raged for years. Some said the mountain was the source of the Nile itself, and it became a focal point of both African exploration and rival European imperialism. In 1861 Baron Karl Klaus von der Decken confirmed Rebmann's sighting, which was followed by another missionary, Charles New, who climbed to the snow line in 1871. Land

treaties were eventually made with the Chagga to the south of the mountain by the German Carl Juhlke, and similar British deals with the people of Taveta in the east. When the two governments met in 1886 to divide Africa into spheres of influence, both claims were recognized — creating the kink in the border between Tanzania and Kenya.

Burton, Speke, and the inland seas
In late 1856, back at the coast, Rebmann was visited by Richard Burton and John Hanning Speke seeking advice on travel in the interior where they hoped to establish the source of the Nile. The two explorers arrived in Zanzibar on 20 December 1856.

Burton was larger than life and charismatic in the 'mad, bad, and dangerous to know' style. In Speke, he chose his own complete opposite. This incompatability was to be their downfall, perhaps fatally so for Speke. On 16 June 1857, they left for the mainland aboard the Sultan's personal vessel.

With 130 men, hired porters, and thirty pack animals bought at Bagamoyo, they headed south-west — to avoid the Maasai — on a trek that lasted five months. They were told about a large lake to the north called Nyanza but chose not to visit it, convinced that the answer to the Nile riddle lay within the interior.

After resting a month at Tabora, Burton and Speke continued on their westward march, reaching Lake Tanganyika near Ujiji on 13 February 1858. By the time they arrived both men were in poor shape. Speke was almost blind and Burton could hardly speak due to an ulcerated jaw. When Speke recovered his sight after a few days rest the two explored the lake by dugout only to find that the Ruzizi River flowed into the lake from the north. Disappointed, they returned to Tabora, where Burton was content to write about his findings on Lake Tanganyika, which he believed might feed the Nile from another point. The restless Speke, however, set out for Nyanza, which he named after the British queen, and returned six weeks later with the unshakeable conviction that he had solved a 'problem which it had been . . . the ambition of the first monarchs of the world to unravel'.

Unconvinced by Speke's claim, Burton declined to see the lake for himself and ordered their return to Zanzibar. But Speke reached England first and presented his claim to the Royal Geographical Society.

When Burton returned in May 1859 he discounted his former colleague's 'evidence'. Speke, however, had already found friends for a second expedition. With companion James August Grant he returned to Africa, this time travelling to the western and northern shores of Lake Victoria.

Alone, on 21 July 1862, Speke found the White Nile north of Victoria sixty-five kilometres (40 miles) downstream. He then marched upstream to name the waterfall, where it left the lake, Ripon Falls, after one of his sponsors.

Sending a telegram — 'the Nile is settled' — ahead of him, Speke arrived home to a hero's welcome. His glory was short-lived.

Geographers and journalists, outraged by his claims to have single-handedly discovered that Lake Victoria was the 'source of the holy river', pressed him to face Burton in public debate.

He could not back down. The September day before the two were to meet in 1864 at the British Association for the Advancement of Science, Speke was found dead, shot through the chest with his own gun. The coroner's verdict was accidental death, but many echoed Burton's words: 'By God, he's killed himself.'

Livingstone

The riddle of Speke's death, wrote one journalist, was one 'to compare with the still unsolved mystery of the Nile itself'. Sir Roderick Murchison, President of the Royal Geographical Society, who delivered Speke's eulogy on 22 May 1865, concluded by announcing his intention to settle once and for all the source of the Nile.

He chose Dr David Livingstone, veteran of twenty-two years experience in Africa and the discoverer of Victoria Falls and Lake Malawi. At fifty-two years of age and in robust health, Livingstone landed at Zanzibar in January 1866.

Ahead of him lay seven gruelling years in unmapped Africa. Three years after leaving the coast, almost toothless and wasted by malaria, he reached Ujiji via Lake Malawi and the southern shore of Lake Tanganyika.

Helped by the Arab traders whose atrocities he recorded, Livingstone recovered enough to head west again (without either medicines or adequate provisions) for the Lualaba River which lies beyond the lake in Congo (Zaire). He believed it was the Nile.

There, along the river's banks at Nyangwe, Livingstone saw 400 Africans massacred by an Arab party. Powerless to help, appalled and terribly ill, Livingstone struggled back to Ujiji where he was again restored to health by the Arabs.

During his lengthy travels and illness, Livingstone's progress remained unknown to the outside. Fearing the great explorer might be lost or even dead, an anxious world waited for news from the interior. Unknown to Livingstone, the wait would soon end.

Stanley

On 10 November 1871, the explorer was 'found' at Ujiji by Henry Morton Stanley, who greeted him with the most famous line in the annals of exploration:

'Dr Livingstone, I presume?'

Stanley was a Welsh-born American journalist on the *New York Herald* and, in finding Livingstone, he also found the fame he craved.

The two became friends and together travelled to the northern shores of Lake Tanganyika to confirm what Burton had always been so reluctant to believe — that the Ruzizi flowed into the lake and was therefore not the Nile. This only served to strengthen Livingstone's conviction that the Lualaba was the Nile. The old doctor declined to return with Stanley to Zanzibar but agreed to travel as far as Tabora to buy provisions for the return to the river.

Stanley gave Livingstone all the men and stores he could spare and promised to send more from the coast if Livingstone would wait. When they parted he carried with him Livingstone's journals and diaries that overnight were to establish Stanley's

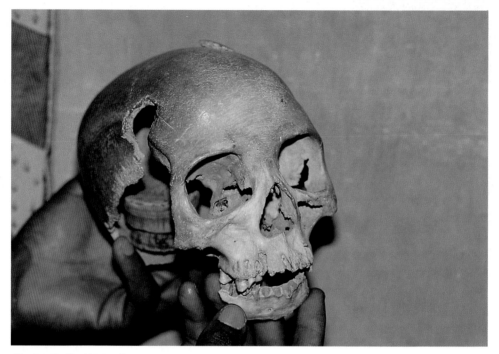

Above: Skull of Hehe Chief Mkwawa who rebelled against the Germans. When finally cornered in July 1898, Mkwawa put a bullet through his own head.

Opposite: Despite its abolition, slavery persisted. Within this cave on Zanzibar Island slaves were held until after dark, then ferried to waiting ships.

reputation as both journalist and explorer.

Five months later fifty-seven porters arrived at Tabora and Livingstone, now fifty-nine, wasted no time in leaving with his faithful servants, Abdulla Susi and James Chuma. (See 'Glory Days', Part Two.) By the end of April 1873, eight months after leaving Tabora, he was close to Lake Bangweulu where he hoped to find a feeder stream that would confirm his faith in Lualaba as the headwaters of the Nile. But, worn out by sickness and travel, on 1 May 1873 Susi and Chuma found him dead by his bed, as if in prayer. They cut out his heart and buried it under a tree, then dried his body in the sun for a fortnight before sewing it in sailcloth and placing it inside a bark cylinder. With his remaining men they walked for eleven months more than 1,600 kilometres (1,000 miles) back to the coast. From there his body was shipped to England for burial in Westminster Abbey.

The mystery of the Nile had eluded him, but Livingstone's report of the massacre at Nyangwe helped end the Zanzibar slave market. He once said, 'If my disclosures should lead to the suppression of the slave trade, I shall regard that as a greater matter by far than the discovery of all the Nile sources together.'

Imperial ambitions

Fuelled by the rapacious Industrial Revolution, European powers of the late nineteenth century began to look further afield for raw materials and cheap labour. Inspired by such explorers as Stanley, who was an evangelical proponent of European domination over the 'Dark Continent', their hungry gaze fell upon Africa.

In 1875, with an imperial glint in their eye, the Germans looked to East Africa, particularly the area south of Kilimanjaro, as a site for potential colonization.

Expeditions were organized to make inroads into the region. The most energetic of these German pioneers, Dr Karl Peters, went to East Africa under an alias disguised as a mechanic. By ruse and double-deal, he made 'treaties' with local rulers who effectively signed their land away to Peters' Society for German Colonization. (See 'Dodoma: Future Capital?', Part Two.)

When he presented the treaties to Bismarck in 1885, the German leader declared the lands a German Protectorate and authorized Peters to establish the German East Africa Company. The Sultan of Zanzibar appealed to the British for help in resisting the Germans, but to no avail.

The German East Africa Company met fierce resistance on the mainland. Led by a red-bearded Arab settler, Bushiri, and an African of the Zigua tribe, Bwana Heri, African 'rebels' successfully regained all the coastal towns from the company with the exception of Dar es Salaam and Bagamoyo. In response Germany assigned Major von Wissman to lead troops against Bushiri and Bwana Heri.

Only after their betrayal and surrender was the coast regained. On 1 January 1891, the Sultan of Zanzibar ceded the Tanganyika coast for £200,000, and Dar es Salaam became the capital of German East Africa under the direct rule of the German government.

Internal resistance

Despite the German's coastal domination, continued resistance inland became a nagging thorn in the imperial German flesh. The tribes centred around Tabora fought long and hard under their leader Isike who, rather than be captured, blew himself up using his own powder magazine.

In the south the Yao chief, Machemba, sent a letter to von Wissman stating, 'I can find no reason to obey you — I would rather die first. I will not come to you, and if you are strong enough, come and fetch me.' He defeated several German patrols before being compelled to make peace in 1899.

But the German's greatest barrier to complete rule was the warrior Mkwawa,

leader of the Hehe. Both he and von Wissman wanted a nonviolent solution to German rule and Hehe independence. In 1891 after Mkwawa refused to go to the coast for talks, von Wissman sent an armed force to Heheland to negotiate. They were met by Hehe envoys bearing peace offerings as they approached the land around what is now Iringa, but their intentions were misinterpreted by the German commander who ordered an attack on the unarmed Hehe. Mkwawa retaliated by ambushing the German contingent at Lugalo, leaving few survivors.

The Germans returned with a large force intent on capturing the Hehe stronghold of Kalenga (see 'Iringa: Highland Haven', Part Two.) After heavy fighting they succeeded. But Mkwawa escaped and continued a guerrilla war for another four years.

Finally, in June 1898, the great warrior shot himself after being found by a German patrol. It was the end of a long manhunt. Mkwawa's head was cut off and sent back to Germany and the body returned to his people.

All resistance ended with the breakup of the Hehe Chief's Council and the exile of the remaining tribal leaders. The Germans then consolidated their rule by building forts at strategic points throughout Tanzania and imposing taxes. The money was usually collected by coastal Arabs and Swahili who were early collaborators with the Germans. Called *Akidas*, these colonial agents were harbingers of a new period of indirect rule.

The iron fist

Deutsch Ost Afrika was far too large to administer using strictly German manpower. Instead, *Beziksamtmann*, District Officers, were appointed to oversee nineteen districts, judge disputes, and discipline *jumbes*, or village headmen. They were all-powerful and, ever mindful of unrest, each maintained between 100 and 200 troops to help collect taxes.

German administration was generally heavy-handed. General von Liebert, the Governor, admitted that, 'It was impossible in Africa to get on without cruelty'. As Germany tightened its grip, pressure

Above: Graves of those killed during World War One. More than 100,000 people died as a result of the East African campaign.

mounted in Berlin for the colony to be at least self-sufficient. But efforts to attract investment failed. Even so, railways were built, mainly for rapid deployment of troops. By 1911 the Tanga to Moshi line was finished, and the final spike was driven in the Central Line, linking Dar es Salaam with Kigoma on Lake Tanganyika, in 1914. (See 'Track to the Interior', Part Two.)

An agricultural economy was established and Europeans urged to settle and farm the Highlands. Those expatriates who took land paid the locals poor wages but made fortunes from coffee, sisal and rubber. Africans were left to grow cash crops, often under duress, to pay taxes.

Maji Maji Rebellion
In 1902 the oppressive Governor launched a cotton scheme. For three years the local headmen in the south had been forced to grow the crop on unsuitable land, achieving poor yields and making little profit under the supervision of the hated *Akidas*. On the night of 31 July, simmering dissent boiled over and the Matumbi Highlanders drove out their *Akida* in what became the Maji Maji Rebellion. *Maji* was a sacred water drunk by the rebels to unite them in their struggle and protect them from bullets. The revolt spread quickly throughout the south. Two months later 8,000 Mbunga and Pogoro tribesmen were massacred when they stormed the town of Mahenge. *Maji* proved little use against machineguns.

The Germans responded to the uprising with a scorched earth policy. By November the rebellion had been effectively crushed. Casualties from the actual fighting were relatively few, but the destruction of crops and villages resulted in widespread famine that left an estimated 60,000 Africans dead.

The British and World War One
Despite the unseemly scramble for African land and wealth, European governments — through the division of the continent into 'spheres of influence' — did cooperate to some degree in the matter of whose flag should fly where.

Above: Reception on the Central Line, Kigoma, 1914.

In this 'gentlemanly' manner the Anglo-German agreements of 1886 and 1890 made way for the birth of German East Africa, while Zanzibar, subject to growing British diplomatic activity since the time of Sayyid Said, became a British Protectorate.

Although the Sultan's pleas for help against the German occupation of the mainland had been ignored, naval protection was provided for Zanzibar and Pemba, giving Britain 'rights' to the islands. When the British consul took office he found the Zanzibari government 'an embodiment of all the worst and most barbarous characteristics of a primitive Arab despotism'. He put an end to the Sultan's rule by replacing him with an educated Arab civil servant.

At the outbreak of World War One the British controlled Zanzibar, Uganda, and what were to become Malawi, Zambia and Kenya; German East Africa was effectively surrounded and her troops outnumbered. The outcome should have been quickly decided, but the British were thwarted by the inspirational leadership and military genius of the German Commander-in-Chief, General Paul von Lettow-Vorbeck.

He conducted a brilliant guerrilla campaign using mainly African troops and was pursued the length and breadth of German East Africa by the Allied forces.

By the end of 1916, although British and Belgian forces controlled all the land north of the Central Line, they continued to be harried by Lettow-Vorbeck in the south. The general did not surrender until 16 November 1918, five days after the armistice in Europe. The East Africa campaign left the country ravaged. More than 100,000 troops and tribespeople died as a result of the conflict, either during the fighting or from the subsequent famine.

Tanganyika

Under the Treaty of Versailles, Germany surrendered all her overseas territories to the Allies. German East Africa was assigned to the British Government under a League of Nations mandate, while Rwanda and Burundi, also German, were given to the Belgians.

Tanganyika Territory, as the British renamed it in 1919, was to be governed as a Trust Territory in the interests of the 'native inhabitants'.

Though ultimately the responsibility of the League of Nations, in effect Tanganyika became another country coloured pink on world maps illustrating the British Empire, and was administered by the Colonial Office.

One of Britain's first actions was to end slavery. The German administrators had stopped short of total abolition, fearing a backlash from the Arabs and Swahili.

Slavery was finally abolished in 1922.

During their rule, the Germans instituted various reforms which included placing the country under civil rather than military authority, divided into twenty-one districts governed by a commissioner. In 1926 the British reorganized these into provinces reporting to the Governor, Sir Donald Cameron.

Conscious of emerging nationalism in Empire territories, Cameron attempted to give sufficient authority to tribal leaders and include them in local decision-making, while at the same time denying them access to central government. This adaptation of the original German 'indirect rule' was bolstered by giving chiefs authority over 'native' courts. For a while the system worked.

With such a well-organized economy and a tolerant legislative system, Tanganyika enjoyed stability and prosperity in the 1920s, resulting in an increase in the number of educated Africans. Motivated by their own advancement and politically aware, they founded such clubs as the Tanganyika Territory African Civil Service Association of Tanga in 1922, and the Tanganyika Africa Association in 1929. Ostensibly social organizations, they were in fact the core of the nascent nationalist movement.

The birth of TANU

If the First World War had catastrophic consequences for Tanganyika, the Second World War contributed to the country's development by increasing world demand for sisal, cotton and pyrethrum.

Above: Teacher Julius Nyerere became Tanzania's first president in 1961.

At war's end in 1945 the first Africans were appointed to the Governor's enlarged Legislative Council. The British Empire was in its sunset years and, with the advent of Indian independence in 1947, post-war British colonialism entered a new phase.

The same year also saw Tanganyika become a Trust Territory of the United Nations and the linking of local and central government that Sir Donald Cameron had been so careful to avoid in 1926. Implicit in any colony's trusteeship status was the goal of independence. Tanganyika was no exception and under the watchful eye of visiting UN missions the colonial administration was expected to work towards this end.

Tanganyika also became involved in the abortive ground-nut scheme. Intended to supply vegetable oil to a hungry post-war world, the operation became a symbol of well-intentioned but badly planned development. It was an agricultural and economic disaster and by 1950 collapsed at a huge cost to Tanganyika and overseas aid donors.

Above: In January 1963, the Afro-Shirazi party ousted the Arabs from Zanzibar in a revolution.

Despite the country's involvement in the scheme, agricultural output increased dramatically, as did the number of farming cooperatives. These societies, along with tribal organizations such as the Bukoba Bahaya Union (which opposed government-appointed chiefs), and even football clubs, actively contributed to the growing voice for self-government.

In 1953 Julius Nyerere, a teacher, was elected President of the Tanganyika African Association. He immediately redrafted its constitution and in 1954 the association changed its name to the Tanganyika African National Union. The central aim of TANU was to subject the British authorities to increasing political pressure for self-government and independence.

Nyerere was given encouraging support during his election year when a United Nations mission proposed a twenty-five-year timetable for independence. The British objected and Nyerere considered the pace too slow.

He effectively lobbied the UN, but even more persuasive was the popular support shown for the aims of TANU and its slogan — *Uhuru na Umoja*, 'Freedom and Unity'. At the country's first general election in 1958, five TANU candidates became ministers.

The momentum gathered force and two years later at the next election TANU candidates were returned in all but one of the seventy-one seats. The message to the UN and the British was clear. After various constitutional and parliamentary changes in which the Governor lost all effective power, a constitutional conference held in London set the date for independence at 9 December 1961. Not a shot had been fired. As the green, black and gold flag (representing the land, its people, and natural resources) was raised, Tanganyika achieved full independence from Britain.

Revolution

Only one thing stood in the way of complete unity — Zanzibar remained a British Protectorate.

The Arab civil service formed itself into the Zanzibar Nationalist Party with the aim of creating an Islamic state. In response to this unpopular move by the disliked Arab elite (headed by the Sultan), the Africans and Shirazis created the Afro-Shirazi Party. In December 1963, Zanzibar was granted independence, and, a month later, after mounting hostility between the two parties, the Sultan was deposed in a bloody revolution. Most of the island's Arab population was either killed or exiled like the Sultan and the ZNP was ousted by the revolutionary council of the ASP.

Three months later a band of blue, representing the sea, was added to the flag and Zanzibar and Pemba joined with the mainland to become the United Republic of Tanzania.

Nyerere and radical socialism

After independence Nyerere began the long and difficult task of rebuilding a country that had experienced two periods of colonial rule lasting almost 100 years.

Of the East African territories, Tanzania had always been the poor relation until the boom years of sisal following the Second World War. Education, a low priority, had been virtually ignored — at independence there were only 120 graduates in the entire country.

Adopting a Chinese model of socialism, *Mwalimu* (teacher) Nyerere embarked on a courageous and idealistic programme of social reform and economic development in which *Ujamaa*, or familyhood policy, was the key. The principles were announced during the famous 1967 Arusha Declaration which was nothing less than an agenda for a radical experiment in socialist economics. Nyerere outlined his policy for the widespread nationalization of banks, industries and rented properties; fixed producer prices; and the redistribution of individual wealth through selective taxation. Corruption and elitism were to be eliminated, and he started at the top by banning ministers from having business interests in companies or from drawing more than one salary.

Ujamaa, however, was the keystone of Nyerere's plan. Based on the fundamental African socio-economic unit — the village — his aim was to build self-reliant communal enterprises in which basic commodities were produced by individuals for the village as a whole. In an effort to decentralize government the villages would be self-managed and administered.

Bolstered by an education system that taught cooperative values and equality, the manifesto was immediately put into practice. Initially it worked. The foundation for Tanzania's enviably high literacy rate (more than ninety per cent) was laid, poverty was alleviated, and a strengthened medical service embarked on a health education and disease treatment programme.

But a combination of circumstances — a lack of personal incentive in state socialism, the oil price rise of the early 1970s, and several periods of drought — all had a damaging impact.

By 1974-5 the system, where it worked at all, was creaking. In an effort to correct the situation, the *Ujamaa* communities were brought under state control and massive 'villagization', or forced resettlement, was instituted. The widely dispersed rural communities were moved into 'villages of development', in theory so that drinkable water, schools, hospitals, and irrigation could be more easily provided in an effort to revitalize the agricultural economy.

During the most intense period of *Ujamaa* in the 1970s, ninety per cent of the rural population were living in 8,000 registered villages.

Not surprisingly, Tanzanians objected to resettlement without compensation or consultation and the government — in the absence of any significant overseas aid — simply did not have the financial wherewithal to provide the essential services it promised.

Despite the unpopularity of the scheme, Nyerere remained a popular leader. In the 1975 one-party election he attracted over ninety per cent of the vote. Since then a revised system of *Ujamaa* has been tried with greater success, but Tanzania has faced other difficulties that continue to make development an uphill struggle. It is listed by the World Bank as one of the world's least developed countries.

Although the West commended Nyerere's vision his radical policies were

Above: The TANZAM railway, running from Dar es Salaam to Tunduma and on into Zambia, as its name implies, was built with the assistance of the Chinese government.

too close to the Communist model for the comfort of major aid donors and development money was not forthcoming during the 1970s. So Nyerere turned to the East. China came to his aid with a project that was the envy of East and southern Africa. At a cost of US$230 million, the Chinese completed in 1975 a major engineering feat by laying 1,870 kilometres (1,160 miles) of the Great Uhuru Railway — also known as TANZAM or TAZARA — from Dar es Salaam to Kapiri Mposhi in Zambia. (See 'Great Uhuru Railway', Part Three.)

The line provided a major boost to the southern economy and relieved the Zambian copper industry of their dependence on the railways of white-ruled Rhodesia and South Africa.

Then came the oil crisis, financial restrictions and fuel shortages. Tanzania was hit badly and the TANZAM/TAZARA line could only afford the most essential maintenance. It fell into disrepair but with recent aid donations and funding from Austria, rehabilitation is under way.

East African Economic Community

In the idealistic days of post-independence, Tanzania, Kenya, and Uganda were all linked by the East African Common Services Organization. As the name implies, it was a union in which services such as airlines, telecommunications, transportation and immigration departments were shared. Shortly after the Arusha Declaration in June 1967, EACSO was upgraded to allow free movement of labour across borders, convertible currencies were introduced and the organization was renamed the East African Economic Community. But differences grew as Tanzania embraced socialism, Kenya developed its capitalist stance and Uganda slipped into Idi Amin's tyrannical chaos.

When the Community fell apart in 1977, Nyerere closed the border with his northern neighbour. The Tanzanian tourist trade suffered dramatically, only adding to the loss of revenue from the collapse of the

EAEC and further stunted the development of the country.

Invasion

Mwalimu Nyerere has long been a vociferous opponent of apartheid and, as the 'conscience of black Africa', has been an active supporter of African liberation struggles. During the Amin years in Uganda, Milton Obote and Yoweri Museveni, the current president, both sought refuge in Tanzania while their country was being ravaged by the despot's army. This support cost Tanzania dearly.

In October 1978 Amin invaded Tanzania and occupied the region east of the Kagera River. The lake ports of Bukoba and Musoma were bombed in retaliation, Amin claimed, for Nyerere's support of exiled Ugandan insurgents. In reality the invasion was a diversionary tactic by Amin whose dangerously undisciplined army was on the brink of mutiny — but Tanzania had to respond.

During the next few months, a people's militia was assembled and hastily trained in the virtual absence of a regular army of any size or effectiveness. The Tanzanians seemed doomed — the Ugandans were known to be better equipped and well trained. But their reputation was undeserved; they fled from the scratch army in disarray and the Tanzanian forces marched into the Ugandan capital, Kampala, virtually unopposed. An occupying force of 12,000 men remained in the country to maintain law and order and allow Nyerere to decide who should take over from Amin. Although the West and other African countries also influenced this choice, no contributions to the cost of the war were ever made by them and the Organization of African Unity even criticized Nyerere for his action. The war cost Tanzania an estimated US$500 million.

The future

In November 1985, Julius Nyerere, father figure of Tanzania for more than twenty years, resigned from the post of president to become party chairman, handing over the reins to Ali Hassan Mwinyi.

In 1992 Parliament voted to abolish three decades of one-party rule. Multi-party elections were duly held late in 1995 and saw the election of Benjamin Mkapa, a protege of Nyerere, as president.

The 1995 elections effectively dismantled the monolithic socialist state established by former President Julius Nyerere. However, President Mkapa is a member of the long-established ruling party, Chama cha Mapinduzi (CCM), which still retains considerable power.

Under the 1964 Constitution, five ministries — foreign affairs, defence, home affairs, finance and higher education — operate for the union as a whole. All other matters are handled by the mainland and Zanzibari governments separately.

In recent years Tanzania has been one of the largest recipients of non-military aid in the world, yet the country remains one of the poorest.

Above: Benjamin Mkapa, President of Tanzania since November 1995.
Overleaf: Abundant wheat fields in northern Tanzania, near Ngorongoro Conservation Area.

The Land: Dazzling in all its Beauty

Up from the green rocky shores of Lake Manyara the rough road cuts sharply in and out of the gullied slopes before cresting the lip of a gently sloping plateau. From this viewpoint the eastern arm of the Rift Valley escarpment plunges down to the glassy waters of the lake.

The road continues through the rolling farmland of Mbululand, where the well-drained soils support wheat, maize, beans, and cattle. Gaining height, the deeper valley sides are covered with coffee bushes that give way to evergreen forest and mixed scrub.

Climbing into the cloud zone the track is flanked by dense upland trees hung with the lichen 'Old Man's Beard' or *Usnea*. Suddenly, you are on the rim of Ngorongoro Crater. Through breaks in the trees there are vertiginous glimpses of open space drawing the eye down to the ochre plain far below. Rock walls reaching 600 metres (2,000 feet) arc away to the left and right in an unbroken line to form the world's largest perfect caldera, eighteen kilometres (11 miles) across. Down on the crater floor a shallow soda lake reflects the high, white cumulus clouds that boil up during the day to bring rain and mist to the highland ridge.

The Great Rift Valley

Like other countries in East Africa, the landscape of Tanzania has been defined by the tectonic movements that resulted in the formation of the Rift Valley. It is the country's major geographical feature, a constant reminder of the forces which throughout millions of years have squeezed, lifted, torn and moulded the Earth into the topography seen today.

Satellite photographs of East Africa show Tanzania as a vast central plateau sloping down to an 800-kilometre (500-mile) coast on the Indian Ocean. This high hinterland is just a small part of a land mass that stretches in a broad swathe from South Africa to Ethiopia. Snaking through this flat land of ancient rock, clearly visible

from space, is the Great Rift Valley. More than 9,700 kilometres (6,000 miles) long, the Rift stretches in a broken scar from Mozambique to Jordan. Formed by intense subterranean pressure and movement over the last twenty million years — relatively recent in geological terms — the valley emerged as the continental masses of the Middle East and Africa shifted and buckled. A string of narrow, shallow lakes flanked by steep walls marks the Rift's progress until the valley sides recede and flatten out south of Lake Malawi.

The Crater Highlands, including Lake Tanganyika, Ngorongoro, and Lake Manyara, all owe their existence to this great fracture in the Earth's crust. It is in Tanzania that the valley's lesser western branch, containing Lake Tanganyika and Lake Albert among others, divides from the main eastern branch.

The main branch then continues up the continent and includes lakes Manyara and Natron in Tanzania; Magadi, Naivasha, Elmenteita, Nakuru, Bogoria, Baringo and Turkana in Kenya.

Some major faulting took place within the last 10,000 years, and there is still violent activity today.

The 2,400-kilometre (1,500-mile) stretch from the Danakil depression in northern Ethiopia to Lake Manyara contains thirty active or semiactive volcanoes, including Ol Doinyo Lengai in Tanzania and countless hot springs and geysers spewing boiling water from underground fissures and pipes.

It was not until the 1880s that serious exploration of the Rift and the interior took place as European imperial and individual ambitions drove a small group of determined travellers to explore this part of 'Darkest Africa'. Although their intentions did not specifically uncover the Rift, their

Opposite: Verdant forest skirts the lower slopes of Mount Kilimanjaro where ninety-six per cent of the mountain's water originates.

frequent crossing and mapping of the valley led to a substantial revision of earlier maps.

In 1883 German naturalist Dr Gustav Fischer entered Maasailand in northern Tanzania for the first time, adding new information about the volcano Ol Doinyo Lengai (the Maasai 'Mountain of God', which erupted in 1966) and the country north to Lake Naivasha in Kenya, the highest and the coolest lake in the Rift.

His countryman, a German adventurer named Baumann, was simultaneously filling in the maps' white space around Lake Manyara, where the sides of the valley begin to recede. With the discovery and naming of Lake Rudolph (now Lake Turkana) by the Hungarian aristocrat and explorer Count Samuel Teleki in 1887, another link in the chain of valley lakes was forged.

It took the Viennese geologist Edward Suess — who had never visited Africa — to finally piece together the available information and conclude that a line of earth movements travelled down the length of Africa. He termed it *Graben* or grave.

One of Suess' enthusiastic followers was the young Scottish-born, John Walter Gregory. He agreed with Suess that it was the break-up of the super-continent, Gondwanaland, that formed the present southern continents and which, in the process, partially tore Africa apart. After an expedition to assess Suess' *Graben* (during which he met with hostile tribes and malaria), Gregory returned to England where he coined a new term for the vast feature he had surveyed — Rift Valley.

From the earliest days of the planet's formation, radioactively heated rocks rose up from the centre of the Earth and flowed outwards underneath the surface crust, like liquid wax at the base of a candle flame. Over immeasurable periods of time cracks appeared in Gondwanaland as the liquid

Opposite: Sentinel splendour of a giant groundsel among the heathers above 2,800 metres (9,200 feet). Normally tiny Alpine plants, they can grow up to four metres (13 feet) high on Kilimanjaro.

rock below tugged in opposite directions at weak points in the newly formed land. Molten rock then gushed out of the fissures and the land masses on either side were slowly pushed apart to form land rafts of varying sizes. Madagascar and Australia are just such rafts.

When a massive outpouring of rock occurred on the Earth's surface, subsidence was likely to take place elsewhere. The Rift Valley is thought to be the consequence of movement out from under East Africa as the Indian Ocean was created. Forty million years ago this subsidence resulted in some of the major Rift lakes being formed as water flowed into the areas where blocks of the Earth had dropped. Subsequently, eleven million years ago, the rifts were fractured by a period of faulting. The lifting of the valley's sides is believed to have taken place only after more faulting less than one million years ago.

The high plateaux through which the Rift runs are incredibly ancient shield rocks up to three billion years old, often eroded down to the type of flat landscape encountered around Tabora and Dodoma in central Tanzania.

In essence, the Rift Valley is a new crack on the very old face of Africa.

Brimstone and bitter waters
Although most of East Africa's volcanoes are extinct, a few dozen remain to remind us of the awesome forces still shaping our environment.

In 1966 Ol Doinyo Lengai, the Maasai's Mountain of God, erupted. For several weeks the volcano had rumbled ominously. Inside, molten rock mixed with gas built up within the 600-metre (2,000-foot) cone until the pressure became too great and the main vent blew.

After the initial shower of white-hot boulders and black lava spray had subsided, Lengai continued to spew out a dense plume of gas and fine cinders to a height of 1,500 metres (5,000 feet).

Within forty-eight hours the black lava had been bleached white by contact with the air, leaving the mountain coated with caustic ash like a fresh snow-fall that obliterated all vegetation. Now the plants

have returned to face an uncertain future in one of the most wildly beautiful parts of East Africa.

A few kilometres to the north lies Lake Natron, a shallow Rift Valley lake; forty kilometres (25 miles) long by ten kilometres (six miles) across.

The lake takes its name from the chemical for natural sodium carbonate, trona. Soda is fed into the waters from lake-bed springs and by waters flowing through the surrounding soda-rich soils off the foothills of two extinct volcanoes, Shombole and Gelai.

Under the midday sun the low-lying area is a shimmering inferno and vapourizing water seems to flow upwards into the thickly shifting air. The algae that live in the bitter soda solution are food for the large resident population of flamingos — the only significant wildlife population that can tolerate Natron's harsh environment.

There the Rift is arid and with temperatures sometimes climbing to 66°C (150°F) the lake is a boiling pan. Forty-one centimetres (16 inches) of rain falls there yearly, while 330 centimetres (130 inches) evaporates from the basin that has no outlet. The water disappears to leave acrid zones of glaring white crusts of soda that, further north at Kenya's Lake Magadi, is commercially extracted for use in the chemical industry.

But here the lake is too remote for such pragmatic use; Natron lies in its infernal basin, a testament to the extremes of nature.

Central Plateau

Almost seventy-five per cent of Tanzania's 945,087 square kilometres (364,898 square miles) consists of dry season savannah. The Central Plateau is no exception. Perched above 1,000 metres (3,280 feet) in the interior of the country, the area is known in Swahili as *nyika*, or 'wasteland'. It consists of dry season savannah, sparse woodlands

and in many places the dreaded tsetse fly. For six to seven months each year the land remains parched and brown, starved for the moisture of the long rains which arrive in November. Temperatures often reach 32°C (90°F). As the heat shimmers in waves across the flat land, only an occasional granite outcrop relieves the monotony.

Toward the north the plateau rises steadily to the Pare and Usambara mountains, eventually culminating in 5,896-metre (19,340-foot) Kilimanjaro, the highest mountain in Africa.

The coast and islands

In direct contrast with the arid interior is the lush, 800-kilometre (500-mile) strip of ocean coast. It has an average rainfall of 1,150-2,000 millimetres (45-78 inches) and, along with Zanzibar and the offshore islands, remains green and tropical year-round. A fertile plain up to sixty-five kilometres (40 miles) wide stretches along the coast. Humidity is broken by heavy downpours and the temperature averages between 21-26°C (70-80°F).

Inland waters

Within Tanzania's borders lie 52,000 square kilometres (20,000 square miles) of water — more than any other African country. Down the western side is Lake Tanganyika, the continent's deepest freshwater body of water. To the north is Victoria, the second-largest lake in the world. Three great rivers, the Nile, Congo and Zambezi, gather their momentum from the Tanzanian watershed.

The mighty Rufiji River and its tributaries, the Great Ruaha, Kilombero, and Luwegu, make up Africa's largest river basin, draining an area of 177,400 square kilometres (68,500 square miles). Each year it dumps millions of tons of silt into the Indian Ocean south of Dar es Salaam, creating a hand-shaped delta sixty-five kilometres (40 miles) wide.

Previous pages: The meandering Rufiji River drains an area equalling 177,400 square kilometres (68,500 square miles), finally emptying into a delta 65 kilometres (40 miles) wide at the Indian Ocean.

The People: 120 Pieces of an Ethnic Puzzle

From the tropical Arabs of Zanzibar to the Chagga of snow-capped Kilimanjaro, Tanzania's people are as diverse as the country they inhabit. More than 120 tribes exist, all differing in culture, customs and language. About a dozen tribes form half the country's population, but no one ethnic group dominates. This has resulted in a balance of power throughout the country and a much lower level of ethnic conflict than elsewhere in Africa.

Kiswahili, which is the mother tongue of Zanzibaris, Pembans and many of the coastal people, has also worked as a unifying factor. Adopted in 1963 as the national language, Swahili is now spoken by more than ninety-five per cent of the population. The vast majority of Tanzanians live in rural areas.

The major part of their waking hours are preoccupied with subsistence needs: producing food, building houses, making basic tools, gathering fuel and hauling water. Any cash earned for small purchases, fees, or taxes, is usually obtained by selling surplus crops or animals.

Hadzabe (Khoisan)

An exception to this are the Hadzabe. Located in northern Tanzania beside Lake Eyasi, the remaining few hundred that form this tribe practice neither agriculture nor own cattle. Their society is based simply on hunting and gathering food.

The following are Tanzania's major tribes:

Iraqw (Cushitic)

Buffered between the Maasai to the east and the Hadzabe to the west, the Iraqw display more obvious signs of their Cushitic origin than any other Tanzanian tribe.

Living in the green hollowed core of the central highlands of Mbulu, the Iraqw are known for their statuesque, immobile posture and their sharply defined features. A withdrawn people, they grow their own food and tend cattle, selling off crops or an animal only when it is essential.

Maasai (Nilotic)

Dominating northern Tanzania and the area known as the Maasai Steppe, these tall, proud people are easily recognizable by their single toga-like piece of clothing — usually bright red or blue — and their ochre-covered bodies. To the Maasai, cattle are all important, determining a man's wealth and prestige. As the main residents of the Ngorongoro Conservation Area, these pastoralists — who also herd sheep, goats, and donkeys — are constantly on the move to find grass and water. In recent years the Maasai have been encouraged to settle, and increasingly are supplementing their traditional diet of milk, blood and meat with grain.

Chagga (Bantu)

To the north of the Maasai Steppe, the Chagga people — Tanzania's third-largest group — live on the slopes of Kilimanjaro where thriving banana groves provide a main staple. Cultivating the mountainside, the Chagga are noted for their enterprise and hard work, early on developing an irrigation system to carry water up to 180 metres (600 feet) above the river level, enabling them to sustain the *mbeke* plant from which they brew beer. Among the earliest groups influenced by the Roman Catholic and Lutheran missionaries, Western education and cash cropping — mainly coffee — through cooperative farming they have achieved substantial incomes and are better compensated than other ethnic groups.

Gogo (Bantu)

The Gogo, south-west of the Maasai Steppe near Dodoma, have been hindered by a serious lack of water. A dam built in 1955 provides for the town, but the Gogo in the surrounding countryside have become accustomed to periodic famine. Between 1953 and 1955

Above: Maasai family outside their mud and dung home. Strong codes of discipline and stoicism enable the Maasai to live cheerfully in their harsh environment.

they were hit by one of the worst droughts in history. The government responded with a rescue campaign, but the bill went to the poverty-stricken Gogo.

Hehe (Bantu)

South of the Gogo, the Hehe make their home in the Iringa district's highland grasses, 1,500-2,000 metres (4,920-6,560 feet) above sea-level. These warlike people spent much of the late nineteenth century fighting and on one famous occasion defeated the invading German colonists. Today the Hehe sustain their military legacy by supplying a large proportion of recruits to the national army. The plateau on which the Hehe live supports a thin population on corn, beans and cattle. Surplus crops are sold to raise any needed cash. Since World War II the Hehe have been enthusiastic about education, with many of their chiefs setting the example.

Makonde (Bantu)

The Makonde, internationally famous for their imaginative woodcarvings, are one of the five major tribes in Tanzania. Located south-east of the Hehe along the coast, they remain relatively isolated on the Makonde Plateau and were perhaps least affected by colonial and postcolonial development.

They have a reputation for cultural conservatism and a willingness to defend their territory and way of life.

Because of their isolation and resistance to outside change, the Makonde have developed a high degree of ethnic self-consciousness. (See 'Makonde Treasures', Part Three.)

Sukuma (Bantu)

The Sukuma (meaning 'people to the north') are Tanzania's largest tribal group and live in the north-western part of the country, just south of Lake Victoria. They remained isolated from missionary influence, modern education and cash cropping until well into the twentieth century. More recently, however, they have

Above: Ferry boat replaces city bus for Tanzanians living along the shores of Lake Tanganyika.

prospered under a mixture of cotton growing and cattle herding. The Sukuma harvest the cotton, use their own gin for processing and sell the final product. The nearby port of Mwanza has prospered under the growing commercial activities of the Sukuma (see 'Out West', Part Two.)

Nyamwezi (Bantu)

South of the Sukuma tribe near the Tabora area live the Nyamwezi. Their name, given to them by Swahili traders of the coast, means 'people of the moon', probably due to their location in the west. Although primarily cultivators, with some cattle, the Nyamwezi were once great traders. Their bartering talents earned them a reputation among nineteenth-century European explorers as the most powerful tribe in the interior. The Nyamwezi were sufficiently organized to threaten the commercial power of the Arabs and in 1880 attacked Tabora, the Sultan of Zanzibar's base.

Recent years have seen their decline. The area sustains little except the tsetse fly and Tabora suffers from an inadequate water

supply, lack of irrigation and sparse land development.

Haya (Bantu)

North-west of the Nyamwezi tribe the Haya make their home in the rich soil along the shore of Lake Victoria. Coffee was grown and traded by the Haya long before the Europeans arrived to buy the crop. Today local coffee and tea processing plants make it possible for the Haya, living 1,400 kilometres (868 miles) from the coast, to export the coffee in powdered form.

Haya women are considered excellent craftswomen and are proud of their hairdressing abilities.

Ha (Bantu)

Along the Burundi border between Lake Victoria and Lake Tanganyika is a land of forest and bush infested with tsetse. There the Ha live in scattered solitude tending their long-horned cattle. Children often wear nothing and adults are clad in hides or fibres of bark for special occasions. The Ha retain a deep belief in the mystical. Outside

Above: Zanzibari girl shields her face with the Islamic *buibui* worn by East African Muslim women.
Below: One of the many colourful and friendly faces of Tanzania.
Opposite: Tribal dancers perform the *Ngama*, with the help of a live python.

each beehive hut a collection of sticks (where food and drink are left) serves as a shrine to the family's ancestors. Attempts to move the Ha away from the tsetse-infested land to better-watered areas have failed. Perhaps because of their remoteness, artistic expression among them has flourished. Their dances and celebrations can continue for several days and nights. Music is made using drums and gourds while dancers beat out complicated rhythms with their bare feet.

Non-Africans

Roughly one per cent of the population is non-African: Europeans, Asians (Indians, Pakistanis, Goans), and Arabs. The majority of non-Africans are Shirazi, a mixture of Arab and the local population, and are well established on the coastal islands of Zanzibar, Pemba, and Mafia. Strongly Islamic in religion, the islands' residents speak Swahili and maintain a different culture from that of the Middle East.

The foregoing is only a cross-section of the country's 120 tribes which, with an annual growth rate of 2.8 per cent, is destined to see the population increase to thirty million by the year 2000.

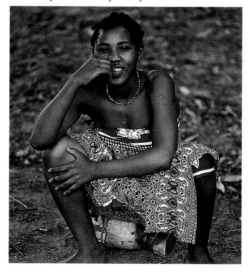

60

PART TWO: PLACES AND TRAVEL

Above: Cloves laid out to dry in the Equatorial sun. Together the two islands of Zanzibar and Pemba produce the majority of the world's cloves.

Opposite: Ornate latticework is typical of the old wooden Zanzibari homes.

Coastal Islands: The Life of Spice

Zanzibar conjures up exotic images of dhows, lateen sails set against a dawn sky, whitewashed Arab houses embracing an azure sea and tall palm trees swaying on a warm tropical breeze redolent with the aroma of cloves and frangipani. The reality is satisfyingly similar and Zanzibar continues to luxuriate in its reputation as a tropical idyll latent with romance. Yet how different is the chequered history of this island which reveals a far from tranquil story.

Known as the Spice Island because of its long-standing clove industry, this low-lying stretch of land — crab-claw shaped thirty-seven kilometres (23 miles) off the coast of Tanzania — has always exerted a powerful fascination as well as influence on the mainland. There is an old saying, 'When they pipe in Zanzibar, people dance on the Lakes' (a reference to lakes Victoria and Tanganyika).

Travellers, traders, raiders and colonizers from around the world have been drawn to Zanzibar throughout the centuries. Sumerians, Assyrians, Egyptians, Phoenicians, Indians, Chinese, Malays, Persians, Portuguese, Arabs, Dutch and the British have all set foot on the island's beautiful white beaches, each leaving behind a different legacy.

The original inhabitants of the 1,660-square-kilometre (640-square-mile) island were the Bantu, who probably migrated from the mainland across an ancient land bridge. The first mention of Zanzibar comes from the Greek mariner's guide, *Periplus of the Erythraean Sea*, written around AD 50. Referred to as Menouthais, the island was described as being 'low and wooded, in which there are rivers and many kinds of bird and the mountain-tortoise.

'There are no wild beasts except the crocodiles; but they do not attack men. Here, there are sewed boats and canoes hollowed from single logs, which they use for fishing and catching tortoises. Fishermen also catch them in a peculiar way, in wicker baskets, which they fasten across the channel opening between the breakers'.

The origin of the name Zanzibar remains obscure, possibly coming into use with the arrival of the first Persian settlers around AD 1200. Some attribute it to the mixing of the Persian words *zangh* (negro) and *bar* (coast). According to explorer Richard Burton, the Arabs claim to derive the word from the phrase *zayn za'l barr* meaning 'fair is this island'.

The first Muslim influence permeated Zanzibar via the trade winds of the Indian Ocean. Persians and Arabs from the Gulf sailed between the months of November and March, when the dry monsoon blew from the north-east, and returned on the wetter south-east monsoon. By AD 700 some Arabs were staying to settle and build their stone houses and by 1107 the *muezzin* was wailing from the coral stone mosque at Kizimkazi in the south-west.

The Arabs, mainly from Oman, intermarried freely with the locals to form the foundations of the Swahili people. The Shirazi, settlers from the Persian Gulf, arrived around AD 1200, adding yet another ingredient to the Zanzibar melting pot — a mixing of races and cultures reflected in the faces of the Zanzibaris today.

The arrival of the piratical Portuguese was heralded by the voyage of Vasco da Gama, who passed by *Jamgiber* in 1498. The maritime Europeans soon came to dominate the entire coast through a combination of warfare, pillaging, and false treaties. For the next 200 years they clung onto their shaky empire in East Africa.

The walls began to crumble, however, when the Omani Arabs sacked Zanzibar in 1652. The Portuguese power structure collapsed with the surrender of Mombasa in 1698, but turmoil persisted throughout the next century and trade stagnated.

Slaves

One factor was to change all this — slavery. Demand for slaves had been steadily growing as the colonial powers expanded

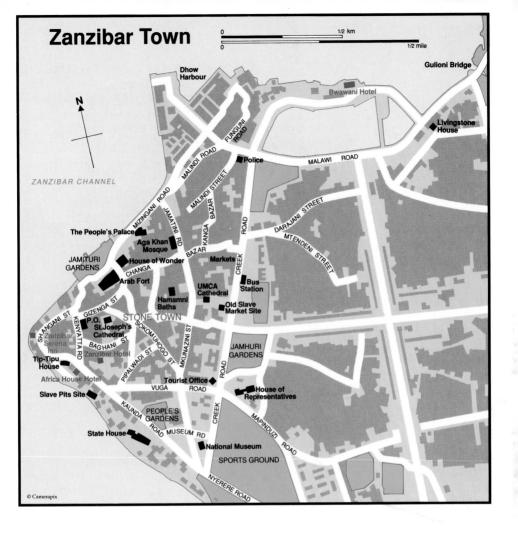

Zanzibar Town

their domains. Omani Sultan Sayyid Said recognized a profitable business opportunity when he saw one and moved his court from Muscat in Oman to Zanzibar in 1840.

Under the Sultan's rule Zanzibar town grew to 25,000 people — swelling to 40,000 during the dhow season — and Zanzibar overtook Kilwa as an entrepôt for slaves. In response to the island's growing power and wealth, the caravan routes shifted north to Bagamoyo, the mainland town closest to the island. From there, those slaves who had survived the trek from the interior were shipped to Zanzibar and sold as labourers for the island's expanding clove plantations, or sent onward to serve as domestic servants overseas. Trade in human beings had replaced Zanzibar's traditional exports of ivory, gum copal, cowries, hides, and cloves.

By the middle of the nineteenth century Zanzibar was the most important town on the east coast of Africa with as many as 50,000 slaves a year being sold in the town's market. Conditions on the island at this time were appalling.

Venereal disease was endemic, cholera and malaria raged and rubbish lay in piles everywhere. Livingstone, who regarded slavery as the 'open sore of the world', thought that Zanzibar should have been called 'Stinkibar'.

Livingstone frequently led the protesting voice of conscience concerning the treatment of slaves. During his later visits to Africa he kept detailed records of the

Above: Church of Christ Cathedral, built on the site of the old Zanzibar slave market. The church altar occupies the spot where the whipping block once stood.

atrocities committed by the Arabs and their African right-hand men — often members of the Yao tribe — which helped lead to the suppression of the trade in the Indian Ocean.

Demonstrating Victorian hypocrisy at its highest level (bearing in mind Britain's use of child labour) the British led the fight to eradicate the slave trade. Thanks to Her Majesty's Royal Navy, which ruled the waves during that era, the new Sultan Sayyid Barghash capitulated in 1873, agreeing to outlaw the export of slaves from the island.

Despite the elimination of human sales, the Omani sultanate managed to weather the storm of change for almost another century. An overnight revolution in January 1964 — only one month after independence from British rule — toppled the Sultan's plain red flag and Zanzibar and Pemba became a people's republic.

On 24 April 1964, the republic was united with Tanganyika and the joint name of Tanzania was adopted.

Getting there

There are regular flights from Dar es Salaam, Mombasa and Nairobi. Catamarans and, from the Malindi Wharf on the Dar es Salaam main seafront, hydrofoils — speedy and comfortable — travel back and forth. The Zanzibar Shipping Corporation's *MV Mapinduzi* sails twice weekly carrying passengers and freight. The journey takes four/five hours, though customs and immigration can add another two.

Dhows are also popular for crossing the channel, leaving when the wind and tide are right. Crossings can be rough and, in a dhow without an engine, may take longer than the normal six hours. Book in advance at the shipping office on Malindi Wharf, Dar es Salaam, or in Zanzibar.

Departure times are approximate, but be there on time just in case.

When to go

Zanzibar enjoys a typical equatorial climate. Between December and March the

Above: Interior of the Church of Christ Cathedral. The small crucifix on the pillar to the left of the chancel is made from the wood of the tree under which Dr Livingstone died.

Overleaf: Lateen sails set, fishing dhows leave Zanzibar harbour in convoy. In the background is the house used by Livingstone in 1866 before he set out on his final expedition.

weather is hot and relatively dry. The cooler, dry period from June to October is also pleasant, with temperatures averaging 25°C (77°F). Expect heavy rains from March to the end of May and short rains during the month of November. Humidity averages seventy-eight per cent.

Where to stay

All accommodation must be paid in US dollars. Hotels with history and a lingering colonial feel include the 52-room Zanzibar Serena Inn, Africa House, Zanzibar Hotel and the Spice Inn, all in Zanzibar Town. The Victoria Guesthouse, Malindi Guesthouse and Emerson's House are suitable alternatives, as well as the High Hill and Hotel Clove. (The Hill and Clove do not serve alcoholic drinks.) The 118-room Bwawani Plaza Hotel overlooks Funguni Creek along the edge of the town. Apart from the hotels there are a number of other guesthouses in town including the Warere and Flamingo,72 which offer rooms at reasonable rates with breakfast included.

The Mnemba Club, on 1.5 kilometre, private Mnemba Island off the north-eastern coast of Zanzibar, has ten thatched cottages. The Zanzibar Tourist Corporation maintains self-catering bungalows on the following beaches: Bwejuu, Chwaka, Jambiani, Uroa, and Makunduchi. The bungalows have no electricity or running water. (See Listings for 'Accommodation').

Sightseeing

Zanzibar Town was the starting point for most major expeditions into the mainland interior; Burton, Speke, Grant, Livingstone, Stanley, and Kirk all came there to assemble provisions and hire porters and guides to take them along the caravan routes. So what better place than the **Livingstone House** to begin an exploration of the island?

Above: *Beit el Ajaib*, the House of Wonders, headquarters for the ruling Zanzibari political party.

The house is located off Malawi Road, 300 metres (327 yards) before the **Gulioni Bridge**. There, between January and March 1866, Livingstone gathered his essential supplies before setting off on his last journey. From there head north by foot (the best way to explore the narrow, winding city streets), keeping the ocean to your right. You'll soon pass the luxurious **Bwawani Hotel** overlooking **Funguni Creek**.

West from the hotel along the water's edge lies **Dhow Harbour**, a bustling hub of sailing activity. From there you can watch sacks of Zanzibar cloves being loaded onto waiting ships or dhows that have arrived with the trade winds from India. The harbour is also the place to hire a ride to the **offshore islands** or, for true adventurers, a lateen-powered trip all the way back to the Tanzanian mainland.

From the harbour continue south-west along **Mizingani Road**, past the **University of Dar es Salaam Institute of Marine Science** and the **Port and Customs offices**, until you reach *Beit el Ajaib*, also known as the **House of Wonders**. Positioned behind **Jamituri Gardens** — a favourite venue for an evening stroll and site of a mouthwatering night food market — the palace was constructed in 1883 by Sultan Barghash. The four-storeyed building (the tallest in Zanzibar) has slender pillars, broad fretted balconies, and marble staircase and floors imported from Europe. The doors, however, are uniquely Islamic, covered with intricate carvings and bearing inscriptions from the Qur'an.

Despite the **cannons** that guard its steps, the building was damaged in 1896 when the British — flexing their colonial muscle — bombarded it in order to place their choice for Barghash's successor on the throne. The war was one of the shortest in history (forty-five minutes) and the Sultan acquiesced. In 1911 the Sultan and his family moved across the street to the more modest **People's Palace** and the House of Wonders was taken over by the British. Today *Beit el Ajaib* is the headquarters of the ruling Afro-Shirazi party which came to power in the bloody revolution of 1964 (see 'History: From the Cradle to Independence', Part One).

Above: Zanzibar Museum, a repository of local information and home to a number of Dr Livingstone's possessions.

Located next to the House of Wonders, across **Sokokuu Street**, is the **Arab Fort**. After the Arabs of Oman sacked Zanzibar in 1652 the Portuguese were booted out and the victors quickly moved in. They tore down a Portuguese church and built in its place the Arab Fort. Public executions (beheading by the sword) took place behind it, the last one in the final decade of the nineteenth century.

Surrounded by towering orange stone walls, the fort was later used as a prison, barracks and finally repair shop for the short-lived **Bububu Railway**. The ornate doorways at the back of the fort lead out into two large courtyards. The courtyard to the left contains, yes, a basketball court. Renovated in 1946, the fort is once again undergoing a face-lift, but can still be toured despite the construction.

Stone Town

Considered by many to be the heart of Zanzibar, **Stone Town** is the only functioning historical town in East Africa, much the same today as it was 200 years ago.

It is the oldest section of Zanzibar Town, made up of winding lanes and unique stone houses. The area was originally a small island divided from the mainland by a creek, which was eventually filled in to become Creek Road. Captain James Frederic Elton, a former British Vice-Consul in Zanzibar, wrote the following about the area in 1879: 'An architectural background of Arabian arches, heavy carved wooden doors and lintel posts, circular towers, narrow latticed windows, recesses and raised terraces, combined with and worked into tortuous lanes and sharp turnings, wells in unexpected corners; squalor, whitewash, dirt, and evil smells as you penetrate further into the heart of the town.'

The Arab homes that form the backbone of Stone Town are as much a part of the island's culture as the dhows that ply the local waters. It is said the Arab owners used to vie with one another in the extravagance of their building. There is even one home, local legend claims, where the sand and other materials were mixed with egg whites.

71

Pity the poor hens, for the walls are very thick. It is also said that slaves were often buried alive in the walls or floors, to ensure against bad luck (but not for the slaves).

The size of a room depends on the length of the mangrove poles supporting the ceiling. Impervious to the white ant, the poles are still shipped out from Zanzibar to Arabia. How they are used can be seen in the finely preserved rooms of the **Zanzibar Hotel,** in Stone Town off **Baghani Street.**

The crowning glory of each stone home is the front door. Made from teak and set with great brass studs, each door, with surrounding frame and lintel, is elaborately carved. Traditionally, when a house was built, the door was erected first and the quotations from the Qur'an and representative carvings covering it were supposed to exert a benign influence. Favourite motifs include the lotus (reproductive power), the fish (fertility), the chain (security), the date (plenty) and the frankincense tree (wealth). There are more than 560 carved doors in Zanzibar. Their historical and cultural importance is now being realized and many of them are being restored.

A good place for Arab doors is near **St Joseph's Cathedral**. From the Arab Fort head due south. Rather than attempting to follow the street signs — in English, Swahili, or Arabic — search the skyline for the cathedral's twin white spires.

For atmosphere, wander the narrow streets that once rang with the sound of the slave masters crying the virtues of their wares.

Today these same alleys are filled with bazaars, women draped in *buibuis*, shops, tailors at treaddle-powered machines, playing children, jewellers, carpenters, local sweetmeats, hawkers selling curios, old men and the coffee seller rattling by with his cups and liquid energy. Beautiful mosques — such as the **Aga Khan** — are suddenly revealed around an unlikely corner.

Directly behind the **city market,** in the very heart of Stone Town along **Hamamni Street**, are the **Hamamni Baths**, built by Hadj Gulamhussen. These public baths (which were closed in 1951) were commissioned by Sultan Barghash who reigned between 1870 and 1888. An unobtrusive door with a plaque overhead marks the entrance to the baths. The cramped entry soon spills out into a spacious maze of marble-floored changing rooms, massage rooms, refreshment areas and, of course, the baths themselves, made from stone covered with lime plaster. Tours can be arranged by inquiring at the shop to the left of the baths as you face the entrance. The charge is a donation to the restoration project currently under way.

When the claustrophobic lanes of Stone Town begin to close in, follow the setting sun to the town's (and island's) most westerly point. There, along **Shangani Street** south of the **External Communications Building**, sits the **Africa House Hotel**, once the former British Club. Redolent with cedar wood and teak, marble floors and past members' cigar smoke, the hotel's signs still announce 'Ladies' Powder Room' and 'Gentlemen's Cloak Room'. This is the best place to come for a sundowner before dinner, but be forewarned . . . the snooker table is permanently under dust covers!

While all the world seems peaceful and idyllic on the porch of Africa House, only a building away sits a reminder of darker days — the **house** of the notorious slave-trader **Tippu-Tip** (Hamed bin Muhammed bin Juma bin Rajad el Murjebi). Of Arab descent but with an African great-great-grandmother, his dealings in ivory and slaves made him a powerful figure in East and Central Africa.

A scant 150 metres (164 yards) south of his home, where the **Tumekuja School** now stands, is the former site of a **slave pit**, where men like Tippu-Tip made their fortunes causing untold misery along the way.

Opposite: A blending of Portuguese and Arabic architecture on Zanzibar. Although the Portuguese stayed only 200 years, their presence remains.

Above: These woven coconut palm fronds will later be used for mats or in the construction of a Zanzibari home.

Continue south along **Kaunda Road**, past the **People's Gardens** on the left and **State House** on the right. At Creek Road turn left then look left for the **National Museum**.

While most visits to the museum begin at the front door, it is worthwhile to begin this tour at the back. Behind the museum the **oldest carved door** on the island can be found, dating from AH 1112 (AD 1694). Once inside the museum, which opened in 1925, exhibits of local wildlife, dhow construction, traditional carving and relics from the time of the Sultans and the early explorers can all be viewed, including Livingstone's letters and medicine chest.

Slave trade

While trade transformed Zanzibar Town from a simple fishing village into a bustling commercial centre in the seventeenth century, the nineteenth century saw the slave market boost Zanzibar's influence to that of the utmost importance in the western Indian Ocean.

The site of the **old slave market** lies north of Haile Selassie School along Creek Road. During the trade's heyday the market itself was described as having been an irregular, oblong space some fifty yards by thirty yards, surrounded on three sides by thatched palm huts and on the fourth by stone buildings. Sales were held at 4.00 pm. The British government official and intrepid explorer, Captain James Frederick Elton, records for posterity:

'When you go at an early hour and look at the strings of men, old women, and children sitting upon the ground in lots, and the rows of younger, better favoured and higher priced girls, bedecked for the occasion with heavy earrings and bangles and bright-coloured robes — all the faces marked with that vacant stare common to the slave population — I protest the sight is a revolting one, and it is rendered doubly so when, as is often the case, some of the recently imported wretches are mere skeletons of skin and bone, festering with sores and loathsome skin-diseases, and looking as if they were on the very threshold of death.'

Above: Boat yard on Chole, one of Tanzania's many offshore islands.

In 1873, Sultan Sayyid Barghash prohibited the export of slaves from Zanzibar. The same year Anglican Bishop Steere laid the foundation stone for the **Church of Christ Cathedral** in the old slave market. Inside the church the altar occupies the spot where the whipping block used to be. Take a minute to notice the massive **marble pillars** (accidentally placed upside down) and the quality of the **stained-glass windows**. A small **crucifix** at the left side of the chancel is made from the wood of the tree under which Livingstone died in 1857 — a tribute to the man for whom the abolition of the slave trade meant so much.

The outside of the church is dominated by a **clock**, donated by the Sultan on the condition that the bell tower did not exceed his palace in height. The walls and wide, barrel-shaped ceiling of the church are built from coral and Portland cement. During its construction Arabs prophesied the roof would collapse and crush the Christians, but the church remains, a potent symbol to the defeat of slavery.

From the Church of Christ Cathedral

continue north along **Creek Road** approximately 150 metres (164 yards) to the island's **bus station**. Just beyond the buses to the left lies the **market**, opened in 1904. There the heartbeat of Zanzibar thumps wildly as vendors vie for the buyer's attention. Whether you are there for fish, fruit, flowers, vegetables, souvenirs, or spices, this is the place to look. Shopping begins as early as 07.30 and continues until 18.00, with a long break at midday.

Islands off the island

For the perfect picnic getaway on a sunny tropical afternoon, the tiny **deserted islands** lying a few kilometres off the western tip of Zanzibar Town are made to order. They can be reached by an organized visit through the tourist office or, for the more adventurous, by hired dhow from Dhow Harbour where the cost depends on your bargaining skill.

One of the more popular destinations is **Chunguu Island**, also known as **Prison Island**. The coral outcrop was formerly owned by an Arab who used it to detain

recalcitrant slaves. In 1893 a **prison** was built there (hence the name). Although it was never used the **ruins** can still be seen.

A relaxing walk around the island, past peacocks and mango groves, takes about half an hour. Goats, gazelles and birds inhabit the woods, but the most famous residents are its fifty giant land tortoises, probably brought from Aldabra in Seychelles near the end of the last century. There is a **bar** and **restaurant** on Chunguu, as well as a small **guesthouse**.

Another well-known spot — despite its gruesome name — is **Grave Island**, famous for its beautiful beaches, swimming snorkelling and sunbathing. The island has been reserved as a European cemetery since 1879 and among the **graves** are those of men killed on HMS *Pegasus*, sunk in Zanzibar Harbour by the German cruiser *Königsberg* during the First World War.

Other islands include **Bat Island**, from which the flying foxes cross the water to Zanzibar every evening to feed on the fruit trees, and **Snake Island**, which most dhows choose to simply sail by.

Zanzibar Island: A Tour of Paradise

The Zanzibar experience would not be complete without a sojourn on the island's famous sandy white beaches, an exploration of the ancient Arab ruins, a sail to the offshore islands and then a fragrant tour through the clove countryside.

The fertile soils of this tropical refuge are replete with nutmeg, lemon grass, black pepper, cardamom, cinnamon — and the omnipresent clove which earned Zanzibar its sobriquet, the Spice Island. Although the clove arrived late to the islands (it was not introduced until 1818), today Zanzibar and neighbouring Pemba Island supply seventy-five per cent of the world's crop.

The fragrant smell of the island's major export hangs heavy over the island during the harvest season between July and December. The clove is actually the unopened bud of the tree, which grows as much as fifteen metres (50 feet) high and blossoms with crimson flowers. Pickers climb the trees using ropes and ladders if necessary and snap off clusters of greenish or yellowish-red buds. The spice is collected in baskets and laid out to dry in the sun for four to seven days. When the buds have turned from a golden brown to a deep, dark brown they are graded, packed and loaded in Zanzibar harbour for export.

An organized tour which stops to see, smell and taste the tropical fruits and spices (usually ending with ginger tea in the afternoon) is probably the most practical way to tour the local plantations.

Alternatively, hop on a bike or bus and follow your nose (and the road north out of Zanzibar Town). Within a few kilometres the town falls behind and the clove countryside unfolds. Ask permission before you cross private property.

Getting there

The Tanzania Tourist Bureau arranges half-day and full-day tours throughout the island. To explore on your own, hire a taxi or hitch a ride on the buses and *matatus* that cover most of the island. But do not be in a hurry. Many interesting sights are within biking distance and you can hire a bicycle, either a Chinese sit-up-and-beg 'Flying Pigeon', or a black, steel-framed Indian import. The locals use them to transport everything from chickens to whole tuna and they are colourfully customized and ingeniously maintained by the dozens of bicycle shops and *jua-kalis* (outdoor artisans).

Sightseeing

Begin a tour of the **southern portion** of the island by following the **main road south** out of Zanzibar Town toward the **airport**. Lying on the city outskirts is the **home** of

Opposite: Dhows have traded between Zanzibar, India and the Middle East for thousands of years. This one, its lateen sail filled by the monsoon wind, heads towards the port of Dar es Salaam.

Above: Little has changed during the passage of time in the Old Town of Zanzibar, the capital of the island of spice.

Sir John Kirk, namesake to the island's rare red Kirk's colobus monkey of which no more than 500 remain. Kirk accompanied Livingstone on his earlier expeditions and later became Vice-Consul in Zanzibar. He was an accomplished botanist responsible for introducing rubber, mahogany and eucalyptus trees to the island from Kew Gardens. Kirk also tended an experimental garden to improve local food plants and trees. The **house,** which can be seen at **Mbweni,** was built for him by Sultan Barghash.

About five kilometres (three miles) further south, the road ends at **Chukwani**. There the **Chukwani Palace** can be viewed as well as some picturesque coral cliffs.

To catch the principal southern road to **Makunduchi**, however, it is necessary to backtrack to Zanzibar Town and then head south-east towards **Fuoni**. Thirty-five kilometres (twenty-two miles) from the town, near **Pete**, is the **Jozani Forest**, the last **Zanzibar red colobus sanctuary** in the world. There are now only five groups of

this endangered sub-species remaining. The reserve covers 484 acres adjoining a forest of 1,500 acres. The high water table encourages the growth of lush tropical vegetation including Alexandrian laurel, screw pine, eucalyptus and a variety of palms and figs.

From Jozani continue south along the main road another twenty kilometres (twelve miles) past **Muungoni**, **Kitogani**, and **Muyuni** until reaching **Kufile**. There the road forks. Turn right and after another three kilometres (two miles) the route arrives at the ancient **Shirazi Mosque**.

Built in the walled city of **Kizimkazi**, the mosque was the first to be constructed on the East African coast. Renovations have taken place in recent years, including a new tin roof, but the northern wall still contains the original mihrab (the alcove that faces Mecca from which the imam leads the prayers) and two layers of **Kufic writing**.

According to the inscription, dated AH 500 (AD 1107), the mosque was 'ordered by Sheikh Abuu Amran bin Mussa Ibn Mohammed, May God grant him long life

Above: Red colobus monkey in the Jozani Forest.

and destroy his enemy'. While other forms of this very old Arabic script can be found in different mosques along the East African coast, the example at the Shirazi Mosque is the longest as well as the oldest.

From the **fork at Kufile** it is nine kilometres (six miles) to the main southern town of **Makunduchi**. Near the town, at **mile thirty-six**, is an **underground cave** featuring formations of **stalagmites**. The other sights worth seeing at Makunduchi are its famed **coral beaches** and abundant **sea-life**. Self-catering bungalows can be rented for those who wish to remain and enjoy the sunny disposition of the islanders. (See Listings for 'Accommodation').

Northern ruins

By bike, bus, or tour, the **Mtoni Palace** should be the first stop on an exploration into the northern hinterland of the island. This historic site lies six kilometres (four miles) past the **Bwawani Hotel** and **Livingstone's house** along the road to **Bububu**. The palace was built early in the nineteenth century by an Arab merchant called Saleh bin Haramili. Unfortunately for Haramili, Sultan Sayyid Said accused him of dealing in slaves. As punishment, his residence and surrounding lands (rich in clove trees) were confiscated. The Sultan's treasury expanded. Poor Haramili died a pauper.

During the palace's period of affluence it accommodated 1,000 people. Now it is a courtyard with a row of stone baths at one end and the aqueduct that brought water to the house. Down on the beach, embedded in coral sand, lie some of the **old guns** that were used as flagstaff stays in the garden. The Mtoni gardens are now ocean foreshore.

A mile north from the palace, on the left of the road, are the **Maruhubi Palace ruins**. Built between 1870 and 1888 by Sultan Barghash (who also constructed the House of Wonders), the palace was used to house the ruler's harem. Unfortunately it burned down, aqueducts and all, in 1899. Only a few rooms and arches of the magnificent nineteenth-century building remain. Next to the palace is the **Maruhubi Restaurant**, where a cold drink can be enjoyed before continuing on towards Bububu.

Above: Some of the best diving waters in the Indian Ocean can be found around the country's main offshore islands.

Bububu was the terminus for one of the **world's shortest railways,** running from Zanzibar Town to Bububu, a total of fifteen kilometres (nine miles). An American company had convinced the Sultan that no civilized country should be without a railway and it was completed between late 1904 and December 1905. As a white elephant it was not expensive, but had a short life. It was closed in 1929 and most of the rails have long since been taken up.

Not far from Bububu a **track** leads off to the right through a coconut plantation and a mile or so up a slope to the **Persian Baths of Kidichi**. Situated on the island's highest spot at 153 metres (504 feet) above sea-level, this remarkably preserved series of **domed bathhouses,** with deep **stone baths** and **massive seats** set in the walls around them, were built by Sultan Sayyid Said for his second wife at the beginning of the nineteenth century. From the Persian Baths head back to the main byway and turn north. Six kilometres (four miles) later the road forks at **Chuini**. The right turning

leads twenty-two kilometres (14 miles) to **Mkokotoni,** and from there a boat can be taken to **Tumbatu Island** to view the **Shirazi Ruins,** a large ancient town dating from the twelfth century that contains forty stone houses. The left turning leads toward **Makoba** and past the nefarious **Mangapwani Slave Caves**.

Although Sultan Sayyid Barghash was coerced into outlawing the export of slaves from Zanzibar in 1873, such a profitable business did not end overnight, it simply went underground — literally.

At Mangapwani a **cave** with a **tunnel** to the sea was used to hold captives until the dhows could slip past the British blockade under the cover of night. According to local legend the cave was discovered one day when a boy, searching for his master's lost goat, heard cries emanating from the cave.

Eastern beaches
For those who truly wish to 'get away from it all', there's no better place than eastern Zanzibar Island. Strung along the sunrise

Above: Warm sunlit waters ensure a profusion of coral and marine life, such as this roving Coral grouper.

coast are a number of picturesque fishing villages, remnants of an earlier, simpler era. The villagers live in basic coral homes under swaying coconut palms. While they grow some staples, their main subsistence is derived from fishing. Women supplement the family income by making intricately embroidered Muslim caps that are sold to the pilgrims in Mecca each year.

The quickest route to the other side of the island is along the **main road** heading straight east out of Zanzibar Town towards **Chwaka**. Halfway along the route, approximately fifteen kilometres (nine miles) from both towns, lie the **Dunga Ruins**. The palace that once stood on the site was built by the last and most feared ruler of a long dynasty of local chiefs, Ahmed bin Mohamed bin Hassan el Alawi. It is said that he held such absolute control over his subjects that they were only allowed in his presence on their knees crying *Shikamu*, 'I clasp your legs'.

The construction of his **royal residence** and **mosque** began in 1845 and was finished in 1856. At the consecration of the mosque many slaves were sacrificed on its foundations; a meshing of old and new religious beliefs. **Treasure** is rumoured to be buried at Dunga, but few Zanzibaris visit the ruins for fear of ghosts.

Along the east coast there are few tourist sites or cultural attractions — only beautiful beaches, aquamarine waters, and friendly inhabitants. Self-catering bungalows (no electricity or running water) are available for rent at Uroa, Chwaka, Bwejuu, Jambiani, and Makunduchi.

Local residents are usually more than happy to prepare a fresh fish meal for a minimal cost. If you desire more than tropical fruits or the ocean's bounty, however, take it with you.

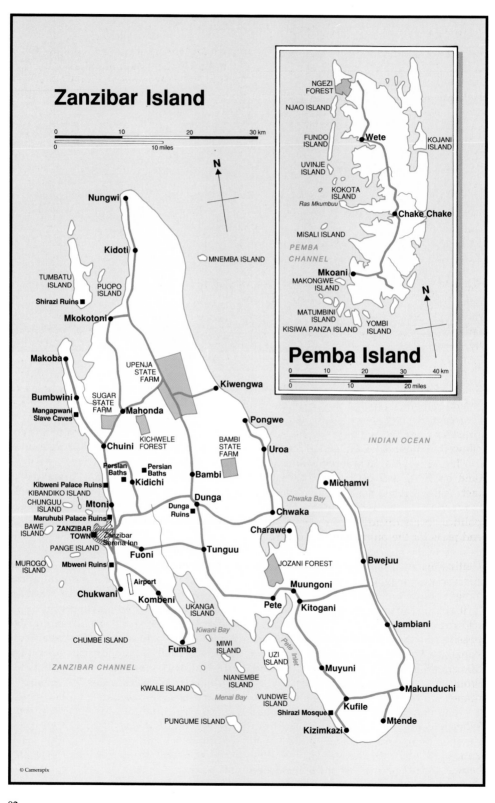

Zanzibar Island

0   10   20   30 km
0   10 miles

N

Nungwi

Kidoti

MNEMBA ISLAND

TUMBATU ISLAND
PUOPO ISLAND
Shirazi Ruins ■

Mkokotoni

Makoba

UPENJA STATE FARM

Bumbwini

SUGAR STATE FARM

Mangapwani Slave Caves ■
Mahonda

Kiwengwa

Chuini

KICHWELE FOREST

Pongwe

BAMBI STATE FARM

Uroa

Persian Baths ■
Persian Baths ■
Kidichi

Kibweni Palace Ruins ■
KIBANDIKO ISLAND

Bambi

Dunga

Michamvi

CHUNGUU ISLAND
Mtoni

Dunga Ruins ■

Chwaka Bay

Maruhubi Palace Ruins ■
BAWE ISLAND
ZANZIBAR TOWN
Zanzibar Serena Inn

Chwaka

Charawe

PANGE ISLAND
Fuoni

Tunguu

JOZANI FOREST

Bwejuu

MUROGO ISLAND
Mbweni Ruins ■

Airport

Muungoni

Chukwani

Kombeni

UKANGA ISLAND

Pete

Kitogani

Jambiani

CHUMBE ISLAND

Kiwani Bay

MIWI ISLAND

UZI ISLAND

Pete Inlet

Muyuni

ZANZIBAR CHANNEL

Fumba

NIANEMBE ISLAND

KWALE ISLAND

Menai Bay

VUNDWE ISLAND

Makunduchi

Kufile

Shirazi Mosque ■

Mtende

PUNGUME ISLAND

Kizimkazi

INDIAN OCEAN

NGEZI FOREST

NJAO ISLAND

FUNDO ISLAND
Wete

KOJANI ISLAND

UVINJE ISLAND

KOKOTA ISLAND

Ras Mkumbuu

Chake Chake

MISALI ISLAND

PEMBA CHANNEL

Mkoani

MAKONGWE ISLAND

N

MATUMBINI ISLAND
KISIWA PANZA ISLAND
YOMBI ISLAND

Pemba Island

0   10   20   30   40 km
0   10   20 miles

© Camerapix

Pemba Island: Clove Capital of the World

Half a day's dhow ride, fifty kilometres (31 miles) north of Zanzibar, is the true clove capital of the world — the seldom visited island of Pemba. Although smaller in size than Zanzibar, Pemba's abundant rainfall and rich soil support the same number of people and three times as many clove trees. It is known as *Al Kuhdra* — the Green Island — and only its irregular coastline, thick with mangroves and poor natural harbours, explain the greater importance of Zanzibar.

Along with a plenitude of cloves, the island is also blessed with a multitude of fish. The Pemba Channel, located between the island and the mainland, is up to 400 fathoms deep (2,400 feet) and recognized by game fishermen as some of the finest waters off the east coast of Africa.

Despite its close proximity and historical links to Zanzibar, Pemba remains a distinct community. It is reputed to have been the centre of witchcraft on the East African coast and perhaps that is why it was allowed to administer itself as late as 1895.

The age of the clove trees on Pemba (and on the island of Zanzibar), plus the fact that Zanzibar's share of the world clove market is declining, has led to political pressure towards diversification and pleas for the promotion of tourism.

Getting there
Air Tanzania flies from Dar es Salaam and Tanga to Chake Chake.

If you are not pressed for time (plan on allowing at least twelve hours) it is also possible to take a dhow from Tanga or Zanzibar. The trip from Zanzibar ends at Mkoani, the island's most southerly town. From Tanga dhows dock at Wete in the island's north.

When to go
Pemba enjoys the same climate as Zanzibar, with the rainy season falling between March to the end of May and also during the month of November.

Where to stay
There are government-owned hotels in each of the island's three main towns: Chake Chake, Mkoani, and Wete. (See Listings for 'Accommodation'.)

Sightseeing
Whether you travel around Pemba by bus, hired taxi, or foot, the smell of cloves — the mainstay of the economy — will follow you everywhere. Once covered by primeval forest (of which the **Ngezi Forest** in the north is a remnant), the island today is dominated by three-and-a-half million clove trees grown on terraces that corrugate the steep-sided valleys.

There are few large **plantations** on Pemba: most farmers own ten to fifty trees (many of which are more than 150 years old). If you visit the island during the harvest season, which occurs every five months, you'll find the schools closed and everybody lending a hand. Collected in baskets, the clove buds are laid out to dry in the sun wherever there is a flat surface: mats in front of houses, tables, concrete yards, roadsides, even the local football pitch is conscripted.

The dried clove is then sent to **Wete** in the north, with its handsome German *bomas* overlooking the **harbour**, and shipped east for use in cigarettes and to produce painkilling oil of cloves, as well as the familiar cooking spice without which any apple pie is unworthy of its name.

Chake Chake
Located in the centre of the island, **Chake Chake,** the principal town of Pemba, contains a new **airport,** a few streets lined with **administration buildings,** several **shops** and an **eighteenth-century Muslim fort** which has been converted into a **hospital**. Pemba's earliest **ruins** are located near Chake Chake, on a peninsula to the west of the town called **Ras Mkumbuu**.

First settled around AD 1200 by the Shirazi, the site contains several **houses, three pillar tombs**, and a great **fourteenth-century mosque**, one of the finest congregational mosques on the east coast of Africa.

Although Pemba never played an

Above: Cloves laid out to dry in Pemba. Every five months the entire population turns out to pick the spice from the island's three-and-a-half-million trees.

influential role in the development of East Africa, invaders from the distant Maldives still considered the island sufficiently important to conquer. In the fourteenth century at **Pujini**, located eleven kilometres (seven miles) north of Chake Chake, the conquerors built a **fortified settlement** ruled by one Mkame Mdume, whose name translates into 'he who draws milk from men'. Among his many legendary cruelties, it is said that Mdume forced toothless old men to crack nuts with their gums.

Luckily all that remains from the despot's era are ruins: a **citadel, mosque,** several **graves,** and a **lily pond.** Pujini, not surprisingly, is said to be haunted, and Mkame Mdume's name is used today as a children's bogeyman. Other relics on the island include **Harun's Tomb,** located in the north-east at Chwaka.

The traditional pillar tomb, three metres (10 feet) high, is believed to be the memorial to a Shirazi prince. Another burial site, whose origin remains shrouded in mystery, is the **Lonely Tomb,** close to

the village of **Vitongoje** between the beach and the jungle. It is rumoured to be the resting place of a former settlement's leader who died suddenly. His followers, distraught at such a catastrophic loss, took to their ships and sailed away.

When the Portuguese arrived in 1520 they set about destroying any existing structures. Their reign was short-lived, however: the only remnants left from their time during the sixteenth and seventeenth centuries include the **ruins** of a **fort** in Chake Chake and the sport of bullfighting.

The fights are held during the hot months of December, January and February when the ground is hard. Luckily for the bulls, the sun also rises the morning after a fight for, as in Portuguese tradition, the animals are not killed.

Mafia Island: The Fisherman's Paradise

Situated 160 kilometres (100 miles) south of Zanzibar is Mafia, the most southerly and smallest of the main Tanzanian islands. It sits at the mouth of the Rufiji River where tonnes of silt deposited each year have created a delta sixty-five kilometres (40 miles) across. It is a favourite haunt of big-game fishermen and scuba divers, for whom record catches and resplendent coral make this a watersports paradise.

At 394 square kilometres (152 square miles), Mafia is actually the largest island in a small green cluster that is administered by the mainland.

The name has nothing to do with the Italian crime syndicate, but probably comes from the Arabic *morfiyeh*, which means a group, and refers to the archipelago of which it is a part. A second theory is that it is a contraction of the Swahili *mahalia pa afya* meaning, a healthy place to live.

Like the rest of the coast, Mafia experienced several waves of settlers and invaders. A centre of Shirazi domination between the twelfth and fifteenth centuries, it gradually lost most of its influence and was subsumed into the Portuguese empire. Its fame must have spread, however, as the poet Milton made reference to it, calling the island Monfia.

Mafia also made history in 1915 when the British used the captured island as the first place in Africa to launch assembled planes for reconnaissance missions. Their greatest success was in finding the German battleship *Königsberg* skulking up the Rufiji delta.

They were helped in their search by intelligence provided by the elephant hunter Pieter Pretorius. His hunting lodge had been commandeered by the Germans — which may have influenced his decision to join the other side. He boarded the vessel disguised as an Arab selling chickens and passed the *Königsberg*'s position to the British.

In a combined air and sea operation in July 1915, the *Königsberg* was shelled and critically damaged by fire and was finally scuttled by her German captain, Max Looff. Until floods broke up the ship in 1978, her listing funnels still showed above the water, a reminder of an historic Great War 'first'.

But the main reason to visit Mafia is for some of the best game fishing in the world. Following in the footsteps of Ernest Hemingway, sports fishermen come for the superb specimens of kingfish, marlin, horse-mackerel, sailfish, and huge rock cod weighing up to 227 kilos (500 lbs). The world record for a dolphin, thirty-four kilos (seventy-five pounds), was set there in 1952.

A contender for the origin of the mermaid legend, the dugong breeds among the grasses of the Mafia Channel. The channel is also the breeding ground of the awesome great white shark. On the coralline beaches of the smaller islands to the east of Mafia, giant turtles lay their eggs during the north-east monsoon.

These rare, armour-plated reptiles are under threat, however. The increasing use of dynamite in fishing and the collecting of shells may soon disrupt the finely balanced ecology of the local coral reef and the whole marine system that depends upon it for survival.

Getting there
Air Tanzania flies once a week from Dar es Salaam. The Tanzania Coastal Shipping Company regularly serves Mafia from Dar es Salaam, but there is no fixed schedule.

Where to stay
Unless you plan to pitch a tent, the thirty-room, air-conditioned Mafia Island Lodge offers the only accommodation. (See Listings for 'Accommodation'.)

Overleaf: Rose-tinged shores of Bawi at sundown, another of Tanzania's little-visited island retreats.

Above: Sandy shores of Mafia Island double as a busy boulevard for residents.

Sightseeing

At **Ras Kisimani** on the south-western tip of the island, **ruins** exist which indicate a settlement flourished there between the ninth and fourteenth centuries. A **thirteenth-century mosque** has been excavated and fragments of **Chinese pottery** can still be found among the foundations.

Other ruins dating back to the fourteenth century have been discovered to the south-east on neighbouring **Juani Island**. In 1829 the entire town was sacked by the Sakalava cannibals who paddled their canoes from Madagascar. The victorious and resourceful Sakalava promptly ate most of their vanquished foes.

Mafia's modern history, as a World War battle front, proves even more dramatic. During the first war the German district commissioner, along with fifty *askaris* (guards), was surrounded in a **coconut plantation** at **Ras Mbiziby** by 500 British troops who forced his surrender. The palm trees still bear the bullet holes of the skirmish.

Above: Unlike her Muslim sister, this islander does not wear the traditional black *buibui* covering, a testimony to the tolerant religious atmosphere found along the coast.

The Coast: From Ancient Ruins to Modern High-Rise

Dar es Salaam: A Haven of Peace

Seen from the deck of a dhow returning from Zanzibar, Dar es Salaam drifts into view across the warm azure straits separating the island from mainland Tanzania. The boat sails parallel to the white sands of the beaches north of the city where tourists and city-dwellers spend their leisure time sunbathing, snorkelling, or swimming out to the coral reefs.

As warm breezes propel the boat along by its huge lateen sail, individual buildings on the foreshore can be picked out against the green backdrop of forest that rises gently around the city to a low, undulating horizon. The Gothic Lutheran church; the white spire of the Roman Catholic St Joseph's Cathedral just behind the main sea-front road, Sokoine Drive; the three-storeyed, old colonial post office; and on Observatory Hill the campus of the new university — can all easily be identified.

The dhow creaks and wallows around a curving headland past the bustling ferry quay and the swell of the Indian Ocean is left behind as you enter one of the finest natural harbours in the world: Kurasini Creek. There freighters, cargo boats, launches and yachts are anchored in the deep water that can accommodate container ships as well as the largest dhows on the coast, the 100-ton *jahazis*. Dugouts quarter the harbour, their bilges slick with freshly caught fry, and the rusting orange ribs of early steel ships rise from the beach like claws.

Toward the hydrofoil base and derricks and cranes of the freight terminal to the south, the main dhow loading area, Malindi Wharf, is a transient floating village of oily decks, rigging and sweating stevedores who work through the heat of the day to load dhows with dried fish, cement, mangrove poles and soft drinks for an evening departure. It was the natural harbour and its central position on the East African coast was responsible for the birth of Dar es Salaam — Swahili for Haven of Peace — in the late nineteenth century.

In 1866 the Sultan Majid bin Said of Zanzibar made plans to develop the harbour into a safe-water port and trading centre. He proceeded to build a palace of coral (imported from Changuu Island off the coast of Zanzibar) which he named Dar es Salaam. The Sultan died before it really took off, however, and his successor did not realize the Sultan's ambition.

A further brief spurt of development took place when the anti-slaver William Mackinnon began an ambitious project to build a road to the recently discovered Lake Malawi. After only 118 kilometres of the 645 (73 miles of the 400) were completed, the scheme was abandoned.

Ten years later, recognizing the potential of Dar's location, the German colonists revived the Sultan's plan. In 1887 they threw out the Arab rulers and fought off the Bushiri uprising, firmly establishing their Teutonic presence which is reflected today in the disciplined lines of the city's administrative offices. (See 'From the Cradle to Independence', Part One.)

Confident that the city had a promising future, the German imperial commissioner moved his headquarters from Bagamoyo, seventy-five kilometres (47 miles) up the coast, to the nascent Dar es Salaam. With the Germans firmly in control, the Benedictines and Lutheran missionaries capitalized on the stability to build their churches. The foundation stone for the Roman Catholic St Joseph's Cathedral was laid in March 1898; the Lutheran Azania Front church was consecrated in 1902.

A hotel, the Kaiserhof, was built for the trickle of travellers and merchants who came to establish trade links. The real business flow did not emerge until after

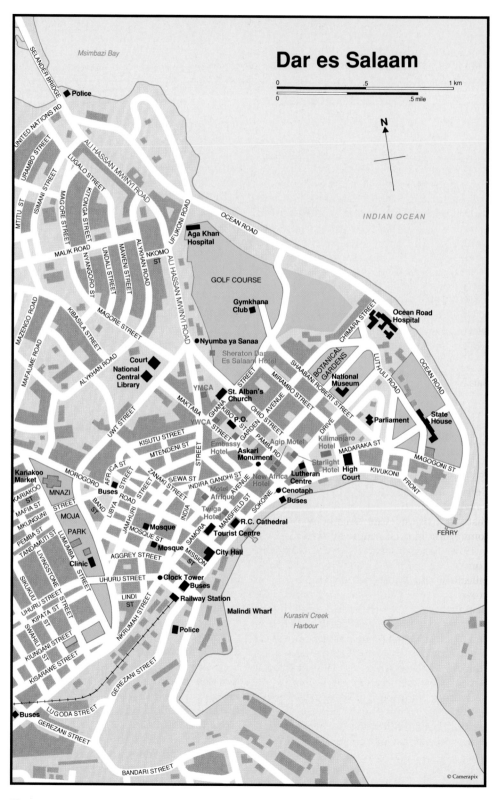

Dar es Salaam

Msimbazi Bay

INDIAN OCEAN

SELANDER BRIDGE
Police
UNITED NATIONS RD
URAMBO STREET
MTITU ST
ISIMANI STREET
LUGALO STREET
MAGORE STREET
KITONGA STREET
ALI HASSAN MWINYI ROAD
UFUKONI ROAD
OCEAN ROAD
Aga Khan Hospital
NKOMO ST
ALI HASSAN MWINYI ROAD
MALIK ROAD
NYANGORO ST
UNDALI STREET
MAWENI STREET
ALYKHAN ROAD
MAZENGO ROAD
MAFAUME ROAD
KIBASILA STREET
MAGORE STREET
ALYKHAN ROAD

GOLF COURSE

Gymkhana Club

Ocean Road Hospital

CHIMARA STREET

Nyumba ya Sanaa

Sheraton Dar
Es Salaam Hotel

BOTANICAL GARDENS

National Museum

LUTH'ULI ROAD

OCEAN ROAD

Court
National Central Library
UWT STREET
KISUTU STREET
MTENDENI ST
AFRICA ST
MOROGORO
ZANAKI STREET
KISUTU STREET
YMCA
MAKTABA STREET
GHANA STREET
St. Alban's Church
KIBO ST
P.O.
YWCA
GARDEN AVENUE
OHIO STREET
MAKTABA STREET
PAMBA RD
Agip Motel
Embassy Hotel
Askari Monument
MIRAMBO STREET
SHAABANI ROBERT STREET
DRIVE
Kilimanjaro Hotel
MADARAKA ST
Parliament
State House
MAGOGONI ST

Kariakoo Market
KARIAKOO ST
MNAZI
MAFIA ST
MKUNGUNI ST
PEMBA ST
TANDAMUTI ST
MOJA
PARK
Clinic
LIVINGSTONE STREET
LUMUMBA STREET
Buses
LIBYA ROAD
BAND
JAM'HURI ST
MOSQUE ST
Mosque
Mosque
AGGREY STREET
SEWA ST
INDIRA GANDHI ST
INDIA AVENUE
SAMORA AVENUE
MANSFIELD ST
MISSION STREET
New Africa Hotel
Motel Afrique
Twiga Hotel
Lutheran Centre
Cenotaph
Buses
SOKOINE
R.C. Cathedral
Tourist Centre
City Hall
Starlight Hotel
High Court
KIVUKONI FRONT

FERRY

UHURU STREET
LINDI ST
Clock Tower
Buses
Railway Station
Malindi Wharf
NKRUMAH STREET
SIKUKUU STREET
UHURU STREET
KIPATA ST
SWAHILI STREET
KIUNGANI STREET
KISARAWE STREET
Police

Kurasini Creek Harbour

Buses
GEREZANI STREET
LUGODA STREET
GEREZANI STREET
BANDARI STREET

© Camerapix

90

Above: A natural deep-water harbour and central location on the Indian Ocean make Dar es Salaam one of East Africa's busiest shipping centres.

Overleaf: As well as being Tanzania's largest city — boasting almost two million residents — Dar is also home to the country's major industries.

1905, however, when work began on the Central Railway linking the coast with Lake Tanganyika, thereby traversing the vast country and dramatically improving communications. The railway was finished in 1914 when the last spike was hammered home in Kigoma, 1,248 kilometres (775 miles) away. Now nothing could stop the growth and influence of the town, and the rush was on.

After the First World War, when Tanganyika was handed over to the British, it was natural that they should base their administrative and commercial centre there — and that they should also rename the Kaiserhof. It became the New Africa Hotel.

Business boomed and the population expanded with it. Today Dar es Salaam has nearly two million inhabitants who live and work in buildings that reflect the architectural styles of at least two foreign cultures laid over its original Swahili foundations. The city is a dynamic patchwork of past and contemporary cultures. India Street, is distinctly Eastern with its Asian speciality shops and bazaars.

The German influence can be seen in the almost Bavarian-style railway station, the old post office (a former administrative centre), and the telegraph office whose verandahs list the dead from the East African campaigns. The British brought their passion for gardening and left a legacy of bougainvillea, fragrant frangipani, Indian laburnum, oleander, hibiscus, jacaranda and brilliant flamboyants to line the avenues and provide shade.

As well as the cheap and tasty Swahili and Asian convenience foods served up to workers and the budget traveller, Dar es Salaam offers all you would expect of a capital city, though its culinary strength lies again in its Afro-Swahili origins. Fish is available in every shape, size, and variety;

Above: The Sheraton Dar es Salaam keeps pace with Tanzania's reputation as being one of Africa's prime tourist destinations.

and all have one thing in common: freshness. Dishes range from fish soup (whose main ingredient is the dried silver *dagga* laid out on sacking in the markets), to smoked octopus served up in newspaper triangles, to sea bass, sailfish and snapper, usually cooked in the traditional Swahili manner with aromatic and hot spices and garnished with coconut. (See 'Tastes of Tanzania', Part Three).

Getting there

In addition to the regular dhow service from Zanzibar and Pemba and the less frequent dhows from as far north as the Gulf, Mogadishu and Mombasa, Dar es Salaam can be reached more conventionally by air. International airlines including Aeroflot, Air France, Air India, Air Malawi, Air Tanzania, Air Zimbabwe, Alliance Airways, British Airways, Egypt Air, Ethiopian Airlines, Gulf Air, Kenya Airways, KLM, New ACS, Royal Swazi and Swissair, all service Dar es Salaam International Airport and many travellers use this route as a gateway to the rest of Africa. Air Tanzania Corporation

(ATC) services internal routes.

By rail the only viable route from outside the country is from Zambia on the TANZAM, one of the classic rail journeys of the world. The train runs in each direction twice weekly. (See 'The Great Uhuru Railway', Part Three).

International buses and express coaches ply the roads between Nairobi and Dar as well as Mombasa and Dar. Buses generally leave early in the morning and arrive early the next day. Most of the main arterial roads are now in good condition, making this an acceptable mode of transport.

When to go

The best months to visit Dar are between June and September, when cooling breezes help keep the temperature and humidity bearable. The summer months (January to March) in Dar es Salaam are nothing short of an endurance test.

Where to stay

Sheraton Dar es Salaam is conveniently located 10 Kms from Dar es Salaam

International Airport and close to the central business district.

Opened in 1995, the Sheraton Dar es Salaam boasts a swimming pool, two restaurants, two bars, coffee shop and shopping plaza.

The spacious air-conditioned rooms, beautifully furnished with colour television and satellite channels, safety deposit boxes and equipped mini bars are the last word in style and comfort.

And like all really top-class hotels the Sheraton Dar es Salaam also offers excellent conference and banquet facilities.

Reservations for any hotel owned by the Tanzania Tourist Board (New Africa Hotel, Kilimanjaro Hotel, Kunduchi Beach Hotel) can be made at their main office which is on Maktaba Road near the Askari Monument. The TTB offers large discounts during the off-season. Other top hotels include: Oyster Bay, The Twiga, Bahari Beach, Motel Agip, Baobab Village, Hotel Embassy, Starlight and Hotel Mawenzi.

For those on a budget, the YWCA offers clean rooms with mosquito nets and fans. Female travellers as well as couples are allowed to stay. (See Listings for 'Accommodation'.)

Sightseeing

With the decline of Tanzania's economy the 'Haven of Peace' has fallen on hard times. Yet Dar still has plenty to offer those willing to look beyond the peeling paint and pot-holed roads. The people are extremely friendly but, as in most African cities, Dar has its quota of thieves, conmen, street children and beggars.

Partly due to the nature of the Tanzanian, everyone has time to stop and chat and unfolding a map on a city street will draw sympathetic response and help.

The best place to begin a tour is at the very heart of the city: the **Askari Monument**. Surrounded by flowerbeds, the memorial bears the words of the German General Paul von Lettow-Vorbeck: 'In memory of native African troops who fought, To the carriers who were the feet and hands of the army, And to all other men who served and died in German East Africa 1914-1918, Your sons will remember your name.'

Head south away from the monument along **Maktaba Street** and immediately to the left is the **Tanzania Tourist Board**. Maps of the city are in short supply but this is a good place to try and procure one. If none are available chances are the friendly people will be able to point you in the right direction.

Across the street from the TTB is the **New Africa Hotel**, constructed in 1906 but recently rebuilt. City maps are definitely available in the lobby but at a price.

There is a thriving black market for foreign currency with many of the transactions taking place outside the New Africa Hotel. While it is possible to receive higher rates than are given by the banks or bureaux de change, where rates vary, be warned: there are plenty of conmen around waiting to rob unsuspecting tourists.

Maktaba Road ends at the **harbour**, and a left turn puts you on **Kivukoni Front**. On the corner stands an imposing **Lutheran church**, one of the first buildings constructed during the German occupation.

Continue along Kivukoni, enjoying the bustling **waterfront** to the right where entrepreneurs selling peanuts, candies, and stalks of sugarcane hawk their wares.

For something more substantial there is no better place to enjoy lunch than the **restaurant** on the **corner of Kivukoni and Ohio Street**, the former Dar es Salaam Club where Evelyn Waugh once stayed. The establishment is recognizable by the red, orange, and white striped umbrellas on the outdoor patio facing the water. The sign above the door reads 'Ministry of Lands Natural Resources and Tourism', but do not be put off. Underneath in smaller print is '**Hotel and Tourism training institute**'. Apprentice chefs, hard at work, can be counted on to serve up one of Dar's more memorable meals.

Next to the restaurant is the **Kilimanjaro Hotel**, billed as the city's most luxurious accommodation. But do not be too optimistic. The hotel hosts an adequate restaurant and is clean. Its real asset is the bank in its lobby. Although they rarely open on time (09.00), the hours they keep are longer than normal and you can

usually have your business transaction completed within five minutes — nothing short of a small miracle in Africa.

Continue along Kivukoni Front until the road ends. There you'll find the *Kivuko ferry* shuttling people, produce and vehicles across the harbour entry to **Kigamboni**, a large fertile **peninsula** where mangoes, pawpaws, cassava, bananas and coconuts grow right down to the beautiful beaches. **Ocean Road** leads away from the ferry, along the water's edge, home to the bustling **Kivukoni fish market**, the best place to buy red snapper, lobster, prawns, squid, barracuda and shellfish straight from the sea.

State House lies past the fish market along Ocean Road. Don't even think about pointing your camera in this direction. Built in 1922 on the foundation of the old German palace, this well-maintained government residence is a blend of African and Arabic architecture. Shrubs, trees and a profusion of blooming flora make it one of the most attractive buildings in Dar.

Botanical beauty

Continue north along Ocean Road followed by a left on **Chimara Street**. Directly ahead lies the inviting green of the city's **Botanical Gardens**. Located right next to the city centre, this oasis of vegetation is surprisingly peaceful. Within the garden bloom bougainvillea, yellow Indian laburnum, mauve jacaranda, scarlet flamboyant, red hibiscus and pink oleander.

Across the street from the Botanical Gardens is the **National Museum**, an interesting cultural centre as well as another retreat from the heat. Established in 1940, the museum boasts archaeological collections displaying some of the most important fossil hominid finds ever excavated, notably the partial **skull** of *Zinjanthropus*, 'Nutcracker Man', unearthed by Mary Leakey at Olduvai Gorge. Tanzania's more recent cultural history is well represented by the **ethnographic displays** of tribal **masks**, **weapons**, **witchcraft totems** and traditional **musical instruments**.

As you emerge from the museum back into the enveloping heat, take a left on **Samora Machel Avenue** (formerly Independence Avenue), renamed after Samora Machel, a former president of Mozambique. This stretch of tree-lined avenue leading back towards the city centre is one of Dar's most pleasant. Two blocks from the museum, Ohio Street crosses Samora. To the right is the **Air Tanzania Corporation** terminal, the place to book internal flights. Reading matter in the form of the latest British newspapers and magazines will be found at the **British Council** on the corner of Samora and Ohio Streets.

One block further west along Samora, on the left-hand side, is the **The Selfservice Supermarket**. The amazing variety of products is a sure sign that import restrictions are relaxing in Tanzania.

Adjacent to the supermarket is the **American Cultural Centre**, a good place to catch up on news from the States. **British Airways** is next door to the cultural centre and beyond the airline office the **Askari Monument** looms from an easterly vantage point.

Main street

This time leave the monument, heading west along Samora Avenue, and enter the **central business district** of Dar. There, stores, banks, travel agents, curio shops, government offices, restaurants and businesses dominate, mixing high-rise buildings with the low, red-roofed Swahili architecture.

In the four short blocks between the Askari Monument and Morogoro Road are several fine eating establishments: **The Alcove**, known for its Indian food; the **Salamander**, a popular lunch stop and the **Rendezvous Restaurant**, with its wide variety of reasonably priced meals all served in air-conditioned comfort. The restaurant on top of the **Twiga Hotel** also offers some fine food.

Opposite: Askari Monument in the centre of Dar es Salaam: a tribute to the Africans who fought and died in the First World War.

Above: Fresh fish are available every day at Kivukoni market.

Directly behind the Twiga Hotel on **Mansfield Street** is the not to be missed **Sno-Cream Parlour**, an establishment gaining a cult following among Western travellers. A walk into the Sno-Cream is a walk into Disneyland. Donald Duck, Mickey and Minnie, Bambi, and Peter Pan and Tinkerbell are all there to greet you, along with every sundae flavour you could wish for. Continue around the block back to Samora Avenue. Down the street from the Twiga, on the left, is the **Minister of Tourism's office**. Pamphlets, brochures, maps . . . are all in short supply, but if you have a specific question they may be able to answer it. Samora and the heart of the business district ends several blocks further west at the **Clock Tower**. The monolith was 'erected by the citizens of Dar es Salaam to commemorate city status 11 December 1961'.

To the left of the clock tower is the **bus station** and one block beyond the bus station toward the ocean is the **railway station**. From the station it is only a stone's throw to the bustling **Malindi Wharf**, Tanzania's busiest port. While it may seem perfectly harmless to take photographs, local officials will probably disagree.

Asian district

Running off Samora Machel Avenue in a north-west direction is another of the city's main thoroughfares, **Morogoro Road**. The first block to cross Morogoro Road is **Ali Hassan Mwinyi Road** (formerly **India Street**). On the corner is a shop called **Wine & Spirits**, whose contents need little explanation. If it can be imported, chances are you will find it there. The second street to intersect Morogoro heading north is **Indira Gandhi**. Take a right for the city's best selection of **gold** work and **textiles**. Three blocks along Gandhi Street, where it intersects India, look for the brightly lit **7UP sign**. Around the corner, on **Sewa Street**, is a matching **Pepsi sign** and entrance to the area's most popular **pizza parlour** with a take-away service. The **Open House** restaurant on Sewa Street specialises in Indian and Chinese Dishes.

For the more exotic, continue north

along Morogoro two blocks to the **Jamhuri Street** intersection and the **A Tea Shop**. Although it looks a little dark and dingy, different varieties of Indian tea can be sampled there. The shop is especially favoured by elderly Asians.

North two more blocks along Morogoro take a left on **Mkunguni Street** (there are no street signs). Sandwiched between **UWT** and **Band streets** is the **Starlight Hotel**, one of Dar's undiscovered treasures. For approximately US$26 dollars you can stay in one of the cleanest, coolest hotels in the city — and they accept Tanzanian shillings. There is a small **market** right outside the front door of the hotel where fresh fruit and vegetable snacks can be purchased. From the Starlight follow UWT back across Morogoro, continuing north-east one block until the **Zanaki Street** intersection. There, perched on the corner, is the **Nights of Istanbul** restaurant. Inside, waiters dressed in jewelled vests, velvet fezzes and billowing trousers await your order. While you may expect a restaurant with the word Istanbul in it to feature Middle Eastern food, this is not necessarily true in Dar.

Nights of Istanbul began as a pizza parlour and its varied menu now covers such non-Middle Eastern delights as fish and chips, lobster thermidor and Indian curries. The atmosphere is fun, the restaurant clean and the food enjoyable.

From Istanbul head south one block along Zanaki to **Kisutu Street** and a real local treat. Next to the **Amrapali restaurant** is a bright blue building (shack) painted baby blue inside. The **teashop** belongs to **Bhupu**, who serves up delicious samosas with a spicy coconut dip, washed down by hot sweet tea or a soft drink. The shop is only open until 15.00/16.00. If you arrive late, look across the road. Usually Bhupu can be found street-side, hard at work on an open table grilling meats and eats for those passing by.

The **Best Buy Supermarket**, also located on the **Kisutu-Zanaki corner**, is a great place to stock up on essentials or, alternatively, try **Dallas** just round the corner on **Mtendeni Street**.

For the ultimate natural drink, try a **coconut** available at one of the numerous street corners. The coconut stops are easy to spot; look for the huge pile of fibery fruit and a *panga*-wielding youth. The top of the coconut is lopped off and a straw stuck into the milk. It is delicious and refreshing.

After tossing your empty coconut on the pile, walk east along Kisutu Street. Many of Dar's **Hindu temples** are located along this short strip of pavement and, while unassuming from the outside, they are beautifully crafted inside. Visitors are welcome.

Kisutu ends at **Ali Hassan Mwinyi Road**. Turn left and head north until you reach the second roundabout. There on the left the **Tanganyika Motors Building** is home to the majority of **airline offices**. Across the street is the **Bushtrekker Restaurant**, featuring a nice view through oceans of glass. The food is good but a bit pricey.

To the right of the roundabout lie the green fields of the **Gymkhana Club**, Dar's main sports and recreation centre, which is open to all including temporary members. It offers a challenging **eighteen-hole golf course**, tennis, rugby, cricket, football, hockey, squash and table tennis.

Nyumba ya Sanaa

Near the entrance to the Gymkhana Club is the **Nyumba ya Sanaa**, House of Art, a 'must' stop on any tourist itinerary. The self-supporting handicraft centre was begun by an American nun, Sister Jean Pruitt, in 1972. Today the non-profit organization supports 150 young artists whose paintings, chalks, clothing designs, carvings, cards, batiks, pottery and weavings are displayed at the centre.

As you browse through the craft area you can watch the students hard at work, carving, sewing and painting. If a specific work catches your eye, ask about the particular artist. If they are around they will be more than happy to give you a private viewing of their accumulated works, as well as the history behind each piece.

Take a break after shopping, at the **restaurant** located in the House of Art for a delicious fresh fish lunch or a cold drink.

Leave the art centre from the same direction you entered; head along **Ali**

Above: Along the coast wooden dhows are still used by local fishermen to troll the Indian Ocean waters.

Hassan Mwinyi Road and, after one block, which passes by the **YMCA**, take a left on **Maktaba Street**. The **YWCA** and **General Post Office** are on the left and the ubiquitous Askari Monument lies straight ahead.

To market to market

Although Dar es Salaam is a bustling port, economic centre and home to many international conglomerates, Tanzania's rural roots still show through the concrete and tarmac.

Upcountry farmers bring their produce into the city every day and tribesmen mingle with office workers on the busy streets.

Nowhere is this more evident than at **Kariakoo Market**, a name taken from the Carrier Corps stationed there during World War Two. To reach the market turn right onto **Uhuru Street** at the Samora Machel Avenue Clock Tower. To the right, after the first roundabout, is **Mnazi Mmoja Park** where the **Uhuru Torch Monument** was erected to symbolize the **Freedom Torch**

placed atop Kilimanjaro at independence. **Republic Fountain**, at the end of the **park** next to Uhuru Street, is a tribute to the founding of the republic in 1962.

Cross **Lumumba Street,** remaining on Uhuru, and proceed one more block to **Azam's.** What began as a single ice cream shop has spread rapidly throughout the city. On every corner Azam shops sell bread, meat and ice cream . . . although the one near **Uhuru Street** and **Livingstone Street** is the original.

For Kariakoo Market take a right on Livingstone Street, march north five blocks, then take a left directly across from the monument onto **Tandamuti Street**. There, in an atmosphere heavy with commerce and conversation, all manner of fruit, vegetables, fish, meat, herbs, traditional medicines and livestock change hands. The surrounding bazaar is an extension of this honeycomb, where utensils, clothes, furniture and crafts are made. Caution is recommended in this area. It is not wise to leave your own or a hired car unattended.

Above: Shady streets and an ocean breeze help offset the searing heat of Dar's tropical climate.

City outskirts

There are several worthwhile excursions beyond the city limits of Dar, the first to the **Village Museum** located ten kilometres (six miles) north along **Bagamoyo Road**.

Traditional houses there represent the homes of the different tribes. Building materials range from sand, grass, and poles to mud and rope. Villagers can usually be seen demonstrating their ancient carving and weaving skills, offering the finished products for sale. On special holidays cultural groups perform such traditional **dances** as the snake and stilt.

Further north along Bagamoyo Road lies the **University of Dar es Salaam**, laid out amid green lawns and colourful gardens atop **Observation Hill**. Beautiful views of the coast and city stretch out below the campus, which was established in 1970.

Below the University on **Mpakani Road** is the famous **Mwenge Handicraft Centre** where **Makonde carvers** carry on a centuries-old tradition. You may have to fight a path through the tourist buses, but the effort is worth the reward. Each carving is a unique piece of art, some reflecting day-to-day themes, others abstract images. There are no price tags, so be prepared for some hard bargaining. (See 'Makonde', Part Three.)

The beaches

The heat, the humidity, the crowds — why do people live in Dar es Salaam? Head north out of the city centre along **Bagamoyo Road** and within six kilometres (four miles) the answer becomes apparent — white beaches, palms swaying and surf pounding.

Oyster Bay is the nearest beach to the city and at weekends is the place to be. But watch your valuables and clothes. Asian families arrive by the car load to visit, swim and enjoy the scenery. Behind the beach is the **Oyster Bay Hotel** with a dining room overlooking the ocean and a congenial bar. There is a pleasant shopping complex just behind the hotel including the wine and spirits stockists **Mohans**.

The rustic fishing village of **Kunduchi**, eighteen kilometres (11 miles) further up the road, offers an even more beautiful choice of accommodation at the **Kunduchi Beach**

Above: Unique porcelain bowls were discovered in Kunduchi ruins, indicating past trade links with China and England.

Hotel — noted for its exemplary Swahili architecture. For a nominal fee anyone can use the beach and bar facilities.

Other outstanding beach resorts include **Bahari Beach**, **Silver Sands**, **White Sands** and **Rungwe Oceanic**. Most of these hotels offer boat trips by *ngalawa* out to nearby **reefs**, coral **atolls**, and **islands** such as **Mbudya** where the snorkelling is excellent.

The only disadvantage of staying at the beach resorts is the twenty-four-kilometre (15-mile) trip to town.

Kunduchi ruins

Slightly inland and adjacent to Kunduchi Village are some of the finest examples of early **Arabic tombs** on the whole East African coast. Among the baobabs and lush coastal vegetation are the scattered remains of eighteenth- and nineteenth-century tombs where notables of the now defunct settlement were buried. Their names, status, and Islamic chronologies are inscribed on **pillars** — a unique feature for this type of mausoleum.

The pillars, which are similar to obelisks, contain **porcelain bowls** and symbols that remain obscure even to modern-day scholars.

Although African in inspiration, the pillars contain such puzzling features as heavy **stone caps**, leading to speculation that they represent turbans. Other researchers claim the caps are phallic, while it is also possible that they acted as primitive land markers for dhow captains.

The bowls contribute to the pillars' unique aspect and, sunk to their rims in plaster, may denote the wealth of the tomb's occupant. One **tomb** contains a **bowl** with an eighteenth-century design showing the Chinese character *shon*, meaning long life, while another earthenware plate carries a pink design called 'Caledonia', produced around 1830 by the English firm of Adams of Tunstall.

Whatever their actual meaning, the fine porcelain pottery suggests a high degree of material wealth among the coastal Arabs and evidence of trading links extending as far as China and England.

The Kilwas: South to the Border

While today Dar es Salaam is the centre of trading and hub of financial activity, centuries ago it was nothing more than a backwater fishing village, unknown and unnoticed by the powerful Sultans to the south. There are actually three Kilwas: Kilwa Kivinje, meaning 'Kilwa of the Casuarina Trees'; Kilwa Masoko, 'Kilwa of the Market' and finally Kilwa Kisiwani, an island separated from the mainland by a narrow one-kilometre channel.

The heyday of the Kilwas began as early as the twelfth century with the arrival of traders from the Persian Gulf and continued well into the 1800s, finally ending with the abolition of the slave trade. A shift in power soon followed and remnants of the Kilwas' former glory remain only in the fabulous ruins that grace the coastline.

Kilwa (taken from Arabic) was probably founded in the twelfth century by settlers from the Persian Gulf. By the fourteenth century Kilwa traders had captured the gold trade from Sofala (near present-day Beira in Mozambique), paving the port's way to power and riches. By the time Vasco da Gama arrived in 1502, he estimated the population of 'black Moors' at 12,000.

A Portuguese fleet returned in 1505 and, when the local emirate refused to pay tribute, the Europeans took the town by force and hastily built a strong fort to consolidate their power.

They called the town Quiloa, which receives mention in Milton's *Paradise Lost*. After the Portuguese gained control of the Indian Ocean trade, Kilwa slipped into decline.

A fate befell the town in 1587 that could have been taken from the pages of fiction but which was, unfortunately, gruesomely true.

The Zimba, a cannibal tribe from the Zambezi region, laid siege to the island. With the help of a traitor the warriors crossed over in the dead of night to slay 3,000 of Kilwa Kisiwani's Portuguese, Arab and African inhabitants. It needs little imagination to realize what befell the vanquished.

Getting there

South of Dar es Salaam travel is hampered by the great delta of the Rufiji River which flows into the sea opposite Mafia Island. A four-wheel-drive vehicle is a distinct advantage even during the dry season.

The bone-jarring drive south from Dar is enough to tax the patience of the hardiest adventurer, bumping, thumping and jumping over countless potholes, ditches and rocks. During the wet season abandon all thoughts of driving and fly with Air Tanzania or by air charter.

The Tanzanian Coastal Shipping Line, located on Sokoine Drive in Dar, also sails to Kilwa every other week.

The best and most rewarding way to explore the southern coast of Tanzania — if time and comfort permits — is by dhow. These ancient craft regularly ply up and down the Indian Ocean, rarely losing sight of land and running to an age-old timetable determined by the tides, the wind and availability of cargo.

From Dar es Salaam the dhows have an easy time sailing south on the north-east monsoon that blows from October to February.

At other times of the year laborious tacking makes the trip to Kilwa, via Kwale Island and Kilindoni on Mafia Island, much slower.

Carrying cargoes of timber, mangrove poles, cement, hewn coral, cashews, dried fish and passengers who find space where they can, the *jahazi's* principal destination of Kilwa is 300 kilometres (186 miles) south of Dar as the dolphin swims.

Where to stay

There are hotels at Kilwa, Lindi, and Mtwara, but take a tent if you have one.

Sightseeing

The coastal town of **Kilwa**, a once-thriving port, which boasted its own Sultan and minted coins, still remains beautiful despite its loss of prestige.

Situated south of where the **Matandu River** meets the ocean, **Kilwa Kivinje** can be approached by water, but it is necessary to anchor offshore and wade in through the mangrove swamps. Like the rest of the southern coast, Kilwa has known better days. During the nineteenth century an unbridled prosperity swept through the city, carried along on the backs of the slaves taken from the interior. As the **terminus** for the **southern caravan route** from **Lake Malawi**, Kilwa Kivinje exported 20,000 humans annually during the 1860s.

Kilwa Kivinje was also the site of the **German's southern administrative headquarters**, but all that remains are pieces of **carved wooden panelling**, crumbling two-storey buildings and the **iron gate** from the **hospital**. Today the town slumbers again in a lingering air of melancholy hard to dispel. Perhaps it can be traced to the **Muslim graveyard**, located in the south end of town, which contains some of the wealthier victims who succumbed to the tropical scourge — cholera. Richard Burton described an outbreak in 1859:

'Corpses lay in the ravines and dead negroes rested against the walls of the Custom House. The poorer victims were dragged by the leg along the sand to be thrown into the ebbing water of the bay; those better off were sewn up in matting . . .

Limbs were scattered in all directions and heads lay like pebbles on the beach.'

Kilwa Masoko

At the southern end of the **Kilwa peninsula**, twenty-nine kilometres (18 miles) from Kivinje, is the thriving town of **Kilwa Masoko**, which takes its name from the vibrant and colourful **market** held there daily in the **square**.

Under the shade of **mango trees** the Muslim population — the men dressed in white robes, the women in black *buibuis* — can be found selling, buying, or trading fresh produce, goods, and the day's local catch. The town boasts an **airport, jetty, college, bank, hotel**, and **timber mill**.

A recent discovery of **natural gas** on nearby **Songo Songo Island** — and the profits it will soon bring — should prove to be a boon to Masoko and cement the town's position as a rising economic centre.

Kilwa Kisiwani

Most visitors who make the long trek down the coast come to see the spectacular **ruins** of **Kilwa Kisiwani**. Located on a **small island** ten minutes by *ngalawa* from Masoko, the ruins are the finest and most intact collection of Islamic architecture south of the Sahara.

By the nineteenth century and arrival of the slave trade, Kilwa Kivinje had replaced Kilwa Kisiwani as the pre-eminent power on the southern coast. Today only a small **fishing village** marks the former seat of power.

Among the crumbling remains, the most famous structure is the **Husini Kubwa**, a fine example of early Arabic architecture and the largest pre-European building in equatorial Africa. The roof is dominated by a **conical dome** rising approximately thirty metres (100 feet) above the sea. Consisting of more than 100 rooms — including a bathing pool — the palace was built for Sultan al Hasan ibn Sulaiman during the fourteenth century. Today it stands as a reminder of the rich trade which once plied the coastal waters of Tanzania.

Other outstanding ruins include the **Great Mosque**, built in the twelfth century and reconstructed on its original foundations 300 years later. Nearby is the **Small Domed Mosque**, the most ornamental and best preserved on the island. Its central **dome** and **vaults** decorated with **porcelain bowls** make this fifteenth-century structure an archaeological treasure.

Other buildings worth seeing are the *Gereza* — prison in Swahili — located in the northern part of the island; the seventeenth-century **Place of Great Walls**; and a reconstructed **fifteenth-century house**.

Taken together with the **stone town ruins** of comparable importance on **Songa Mnara Island**, located a few kilometres to the south and the ancient **oblong houses** on long-uninhabited **Sanje ya Kati**, this

Above: The Great Mosque on Kilwa Kisiwani dates from the twelfth century, although most of what remains was rebuilt in the fifteenth century. It is the largest, and considered by many to be the most beautiful mosque of this period.

area is the historical jewel of the south; a glorious monument to the achievements of a culture that flourished while Europe struggled to emerge from the Dark Ages.

The sleepy coast

Few tourists venture south of the Kilwas. Terrible roads, time constraint and general lack of interest in the area being the main reasons for their absence. Small fishing villages predominate along the water's edge, unchanged by events taking place in the worlds-away cities to the north.

The town of **Lindi**, approximately 160 kilometres (100 miles) south of Kilwa Kivinje, was once the main port of the southern province. Today the area is known for its excellent **fishing** and fine **beaches**.

The main **southern port** is now located at **Mtwara**, approximately ninety kilometres (56 miles) further south. The **natural harbour** has two deep-water berths, capable of accommodating the largest ships afloat. The **Mtwara Beach Hotel** offers good swimming and snorkelling.

Eleven kilometres (seven miles) west of Mtwara is the village of **Mikindani**, an old Arab seaport filled with narrow winding streets and lined with small **shops** and **mosques**. While Mtwara is the hub for modern shipping, Mikindani remains a busy centre for the trusty ancient dhows that still ply the Tanzanian coast.

Bagamoyo: Glory Days

Opposite Zanzibar, seventy-five kilometres (47 miles) north along the coast from Dar es Salaam, lies Bagamoyo, the former capital of German East Africa and once an important and powerful trading centre.

Before the mid-eighteenth century, Bagamoyo was nothing more than a small trading post handling dried fish, gum copal and salt. Then came the slavers. Capitalizing on its existing trade links, Bagamoyo was able to expand and consolidate its routes. The town's importance as an entrepôt was confirmed when Sultan Sayyid Said decided to relocate his capital from Oman to Zanzibar in 1840.

Bagamoyo, located directly across from the island, became the mainland terminus for the slave caravans (see 'Zanzibar Island', Part Two.)

Bagamoyo means 'lay down your heart'; a poignant reminder that the town's wealth was built using the sweat of the slaves who carried ivory from the interior to be sold and were then placed on the auction block themselves.

In the shade of a tree which still grows in the town, slaves were sold before being transported across the Zanzibar Channel to the island or crushed in the dank holds of slave ships destined for Arabia, Persia, or India.

As well as a terminal, Bagamoyo was also the starting point for the first European explorers on their way to discover the source of the Nile and the secrets of the inland seas. Livingstone, Burton, Speke, Stanley, and Grant all set foot there. Livingstone returned to Bagamoyo, but under less than pleasant circumstances. On 15 February 1874, his sun-dried body was carried into town by the two African bearers — Abdulla Susi and James Chuma — who had stayed with him throughout his seven-year travels, including the eleven months it required to carry his remains more than 1,600 kilometres (1,000 miles) from what is now central Zambia. Seven hundred slaves came to see his body in Bagamoyo before it was shipped back to England for burial in Westminster Abbey.

As the major port on the coast during the late nineteenth century, it was only natural that Bagamoyo was chosen (in 1888) as the site for the capital of the new German colony. Its exalted status was short-lived, however. Lacking a deep-water harbour, the capital was eventually moved to Tanga, 161 kilometres (100 miles) to the north.

Getting there

Buses and *matatus* ply between Dar and Bagamoyo.

Where to stay

The Gogo Hotel or the Bedego Beach Hotel.

Sightseeing

While Bagamoyo is quiet these days, there are some sites worth seeing. The **first Catholic mission** in East and Central Africa was built in Bagamoyo in 1868 by the Fathers of the Holy Ghost. It was to there that **Livingstone's body** was carried before beginning the journey back to England.

Originally the church was built to house orphans from the slave trade, but by 1872 had expanded to include a church, workshops, schools and agricultural projects.

Part of the church is now given over to a small **museum** of slave artefacts that includes stone **pens**, **shackles**, **chains**, **whips** and **freedom certificates**, as well as documents about explorers, foreign rule and freedom.

In 1983 one of the town's oldest inhabitants could proudly show visitors his own freedom certificate given to him in 1897 at the age of one by the mission fathers.

The present **police station**, located near

Opposite: A young Tanzanian rests on the statue outside the first Catholic mission erected in East and Central Africa. The church was built in 1868 to house orphans from the slave trade.

Above: Faded elegance of this building in downtown Bagamoyo bespeaks a more imposing past. It was once the headquarters for Germany's East African colony.

the shore, was once the **old prison** where slaves were held in the back courtyard, then herded blindfolded through underground tunnels to the waiting dhows. Today the scruffy lower floors of the station are used for mundane administration duties while the loft is occupied by bats. Next to the police station sits the imposing 'State House', the former **headquarters** for the German colony. Even today the building on **India Street** dominates Bagamoyo's low, thick-walled houses set among narrow and winding streets.

The German East Africa Company was grudgingly granted the right to collect custom duties along the coast by the Sultan of Zanzibar in 1888. When local leaders protested, the company enforced the treaty using the gunboat *Leipzig* based at their new Bagamoyo headquarters. The German flag was raised, money collected and a **guardhouse** built that still remains.

Near the decaying German headquarters is a **memorial** that commemorates the German soldiers who died between 1889-

1894. Many are buried in the **graveyard** near the shore. This open space was also the site of punishment for anyone breaking penal codes. The Arab sentence usually consisted of twenty-four lashes. When the Germans took over as ruling colonials, the number was increased to twenty-five, adding 'one for the Kaiser'. Their rule was often harsh. An uprising, led by Bushiri who built a **stronghold** ten kilometres (six miles) from Bagamoyo at **Nzone**, was put down by the Germans with Zulu and Sudanese troops. Bushiri was hanged five months later in 1897 at **Pangani** near Tanga (see 'History: From the Cradle to Independence', Part One.)

Several seafront fortified buildings erected by the Germans, along with the **'hanging tree'** opposite the prison, have outlasted their stay and serve to remind the visitor of Bagamoyo's Teutonic era.

Kaole ruins

Five kilometres (three miles) south of Bagamoyo are the remains of the once

Above: Sail of the centuries; wind power remains the most popular form of transport between the smaller settlements along the southern coast.
Below: Typical architecture of Kilwa, which once had strong trade links with Kaole.

prosperous town of **Kaole**. It was founded before the thirteenth century by immigrant Shirazi Arabs who trace their ancestry to the town of Shiraz in Persia. The settlement was the forerunner of Bagamoyo as the coastal capital. It thrived until the fifteenth century and the arrival of the maritime Portuguese who roamed the coast hellbent on disrupting trade where they themselves could not control it.

Kaole's trading association with **Kilwa**, south of Dar es Salaam, was rapidly crushed and the town went into decline. All that remains today are some intriguing **double 'love' graves** dating from the eighteenth and nineteenth centuries, a **fifteenth-century house**, and many **mosques**.

It has been suggested that one of the mosques, the **West Mosque** — with its unusual external staircase for the muezzin to ascend — may have been the first constructed on the mainland.

Above: Bagamoyo, final resting place of a German soldier killed in 1918.
Opposite: Hanging Tree at Bagamoyo, where Arabs brought their slaves from the interior before transporting them across the channel to Zanzibar.

Tanga: A Wealth of Ruins

One major obstacle stood in the way of Bagamoyo's development as the capital of the new German territory — the lack of a deep harbour. Commissioner von Wissman, explorer and warrior who defeated the Bushiri insurgents, therefore decided that Tanga, 160 kilometres (100 miles) to the north, would be the main port. The railway to Moshi began in 1893 and as the tracks were laid the population grew quickly. In 1914 the maverick von Lettow-Vorbeck, commanding a small number of Germans and African *askaris*, soundly defeated a British and Indian expeditionary force at Tanga. (See 'From the Cradle to Independence', Part One.)

To add to their troubles in the hot and unfamiliar country, the invaders were attacked by swarms of killer bees as they advanced, a story which forms the opening episode of William Boyd's historical novel, *An Ice-Cream War*.

Despite the sleepy appearance of the town and its inhabitants, Tanga remains the country's second-largest commercial port after Dar es Salaam, relying on the export of sisal (Tanzania is the world's largest producer) to maintain its position.

Getting there

Tanga is 352 kilometres (218 miles) from Dar and 435 kilometres (270 miles) from Arusha. From Tanga to Nairobi the road routes are either via Korogwe, Moshi and Arusha crossing the Kenya border at Namanga, or via Mombasa crossing the Kenya border at Lunga Lunga. The surfaces are good with the exception of a short stretch between Korogwe and Mombo. Rail connections link Tanga to Nairobi and Dar.

It is also possible to reach Tanga by air or boat. Air Tanzania flies regularly to Tanga from the country's major towns and the Tanzanian Coastal Shipping Line sails twice a week.

111

Above: Making a living from the sea: Tanzania's coastal towns abound with expert sailors and fishermen.

Opposite: Young Zanzibari brings home a fine catch of fish, the most important source of protein for coast and island inhabitants.

Where to stay

A town of decadent, relaxed charm, accommodation includes the 1950s Sir William Lead Memorial Hall, converted by Bushtrekker Safaris into the main building of the Mkonge Hotel overlooking Tanga harbour. Other hotels include the Planters on Market Street, an old, rambling wooden building surrounded by a verandah; the Bandorini Hotel on Independence Avenue with a view of the ocean; the Sunset and Equator guesthouses; the Marina Inn; and the Baobab Beach Hotel, about five kilometres

(three miles) from the town centre.

Sightseeing

Reasons for visiting Tanga include: to catch a dhow to Pemba, visit the **Amboni Caves** and **Galanos Sulphur Springs** and, to the south, explore **Tongoni Ruins** and **Pangani** at the mouth of the **Pangani River**.

The hot springs and Amboni Caves are located ten kilometres (six miles) north of the town centre off the coast-hugging road via Moa to **Lunga Lunga** and the **Kenyan border**.

In the 1950s the Greek 'sisal baron' Christos Galanos, who claimed to have been cured of various ailments after bathing in the springs, was persuaded by the Tanga Municipal Council to finance — as his own memorial — a small spa for the use of which a nominal fee would be charged. It was visited by many tourists from Europe, America, India and Africa, but soon fell into disrepair. In the 1980s thieves stole electrical parts, disabling the generator.

The limestone **Amboni Caves** are notable for their bat colonies, beautiful **stalactites** and **stalagmites** and animal paintings on the ceiling. Of the ten caves, only one, leading to **Kange** seven kilometres (four miles) away is open to tourists. Fifty kilometres (31 miles) south of

Tanga lies **Pangani**, with its six-kilometre-long (four-mile) sandy, palm-fringed bay. This picturesque village with a well, mosque and ancient Arabic buildings, is surrounded by the Bushiri legend.

Twenty kilometres (twelve miles) south of Tanga, on the way to Pangani, are the **Tongoni Ruins** — the greatest concentration of ancient **burial sites** on the East African coast. The area was a former Shirazi settlement and comprises more than **forty tombs** and a large ruined **mosque**.

Like so many ancient sites in Africa, the history of Tongoni remains shrouded in mystery and estimates about the actual age of the once prosperous town vary from the tenth to the fifteenth century.

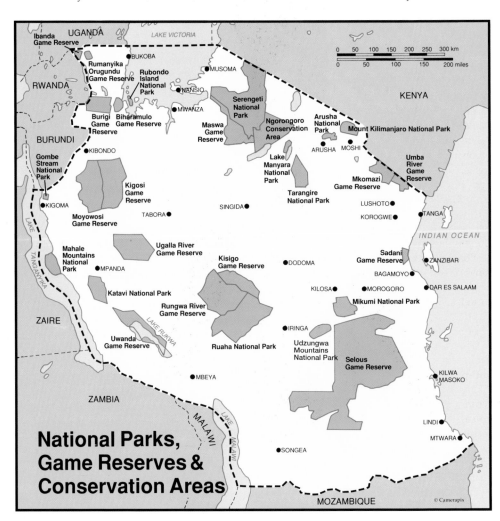

National Parks, Game Reserves & Conservation Areas

The Northern Circuit: Life of the Wild

A full moon over savannah; vast reaches of untouched land; the waterhole where the hunter and hunted come to drink. For most people a safari to Africa is a once in a lifetime opportunity — a three-week escape from the stress of a high tech, high speed world to the pristine wilderness of a bygone era. Only in Africa can twentieth-century man return to the land as it used to be, before his intrusive hand began to reshape the continent and its inhabitants.

Northern Tanzania remains one of the last strongholds of nature, from the great wildebeest migrations of the Serengeti to the brilliant pink flamingos of its numerous alkaline lakes.

Despite the importance of these national sanctuaries and the Tanzanian government's commitment to preserve them for future generations, problems persist that threaten to destroy the parks and their animals.

Poaching has become an open sore on the African landscape. Worst hit are the elephant and rhino; the former for its ivory tusks, the latter for its horn. Between 1977 and 1987 the elephant population declined from 316,000 to 87,000. The rhino population has been reduced by more than ninety-eight per cent and those surviving now number in the low hundreds.

Poaching for meat has also emerged as a new threat. In the northern section of the Serengeti, for example, organized meat poaching has reduced the buffalo population from over 30,000 in the 1960s to approximately 1,500 in the mid-1990s.

The situation had improved a little since then, however, with the establishment of anti-poaching patrols, manned by the army. Along with these came a new commitment from the government to develop the country's tourist infrastructure and resources.

Illegal tree cutting in forested areas has also taken its toll in reserves such as Arusha National Park, which is surrounded by human settlement and agricultural development. Rural people traditionally use wood or charcoal to cook with and, as the population increases, so does the demand for fuel. Axing trees for building is also stripping the land of valuable flora.

Domestic stock competing with wildlife for grazing is an additional threat. Expanding populations situated along the edge of the national parks use the land to feed their cattle, sheep and goats, reducing the amount of food available and, especially when accompanied by dogs, disturbing the local wildlife.

At the root of the problem is the hard-pressed Tanzanian government's inability to provide adequate funding to the departments responsible for managing the game reserves and institutions in charge of training future managers.

Underpaid employees and ineffective management have resulted in corruption in the park system. This is especially applicable for those on a do-it-yourself safari where park entrance fees and lodging are not part of a package deal. Before you set out on your adventure find out from the National Park Headquarters, PO Box 3134, Arusha or any reputable travel agent the exact prices charged for entry to the park, camp sites, and the cost of taking your own vehicle into the reserves.

Do not be tempted to make a 'deal' with any park official to save money. This not only encourages corruption but directly robs the parks and reserves of much-needed revenue.

A quarter of the country is devoted to national parks, game reserves, and no shooting areas, where almost every species of African wildlife can be viewed, from the elephants of Tarangire to, more rarely, the tree-climbing lions of Manyara.

The Tanzanian government, along with such organizations as the African Wildlife Foundation, Tanzania Wildlife Protection Fund, Wildlife Conservation Society of Tanzania and the World Wide Fund For Nature, are working to eliminate the problems threatening the future of the parks and wildlife.

Mkomazi Game Reserve: Mountain Majesty

While most people approach the northern game circuit via Nairobi or Arusha, for those with time, inclination and stamina, an overland trip through the Usambara Mountains, Pare Mountains, and Mkomazi Game Reserve to the wildlife parks is an adventurous alternative.

Sweeping down in a semi-circle known as the Eastern Arc Mountains, these northern highlands include not only the Usambara and Pare ranges but the Taita, Nguru, Ukaguru, Uluguru, Rubeho, Udzungwa, and Mahenge mountains as well. Together they hold ninety per cent of the endemic plants of Tanzania and their montane forests have been listed by the US National Research Council as one of the eleven most important zones of biological diversity in the world. In the eastern Usambaras alone the rate of endemism has been calculated at forty per cent.

Getting there

The main road from Tanga to Moshi is approximately 375 kilometres (233 miles) and runs through the heart of the highland country. The tarmac is good with the exception of the short section between Korogwe and Mombo, at the foot of the Usambaras. It is also possible to travel by bus or train from both Tanga and Dar es Salaam.

When to go

The long rains fall between March and June, when dirt roads are often rivers of mud.

Where to stay

A variety of accommodation is available in either Moshi or Tanga but there is little in between. There are unfurnished rest houses at Mombo and Mkomazi. At Same, a small motel with a bar and restaurant (The Elephant) provides a handy base for day trips into the Mkomazi Game Reserve.

In scenic Lushoto, at the head of a sheltered Usambara valley, there are several medium-class hotels which, alas, have obviously seen better days. In the Mkomazi Game Reserve a two-room bungalow with furnishings and a kitchen is available, but reservations need to be made well in advance. Camping is also allowed. (See Listings for 'Accommodation').

Fees to pay

Fees must be paid in foreign currency and are subject to change. Up-to-date information about the current fees charged for accommodation and entry to the national parks can be obtained from tour operators or the National Park Headquarters.

Sightseeing

Head west out of **Tanga** for the **Usambara Mountains** where visitors often compare the magnificent scenery with the Alps — without the snow. Winding roads up from **Muheza** (for **Amani**) and from **Mombo** (for **Soni** and **Lushoto**) curve around the mountainsides, offering breathtaking views into the valleys below.

Rising gently behind the narrow coastal plain, the moist maritime wind blows over these mountains for much of the year and the abundant rainfall encourages a rich forest that once stretched from the Congo basin in a wide band to the East African coast.

Now, after climatic change and violent earth movements, these upthrusts are left with a unique relict flora and fauna that reflects millions of years of environmental isolation. There are types of plant there whose nearest relatives are found only in the rainforests of West Africa: the **Eastern Arc Mountains** are a continental Galápagos.

Such conditions are ideal for the formation of new species and of the 2,000 plants classified so far — with perhaps hundreds still to be discovered — thirty per cent exist nowhere else in the world. The Usambaras are a repository of rare and indigenous smaller amphibians and reptiles, and also of the endemic robin-like Usambara alethe and the Usambara weaver. In the gloom beneath the dense canopy of the reserve's protected forests, the rare Abbott's duiker is most often seen just after dawn among clumps of the shade-loving African violet (*Saintpaulia ionantha*) and the wild coffee tree. The Usambaras are also a centre of the Tanzania tea-growing industry. From the small town of **Amani** nestled in the highlands, **tea gardens** stretch for miles. Amani was famous during the days of German East Africa for its botanical gardens and medical research centre. Visitors can stay at the town's lovely guest house.

These little-visited mountain ranges are a haven for hikers, bird-watchers, and general outdoor enthusiasts. If you are planning to spend more than a day, take water and food.

Mkomazi Game Reserve

Continuing north-west along the road to **Moshi**, the Usambaras eventually meld into the **South Pare Mountains** at the small town of **Mkomazi**. The town's name is the same as the 2,500-square-kilometre (1,000-square-mile) **game reserve** that lies directly to the east. The reserve's **main entrance** is another 100 kilometres (62 miles) north, five kilometres (three miles) east of **Same** town. Entry permits for day visitors are obtainable at the gate, or at the Tanga or Same game division offices. **Ibaya Camp** is sixteen kilometres (10 miles) from the **main gate**.

Separated only by an international **border** from Kenya's vast Tsavo, the **Mkomazi Game Reserve** acts as an important buffer zone for wild animals. Moves are afoot to establish it as a national park. In 1992 Tanzania's Department of Wildlife invited the Royal Geographical Society to undertake a detailed study of the reserve to underpin future management plans. In recent years, however, the lowland plains of both areas have suffered from Maasai pastoralists watering their herds at the few permanent holes. Yet the land remains incredibly beautiful. The rolling South Pare Mountains give way to the reserve's own system of valleys, some containing **small lakes** and numerous wildlife.

At the crest of a 305-metre (1,000-foot) **escarpment** the scene drops suddenly to the vast **Umba Steppe**, seeming to stretch forever to the Indian Ocean.

With the changing landscape the taller baobabs, flat-topped acacia, and fig trees give way to the dwarf thorn bush and vegetation characteristic of semi-arid plains. The reserve accommodates more than seventy species of wildlife including elephant, hartebeest, giraffe, impala, Grant's gazelle, steinbok, packs of wild dog — and a wealth of bird life. Solitude and wilderness are the key words associated with this little-visited area.

Leaving the game reserve at Same, it is 100 kilometres (62 miles) along the main road (past the Northern Pare Mountains) to the highland town of **Moshi** and the start of the world-famous 'northern circuit', home to Africa's greatest concentration of wildlife.

Moshi: In the Shadow of Kilimanjaro

Moshi lies a scant forty-two kilometres (26 miles) from the 5,896-metre (19,340-foot) Kibo dome of Mount Kilimanjaro. As a result, town and mountain are connected not only by location, but also by spirit. From the hotels of Moshi you see the famous snows of Kilimanjaro and make arrangements to conquer the mountain's summit.

Getting there

Moshi is the end of the northern railway line from Dar es Salaam or Tanga. The town can also be reached by bus. For drivers there is a 375-kilometre (233-mile) road from the Tanzanian coast at Tanga. From Nairobi, via either Namanga or Taveta, the drive takes four and a half hours. A regular minibus shuttle service operates Nairobi/Arusha/Moshi. Flights from Kilimanjaro International Airport, located thirty-four kilometres (21 miles) to the west of Moshi, arrive daily from destinations throughout Africa and Europe.

Where to stay

Accommodation ranges from the low-budget Arawa Hotel to the top-of-the-line

Above: Red face and extremely short tail are the trademarks of the bateleur eagle.
Opposite: Lake Chala, a beautiful paradise astride the Tanzania and Kenya border.

Moshi Hotel (formerly Livingstone Hotel). The YMCA is a favourite destination, with a swimming pool (which may or may not have water), lounge, and several rooms with mountain views. It is also a popular place from which to arrange treks up Kilimanjaro. There is a campsite two miles out of town on the main road to Arusha. (See Listings for 'Accommodation').

Sightseeing
Omnipresent Kilimanjaro makes its presence felt in the surrounding farmlands where coffee, wheat, sugar, and sisal flourish on the rainy slopes and fertile volcanic soil.

Moshi itself is a sprawling town with tree-lined **avenues** and owes its existence to the arrival of the railway from Tanga in 1911. It has a bustling **market** and is a good place to stock up on supplies before an assault on Kilimanjaro.

The **market** is situated along the **main street** about three-quarters of a kilometre (half a mile) **south** of the **clock tower** in the city centre. The **YMCA** can be found the same distance to the **north** of the tower.

Also located within a block of the tower are the **National Bank of Commerce**, **Moshi Hotel**, **Air Tanzania** office, **post office**, **bus station**, **White Mosque**, and **Lutheran Centre**.

As well as being the base for climbing Kilimanjaro, Moshi is close to two very different but equally attractive freshwater lakes: Chala and Jipe. **Lake Chala** is a small limpid-blue crater lake fed by the drainage from Kilimanjaro. It lies to the north of the road from **Moshi** to **Taveta** and its waters form the border with Kenya.

Lake Jipe lies south of the same Moshi-Taveta road at the base of the Pare Mountains. Slightly saline, sixteen kilometres (10 miles) long by five kilometres (three miles) wide, it is significantly larger than Chala. Jipe's waters, like Chala's, also form the Tanzania-Kenya border and are rarely visited from the Tanzanian side, only adding to its air of seclusion and mystery.

Mount Kilimanjaro: Roof of Africa

Rising from the surrounding plains like a mirage, the snow-capped peaks of Kilimanjaro — only three degrees south of the Equator — were believed for years to be nothing but fanciful tales. Snow on the Equator? 'Impossible,' snorted the Victorian armchair explorers of London's Geographical Society.

How wrong they proved to be. Kilimanjaro is the highest mountain in Africa and the tallest free-standing mountain in the world. It is actually three volcanoes in one: Kibo, the youngest, highest, and most central point at 5,896 metres (19,340 feet); Mawenzi in the east at 5,149 metres (16,889 feet); and the western Shira, 3,962 metres (12,999 feet). Previously thought to be extinct, the mountain is in fact dormant and may yet have the capacity to erupt as all three undoubtedly did during their formation.

From the time of its first mention several thousand years ago by Ptolemy, the snows of Kilimanjaro have continued to attract explorers, scientists, adventurers, climbers, and tourists from around the world. With its white mantle dominating the horizon, Kilimanjaro, as much as the wildlife that lives and feeds in its shadow, has now come to symbolize the continent of Africa.

History

Kilimanjaro is a comparatively young mountain, about 750,000 years old. The Chagga who live around its base tell the legend of how Mawenzi borrowed embers from his younger brother Kibo in order to light his pipe, suggesting that there may have been fire and brimstone on Kilimanjaro as recently as the Stone Age. Unfortunately myth often suffers at the hands of empirical science, and geological surveys do not support the story.

There are as many explanations for the meaning of the word Kilimanjaro as there are hiking routes up the mountain. One of the more popular translations is the Swahili 'mountains of greatness'. It has also been taken to mean 'mountains of caravans' (kilima = mountain and njaro = caravan); a landmark for the caravans which travelled the interior looking for slaves. A third hypothesis is that while kilima means mountain, njaro is the name of a demon who created cold. The result: 'mountain of the demon Njaro' or 'mountain of the evil spirit'. And finally, that njaro comes from the Maasai word meaning 'springs' or 'water'. Kilimanjaro could then be taken to mean 'mountain of water'.

Caravan, water, evil spirits — whatever the meaning — for such a towering mountain Kilimanjaro managed to stay well-hidden from prying Western eyes for centuries. First mention of it comes from the Greeks, who describe a 'great snow mountain' at the beginning of the common era. A second reference is not found until a thousand years later, when a Chinese chronicler notes that the country to the west of Zanzibar 'reaches to a great mountain'.

Undoubtedly the snowy peaks were being seen by increasing numbers as the Arab search for gold, ivory, and slaves penetrated the interior of the Dark Continent. (See 'History', Part One.)

With the arrival of Vasco da Gama in 1497, the Portuguese soon succeeded the Arabs as the ruling force in East Africa. Based on rumour and Portuguese exploration, Spanish geographer Fernandes de Encisco wrote: 'West of (Mombasa) is the Ethiopian Mount Olympus, which is very high, and further off are the Mountains of the Moon in which are the sources of the Nile.'

It was this same search for the Nile source, along with a burning zeal to spread the word of God, that 300 years later paved the way for the opening of the continent and a first-hand look by Westerners at the majestic Kilimanjaro.

The first European to glimpse the snowy mountain was Johannes Rebmann, a missionary determined to convert all of Africa to Christianity. Armed with his umbrella and Bible, he set off for a land called Jagga to establish a mission.

He had been told that there was a mountain in Jagga full of djins and evil spirits. Gunpowder would not fire on its

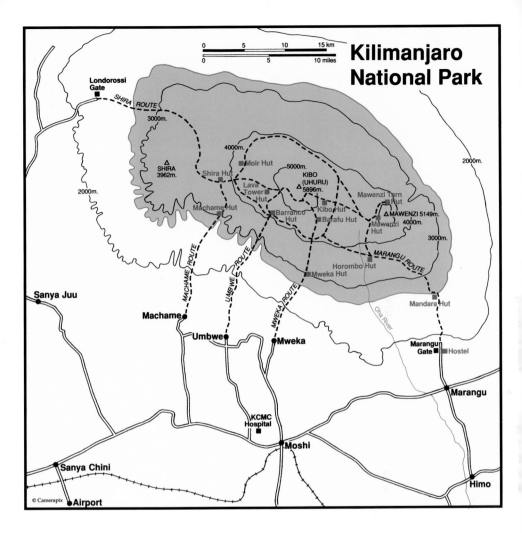

slopes, legs stiffened, and people died from encounters with the *djins*. There was once a king who sent a large number of his subjects to examine the white substance that lies on the top of the mountain. Only one returned, a man named Sabaya. According to Sabaya all his companions mysteriously disappeared during the ascent. He continued until he saw a large door studded with iron spikes. The door was open but he was too weak and frightened to enter. He returned down the mountain, but along the way his hands and feet were destroyed and he became crippled for life. Despite the stories, Rebmann persevered. On 11 May 1848, he approached the high mountains of Jaggaland. 'At about ten o'clock,' he recalls, 'I thought I saw one of them enveloped in a prominent white cloud. My guide simply described the whiteness that I saw as cold (*baridi*); and it was as good as certain to me that it could be nothing else but snow.'

Rebmann's discovery was published in the *Church Missionary Intelligencer* in May 1849, and was greeted with interest and disbelief. Some went to the trouble to prove 'scientifically' that snow at the Equator was

Overleaf: Snowy dome of 5,896-metre (19,340-foot) Kibo, Kilimanjaro's highest point, appears in the background. To the right, Mawenzi at 5,149 metres (16,889 feet).

impossible and the white summit was nothing more than an optical illusion created by the reflection of quartz cliffs, limestone rocks, or crystal. Because of his seemingly far-fetched claims, Rebmann was subject to ridicule and derision and it would take another twelve years before the scientific sceptics eventually conceded the accuracy of his observations.

To the summit

The first attempt to scale Kilimanjaro was undertaken in June 1861 by the German explorer Baron Karl Klaus von der Decken, who climbed to about 4,300 metres (14,108 feet) before turning back near the snow line. The first person to leave his footprints in the snow was missionary Charles New.

He reached an area between Kibo and Mawenzi called the Saddle, which according to New lay at 4,420 metres (14,502 feet). (Today the Saddle is a gravel desert, evidence of the snows of Kilimanjaro's retreat and perhaps the threat of global warming.) New was the first to refer to the five different vegetation zones that exist on the mountain. The summit was first scaled on 5 October 1889 by the Leipzig geographer Hans Ludwig Meyer and the Austrian mountaineer Ludwig Purtscheller.

Between 1889 and 1927 only twenty-three people set foot on the summit of Kibo. Within ten years this figure trebled. After 1928 the numbers began to multiply so frequently it became impossible to maintain any sort of accurate record.

With the construction of huts up the mountain side and the opening of nine main routes, climbing Kilimanjaro has increased in popularity and thousands over the years have attempted to conquer its wintery peaks via the old and well-known paths or, like Rheinhold Messner — one of mountaineering's true stars — by scaling the 1,524-metre (5,000-foot) treacherous Breach Wall. In recognition of the mountain's grandeur and beauty Kilimanjaro was designated a national park in 1973.

Geology

Kilimanjaro owes its existence to the formation of the Great Rift Valley. About 750,000 years ago lava began to flow from deep fractures in the Earth's crust at three main centres: Shira, Mawenzi, and Kibo. Their cones grew for thousands of years, eventually reaching 5,000 metres (16,400 feet) about 500,000 years ago. Shira was the first to become extinct; it eventually collapsed and was covered by material from the other two volcanoes. Mawenzi and Kibo continued to grow, their lava intermingling to form the 'Saddle' which stretches between the two peaks.

Mawenzi was the next to die, but not before an enormous explosion ripped away the entire eastern rim, forming a spectacular gorge. Lava later seeped through the cracks, lending Mawenzi its jagged profile.

Eventually (450,000 years ago) even Kibo succumbed to volcanic ageing and ceased to grow. A huge landslide 100,000 years ago carried away part of the summit and created the huge Kibo Barranco. Then, in one final gush of activity, a puff of smoke placed a perfect cone of ash around Kibo's rim.

Ice, as well as fire, has helped shape the summit of Kilimanjaro. At one point in time an unbroken sheet of ice covered the mountain down to 3,000 metres (9,840 feet). The snows of Kilimanjaro are in fast retreat however, the glaciers have lost their definition and the crater is often bare. Even so, with four square kilometres (1.5 square miles) of glaciers, the mountain possesses about one-fifth of all the natural ice in Africa.

Getting there

Moshi, the major town at the base of the mountain, can be reached by road from Arusha, by rail from Tanga and Dar es Salaam, or by flying in to Kilimanjaro International Airport, located fifty-six kilometres (35 miles) west of the town. From Moshi the road leads east about twenty-eight kilometres (17 miles) to a small village called Himo. Turn left at Himo and ascend the slopes for eleven kilometres (seven miles) to the village of Marangu.

Many hikers choose to skip Moshi and arrange their tour from Marangu, near the park headquarters. Bus and *matatu* ply the forty-eight-kilometre (30-mile) stretch between the two. From Marangu a steep, winding seven-kilometre (four-mile) road threads its way to Marangu Gate, which stands at 1,860 metres (6,100 feet) and is the official park entrance.

When to go

It is possible to climb the mountain at most times of the year, avoiding the two wet seasons; late March to mid-June and October to the beginning of December. The dry months are January, February, July, August and September.

Where to stay

The YMCA in Moshi is known as one of the most economical and dependable places from which to arrange a tour.

In Marangu, the Kibo and Marangu hotels are each pleasant. The Marangu has gardens of interest to bird-watchers and walkers. The Kibo's gardens are smaller but well planned and maintained, with accent on tropical trees and shrubs. Both the offer mountain safaris and arrange hire of porters and guides, and book mountain huts. It is advisable to make reservations well in advance.

The park headquarters are situated at Marangu Gate, the main entry point to the mountain. Porters and guides can also be hired there, but the process may involve up to a whole day, particularly during the busy periods of December and January.

Fees to pay

Budget travellers may have a difficult time financing their way to the top of Kilimanjaro. The park entry fees and hire of guides and porters increase regularly as the cost of living escalates. Add to these the costs of food, equipment and transportation. If you arrange your tour through the Tanzania Tourist Board in Dar es Salaam it will cost twice as much.

Sightseeing

Fishing in the **rivers** of Mount Kilimanjaro is crystal cold delight. Runs, pools and waterfalls all follow in quick succession. **Two streams** administered by Tanzania National Parks on the eastern side of the mountain under **Mawenzi peak** are easily reached by car. Anglers can expect to find trout from 1,520 metres (4,986 feet) up to 2,000 metres (6,560 feet).

The majority of tourists who travel to Kilimanjaro, however, come to tackle the great mountain itself. One of the most interesting aspects for anyone walking up the slopes is the textbook **vegetational zonation**, a term used to describe the idea that certain plants will only grow at certain altitudes, leading to distinct bands of trees, shrubs and flowering plants that change with height. Within these types of habitat live animals that have adapted to a greater or lesser extent to mountain life.

The vegetation bands range from the lush **forests** that completely encircle slopes to the **permanent ice fields** gracing the peaks of the mountain. Each zone occupies approximately 1,000 metres (3,280 feet) of altitude. In general the temperature falls about 1°C for every 200-metre (656-foot) increase in altitude.

The southern slopes receive most of the rainfall from March to May — the trade winds — and the northern slopes are subject to the drier monsoon from May to October. Additionally, moist air condenses as it is forced up the mountain to about 3,000 metres (10,000 feet), producing rainfall as high as 236 centimetres (92 inches) a year below 1,800 metres (5,905 feet). On Kibo only thirteen centimetres (five inches) of rain falls each year.

Zone one: Lower slopes

Extending from 800-1,800 metres (2,624-5,905 feet), the mountain's lower slopes are used for grazing livestock and cultivation. Human encroachment has completely changed the natural vegetation habitat and what was once scrub, bush and lowland forest is now **grassland** or **crop land**.

The scruffy-looking plant growing in tall clumps, often seen with huge faded heads

Overleaf: The three volcanoes of Kilimanjaro: Shira in the background far right, wedding cake Kibo in the centre and the ragged edges of Mawenzi in the foreground.

Above: Glacial steps on the eastern ice field of Kibo.

of small purplish flowers, is most likely a *Vernonia*. You can see and smell the lemony-scented leaves and blooms of the *Lippia* and *Lantana* species — which also grow in clumps — but watch out for the pinkish *Erlangea tomentosa* seeds that can stick fast to your clothing. In these thickets and hedgerows, ferns, clovers, peas and balsams grow, as well as a relative of the original African violet, *Streptocarpus glandulossinus*.

In the cultivated zone large mammals are unlikely to be seen, but small ones abound. At night the galagos — bush-babies — scream and make a terrific clatter as they jump on roof tops, and the genet cat, with its black and white tail flickering through the branches, is also quite common.

Zone one is most notable for its prolific **bird life**. Where the cultivated lands meet the forest there is an abundant food supply and plenty of nesting sites. Keep your ears tuned for the pure flute-like notes of the shy tropical boubou and the crescendo of melodious phrases emitted by the white-browed robin chat at dawn and dusk. Fruit

trees attract hordes of speckled mouse-birds, brown with crests and long tapered tails. In flowerbeds a variety of sunbirds, nectar feeders with curved bills and iridoscent plumage, make themselves at home.

Zone two: Forest
Ranging from 1,800–2,800 metres) 5,905–9,187 feet) the southern slopes of Kilimanjaro make up the richest area of the mountain. Ninety-six per cent of the water that falls on the mountain originates in this zone. Because of the altitude and dampness of the forest, a wide band of clouds frequently surrounds this level. Wild date palms and figs are common in the wetter forest of the southern slopes, while in the drier western and northern forests the characteristic trees are the tall, twisted juniper; two species of olive; and the *Podocarpus* and *Nuxia congesta* species, with their heavily buttressed trunks hung with dense trailing fronds of lianas reminiscent of Tarzan's favourite mode of transport.

The forest zone of Kilimanjaro lacks one type of tree found on most other East

African volcanic mountains — the bamboo. No one has yet been able to explain this oddity. A flower indigenous to the mountain and found nowhere else in the world is the *Impatiens kilimanjari*, a type of 'Busy Lizzie'. This scarlet and yellow flower can usually be spotted along streams.

The forest zone is also home to the majority of the mountain's wildlife, although the thickness of the undergrowth and dense cloud cover can make the animals difficult to spot.

While you may not be able to see such creatures as the blue monkeys or black and white colobus, you will certainly be able to hear them. The colobus' guttural purring echoes through the forest. Leopard and the Kilimanjaro bush pig, as well as elephant, buffalo, bushbuck, mountain reedbuck and the red duiker are all common but elusive.

Birds are more abundant than mammals but equally difficult to distinguish in the lush foliage. Fruit trees attract the silvery-cheeked hornbill — a black and white bird with a loud braying call — and the crimson-winged Hartlaub's turaco which flickers like a flame between the boughs.

Zone three: Heath and moorland
This low alpine zone, ranging between 2,800-4,000 metres (9,187-13,120 feet), is made up of heath and moorland communities. Here the heathers are giants, forming a forest in their own right that reaches up to nine metres (30 feet) high and stretches for 1,000 metres (3,280 feet) to the 4,000-metre (13,120-foot) contour line, becoming more sparse as it is broken by tussock grass.

The most common heathers include *Erica arborea*, with its small, white bell-shaped flowers, and *Philippia excelsa*, more bushy than erica with cup-shaped white flowers. Both species have very tiny leaves.

The higher moorland elevations are characterized by a plant that looks like a mutant bolted cabbage, the forest groundsel, *Senecio kilimanjari*. These giant senecios have tall stems which act as reservoirs for the leaves. When the large leaves die they do not always fall off, but form a dry insulating skirt that covers the trunk.

There are relatively few large mammals found at the low alpine level and those sighted are usually in transit to another zone. Elands, common duikers, African hunting dogs, buffalos and elephants have all been recorded, but it is the small animals that predominate.

Foraging among tunnels in the coarse grasses are the mole rat, the four-striped grass mouse and the harsh-furred mouse. The biology of these and other small mammals of the alpine zone has largely been neglected and there are probably several species awaiting discovery at this altitude.

Rodents are the principal prey of the moorland and alpine zone birds, which include the augur buzzard, Mackinder's owl, Verreaux's eagle, and the lammergeier, a rare vulture with long wings and a wedge tail. Keep a sharp eye out for such scavengers as the white-necked raven — any food left unattended is considered a free meal!

The black silhouettes of the alpine swifts carve through the thin air, mouths agape for insects, which are also the food of the hill chat and the yellow-crowned canary. Scarlet-tufted malachite sunbirds sip nectar from the few flowers and the streaky seed-eater lives up to its name.

Zone four: Highland desert
In the alpine zone of 4,000-5,000 metres (13,120–16,400 feet), only the hardiest life can survive. Nights are below 0°C (32°F) and daytime temperatures can reach as high as 40°C (104°F) in the direct sun. The major problem plants must deal with at this altitude is 'solifluction'. This occurs when the ground freezes and the soilwater expands, causing the soil to move, uprooting plants in the process.

The fifty or so species of plants that live at this altitude have evolved sophisticated ways to survive the extreme environment of high ultraviolet radiation in the day, freezing temperatures at night, high rates of evaporation and occasional snowfalls.

Often plants will grow in protective shapes. The cushioned tussock grasses, for example, keep their roots warm by having a large number of hairlike leaves. Others don't shed their dead leaves but keep them as insulation.

Some of the most common plants, the lichens (a combination of fungus and algae), avoid the soil altogether and encrust the lava rocks. Another plant that avoids putting down roots is the moss ball. Mosses at these elevations curl around soil nodules and form spheres or ovals that can roll freely along while feeding on the soil they enclose and soaking up any available moisture like a sponge.

Animal life is as sparse as the plant life, although sightings of eland, leopard, and hunting dog have been recorded. Ravens and large birds of prey may forage at these heady heights during the day, but few other species can cope with the thin air and shifting currents.

The most abundant forms of life are the small and sedentary insects that remain concealed under tussocks and rocks. Most have short wings or no wings, and there are numerous spiders who feed on the wind-blown and ground-dwelling insects.

Zone five: Summit
This area, above 5,000 metres (16,400 feet), is characterized by Arctic conditions. Oxygen is about half that at sea-level and there is nothing to protect the human skin from the sun's radiation. Surface water is practically nonexistent, with most of the moisture locked up in snow and ice.

The upper limit of flowering plants is 4,900 metres (16,072 feet) on Kilimanjaro and above this level the only vegetation is the crusty lichens that grow one millimetre a year and can live to be hundreds of years old. The one exception to this is the tenacious *Helichrysum newii*. In the warm air and ground around the small vents (fumaroles) of Kibo, this lone plant has managed to surmount the Arctic environment and stake out one tiny warm habitat where life is possible.

At these dizzy heights only a few hardy spiders exist, eking out a precarious living by wrapping themselves in their own webs and catching insects borne on the wind blowing up the mountain. From there on up, conditions are too inhospitable for any visible form of life. One of Kilimanjaro's enduring enigmas, however, was the discovery high on Kibo of a **leopard skeleton**. A convincing explanation of why the animal was there has never been put forward, but the mystery was immortalized by Ernest Hemingway in *The Snows of Kilimanjaro*.

The climb

The most popular route is via **Marangu** and usually takes five days for the round trip. Kilimanjaro can be climbed by almost anyone who is reasonably fit. The youngest person to scale the mountain was aged eleven, the oldest seventy-four.

The summit, for those who persevere until the bitter cold end, is usually **Gillman's Point**, which is 213 metres (700 feet) lower then the actual summit, **Uhuru Peak**. More experienced climbers take the frequently icy and potentially dangerous crater rim ridge walk all the way to Uhuru Peak and the roof of Africa.

Day one: Plan on spending one to two hours at the **Marangu Gate Park Headquarters** for registration and payment of fees. It is best to start early in the morning to avoid afternoon showers. From **Marangu Gate** at 1,800 metres (5,904 feet), the cleared trail leads through lush **rainforest**. Wildlife is limited due to the heavy foot traffic. An alternative route branches off through the forest after the gate and follows the edge of a stream through undergrowth. About an hour and a half from the gate it is possible to cross the stream and rejoin the main trail, or remain walking along the forest trail. Both paths continue on opposite sides of the stream, merging one hour before **Mandara Hut**, located at 2,700 metres (8,856 feet). From Mandara Hut it is a short walk to the **Maundi Crater**. Those with the energy and inclination to visit the crater will be rewarded with beautiful scenery and sight of the massive **protea flower**.

Day two: The morning of the second day is spent walking over the steep slopes and rushing streams of the giant **heather forest**, after which the track opens out onto the

Above: Climbers make the long journey to the roof of Africa.

southern slopes of **Mawenzi**, running through a band of moorland. Five hours and fourteen kilometres (nine miles) from Mandara brings you to Horombo Hut at 3,810 metres (12,500 feet). (To call the Mandara and Horombo accommodation 'huts' is being slightly unfair; they more closely resemble chalets and can sleep 200 people.)

There are a number of good reasons for staying an extra night at Horombo: the most important is to become acclimatized to the altitude and reduce chances of sickness. There are also several interesting features well worth visiting, including the **Zebra Rocks**, a low cliff 1.5 kilometres (one mile) away with vertical stripes of contrasting colours caused by differential rain flow. Below the huts are cul-de-sac **lava tunnels** with glassy walls that are worth exploring. Finally, the number of bunks at Horombo make it the most comfortable of all the huts on the mountain.

Day three: A valley behind Horombo leads straight up to the barren and rock-strewn **Saddle** between Kibo and Mawenzi, passing Zebra Rocks on the way. It is thirteen kilometres (eight miles) and seven hours to Kibo Hut at 4,725 metres (15,500 feet), reached by taking the **left fork** just after a **rain gauge** at the start of the Saddle.

Day four: The trail to the summit lies directly behind **Kibo Hut** to the west. The climb usually begins shortly after midnight for two reasons: 1) to see the sun rise over Mawenzi from the top of Kibo and 2) the loose stone scree is frozen, making it easier to clamber over. The first part of the trail is uneven and leads to **Hans Meyer Cave**, a good place to try and catch what little breath you have left. From the cave the path switchbacks most of the way to the top, with a last scramble over rocks to **Johannes' Notch** and **Gillman's Point**. From there the trail continues along the rim past **Stella Point** to **Uhuru Peak**. After enjoying the view from the top of Africa, hikers make a speedy return to Horombo Hut.

Day five: The descent continues from the Horombo to the Mandara hut, which is reached by lunch time, then proceeds to the park gate and Marangu in the afternoon.

The *Guide to Mount Kenya and Kilimanjaro* edited by Iain Allan and published by the Mountain Club of Kenya, provides much useful information, such as detailing the climbing routes and how to cope with mountain sickness.

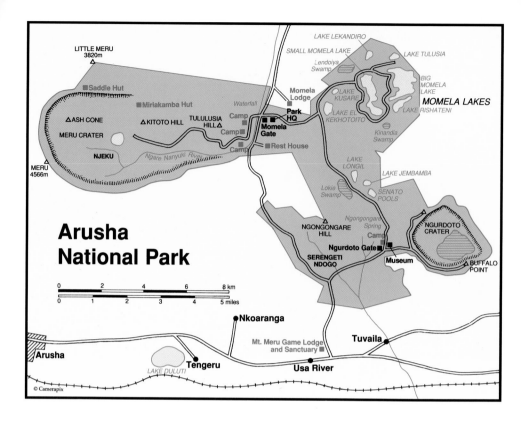

Arusha National Park

| 0 | 2 | 4 | 6 | 8 km |
| 0 | 1 | 2 | 3 | 4 | 5 miles |

© Camerapix

Arusha: Safari Town

Halfway between the Cape and Cairo — situated in the shadow of Mount Meru — lies Arusha, an attractive town that is both a centre of agriculture and the main safari base to the northern parks. Landrovers and Toyotas quarter the town from dawn to dusk, departing to Tarangire, Lake Manyara, Ngorongoro, Serengeti and Arusha National Park, returning with tanned and toughened tourists anxious to relax and chat.

Formerly an old trading post for the local waArusha and waMeru tribes, Arusha has become the administrative centre of an important agricultural region producing coffee, maize, wheat, sisal, pyrethrum and dairy products. The town's busy and colourful market reflects Arusha's rural background, which is a result of the area's fertile soils, temperate climate and ample rainfall captured by the misty heights of Mount Meru.

The town is divided roughly in half by a valley of parkland through which the Naura River runs. To the west is the industrial area of the town, the road to the Kenyan border at Namanga and the market. To the east are the first-class hotels, shops, restaurants, safari companies, and the Arusha International Conference Centre, built to be the administrative headquarters of the short-lived East African Community and now a busy venue for meetings as well as headquarters of the Tanzania National Parks.

Also in this area are the craft shops selling Makonde carvings and local handicrafts as well as the famous meerschaum pipes. Meaning 'sea foam' in German, the rare mineral was used by the Greeks as a form of soap, the Africans used it for building blocks and the Turks have worked deposits sporadically for more than 2,000 years. The mineral was discovered at the Tanzanian end of Lake Amboseli in the 1950s, the largest known deposit of meerschaum in the world.

Above: Clock tower in the heart of downtown Arusha.

Getting there

Arusha is a four-hour drive from Nairobi on good tarmac all the the way via the customs post at Namanga. A regular minibus shuttle service operates Nairobi/Arusha/Moshi and return. From Dar es Salaam buses run to Arusha, taking at least twelve hours to complete the arduous 650-kilometre (400-mile) journey. There is a bus service from Musoma on Lake Victoria through the dirt roads of the Serengeti.

Kilimanjaro International Airport, located east of Arusha, is half an hour away by car. Ethiopian Airlines, Air France and KLM operate regular international flights, while Air Tanzania Corporation operates international and local services.

Where to stay

With over 2,000 hotel beds available, there is no shortage of accommodation in Arusha. Top-class establishments include the Mount Meru Hotel and the Hotel Seventy-Seven, both on the outskirts of town. The New Arusha Hotel, Equator Hotel and New Safari Hotel are clean and comfortable lodgings in the town centre.

Sightseeing

From a small German military garrison established in 1900, Arusha has matured into a sprawling lively centre. Take an afternoon to explore the town between safari departures. A good place to start is at the central **clock tower**, located at the intersection of **Cantonment**, **Malda**, and **Sokoine** roads in front of the Arusha **post office**. Behind the clock tower rises majestic Mount Meru, standing like a sentinel over the town streets.

Between the clock tower and **Ngoliondoi Road** lie many craft shops where the internationally known Makonde woodcarvings can be purchased. Other items for sale include batiks, Maasai bead necklaces, and meerschaum pipes. Head south along Ngoliondoi Road until it intersects with **Sokoine Road**. Turn right and stroll past the local **library** to the left and the **park** to the right. If the jacarandas are in bloom, the park and side streets are awash in pale purple beauty. On top of the

Above: Arusha International Conference Centre, headquarters of the Tanzania National Parks, is also a busy venue for international conferences.

hill in the park sits the stately **Roman Catholic Church**. Two blocks after the park take a right on **Azimio Street**. One block north on the left is the vibrant **market**. Take time to wander through the narrow alleys. The fruit and vegetables so carefully arranged at each stand resemble still-life paintings. Piles of salt, baskets, plastics, fresh fish and meat are all available.

To package the pungent spices, long strips of plastic, made into separate bags by melting the edges with a candle, are hung in row after row from each stand's roof. Drains running through the centre of the market keep the floor clean and the smell fresh.

Around the edge of the market, permanent **shops** house tailors — who treadle to the beat of rap, reggae and Indian music — cobblers, electronic wares, clothing boutiques, and mini-grocery stores. The whole block seems to throb with energy.

After perusing the stands, head north again along Azimio Street until it ends at **Makongoro Road**. At the **intersection** stands the tall **Uhuru** (Freedom) **Monument**.

If it is a Sunday afternoon, turn left and continue along Makongoro Road for the **stadium**, where the chances are you will find a keenly contested football match in progress. For a scenic picnic spot choose **Lake Duluti**, a water-filled extinct volcano 13 kilometres (eight miles) beyond the town to the south of the Arusha-Moshi tarmac.

Arusha National Park: A Small but Brilliant Gem

While Arusha is a pleasant town and home to some of the friendliest people in Tanzania, the real reason most tourists visit this northern town is to arrange a safari to one of the numerous nearby parks.

Among the closest and most beguiling is Arusha National Park. Sir Julian Huxley called this 137-square-kilometre (53-square-mile) area 'a gem amongst parks'. It was established in 1960 and has three distinct zones that contribute to the park's variety and beauty: Ngurdoto Crater, the Momela Lakes, and Mount Meru. Altitudes range from 1,500 metres (4,920 feet) above sea-level at Momela to more than 4,566 metres (14,990 feet) at the summit of Meru. The vegetation and wildlife found in the park are determined by the altitude and geography of the different areas.

Ngurdoto Crater, for example, is surrounded by forest, while the crater floor is swampy. The lakes, like many in the Rift Valley, are alkaline and Mount Meru is a mixture of lush forests and bare rock. Within these diverse habitats 400 species of birds, both migratory and resident, have been recorded.

Arusha National Park is ideal for a day excursion. There is a pleasant walk to the caldera, through the forest, which can be undertaken during a single day of hiking.

If you plan to tackle Mount Meru, however, allow three full days. It is mandatory to have an armed guard with you for the climb, due to the danger of buffalos.

Getting there

Arusha National Park lies twenty-one kilometres (13 miles) from Arusha and fifty-eight kilometres (36 miles) from Moshi along the Arusha-Moshi road. A clearly signposted all-weather road leads from the main road to the park.

When to go

November to May are the months of heaviest rain, with a period of lighter rain between December and February when the views of Kilimanjaro and the park in general, are at their best. During the dry season the skies are often hazy.

Mount Meru is best climbed between October and February and should be booked beforehand as walkers must be accompanied by an armed park ranger.

The address is: The Warden, Arusha National Park, PO Box 3134, Arusha.

Where to stay

For a day trip into the park, Mount Meru Game Lodge, at the Mount Meru Game Sanctuary at Usa River, offers excellent accommodation. The Hotel Tanzanite is also nearby and offers comparable accommodation and camping facilities.

Momela Game Lodge, with views overlooking both Meru and Kilimanjaro, is situated just outside the park at the Momela Gate, and can accommodate forty people.

Near the Momela Gate there is a spacious self-help rest house that can hold five people. Reservations are recommended for the rest house and can be made through The Warden, Arusha National Park, PO Box 3134, Arusha. There are four campsites in the park, all with water, toilets and wood, and a hostel at Kusare for visiting groups. There are two huts on Meru for climbers: Miriakamba Hut, which accomodates forty-eight people and Saddle Hut which accommodates twenty four. (See Listings for 'Accommodation').

Fees to pay

Fees must be paid in foreign currency and are subject to change. Up-to-date information about the current fees charged for accommodation and entry to the national parks can be obtained from tour operators or the National Park Headquarters.

Sightseeing

Turning left off the main **Arusha-Moshi tarmac**, the road soon forks; the right fork leading to **Ngurdoto Gate** and the left fork eventually arriving at **Momela Gate**. The area where the fork occurs is known as **Serengeti Ndogo**, which means 'Little Serengeti' and describes the open grassland — which is the only place in the park where Burchell's zebra can be seen. At Ngurdoto Gate there is a small **museum** and a collection of **mounted birds** commonly found in the park. From there the road forks again; the left fork leading toward Momela and the right fork toward **Ngurdoto Crater**.

Ngurdoto Crater

Fifteen million years ago molten rock was forced to the Earth's surface by super-heated steam, slowly building up a cone around the vent and imprisoning gases from the Earth's core. An explosion eventually resulted from the trapped gases and Ngurdoto Crater was formed. Today the former volcano is a steep-sided bowl three kilometres (two miles) across, and its lush swamps and riverine forest are home to buffalo, baboon, wart hog, olive baboon and the black and white colobus monkey.

The road from Ngurdoto Gate to the crater soon divides, with the steeper left-hand route ending at **Leitong**, the highest point of the crater rim. The right-hand road passes four picnic/observation points, eventually ending at **Buffalo Point**. Both roads can be slippery during the wet season and a four-wheel-drive vehicle is recommended.

Descending into the crater bottom, situated at 1,474 metres (4,835 feet), is not allowed, making it in effect a reserve within a reserve. The well-worn trails visible are used by the animals entering and leaving the crater.

Mosses, ferns, lichens and orchids thrive in the damp, misty atmosphere giving way to mahogany, olive trees, and wild date palms on the drier walls that rise to a high point of 1,854 metres (6,080 feet) at Leitong (which means 'prospect pleases'). Lobelias are also abundant in the high moorland zones of Leitong where, on a clear day — usually between December and March — Kilimanjaro can be seen over the broken canopy of the croton forest below.

There, shy duikers — antelopes hardly bigger than the tiny dog-sized dik-dik — briefly lift their snouts to sniff the cool air in the glades of the forest before disappearing into the bush.

Because the two tracks around the crater do not join, it is necessary to retrace your route back to Ngurdoto Gate before venturing off to explore the rest of Arusha National Park.

Momela Lakes
The **Momela Lakes** lie approximately ten kilometres (six miles) north of Ngurdoto Gate, past **Senato Pools**, **Lake Jembamba**, and **Lake Longil**. These pools frequently dry out but when full are used by all types of wildlife.

Mixed moor and grasslands slope northwards to the Momela Lakes, at 1,500 metres (4,920 feet), the lowest part of the park.

The **seven lakes** — **El Kekhotoito, Kusare, Small Momela, Rishateni, Big Momela, Tulusia,** and **Lekandiro** — are fed from underground streams and are quite shallow. Because they are alkaline, animals do not use them for drinking. The ecology of each lake varies according to its mineral content and all seven lakes support a different type of algae growth, resulting in a different colour for each body of water.

Bird life varies greatly from one lake to the next, even where the lakes are separated by only a thin stretch of land. Blue-green algae blooms in some waters — notably Lake Rishateni — and not in others, providing food for the coral pink lesser flamingo, while the greater flamingo, with its longer legs, can feed in deeper water on crustacea adapted to a different level of dissolved mineral salts.

Above: Entrance to the Mount Meru Game Sanctuary, founded in 1960.

Above: Mount Meru Game Lodge at the base of Mount Meru, Africa's fifth-highest mountain at 4,566 metres (14,990 feet).

The lakes were born when water filled the depressions left after volcanic mud and rubble spewed from Mount Meru down into the valley as far as the foothills of Kilimanjaro. These are the haunt of many species of waterbird, including the common little grebe, African pochard, ibis, heron, and egrets of all varieties. One of the easiest birds to recognize is the Egyptian goose with its brown plumage, contrasting white shoulders and chestnut patch on the centre of the belly and around the eye. Over 380 species of bird have been spotted there, and from October to April huge flocks of wildfowl from northern Europe and Asia winter at Momela.

Mount Meru

At 4,566 metres (14,990 feet), Mount Meru, Africa's fifth-highest mountain, is one of the continent's most rewarding climbs, not only for the achievement itself, but for the beautiful plants and animals found on its forested slopes. Sporting a cone that once matched Kilimanjaro's Kibo in height, a massive explosion perhaps a quarter of a million years ago blew out the whole eastern side, leaving an asymmetric caldera with a distinctive 'toothed' profile. Within the crater is the **Ash Cone**, made up of red and grey gravels and dust that built up gradually after the main explosion. In itself the cone is worth a climb to the summit.

The climb

Ascending Mount Meru once required either a dawn start and a hectic dash to the top followed by a tiring trudge back down in the dying light, or camping on the first and perhaps even the second night. Now the trip can be made in comfort by using the new cabins, **Miriakamba Hut** and **Saddle Hut**. (See 'Climbing and Trekking Advisory', Part Three.)

Day one: From **Momela Gate** — where it is necessary to sign in and pay your fees — the road leads west, fording the **Ngare Nanyuki River** and crossing some open bushy grassland where a resident herd of

Above: Graceful male impalas. They are capable of leaping ten metres (32 feet).
Opposite top: The flap-necked chameleon, master of disguise; one of thirty-nine species found in East Africa.
Opposite: The dinosaur *Triceratops* chameleon is easily recognized by the three horns protruding from its nose.

buffalo regularly graze around the base of an outlier, **Tulusia Hill**. The track skirts the domed hill to the south, past several excellent campsites, and begins to climb through densely forested foothills. Leopard and — in the past — rhino have been seen there, but you are more likely to encounter bushbuck and a fleeting glimpse of a turaco flashing across a glade.

The road continues to wind its way between the buttressed trunks of the lower **montane forest** at about 2,000 metres (6,560 feet). Many of the trees are fig and *Nuxia congesta* species, and the much taller African olive, *Olea hochstetteri*. With its finely curved, tall, and slender limbs, it is a far cry from the stubby, gnarled European olive. Around the base of the tree grows Black-eyed Susan, *Thunbergia alata*. Higher into the upper zone of the forest the trees are predominantly lofty juniper, or African pencil cedar — the world's largest species — and the equally tall podo, or East African yellow wood, both valuable as timber species. The podo provides food for the flocks of raucous red-fronted parrots.

Glades formed by fallen trees and elephants are kept open by buffalo which graze the areas where Lady's Mantle, *Alchemilla volkensii*, and a blue vetch, *Parochetus communis*, thrive in the sunlight.

By the time **Kitoto Hill** is reached the vegetation has become open heath land characterized by the bushy green *Erica arborea* and the grey *Stoebe kilimandscharica*.

From there an alternative trip up the mountain track can be taken westwards towards the crater itself and an area called **Njeku** which lies at the confluence of several streams. *Njeku* refers to an old woman who has the power of rainmaking. In times of drought the Meru people would make a sacrifice to the gods at the base of an ancient juniper tree that stands nearby.

When the long rains do arrive they bring out the 'red hot pokers', *Kniphophia thomsonii*, that glow in the surrounding woods and valleys, along with the pink-flowered balsam, *Impatiens papilionacea*. The

Above: Easily distinguishable from the male, the female waterbuck is slightly smaller and hornless.

short rains in November are soon followed by the spectacular fire-ball lily, *Scadoxus multiflorus*, with its rich red inflorescence.

Travel beyond Kitoto by car means engaging four-wheel drive to reach Miriakamba Hut, four kilometres (2.5 miles) away at the start of the **crater wall**. Miriakamba can be used as a base to explore the **crater floor**, which is reached after an easy walk down into the bowl where the **headwaters** of the **Ngare Nanyuki** collect.

As you emerge from the forest onto the floor of the crater you see old ash flows rising up like talons clawing at the 1,500-metre (4,920-foot) back wall of the crater.

Klipspringer live there and *Hypericum lanceolatum*, a type of St John's wort, is a bright yellow contrast to the burnt grey lava. Another interesting plant is *Hebenstretia dentata*, a plant with white flowers that are scented only in the evening when they give off sweet perfume. It grows with the small twisted tree *Agauria salicifolia*.

Soaring on updrafts from the crater you might catch sight of the rare lammergeier. This large, distinctive bird of prey will lift scavenged bones high into the air and drop them onto rocks to smash them to extract the marrow.

Day two: After spending the night at Miriakamba, there is a steep but relatively relaxed walk up to the **Saddle Hut**, passing through the open north-eastern flanks of the mountain where the red-flowered hagenia trees grow profusely. The trees are sometimes covered in epiphytic ferns, mosses and tree orchids.

Chewing on the woodland leaves are troops of colobus monkeys. Unique among the primates, they have given up the omnivorous habit and live entirely as vegetarians, evolving complex digestive systems along the way to deal with their high fibre diet of leaves. Unusual also in that they have only a small vestigial thumb, their croaking call of 'horrr, horrr, horrr' can be heard ringing through the forest before a crashing black and white blur advertises their presence completely.

Less obvious, but also sharing the montane forest, are bushbuck, mountain reedbuck and duiker, who forage among the undergrowth and do not venture out into the exposed upper slopes where giant heathers have come to dominate.

The path curves through heath land and the gradient becomes more gentle as the Saddle Hut at 3,600 metres (11,808 feet) comes into view between the crater rim and the peak of **Little Meru** to the north.

Little Meru is only 250 metres (820 feet) higher than the Saddle and can be reached easily by those who feel up to the short scramble to the park's north-western limit. From here, there are superb views of Kilimanjaro, the Momela Lakes and, to the west and north, the wilderness that harbours Ol Doinyo Lengai and Lake Natron.

The heather soon thins after the Saddle to give way to hardy grasses and sedge. But even these cannot survive on the barren sands of the crater rim that curves around along a series of ridges, crags and lava boulders to the rocky knoll of the summit itself.

Above: Newborn wart hog stretches its legs. An average litter is three to four, although a sow will frequently take care of up to eight piglets.

Tarangire National Park: The Long Dry Season

Tarangire National Park derives its name from the Tarangire River that rises in the highlands of central Tanzania and winds its way through the game sanctuary. The river irresistibly lures the herds of plains migrants from the parched surrounding areas to its shrunken — but permanent — brackish waters during the dry season.

The animals come by the thousands from as far north as the shores of Lake Natron, dramatically swelling the resident population with wildebeest, zebra, eland, elephant, hartebeest, buffalo and fringe-eared oryx. As the rainless days continue the Tarangire's pools are clotted with thirsty migrants, and elephants begin to dig for underground streams in the dry river bed. At this time of year the concentration of animals rivals that of the Serengeti to the north-west. The animals share the permanent pools with flocks of Tarangire's diverse bird life: green wood hoopoes, Fischer's lovebirds, white-bellied go-away birds, hornbills, cuckoos and waterbirds such as the goliath heron, purple gallinule, Egyptian goose and giant kingfisher.

With the arrival of the short rains in October the first animals to leave are the herds of wildebeest and zebra which flood out of Tarangire to the north. They are closely followed to the east and south by the bulk of the animals, including Grant's and Thomson's gazelle, buffalo, eland, elephant, oryx and hartebeest.

As the watercourses of the Tarangire fill up, population pressure is relaxed and soon only the resident species are left behind: lion, waterbuck, impala, wart hog, dik-dik, giraffe, lesser kudu and the year-round plague of the park, tsetse fly. In one respect, though, the fly is a blessing in disguise. The wildlife is resistant to the trypanosomiasis (a form of sleeping sickness) the insect carries, but the Maasai's cattle are not. The result is that the Maasai

141

do not use the park as range land and the wildlife has remained undisturbed. When the second and longer rains are at their heaviest in early April the animals are dispersed throughout an even greater area — 20,000 square kilometres (7,722 square miles) — taking in Lake Manyara to the north-west, the Maasai Steppe in the south-east and the badlands to the south and west of Lake Natron. In June when the long rains come to an end and the plains grasses dry up the animals once again feel the pull of the river.

Getting there
Tarangire National Park is 114 kilometres (71 miles) from Arusha along the Arusha-Dodoma tarmac. After 106 kilometres (66 miles) there is a left turn, marked by a sign post at the village of Kwa Kuchinja. The park entrance is eight kilometres (five miles) along this dirt road. The park also maintains an airstrip for charter planes.

When to go
Prime viewing months are between September and December.

Where to stay
On the east side of the Tarangire River, there is luxury accommodation at Tarangire Sopa Lodge which has 75 double suites on a hillside site of fine baobabs and natural rock formations. Luxury tented accommodation is at Tarangire Safari Lodge, 29 double tents and eight cabins all with private bathrooms. Several campsites overlook the river and booking is advisable during the peak dry season: Tarangire Ltd, PO Box 1182, Arusha. (See Listings).

Fees to pay
Fees are payable in foreign currency only and are subject to change. Up-to-date information about the current fees charged for accommodation and entry to the national parks can be obtained from tour operators or the National Park Head-quarters in Arusha.

Sightseeing
Present development is currently limited to the **northern section** of the park with plans to extend the **main road** to the south which would allow access to the **Kolo rock paintings**. Many of the current roads become impassable during the wet season.

Stepping out of your vehicle in open areas is allowed, but make sure there are no animals or thick bush (where animals may be hidden) nearby.

Lemiyon and Matete
Tarangire National Park is divided into **eight zones**. **Lemiyon** is the most northerly, distinguished by undulating hills where giant baobabs with their elephant-grey bark grow in profusion, and a small area of long-grass plains infested in places by tsetse flies.

The Maasai believe that the baobab was the first tree of creation, but it soon became restless and began to wander about the Earth. To put an end to its meandering God replanted the tree — upside down — and its naked roots now wave in the air. The baobabs provide nesting sites for barn owls and the hollow trunks are home to the area's ten species of bat some of which pollinate the tree's flowers.

Matete is located south-east of Lemiyon and contains the park's **lodge**, **campsites** and beautiful views of **Lolkisale Mountain**, which towers outside the park to the east.

Both areas consist of open grasslands with flat-topped acacia trees and black cotton grasslands. 'Black cotton' is a heavy clay common in Africa. When it dries, enormous cracks — often two metres (seven feet) deep — are formed. Once the rains begin the soil absorbs the water rapidly, soon becoming a sticky mess just waiting for an unsuspecting driver. The grasslands support a wide variety of animals including baboon, zebra, elephant, hyena, lion, leopard, wart hog and vervet monkey.

Burungi and Kitibong
Known for its eighty-kilometre (50-mile) **game circuit**, **Burungi** is a mixture of grasslands, woodlands and the **Tarangire River**. **Black rhinos** are sometimes seen in this northern area of the park, but poaching has made them a rare sight. You are more likely to spot a **candelabra tree**, with its

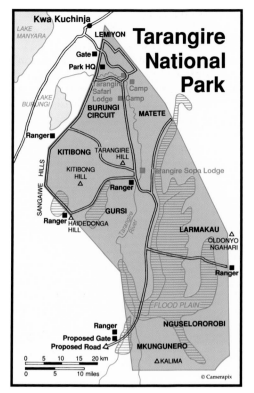

Tarangire National Park

Map labels:
Kwa Kuchinja, LAKE MANYARA, LEMIYON, Gate, Park HQ, Tarangire Safari Lodge, Camp, Camp, BURUNGI CIRCUIT, MATETE, LAKE BURUNGI, Ranger, KITIBONG, TARANGIRE HILL, KITIBONG HILL, Tarangire Sopa Lodge, Ranger, SANGAIWE HILLS, GURSI, Ranger, HAIDEDONGA HILL, Tarangire River, LARMAKAU, OLDONYO NGAHARI, Ranger, FLOOD PLAIN, Ranger, NGUSELORORORBI, Proposed Gate, Proposed Road, MKUNGUNERO, KALIMA

0 5 10 15 20 km
0 5 10 miles
© Camerapix

dark green succulent branches fanning upwards to the sky. The trees are readily eaten by rhinos if they are knocked or blown down, but otherwise remain undamaged by animals.

South of Burungi lies **Kitibong**, an area of acacia parkland (grasslands) and woodlands. Within this zone the **Sangaiwe Hills** can be seen off to the west outside the park's boundaries. Buffalo are often found on the east side of this area, usually in mixed breeding herds, as male animals live alone or in bachelor herds. Because they need to drink regularly and are fond of wallowing, they tend to stay close to the water.

More than **300 species of birds** have been recorded in the park and Tarangire boasts the highest recorded number of breeding species for any habitat in the world. One of the more interesting is the **ground hornbill**. Resembling a black turkey, it spends much of its time on the ground feeding upon insects and lizards. At a distance the call sounds similar to drums. A Maasai folk story translates the sound as a man speaking to a woman saying 'I want more cows', to which she replies, 'You'll die before you get them'.

Gursi and Larmakau

Together these two zones make up the **central section of the park**. Gursi (to the west) contains the same vegetational zones as Kitibong, along with an additional strip of woodland that runs parallel to the river. **Large grass fires** are known to sweep through this area and controlled burning is carried out to minimize the damage.

Larmakau is a corruption of the Maasai *Ol Makau*, which means hippopotamus. The black cotton grasslands become a *mbuga* (huge swamp) during the wet season and indolent hippos can be seen wallowing to their hearts' content. Some years the swamp never dries and waterbirds and mammals remain there all year-round. Larmakau is also home to the **tree-climbing pythons**, a rare occurrence in any of the other parks.

The ostrich (the largest bird in the world) and the kori bustard (the heaviest bird that can fly) are two special residents of the area along with buffalo, elephant, giraffe, ground squirrel, hunting dog, hyena, impala, lion and wart hog.

Nguselororobi and Mkungunero

Making up the most **southern portion of the park**, these two areas are a mix of open plains, woodlands, black cotton grasslands and **freshwater pools**.

In such a dry stretch of country, these pools are a welcoming sight to a wide variety of **waterbirds**.

The crowned crane, Egyptian goose, jacana, long-toed lapwing, purple gallinule and saddle-bill stork all make their home among the water weeds.

Another visitor is the **hammerkop** or hammer-headed stork. This brown bird, with a dark bill and feet, is easily recognized by the shape of its head. Many legends surround this fish- and frog-eater and it is considered unlucky to kill one.

Unfortunately the main road does not yet extend into these far-flung southern areas of the park.

Above: Tree-climbing lion of Lake Manyara National Park.

Manyara: Tanzania's Water Wonderland

From whichever direction you choose to approach Manyara — either through Arusha or by dropping down into the Rift Valley along the Ngorongoro road — the views are guaranteed to be dramatic. Lying in a shallow depression at the base of the western wall of the eastern arm of the Rift Valley, Lake Manyara spreads out in a heat haze backed by a narrow band of forest and the sheer red and brown cliffs of the escarpment. The park's name is derived from the Maasai word for the *Euphorbia tirucalli*, a bush which they grow as a living stockade to keep their cattle from straying.

From the top of the cliffs the 325-square-kilometre (125-square-mile) area spreads out before you, dominated by the lake that occupies two-thirds of what used to be prime hunting country. In *The Green Hills of Africa*, Hemingway described his game-trophy activities throughout the Manyara

lands. In 1960 hunting ceased when the lake district achieved national park status.

The entrance to Manyara is from the village of Mto wa Mbu, 'Mosquito Creek', a market town where several tribes converge to form the richest linguistic mix in Africa. The Mbugwe, Iraqw, Gorowa, Irangi, Tatoga, Chagga, and Maasai have used Mto wa Mbu as a trading post for centuries and it is the only place on the continent where you can hear the Bantu, Cushitic, and Nilotic languages spoken in the same area, perhaps even Khoisan from Lake Eyasi.

Getting there

Lake Manyara National Park lies about 120 kilometres (74 miles) south-west of Arusha along the main road to Dodoma. At Makuyuni turn right onto an all-weather road that leads to the lake and on to Ngorongoro Crater and the Serengeti. The park entrance is a short drive from the handicraft and fruit stalls of Mto wa Mbu.

When to go

The dry season is from June to September,

the short one from January to February. Park tracks are only suitable for four-wheel-drive vehicles during the rainy months.

Where to stay

Lake Manyara Serena Safari Lodge, on the escarpment, offers 65 rooms commanding fine views of the lake and its birdlife. Lake Manyara Hotel, with 212 rooms and a swimming pool, is situated outside the park also on top of the escarpment. There are ten self-help bandas at the park entrance with raised sitting platforms, a central kitchen (with gas if available) and firewood. Maji Moto Camp offers the only luxury permanent camp inside the park. Two campsites are available at the park entrance; both have water, toilets and shower facilities. There are campsites (no facilities) within the park, at Msasa and Bagayo. Permission from the warden is needed to camp there. There is a hostel sleeping forty-eight people at park headquarters. Make bookings in advance for the bandas. (See Listings for 'Accommodation').

Fees to pay

Fees are payable in foreign currency only and are subject to change. Up-to-date

Top: A baby elephant finds comfort and security between its mother's legs.

Above: Powerful front teeth that continue to grow throughout its life help this ground squirrel to make short work of a piece of coconut.

Overleaf: Squabble and beak — petulant male hippos in territorial dispute, watched by unruffled avian arbiters.

information about the current fees charged for accommodation and entry to the national parks can be obtained from tour operators or the National Park Headquarters in Arusha.

Sightseeing

Lake Manyara National Park is an ideal size for a day trip. It is possible to leave the camp or lodge early in the morning, picnic at one of the many picturesque sites and return by early evening. Park roads are suitable for cars during the dry season (June to September and January to February), but use a four-wheel-drive vehicle during the rains. As there is only one entrance, all trails start and end at the gate but you can exit at the south end by special permission. The Manyara area has a highly unreliable pattern of rainfall, ranging from 250 to 1,200 millimetres (10-47 inches) per year. In 1961 the lake dried up; the following year it flooded. The only way for a mature forest to survive in this stressful environment is to have its own water supply. At Manyara, this is provided by springs that bubble out of the escarpment base, having drained through 600 metres (1,968 feet) of the Ngorongoro Highlands.

Ground water forest

Entering the park you will find yourself surrounded by tall trees of the **ground water forest**. In many ways it resembles a tropical rainforest — with its verdant foliage and variety of bird life — the difference being these trees are supported by a water supply from underneath rather than by abundant rainfall. Mahogany, *Antiaris toxicaria*, *Trichilea emetica*, sausage tree and croton all grow there as canopy species. Blue monkeys and male vervets, with their distinctive azure scrotums, pick insects and fruit from the high branches, while the middle layer of the forest is made up of shrubs where elephants come to feed on the fallen fruit of the wild fig, picking them out of the grasses, sedges and flowering plants that cover the forest floor. Where the ground is too wet, reeds and star grass grow in the uninterrupted sunlight. Baboons, bushbuck, waterbuck, the nocturnal aardvark — considered to be

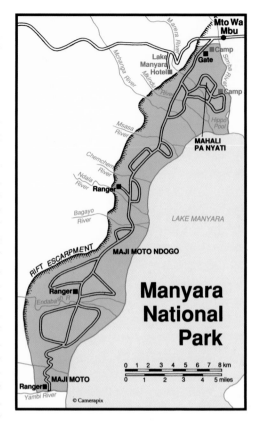

good eating by the Maasai — civet, pangolin and leopard live in the ground water forest, but black rhino are no longer seen there.

Vervet monkeys are a favourite prey of the leopards.

South of the park entrance, half a mile after crossing the **Marera River bridge**, is a left-hand turning to **Mahali pa Nyati**, 'place of the buffalo'. Although buffalo live there, they are difficult to spot from the road as they prefer to keep to the edge of the nearby **Simba River**. There, along the water's edge, a thick blanket of sedge forms the food for large herds of buffalo that can number 300 strong at certain times of the year. Up to sixty kilos (132 lbs) of this sedge is also consumed per day by each of the hippos that wallow in the nearby **Hippo Pool**, also located along the Simba River.

These 3,000-kilo (6,600-lb) animals can remain submerged for up to three minutes at a time and prefer to stay in the water to keep cool, only emerging to forage on the lake flats at night.

Above: The expansive waters of Lake Manyara, one of the Rift Valley's numerous alkaline lakes, stretch to the horizon.

Many of the park's 380 species of birds live in and around the Hippo Pool, including the hadada ibis, saddle-bill stork, knob-billed duck, avocet, Hottentot teal, plover, African pied wagtail and predatory fish eagle, which can usually be seen perched atop a dead tree, scanning the horizon for a likely meal.

Tree-climbing lions

Back on the **main park road** heading south, the thick vegetation of the ground water forest eventually merges into flat-topped **acacia woodland** that stretches between the **Msasa** and **Bagayo rivers**. There browsers and grazers feed and elephant, giraffe, impala and zebra are all easily spotted.

Do not count on it but, during the rains, entire prides of lion are sometimes seen stretched out in the branches of the acacias. No one knows exactly why they prefer the lofty perch; perhaps because it is cooler or maybe because the high vantage point allows them to escape the biting flies, the tsetses and the herds of buffalo and

elephant. It was once estimated that there were seven elephants per square mile in the park, a concentration said to be one of the highest in Africa. As elsewhere in East Africa, however, the once-thriving population has suffered greatly from poaching and from farmers who kill the beasts when they encroach on farmland.

Along with the lounging lion, the acacia woods are also a playground for the banded mongoose. Living in troops of up to thirty individuals, they can sometimes be seen following paths through the bush in single file, hot on the trail of the insects found in elephant dung.

Sixteen kilometres (10 miles) south of the **gate entrance** you cross the **Bagayo River**. There the road comes close to the Rift escarpment and the trees covering the boulder-strewn slope begin to change. Most noticeable are the majestic baobabs, with their large silvery trunks and splindly branches.

Their young leaves are edible and the wood, which has a long fibre, is made into ropes and woven articles. As many baobabs

Above: Luxurious Lake Manyara Serena Lodge stands on top of the Mto Wa Mbu rift wall, and the view stretches far into the East African Rift Valley and onto Lake Manyara.

are hollow, they serve as reservoirs for rain water and are often the site of wild bee hives or nesting hornbills.

Five kilometres (three miles) south of the Bagayo River lies **Maji Moto Ndogo**, 'small hotwater'. These hot springs are about 40°C (104°F). The water is fresh, although gas emissions do occur, and is heated as it circulates through fractures in the rock formed by the Rift Valley faulting.

The lake

South of the hot springs toward the **Endabash River**, the elevation is slightly higher and grand views of **Lake Manyara** can be glimpsed. Following the formation of the Rift Valley, streams cascaded down the rocky walls and, because there was no outlet, a lake formed. It was at its largest about a quarter of a million years ago. The average area of the lake is around 390 square kilometres (151 square miles), varying from year to year. During a dry stretch it is possible to drive across the lake and during rainy years the lake often covers the main road. Wherever you drive in the park, the lake and its attendant bird life is never far away. Although Manyara is fed by freshwater streams and the escarpment springs, its waters are slightly alkaline. A diverse collection of waterbirds gathers in the shade of acacias along the shores, to wash the soda from their feathers.

Pelicans, storks, cormorants drying their outstretched wings, Egyptian geese, spur-winged geese and whistling ducks all congregate in abundance. Out past the beds of sedge and rushes the lake is streaked pink where the flamingos feed and parade.

The end of the park is near when you reach **Maji Moto**, a second set of hot springs that bubble around a scalding 60°C (140°F). If you'd like to hard boil an egg for lunch, this is the place to do it.

Another two kilometres further along is the **Yambi River**, beyond which the park extends incorporating a former farm. The **ranger post**, formerly at Yambi River, is now across the next river further south.

Top: Pelicans roost in a tree near Lake Manyara National Park, the hunting grounds once stalked by Hemingway and described by him in *The Green Hills of Africa*.
Above: Lake Manyara's Hippo Pools, located along the Simba River, are a favourite retreat for these 3,000-kilogramme (6,600-lb) animals.
Overleaf: Intrusive zebra startles a flock of yellow-billed storks along the shores of Lake Manyara.

Ngorongoro Conservation Area: Wonder of the World

In his introduction to the *Ngorongoro Guidebook* of 1980, Professor Bernhard Grzimek — who arguably did more to promote and conserve the area than any other individual — wrote: 'It is impossible to give a fair description of the size and beauty of the Crater, for there is nothing with which one can compare it. It is one of the Wonders of the World.' To call the crater simply one outstanding feature in the vast Ngorongoro Conservation Area (NCA) diminishes its stature.

But the fact remains that it is only one attraction within this huge and diverse area that contains recently active volcanoes, soaring mountains, archaeological sites, rolling plains, rivers, forests, lakes and shifting sand dunes.

Explanations for the name Ngorongoro are as diverse as the area's wildlife. Some say the word is taken from an especially valiant group of Datoga warriors who defeated the Maasai in a pitched battle on the floor of the crater 150 years ago. Others believe it to be the name of a Maasai age set or the name of a Maasai cattle-bell maker who lived in the crater.

The NCA was once part of the Serengeti National Park. In 1956, conflict over the land's use flared between park authorities and the Maasai, eventually leading to the reclassification of Ngorongoro as a conservation area that would benefit both wildlife and pastoralists.

It was an idea ahead of its time but certainly long awaited. The Ngorongoro Conservation Area Authority (NCAA) was established by the government to oversee this pioneering experiment in multipurpose land use and attempt to integrate its many facets. Today the NCAA is responsible for coordinating the wildlife, Maasai grazing, forestry, archaeological sites, education and research — and tourism.

The NCA covers 8,280 square kilometres (3,196 square miles). Of this total the Ngorongoro Crater (which was declared a World Heritage Site in 1978) makes up 260 square kilometres (100 square miles) or three per cent of the area; the Northern Highlands Forest Reserve about twenty per cent; the remainder of the highlands about twenty-seven per cent; and the surrounding plains, bush, and woodlands to the north and west about fifty per cent.

The land is made up of varied geographical and ecological regions, from the shores of Lake Eyasi in the south-west at the foot of the Rift Valley wall, to the central Olbalbal Swamp, to the arid Olduvai Gorge. These distinctly different habitats give rise to a startling variety of animals and plants.

In the same way that habitat determines the species in an area, the climate, particularly rainfall, dictates how the species are distributed at certain times of the year. The great migrations of wildebeest and zebra are driven by the need for water as they move throughout Ngorongoro and beyond.

Climate

Only two seasons exist in the NCA — wet and dry. From November to May — the wet season — virtually all the rain falls, with the east and south sides of the mountains receiving the greatest amounts from the Indian Ocean. The driest parts of the NCA are the plains and Olduvai, which lie in the lee of the mountains in an area known as a 'rain-shadow'. That said, the rains are unreliable and an entire year can be as arid as the dusty dry season — from June to October.

The onset of the dry season brings cold weather and the crater rim, at 2,200 metres (7,216 feet) above sea-level, can be very chilly when the mist shrouds the forest. Yet even in the coldest months of June and July it usually remains bright and clear. By October the temperature starts to rise and with the first rains the skies are blue and views from the crater over Lake Magadi and Oldeani and Sadiman volcanoes are steely bright.

Geology

Today's landscape is the complex outcome of intense earth movement, volcanic activity, and the biggest influence of all — time.

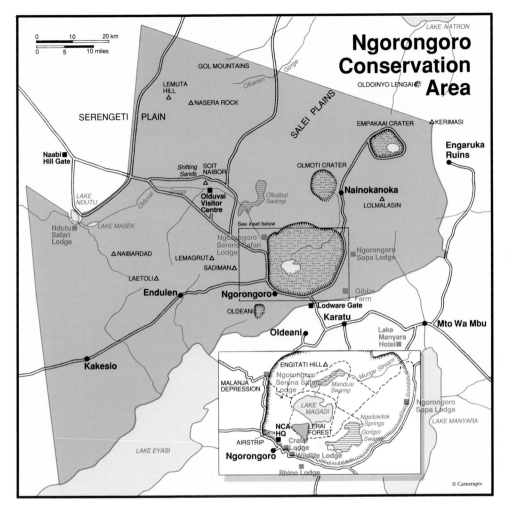

The NCA is essentially made up of two separate rifts shot through and covered by molten rock spewed from volcanoes ancient and modern. A violent landscape that has been softened by aeons of erosion.

The ancient Gol Mountains in the north were relatively untouched by major faulting. They have had their gneiss rocks reduced to smooth hills and kopjes by millions of years of weathering, resulting in such monoliths as Nasera Rock, a 100-metre-high (328-foot) block of granite that squats on the plains, surrounded at its base by evidence of Stone Age habitation. The same ages of hot days followed by cold nights have formed the smooth domed gneiss and granite kopjes of the Serengeti by a process called exfoliation.

To the south of NCA the Eyasi Rift, which forms the 300-metre (984-foot) back wall of Lake Eyasi, was buried over most of its length by upwellings of lava fifteen million years ago. The park's oldest volcanoes were also born at this time: Oldeani, Sadiman and Lemagrut.

As little as 2.5 million years ago the young Ngorongoro Volcano had filled with molten rock that solidified as a crust, or roof. As the lava subsided the solid dome crumpled and collapsed, forming the largest perfect caldera in the world, eighteen kilometres (11 miles) across.

Overleaf: At 18 kilometres (11 miles) across, Ngorongoro Crater is the largest caldera in the world.

The activity continued unabated. Olmoti and Empakaai volcanoes also sank back into themselves like burst bubbles in a vat of hot toffee. The Manyara Rift appeared, running north to south, and a block of land in the east dropped where Lake Manyara and Lake Natron now rest. All across this dynamic landscape molten rock percolated up from deep within the earth and broke from surface fissures, producing small craters, calderas, cones, and the Kerimasi Volcano, which partially sealed over the Manyara crack in the north.

In its dying days Kerimasi threw out clouds of ash that blanketed and preserved the hominid remains at Olduvai and is the building block of today's fertile soils stretching across the Serengeti and Salei plains.

Getting there

Ngorongoro Conservation Area lies 180 kilometres (112 miles) from Arusha. Head south-west out of Arusha along the main road to Dodoma. At Makuyuni turn right onto an all-weather road that leads past the Lake Manyara National Park entrance and on to Ngorongoro Crater and the Serengeti. There is also an airstrip on the crater rim

Above: Freshwater pool quenches the thirst of an Ngorongoro lion.

Opposite: With its three-toed hoof and prehensile upper lip, the rhino is able to forage for food from sea-level to high savannah and montane forest.

Overleaf: Pride of place: The Ngorongoro Crater hosts one of the world's densest populations of large predators — mainly lion.

and another at Ndutu Lodge. Manyara airfield is two hours by car from the southern entry gate.

When to go

Any time of the year, although it may be very muddy in April and May.

Where to stay

On the crater rim, Ngorongoro Wildlife Lodge with 150 beds, Ngorongoro Sopa Lodge with 100 luxury suites and Ngorongoro Serena Lodge all offer unhindered views of the crater and its wealth of wildlife. Ngorongoro Crater Lodge, the oldest and built of logs, retains a

Above: Tanzania's elephant population has suffered dramatically at the hands of ivory poachers.

rustic ambience. Within the NCA but with no view into the crater, Rhino Lodge offers good food and comfortable accommodation. Ndutu Safari Lodge, near the Naabi Hill Gate, has 32 double rooms and six double tents in attractive acacia woodland overlooking Lake Ndutu.

At Karatu, Gibbs' Farm, also known as Ngorongoro Safari Lodge, on the outer slopes of the crater highlands, is small and intimate, with fifteen double rooms, seven in separate garden cottages. Camping is allowed at designated sites in the NCA. Two are on the crater rim.

Camping is permitted along Olduvai Gorge and at Olmoti and Empakaai craters. At Olmoti, after leaving your vehicle at the Ranger Post, the choice of campsite is yours; the rangers will be able to give advice and point out safe drinking water. Empakaai has a number of basic accommodation options. There are camping sites near the Ranger Post or, at the southern edge of the lake, there is a cabin which must be booked at the NCA headquarters before setting off. Spring water is available. Take all food and

provisions with you to both Olmoti and Empakaai. (See Listings for 'Accommodation').

Fees to pay
The official entry points are at Lodware Gate at the southern forest boundary on Ngorongoro Crater and at Naabi Hill Gate on the Serengeti plain. There are other entry points where you do not need to pass through a gate but you must secure permission to use these routes. All fees are payable in foreign currency only and are subject to change. Up-to-date information can be obtained from tour operators or the Conservation Area Headquarters, PO Box 776, Arusha.

Sightseeing
Most people enter Ngorongoro Crater via the **Northern Highlands Forest Reserve** on the south and east slopes of the NCA. The high **montane forest** extends from the **Lodware Gate** to the lip of the crater, partially encircling its outer slopes. As you climb the composition of the trees changes. Crotons, with their pale, low branching

162

trunks and open crowns are common at low altitudes. Red thorn acacias, flat topped and decked with ruby vines, grow on the ridges of the steep and gullied hill side.

Shooting straight up out of the bottom and sides of the canyons are the aptly named pillar-woods. Their unbranched boles are extremely tall and support a bushy growth of branches hung with the lichen *Usnea*, or Old Man's Beard, which prospers in the moisture-laden air.

On the rim itself the gnarled *Nuxia congesta*, with its distinctive fluted trunk and white flowers, is a common sight, especially around **Rhino Lodge** and **Ngorongoro Wildlife Lodge**.

The rim is also the habitat of the strangler fig, so-called because its seeds often lodge in the branches of other trees and envelop their host in a suffocating web of tendrils and roots. The yellow flowers of the climber *Senecio hadiensis* festoon much of the forest by the side of the road.

You might catch sight of a buffalo as it crosses the track — perhaps even a leopard — or of the reclusive bushbuck and duiker. Blue monkeys and olive baboons clamber in the trees, while nocturnal bushbabies are active with the other creatures of the night: civets, genets, servals, porcupines and bats. Elephants come to the forest to 'mine' the earth for the mineral deposits.

Augur buzzards flash their white underparts as they swing over the dense green canopy and crowned eagles may sometimes be seen. Among the branches red-eyed doves, Hildebrandt's francolins, Livingstone's turacos, shrikes, mousebirds, and hornbills call and display or search for food in the partial gloom.

The crater
Be ready for some fantastic views at the crater's rim. Driving west, with the crater on the right and **Oldeani Mountain** to the left, all the world is laid out below. Rhino Lodge is the first establishment passed, then Ngorongoro Wildlife Lodge. Shortly thereafter you encounter the road that exits the crater (this is a one-way route, so don't descend!). Beyond the path out of the crater are the **graves** of zoologists **Bernhard Grzimek** and his son **Michael**.

Grzimek conducted many early pioneering ecological surveys of the Serengeti and Ngorongoro and is largely responsible for bringing this area to the attention of the world, alerting man to the problems of conservation on a vast scale. His son died tragically when his plane struck a vulture and crashed during the filming of his father's book, *Serengeti Shall Not Die*.

Beyond the graves and off the **main track** is **Crater Lodge**, followed by the road leading to the **Ngorongoro village**, **visitor centre** and **petrol station**. Beyond this, on the main road, where the Forest Reserve gives way to more open country, is the **Conservation Area Headquarters**.

As the forest recedes, the crater's vertiginous void opens up with tantalizing glimpses of its vastness. At one of the numerous **viewpoints**, stop to take in the sheer spectacle. The **crater floor** spreads out 600 metres (1,968 feet) below; a microcosm of Africa.

Grassland, swamps, lakes, rivers, woodland, mountains and wildlife are all there. The **Gol Mountains** nudge above the far rim, **Lake Magadi** is centre stage with **Seneto Springs** to the left, **Gorigor Swamp** to the right, and **Lerai Forest** in the foreground. With binoculars it is possible to see the large animals of the crater — rhino, elephant and buffalo — as you scan the vast panorama.

Into the crater
Beyond the NCA headquarters, several kilometres distant, the road drops down from bushy moorland into the **Malanja Depression**. This is an amphitheatre of grassland — carpeted with bright yellow flowers in May — where the Maasai graze cattle under the **Sadiman** and **Lemagrut Volcanos**, landmarks that are visible from

Overleaf: Cheetah usually prey on small animals, such as this impala, although groups of males will attack larger animals.

almost all parts of the NCA except within the crater itself. The road follows the slope of the depression, then passes an opening allowing an eastern view of the crater floor. The area is called **Windy Gap** and it is there the descent into the crater begins, following a steep path that was once an animal track. *Euphorbia candelabrum* and *Euphorbia kibwesensis* line the road of **Seneto Descent**, named after the springs at its base.

The crater supports up to 25,000 large mammals. Grazers dominate: zebra, wildebeest — accounting for almost half the animals — gazelle, buffalo, eland, hartebeest and wart hog. Certain animals are notable by their absence.

Giraffe, for example, stay away because there is insufficient food at tree level; topi because they compete directly with wildebeest (although the Serengeti can support them both, probably due to its much larger area). There are also no impala for reasons that remain unclear.

An odd feature of the crater elephants is that they are almost exclusively bulls. Breeding herds — comprising large numbers of females and young with a few attendant older males — are probably unable to find sufficient quality food in the crater.

Ngorongoro has carnivores in quantity, drawn by the large herds of prey animals. It has the most dense population of large predators, mainly lion — about 100 — and more than 400 spotted hyena, living in eight clans of up to eighty individuals. Both lions and hyenas will scavenge from each other, depending on weight of numbers and another potent motive — hunger.

From **Seneto Springs** at the bottom of the descent trail, most visitors head north to **Engitati Hill** and nearby **Mandusi Swamp**. Just to the east of the road along the way are a small group of pools called the **Goose Ponds**. These are the regular haunt of serval cats who prowl in the marsh for waterbirds. The ponds are also popular with lions and hyenas who come to drink, lounge and prey on unsuspecting grazers. During the dry season you can cut across the marsh to where **Munge Stream** enters the crater's soda lake, or continue on the main route until you come to a loop track that leads off to the left and up **Engitati Hill**. Perched on top, you'll be rewarded with an excellent view of the entire northern side of the crater.

The **Mandusi Swamp**, just south of Engitati Hill, is a marshy flood plain formed by the **Munge Stream** flowing out of **Olmoti Crater**. It is a favourite haunt of elephant, hippo, reedbuck, serval, and occasionally the nocturnal side-striped jackal. Waterbirds are always present and include the spoonbill, jacana, Egyptian goose, black-headed heron and, in the rainy season, widow birds.

Much of the bird life of Ngorongoro is seasonal. The wet months see the arrival of Eurasian migrants at the open pools. White storks, yellow wagtails, and swallows mingle with the local inhabitants: stilts, saddle-bill storks, ibis, ruff, and various species of duck. Lesser flamingos are only there to feed, flying in from their breeding grounds at Lake Natron during the night to filter out the rich blooms of blue-green algae.

The most distinctive grassland bird of the crater — after the ostrich — is the kori bustard, which performs an elaborate territorial display during the breeding season. Another flamboyant show-off, the crowned crane, executes a high-stepping dance in the rainy season when the birds pair.

Also influencing the variety of bird species on display is the ratio of soda to fresh water in the largest expanse of water on the crater floor, **Lake Magadi**, also known as **Makat** (both the Swahili and Maasai words mean soda). The lake is

Opposite: The rock hyrax, a relative of the elephant, hides in holes, crevices, or under rocks, seldom venturing far from its retreat.
Overleaf: The late afternoon sun softens the colours of flamingos in the alkaline waters of Ngorongoro Crater's Lake Magadi.

alkaline due to deposits of volcanic ash thrown out by surrounding volcanoes. During the year the depth of the water is determined by the quantity of water flowing down from the highlands in the Munge Stream, which empties into the lake. When the water is relatively fresh there are more birds, like the little stint, curlew sandpiper, and Kittlitz's sandplover. During the dry season the lake shrinks dramatically and white dust devils whirl over its shimmering glazed surface. Even during the wet season it is never more than three metres (10 feet) deep.

The lake edges are favourite stalking grounds for golden jackals, lions and hyenas that catch birds themselves or steal the meals of other predators.

To the east of Lake Magadi lie the springs of **Ngoitokitok**. Welling up from the earth in abundance, the clear waters form a lake before spreading south into the vast **Gorigor Swamp**. Along the lake shore a lone fig tree makes a pleasant **picnic spot**, and nearby there are several toilets. Beware — African kites here are aggressive enough to snatch food from unsuspecting hands.

The expansive Gorigor Swamp area can be a boggy mess during the wet season and it is mandatory to keep to the main roads on the crater floor. When wet, the swamp's outlet stream is frequented by rhino and vehicles may be subject to a mock charge. The short-sighted animals rush at threatening immobile objects, such as a Landrover, in order to get a sighting on them when they move. In the dry season the lions use the grasslands by the swamp for cover as they ambush thirsty grazers.

Crossing the **Gorigor Bridge** the road enters the **Lerai Forest**. Lerai is a Maasai word that refers to the tall yellow-barked acacias dominating the forest. Years of bark stripping by elephants have left them gnarled and today many are dying — but not from elephant damage. In parts of the forest the ground water level is receding and the trees, unable to obtain enough moisture from the earth, slowly die.

At **Ngoitokitok Springs** rising water levels encourage trees to flourish.

The Lerai Forest could be a wildlife sanctuary in its own right. Eland, elephant, vervet monkey, bushbuck, francolin, vulture and eagle all live side by side there, along with the tree hyrax. Unlike its cousin the rock hyrax, this guinea pig-sized animal feeds only at night. You can often hear its piercing cry (which resembles a horror movie scream) emanating from around the lodges at nights. Many of the fig trees in this area of the crater are considered sacred to the Datoga and Maasai people.

One massive southerly tree, where Fig Tree Camp used to be, is revered as a burial site. According to the Datoga, a warrior was wounded in his leg during a war with the Maasai around 1840. The injured man attempted to crawl back to his *boma*, calling along the way for his wife to bring him a drink of milk. Hearing her husband's pleas, she left the safety of her home and eventually found him and quenched his thirst. He then said goodbye and was never heard from again, nor was his body ever discovered. In the place where he drank his milk the fig tree now stands. The Datoga say the fig grows to offer him shade.

Coming almost full circle around the crater floor by this point, the **ascent road** cuts up the southern wall through a zone of flowering plants and a canyon where large trees such as the pinkflowered Cape chestnut grow. Some of the more striking plants, either for their scent or colours, are the fragrant Lippia and Lantana bushes, the *Aspilia* and *Bidens* (which resemble daisies) and wild banana. *Leonotis*, the orange-flowered 'lion's paw', is a common and attractive plant that grows in stands on the floor, walls and rim of the crater.

As you leave the crater it is important to remember that this living, vibrant ecosystem is in a constant state of flux as it adapts to its changing circumstances. Animal populations are not only seasonal but long-term as well. In the last thirty years the wildebeest numbers have fluctuated

Opposite: The not yet extinct volcano Ol Doinyo Lengai, seen from the still ash-strewn Rift Valley floor.

between 8,000 and 15,000. The now common wart hogs are a recent arrival, not seen at all until 1976. Buffalos have only arrived with the departure of the Maasai and their livestock and today number approximately 3,000.

Man has also had a hand in the fortunes of the crater and its animals. Black rhino numbers have plummeted from 100 in 1965 to less than 20 — due entirely to poaching. Their future survival is critical as poachers become more resourceful and well-armed in their search for huge profits.

Reaching the top of the rise, *Buddleia polystachya*, with its golden flower spikes, drops from view. Looking back over the lakes and plains of Ngorongoro it is both apparent and imperative that this 'eighth wonder of the world' must be protected at all costs for future generations to enjoy.

Even more craters

Although not as spectacular as Ngorongoro Crater, the extinct volcanoes of **Olmoti** and **Empakaai** to the north-east are worth a visit for their scenic beauty and sense of solitude. They are not on the regular 'tourist trail', however, and permission should be sought from the NCA headquarters before visiting them. Both volcanoes are reached from the **ascent road** on the **eastern side** of **Ngorongoro Crater** through thick stands of *Acacia lahai* trees.

To reach **Olmoti Crater** either ask for directions at **Nainokanoka village** or take the **last track leading left** at the end of the village. This will take you to the **Ranger Post** where you can leave your car and hire a guide for the rest of the thirty-minute walk along cattle tracks through buffalo country to the summit.

From the crater rim at about 3,700 metres (12,136 feet), eland and bushbuck can be seen grazing the shallow floor of the grassy caldera. Water collects in this natural basin and flows out of the south side as a **waterfall**, just below the path to the summit. This cascading sheet of water is the **Munge Stream**, named after the Maasai

word given to their ceremonial anklets made from the skin of the colobus monkey. The white water falling down the dark escarpment is analogous to the black and white monkey flashing through the high forest branches.

Oddly though, colobus are not found anywhere in the Ngorongoro forest, even though it is quite a suitable habitat. It may be that the monkey has never crossed the open plains from its nearest home, the western Serengeti.

Whereas Olmoti Crater is relatively shallow and dry, **Empakaai**'s 300-metre-deep (984-foot) caldera is dominated by a soda lake. Unlike most soda lakes, which are quite shallow, Empakaai's is eighty-five metres (279 feet) deep. Even so, the familiar waterbirds like the black-winged stilt, Cape teal and flamingo still dot its shores.

The crater rim of Empakaai can be walked — a distance of thirty-two kilometres (20 miles) — with spectacular views along the entire trek. The walk begins outside of Nainokanoka village, gradually ascending through silent stands of *Nuxia*, figs, crotons, and the high-altitude *Hagenia abyssinica*, with its feathery leaves that collect and drip water from the misty atmosphere.

When skies are clear there are views of the still active volcano **Ol Doinyo Lengai** to the north, **Lake Natron**, and even **Kilimanjaro** far to the east. From the eastern section of the rim a path leads to the crater floor through woodland where sunbirds feed from bright flowers. Beware — buffalo and bushbuck are not uncommon.

The plains

Almost half of the NCA is made up of vast tracts of open **grassland** — dry and barren for most of the year — which swing in an arc from the **Serengeti** in the north-west, through the **Gol Mountains**, to the **Salei Plain** in the north-east.

Beyond the boundary of the NCA the plains extend in an unbroken wilderness as

Opposite: Ethereal silhouette of Ol Doinyo Lengai, or 'Mountain of God', south of Lake Natron on the edge of the Ngorongoro Conservation Area. Lengai erupted in 1966 and 1983.

far north as **Lake Victoria** and the shores of **Lake Natron**. Dry for most of the year as they lie in the rainless shadow of the southern massif, the plains appear windswept and arid as dust devils suck the fine soil up into a blue sky. When the rains do come — sporadically between November and May — the plains undergo a schizophrenic transformation. The soil's latent fertility becomes apparent as nutritious grazing grasses rapidly sprout, attracting huge herds of migrants for as long as the water and green shoots last.

The **Salei Plain** is a wedge of grassland lower and even drier than the Serengeti. Its western edge is the fault line that runs from **Olbalbal Swamp** to the eastern edge of the Gol Mountains and beyond.

Remote, harsh and thinly populated by the Maasai who live mostly outside the boundary of the NCA, the Salei should only be visited by well-equipped parties in four-wheel-drive vehicles accompanied by a guide who knows where the area's renowned sand traps are situated.

The Salei can be reached from the main road at the foot of the outer slope of Ngorongoro Crater. Head eastwards towards **Olbalbal depression**, then turn north towards the village of **Malambo**. The dusty, rutted track crosses the end of Olduvai Gorge and runs along the west edge of Salei and the eastern foot of the Gol Mountains.

Visiting during the dry season is to be avoided, but in the wet season the region has several attractions, not the least being the adventure of travelling through this area of bumpy plains and blowing sand dunes to the pink granite cliffs of the Gol Mountains.

Lying in the shadow of the mountains is **Nasera Rock**, a great granite monolith rising 100 metres (328 feet) above the plains. For thousands of years a shelter from the wind for animals and humans, Nasera is surrounded by archaeological evidence of human habitation from the Stone Age to the present.

During the wet season, wildebeest romp across the green grass and baboons clamber up the precipitous sides of the rock. A wide variety of bird life can be seen and heard in the leafy fig and acacia trees surrounding Nasera's base. If you have energy and determination it is possible to climb the eastern side of Nasera. Look for klipspringers and falcons, residents of these rocky heights.

Another spectacular land form is the **Olkarien Gorge** at the eastern edge of the Gols, nesting site of Ruppell's griffon vulture, and half a day's dusty drive from Ngorongoro Crater through the treeless landscape.

One reason for the lack of trees is that the seasonal — and daily — movement of water up and down through the soil causes a 'hard pan' of limestone to accumulate underground. Plants with shallow roots, like grass, can grow in the upper layer but trees cannot extend their systems deep enough, except where the pan is broken.

Only the hardiest and most drought-tolerant animals stay on the plains during the dry months. The rare fringe-eared oryx is one species that manages to scratch out a living. The striped hyena, also a local inhabitant, only ventures out at night to scavenge with the other nocturnal animals such as the spring hare and the aardvark.

The rains bring the Salei back to life again. Migrants from the highlands, where the forage is more abundant but less nourishing, sweep through the flower-rich new growth.

Thomson's gazelle are followed by wildebeest — which give birth during a precisely regulated period of a few weeks between February and March — then zebra, topi, hartebeest and eland. As the animals arrive the Maasai move their cattle out, fearful of the lethal malignant catarrh the new-born wildebeest can carry.

Predators follow their on-the-hoof food and, after months of near-starvation, turn to gluttony. Lion, hyena, jackal and the five local species of vulture are never far from any carcass.

Olduvai Gorge: Cradle of Mankind

Cutting across the Serengeti and Salei plains in an east-west direction is a narrow fifty-kilometre-long (31-mile) gorge. This is Olduvai, site of some of the most important fossil hominid finds of all time; unearthed remains of our ancestors that have raised as many questions as they have answered.

Olduvai, or more correctly Oldupai (named by the Maasai for the wild sisal plant that is commonly found there), first came to the attention of Europeans in 1911 when a German entomologist, looking for butterflies, found fossil bones in the gorge.

Back in Berlin the remains were identified as being those of a prehistoric and now extinct horse, *Hipparion*. The Kaiser was sufficiently impressed to personally fund an expedition, led by Professor Hans Reck, to find more fossil bones. Unfortunately World War I put an end to Reck's work.

Louis Leakey saw the Berlin bones and became convinced that Olduvai would yield something far more interesting than the skeleton of an ancestral horse. Gathering his tools and family, he began his first dig at Olduvai in 1931 and within a few hours of arriving at the site was rewarded with the discovery of stone tools.

With his wife Mary, he continued excavations for the next twenty-eight years, uncovering hundreds of stone objects and fossil bones. Their hard work finally paid off when Mary discovered the partial skull of 'Nutcracker Man', later named *Australopithecus boisei*, who lived 1.75 million years ago.

A boisei, and the later discovery of *Homo habilis*, or 'Handy Man', arguably became the most important and controversial hominid finds of the time, fuelling academic debate about the origin of the first human for the next two decades. (See 'History: From the Cradle to Independence', Part One.)

Getting there

Olduvai Gorge is located within the Ngorongoro Conservation Area, 180 kilometres (112 miles) from Arusha. Head south-west out of Arusha along the main road to Dodoma. At Makuyuni turn right onto an all-weather road that leads past Lake Manyara National Park, the Ngorongoro Crater and on to the Serengeti. About thirty kilometres (19 miles) past the crater a signpost to the right directs visitors six kilometres (four miles) down a very dusty track to the Olduvai Visitor Centre.

When to go

It is possible to visit the NCA at any time of the year, although it can be muddy in April and May.

Where to stay

Ndutu Safari Lodge is nearest to the gorge on its western side, with 32 double rooms and six double tents when additional accommodation is needed. There are also campsites near the lodge.

Their facilities are only basic and campers should have their own water and be entirely self-contained although the lodge has a bar and restaurant. The campsites overlook the south-west shores of Lake Ndutu. There are other sites along the northern shore.

At Ngorongoro: Ngorongoro Serena Lodge, Ngorongoro Crater Lodge, Ngorongoro Sopa Lodge, Ngorongoro Wildlife Lodge, Rhino Lodge, Gibbs' Farm (Ngorongoro Safari Lodge) and camping sites. There are camping sites along the Olduvai Gorge itself and at Olmoti and Empakaai craters.

At Olmoti, after leaving your vehicle at the Ranger's Post, the choice of campsite is yours; the rangers will give advice and point out drinking water.

Empakaai has a number of basic accommodation options with camping sites near the Ranger Post. At the southern end of the Empakaai crater lake there is a cabin which must be booked in advance at the NCA Headquarters. (See Listings for 'Accommodation').

Fees to pay

The official entry points are Lodware Gate

Above: Olduvai Gorge, the 'Cradle of Mankind' and the site of spectacular archaeological discoveries by Mary and Louis Leakey.

at the southern forest boundary on Ngorongoro Crater and Naabi Hill Gate on the Serengeti plain. There are other entry points that do not require you to pass through a gate but you must secure permission to use them. Fees are payable in foreign currency only and are subject to change. Up-to-date information about the current fees charged for accommodation and entry can be obtained from tour operators or the NCA Park Headquarters.

Sightseeing

Begin a tour of **Olduvai Gorge** at the small but informative **museum** located at the **visitor centre**. From there guides lead **lecture tours** down into the gorge and some of the sites can be seen at close quarters.

The gorge is a uniquely productive site for **archaeological excavations** due to a number of conjoining factors. The area was abundantly inhabited by many species of animals, including a sabre-toothed big cat, two kinds of elephant, a giant giraffe with immense sweeping horns called

Sivatherium, and various predecessors of today's plains game such as giant pigs and wildebeest. Man — the hunter and the hunted — lived in their midst.

Together their bones were preserved in the alkaline mud of the lake that once covered the area — an ideal medium for fossilization. As the years passed, sediment built up as the lake grew and shrank, creating chronological layers that are today easy to interpret. Additionally, the sedimentary mud, which is volcanic in origin, is conducive to radioactive dating methods. Lastly, the layers have been neatly exposed by a seasonal river that cut through the beds like a knife, exposing the historic treasures as if they were currants in a layered cake.

As well as ancient fossils, the work at Olduvai — begun by the Leakeys and now in the hands of the **National Museum of Tanzania** — has revealed evidence of **settlements** and **stone artefacts**. There is a 1.75 million-year-old **circle of stones** that was once the foundation of a **shelter**. These

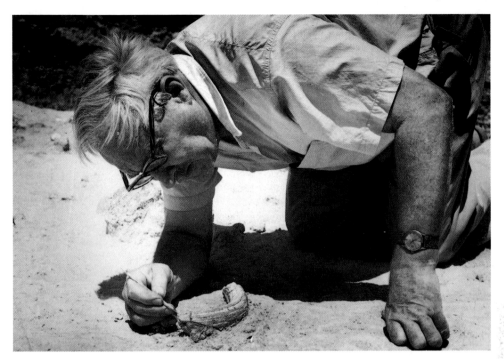

Above: Louis Leakey, working at Olduvai Gorge. He helped elevate African palaeontology to international status.

stones, along with the nearby remains of animal bones and stone implements, suggest that early man lived in the type of social group still evident among the Bushmen. In places the gorge is sixty metres (197 feet) high and the five layers of clay and sand laid down as sediment in the lake, on a base of volcanic rock, can clearly be seen. The bones and teeth of more than 150 species of animal have been excavated from the strata and an almost continuous record of human habitation from the earliest tool users to the Stone Age has been recreated from artefacts excavated.

Shifting Sands

Across the gorge from the visitor centre is a track that passes to the left of a **hill (Soit Naibor)**. Two kilometres further on lies an interesting phenomenon — **Shifting Sands** — a rolling black dune of fine ash blown by the wind from Ol Doinyo Lengai.

About nine metres (30 feet) high and 100 metres (328 feet) long, Shifting Sands is a fine example of a barchan or crescent-shaped dune. The constant dry wind blowing from the east pushes sand grains from the back of the dune, up its steep slope, to tumble over the top. Grain by grain the dune advances across the wide expanses. Look for the dated concrete markers that show the dune's movement. Since 1969 it has covered about seventeen metres (56 feet) each year. When the rains fall the dune stops moving, but rain is so rare in this area of the NCA that plants never have a chance to take root before the dune is off and rolling again.

Nearby lakes

To the west of the Olduvai archaeological site are **lakes Ndutu** and **Masek**. Strictly speaking, Lake Ndutu is within the Serengeti National Park, so the Maasai are only able to use Masek as a watering hole for their cattle; they are not allowed to graze within the Serengeti, which is strictly reserved as a wildlife sanctuary.

The lakes can be reached by following a

Below: Discovery site of *Australopithecus boisei*, believed to have roamed Olduvai Gorge almost two million years ago.

Above: Like the women, Maasai men also wear elaborate beaded earrings through their elongated lobes.

Opposite: These young Maasai girls, who make their home in the Ngorongoro Conservation Area, proudly display the intricate bead work for which their tribe is renowned.

track that branches off the main **NCA-Serengeti road**. Look for a **signpost** six kilometres (four miles) beyond where Olduvai Gorge crosses the **main road**. For twenty kilometres (12 miles) the track traverses the plain parallel to the gorge then dips down into bush before coming out onto a flat area between the lakes at a crossing.

The **Ndutu Lodge** is about three kilometres (two miles) beyond this point. Both stretches of water are soda lakes in the tradition of East African volcanic regions, rendered alkaline either by ancient volcanic dust or by mineral springs.

Lake Ndutu, in particular, has two distinct aspects to its character, changing markedly between the dry and wet seasons. June to November dust blows in from the plain and the region's wildlife — impala, dik-dik, hartebeest and giraffe — congregate around the river and water holes which, depending on the year, may be the only source of water. Elephants also come to the swamp when the drought is at its worst and Ndutu, the shallower of the lakes, is reduced to a baking white salt pan.

At any time, Ndutu's residents are unusual. Yellow-winged bats hang like fruit in the acacias; tortoises resolve themselves out of stones in front of your vehicle and lumber away through the sansevieria; troops of rare wild dogs lope across the plain; serval and caracal cats stalk the bush and genets, relatives of the mongoose, frequent **Ndutu Lodge**. Martial eagles silently hunt through the trees and green and orange lovebirds stand out against the ochre landscape.

At the start of the rains, usually in November, the grazing herds become restless and assemble in the higher elevations of the NCA and surrounding areas for their trek back to the greening plains.

The wildebeest are especially single-minded in their travelling. They cross the lakes in long streams rather than take a small detour around the shores. Sometimes, when calving is at its peak in February and March, the animals will panic and stampede, resulting in many casualties.

Above: With its authentic architectural design, Serengeti Serena Safari Lodge offers new levels of luxury in the wilds of the National Park.

Animals die either from drowning or injury, or because orphaned wildebeest are not adopted by others. For days the lake is a charnel house as scavengers flock in to feed on the dead and dying in the mud.

Insect life undergoes a population explosion during the rains and with it the long-range migrant birds sweep in to feed on the creatures. Terns, white-storks, common and lesser kestrels, and Montagu's harriers leave their European breeding grounds in winter for the abundant southern dining and a lazy African season.

Serengeti: The Great Migration

Between the Ngorongoro highlands, Lake Victoria and Tanzania's northern border with Kenya stretches one of the world's last great wildlife refuges — the Serengeti. The name comes from the Maasai *siringet*, 'endless plains'. The Serengeti's 14,763 square kilometres (5,700 square miles) — equal in size to Connecticut or Northern Ireland — contain about three million large animals, most taking part in a seasonal migration, unparalleled in nature. Not since the great bison migrations across the North American plains have there been such concentrations of animals on the move at one time.

Twice a year, triggered by the rains, 1.3 million wildebeest, 200,000 zebra and 300,000 Thomson's gazelle gather to undertake the long trek to new grazing lands. The migration of the herbivores roughly defines the boundaries of Serengeti National Park

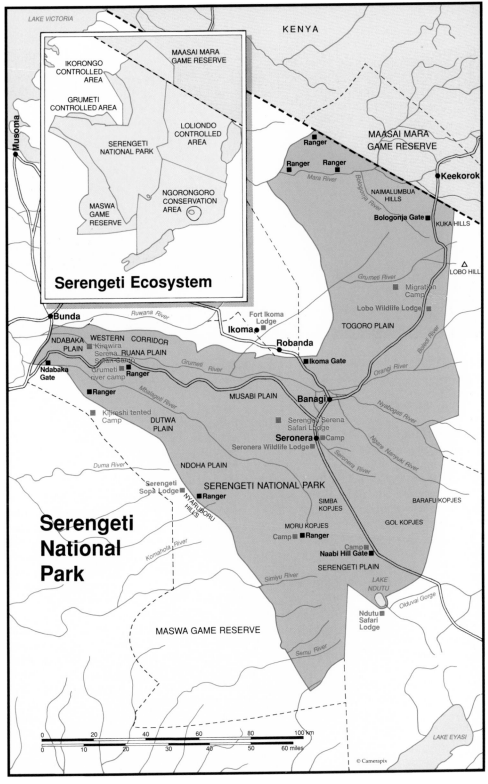

Serengeti Ecosystem

Serengeti National Park

181

Above: The northern woodlands of the Serengeti as seen from Lobo.

which is the central zone of the Serengeti ecosystem, an area that also takes in Kenya's Maasai Mara National Reserve, the Ngorongoro Conservation Area and the Maswa Game Reserve to the west. Within this 25,900 square kilometres (10,000 square miles) of varied landscape live thirty-five species of plains game and 500 bird species.

The park is made up of several different vegetational zones. In the dry south, located in the lee of the Ngorongoro highlands, are the short and long grass plains, where an average of only fifty-one centimetres (20 inches) of rain falls sporadically during the year. In the centre lies the acacia savannah.

The western corridor, a region of woods and pans of black cotton soil, curves off in a great swathe to the edge of Lake Victoria where the rainfall is twice that of the south. To the north is wooded grassland concentrated along watercourses and tributaries of the Grumeti and Mara rivers.

History

One hundred years ago the Maasai first arrived at the Serengeti, bringing their fierce reputation and abundant cattle to graze on the rich grasses. Prior to this the region was uninhabited and only the Ndorobo and Ikoma came there occasionally to hunt.

The Maasai were soon followed by Dr Oscar Baumann, a German anti-slaver who passed through on his way to Burundi in 1892. Other whites were quick to grasp the Serengeti's potential and by 1913 the first European hunters arrived to shoot game. Lions were considered vermin and were so plentiful on the plains that it was not uncommon for a hundred to be killed on a single safari. By 1921 their numbers had been drastically reduced and it became clear that lions and other game needed protection. In response, the area was made a partial game reserve and eight years later a complete reserve.

The Serengeti was one of the first regions to benefit from the growing appreciation that wildlife was not infinitely renewable but needed safeguarding — usually from human interference — and in 1951 the

Above: Rustic and natural, and built of natural materials, Serengeti Serena Safari Lodge is situated on a hill with magnificent views over the central Serengeti.
Overleaf: Every year more than one million wildebeest and zebra gather on the Serengeti plains for the long trek north to greener pastures.

reserve was designated a national park. It was Tanzania's first national park and remains its largest. The Serengeti has also been declared a World Heritage Site, in recognition of its uniqueness as the last stronghold of the great migrations. The original Serengeti also incorporated the Ngorongoro lands. In 1959 the Ngorongoro Conservation Area was created as a separate unit to meet the needs of the Maasai and their livestock who, prior to that, had been denied access to their old grazing lands around the Ngorongoro highlands in the interests of the wildlife.

Getting there

From Arusha it is possible to drive south-west eighty kilometres (50 miles) along a tarmac road, then branch off to the right at Makuyuni to an all-weather road that leads past Lake Manyara, through the Ngorongoro Conservation Area, the Naabi Hill entrance gate, and on to Seronera in the heart of the Serengeti. The total drive of 335 kilometres (208 miles) from Arusha to Seronera is possible by car during the dry season, but a four-wheel-drive vehicle is recommended during the wet months.

Alternatively, from Kenya and the Maasai Mara, entry is via the Bologonja Gate which leads to the Lobo Wildlife Lodge, approximately eighty kilometres (50 miles) north-east of Seronera. From Musoma on the shores of Lake Victoria it is also possible to travel along an all-weather road to Serengeti through the Ikoma Gate.

Several airstrips are maintained throughout the park for those arriving by charter flight. For those without transport there are many safari tour operators based in Arusha.

When to go

The best time to see the heavy concentration of animals on the plains is from January to February. During the rains in

November-December and March-April-May, prepare to use four-wheel-drive.

Where to stay

Timbered Seronera Lodge is imaginatively built around a large **kopje** at the summit of which an observation platform is reached by climbing rock-hewn steps. Eighty kilometres (50 miles) away by good road and comparable in style and comfort, Lobo Lodge overlooks the northern plains. Both have their own airstrips. Eighty-five kilometres west of Seronera Wildlife Lodge and south of the river is Grumeti River Camp, a luxury permanent camp run on solar power. Ninety-six kilometres (60 miles) from the Naabi Hill Gate the newer, luxury Maasai *manyatta*-inspired Serengeti Sopa Lodge gives sweeping views across the plains from the Nyaboro Hills. All the 66 rooms of Serengeti Serena Safari Lodge in the centre of the park command exceptional views.

At Kirawira Camp in the park's western sector 25 luxury double tents are operated by Serena Hotels. Campsites within the park include four at Seronera, three at Moru Kopjes and one each at Lobo and Naabi Hill Gate. Pay camping fees at the gate and take your own provisions and water. To camp in other than designated areas, permission must be granted by the warden. Kijireshi Tented Camp is situated beyond the Ndabaka Gate. (See Listings).

Fees to pay

Fees are payable in foreign currency only and are subject to change. Up-to-date information about the current fees charged for accommodation and entry to the national parks can be obtained from tour operators or the National Park Headquarters.

The Great Trek

If you arrive from the south-east the first view of the **plains** is offered from the slopes of the **Olbalbal escarpment**. The open grasslands and blue African sky stretch as far as the eye can see.

All year-round throughout this vast tract, herds of herbivores move in a constant cycle of grazing, rutting and calving. Life in the Serengeti is a complex and dynamic ecological system in which all animals and plants interact with each other and their environment. No organism exists in isolation or is static — and they are all dependent upon the rains.

There are two distinct seasons: the dry season between June and October and the wet season which starts in November and lasts irregularly until May.

Breaks in the seasons mark the onset of the migrations and the chief protagonist in this journey is the wildebeest. This unlikely looking antelope is the most successful of the Serengeti grazers, despite being characterized as the 'clown of the plains' (said to be made up of a collection of parts left over from other animals). Nature has designed the wildebeest to move rapidly and economically over vast expanses of land in their endless search for food. Their wide set of incisor teeth enable them to harvest more grass a bite than any competitor.

But with all those millions of jaws chomping, the grass cannot grow fast enough to support the large herds. During the rainy season the mineral-rich short grass plains feed 1.3 million wildebeest, along with thousands of zebra and Thomson's gazelle, large numbers of eland, topi and hartebeest, all prey for their attendant predators.

Although the short grasses are highly nutritious, the animals can only stay on the plains for as long as there is standing water. As soon as this dries up and the grass loses its freshness the animals leave.

The precise timing of the migration varies each year, but generally the herbivores congregate and move out at the end of May over a period of weeks, or as little as three or four days, in columns up to

Opposite: Young Maasai herdsman at Ngorongoro. Fiercely independent, the Maasai people have resisted change throughout the century, and continue to hold on to their traditional pastoralist existence.

Overleaf: Supine felines: A pride of lioness and their young sleep on a kopje, preferring to hunt during the cooler evening or early morning hours.

Above: Although these cubs are weaned at ten weeks, they will remain with their mother for up to eighteen months.

forty kilometres (25 miles) long. With the zebra they head mainly westwards into the hills of the **western corridor** on the first leg of a roughly triangular 800-kilometre (496-mile) circuit.

Zebras are outnumbered six to one during the exodus and their migratory urge is not as strong as that of the wildebeest. They move in smaller herds made up of family units headed by a stallion who will defend several females and their young against predators by lashing with his hind legs.

Other hooved animals are either sedentary or, like Thomson's gazelles, semi-migratory. 'Tommies' only move their range as far as the long grasses around **Seronera**, located on the boundary between the plains and the northern woodland. Dik-diks, on the other hand, may spend their entire lives as a breeding pair, surviving off one acre of ground.

As if the start of the wildebeest's journey were not stressful enough, the exodus coincides with the 'rut' or breeding season.

Females are in oestrus and males with territories fight to determine which bulls will breed with which females. In three weeks of frenetic territorial battles and frantic copulation, the plains reverberate with the deep lowing as dominant males breed with ninety per cent of the cows — close to half a million individual animals.

As the dry season becomes more intense the herds drift out of the west, splitting into two loose groups numbering hundreds of thousands. One group swarms north and the other north-east, both heading for the permanent waters of the northern rivers and the Mara. The migration instinct is so strong that the animals often come to grief in the swollen rivers as they dive from the banks, like the proverbial lemmings.

The injured are despatched by crocodiles and the tumbling bodies of the drowned sweep down the **Mara River**, providing easy meals for the predators. Often the course of the river can be followed from the air, as the vultures chase down the coursing water after the carcasses.

Above: The perfect spot — leopards are the most widely distributed of African carnivores. Their successful existence is largely due to a varied diet.

The three or four months leading up to the start of the rains in November see millions of the surviving migrants concentrated in Kenya's Maasai Mara National Reserve. When rains start in the south, the wildebeeste, including the heavily pregnant females, turn like the tide and begin to move south along the eastern and final stage of the migration route. Eight-and-a-half months after the rut, the wildebeest are back on the **short grass plains** and the calves are born. Most antelopes give birth alone and in seclusion but the wildebeest have their young together (eighty per cent of the pregnant cows have their calves within a few weeks of each other) and out in the open. In the mornings the calving grounds are bursting with newly born young. Within three to five minutes of birth the calf totters to its feet and can run as fast as its mother, with whom it lives in close vicinity for the next six months to a year.

The youngest calves are the preferred prey of lions and easy victims of the cheetah and wild dogs. The wildebeests'

main enemy, the spotted hyena, prefer to take calves under two days old since after this age they become very difficult to catch. Along with the new-born calves, many sick or exhausted animals succumb to the predators who follow the herds.

Wild dogs, once prolific but almost non-existent now in the Serengeti, will select a particular animal from the herd. The pack then tirelessly chases it until, exhausted, the prey is brought down, eviscerated, torn apart and eaten, often within minutes.

Lions hunt either individually or in small groups, typically stalking or ambushing their prey before a final sprint at the unsuspecting animal. Small prey such as gazelle are slapped to the ground and quickly killed by a bite to the neck. Zebra and wildebeest are leapt on from behind and pulled down before the lion strangles the animal by gripping its throat. Alternatively, they may also clamp the muzzle of their prey and suffocate the victim. Lions are poor hunters. They average only one kill in every three attempts, or less.

Above: Carrion feasting flock of vultures enjoying another's misfortune. These usually silent birds emit a hideous cacaphony when feeding.

Cheetah stalk from a great distance until, after an explosive ninety-seven-kilometre-an-hour (60-mile-an-hour) dash over the plains, the cat knocks away the legs of its target — usually impala, gazelle, or reed-buck — killing it with a bite to the throat. Even then the cat is not assured a meal; lions and hyenas will often steal the prey after spotting the cheetah's conspicuous hunting technique. Not surprisingly, they are nervous eaters.

Islands of the plains

After a kill, the lions of the Serengeti will often retreat to a **kopje** (pronounced *kop-yee*) — an Afrikaans word meaning 'small head'. These smooth granite domes can be oases of life during the dry season and they support distinct populations of animals that live there or come to drink from their rock pools.

Most kopjes are found north of **Naabi Hill Gate**, and **Seronera Lodge** is built around one.

They provide shelter for a number of plants that cannot grow out on the open

grassland, such as sansevieria, aloes, blue and yellow hibiscus, and the spectacular crimson *Gloriosa* lily. Cheetah use the boulders as lookout points from where they scan the plains for game, and the rock hyrax lives among them in burrows where it remains safe from the leopard, jackal and serval cat.

Agama lizards do press-ups on the hot rocks and, when they are disturbed, their blue bodies and rose coloured heads fade to a uniformly granite grey disguise.

Verreaux's eagles, massive black birds of prey, nest on the upper parts of the **Moru Kopjes** to the west of the plains.

The Maasai species of klipspringer — in which most of the females have horns — live in monogamous breeding pairs among the northern kopjes where they stand motionless for hours, like sentinels, on the tips of their black pointed hooves.

They share the boulders with several species of mongoose. Dwarf mongooses prefer to make their home in abandoned termite mounds but will come to the kopjes in search of grubs, bird eggs, fledglings and mice. Spitting cobras and puff adders lurk in crevices. Around the base of a kopje there will often be pellets of dung concentrated in thick patches. These are the droppings of the dik-dik, a finely built antelope no bigger than a small dog, with a twitching glossy black proboscis.

The nightjar comes to haunt the kopjes, at night, of course. Its Swahili name is *mpasuanda*, 'tearer of grave cloths'.

Hidden among the jumbled boulders are the **rock paintings** of the Maasai. Drawn on the smooth surfaces with charcoal and ochre are shields, antelopes and stick men hunting elephants; images that have survived decades of rain and wind.

Seronera

The Grzimeks' pioneering work, a heightened public awareness of conservation matters and the blossoming new science of ecology led to the establishment in 1962 of the **Serengeti Research Institute** (SRI) at Seronera. There, much of the ecological and ethnological research is done that has made the Serengeti one of the best understood large ecosystems in the world. Seronera is the **park headquarters**, and the **lodge** is centred around a particularly rich variety of habitats and animals.

Hyrax live on the Seronera Lodge kopje alongside the other characteristic animals of the rocks. The hyrax's main claim to fame is the fact that it is the closest living relative of the elephant. In Europe its dried urine was also once used to treat hysteria.

Surveys carried out at the SRI have shown that most of the park's animal populations are stable, if not actually rising. Since the Grzimeks' first count of 250,000 wildebeest in 1960, numbers have increased to 1.3 million, with a high in 1978 of 1.5 million.

Predators have benefited from the extra food and both lion and cheetah are believed to have doubled their numbers.

On a more sombre note, wild dogs were once common, but an epidemic of canine distemper has nearly obliterated them.

Thirty years ago there were no elephants in the park. Now there are 2,000, forced out of their home areas to the north and south by encroaching human activities. Man upsets the balance wherever he has a hand in shaping the environment.

Poaching is a constant problem in the Serengeti. Local people have hunted these lands since the time of the Wandorobo and Ikoma. The poison-tipped arrows that once provided meat for hungry families have now been replaced by the commercial poachers' four-wheel-drive vehicles and assault weapons that are all too often aimed at the park wardens as well as animals.

Despite the capture of 6,000 poachers over the last twenty years, the 1980s saw the black rhino population reduced by ninety per cent and they are now at extinction level.

The increase in the number of Maasai from 115,000 in 1968 to 300,000 in 1986 — and a comparable increase in their cattle — has been a consequence of improved medical and veterinary practice. Yet this improvement in human welfare is ultimately at odds with the future of the park. Where are the additional Maasai going to live and graze their livestock? The work done at Seronera helps to provide the policy makers with the intelligence that enables them to make informed decisions about the future well-being and survival of the Serengeti.

Seronera Valley

The **valley** is justly famous for its abundance of lion and leopard that can usually be seen and photographed without any difficulty. Lions only frequent the plains of the south during the wet season when the wildebeest are easy prey. The rest of the year the intensely social prides stay among the woods and watercourses of the central savannah country around Seronera.

Prides consist of between two and fifteen related adult females, who do most of the hunting within a defined territorial range in which they share the responsibility of raising the cubs.

Adult male lions of the Serengeti — their

characteristic black manes fully developed after four years — lead a very different life. A group of adults, often related, controls a range that is marked and defended against the intrusion of other related groups or individuals that do not have their own ranges.

Although the males are fifty per cent heavier than females and considerably stronger, lionesses do the majority of the hunting. In open grassland this is done at night, while daylight stalking occurs where there is vegetation cover for ambushes.

Males quickly muscle in on kills and can eat up to a quarter of their body weight at one sitting. Cubs take what they can after the adults have finished eating and do not start to feed off a carcass until they have reached three months of age.

But hunting takes up only a small fraction of the day and for the most part the prides spend their hours on kopjes or in the shade playing, nuzzling each other in greeting, swatting at flies, or simply sleeping.

While lions can be sighted on the open plains, look up into the trees for the give-away twitching tail of the leopard. The yellow-barked acacia and sausage trees are usually their favourite haunts. Despite their habit of lounging in the branches, where they also eat their kills, leopards are infrequently seen, their roseate spot pattern serving as surprisingly effective camouflage against the dappled background of a tree.

Leopards are solitary, mainly nocturnal felines, and come with a dangerous reputation. Little is known about their behaviour. They live in a variety of habitats, except the driest country and are the most widespread of the cats, even occurring on the outskirts of urban neighbourhoods where, ironically, they may have been forced to seek refuge by the activities of man.

In the 1960s and 1970s they suffered badly at the hands of the furriers who catered for a fashion boom in leopard skin coats, a trend begun when Jackie Onassis made a public appearance wearing one.

In the Seronera valley, kopjes, large trees near streams, and boulders are their main haunts. They advertise their presence to other leopards with a sawing cough as an intention to avoid territorial fights.

Primarily stalkers when hunting, they also utilize their climbing skills and will leap from trees onto their prey. Afterwards the leopard drags the kill back up into the branches to avoid having the carcass stolen by hyenas or lions.

Western corridor

The western corridor road branches left from the **Seronera-Banagi road** five kilometres (three miles) from Seronera. Following the road west for about 140 kilometres (87 miles) brings you to the **Ndabaka Gate**, near the **shores of Lake Victoria**, and on to the towns of **Musoma** and **Mwanza**. As you travel west the **Grumeti River** (which drains into Victoria) lies to the right; to the left is the **central range of hills**. Thirty kilometres (19 miles) before Ndabaka are extensive clay plains. Known as 'black cotton', this area is a dangerous bog during the wet season.

During and just after the rains beautiful yellow hibiscus plants flower throughout the grasses. While the short-grass plains are at their best during the wet season, the western corridor is more interesting and easier to travel through during the dry months.

Some of the mammals that make their home in this section of the park include baboon, vervet and colobus monkeys, eland, impala, topi, zebra and wildebeest. The crocodile is also a local resident, usually found basking on the sandbanks of the river. Do not venture near the water's edge when crocs are spotted. They can move with surprising speed and once a victim is caught in their vice-like jaws they are drawn underwater and either torn apart immediately, or stored until the reptile can work up an appreciable appetite.

Opposite: Marabou storks enjoy the sunset perched atop an acacia tree in the Serengeti.

Out West: To the Source of the Nile

A glance at a Tanzanian map reveals that the country contains, and is bordered by, large areas of water — a good proportion accounted for by Lake Victoria, the largest lake in Africa and the second-largest freshwater lake in the world. The source of frenzied European exploration during the nineteenth century, this once-elusive lake drains north, its waters carried along by the Nile more than 6,450 kilometres (4,000 miles) to the Mediterranean Sea.

Lake Victoria is an atypical Tanzanian lake; it does not lie in one of the depressed troughs of either the eastern or western arm of the Rift Valley — like lakes Tanganyika, Malawi, Rukwa, Manyara, Natron, and Eyasi — but occupies a large shallow basin about the size of Scotland that averages seventy metres (230 feet) deep. Victoria is also unusual because it is fresh water. As a general rule the lakes of East Africa are fed by rivers that flow off mountains — like Kilimanjaro — that are made of basic lavas containing numerous minerals. The rivers collect these minerals as they course down the slopes, emptying them into the lake where they become concentrated through evaporation. The result is alkaline water.

Discovery

It was in Tabora that explorers Burton and Speke heard tell of a vast inland sea to the north that was far greater than Lake Tanganyika. Burton, recovering from illness, was forced to stay behind, but Speke set out with a few men and great determination. On 3 August 1858, after passing through featureless miombo woodland, he and his weary followers reached the shores of the lake he named Victoria. Speke claimed this was the ultimate prize of Victorian exploration — the source of the Nile.

Burton did not believe him and Speke returned three years later to pursue his claim to its final bitter conclusion. He died under mysterious circumstances back in England the day before he was due to meet Burton in open debate. (See 'History: From the Cradle to Independence', Part One.) Lasting African tributes to his memory are the inlet called Speke Gulf and the scientific name of the local water-loving antelope, the sitatunga — *Tragelaphus spekei*.

Fish and fishing

Noted for its scenic beauty, Lake Victoria is also a fishery of vast potential, the main commercial species being the ubiquitous and delicious tilapia that grows up to two kilos (4.4 lbs) and is known locally as *ngege* or *mbiru*. The genus is found throughout East Africa and has evolved a number of highly successful species, some of which can tolerate the extremely high temperatures and salinity of the Rift's soda lakes, conditions that would quickly prove lethal to any other vertebrate.

Tilapia are members of the cichlid family, a group of fish that includes among its number several species of 'mouth-brooders'.

These fish carry out colourful and elaborate display rituals, including nest building by the male, at which time the eggs are fertilized externally. The female then takes them into her mouth — being careful not to swallow any — where they are brooded for several days. Tiny larval *Oreochromis* hatch and remain close to the mother who will rapidly take the whole shoal back into her mouth at the slightest sign of danger.

Another denizen of these waters that has also evolved novel survival techniques is the lungfish. It is a snake-like creature that can breathe air into its swim bladder, which then acts as a set of primitive lungs. This unique fish, which has survived for the last 300 million years, is believed by some authorities to represent a transitional phase

Opposite: The waters of Lake Ndutu come and go with the seasons. The skull is all that remains of a wildebeest too weak to continue with the annual migration.

between aquatic and terrestrial vertebrates.

Lake Victoria's most prominent lungfish is *Protopterus aethiopicus* which has a mouth composed of two sharp-edged bony plates instead of individual teeth. Commonly reaching two metres (seven feet) in length and weighing as much as forty-five kilos (99 lbs), the *Protopterus* (which bites without compunction) is quite capable of removing human fingers.

This unselective snapper is remarkable for its ability to survive drought. When the pool it lives in begins to dry, the adult fish burrows down into the mud and encases itself in a cocoon of mucus, leaving only a narrow breathing hole to the surface. The fish then aestivates — a type of dormancy — until the rains come, when it wriggles free of its lair.

Tilapia — and other small cichlids like the many species of haplochromines — are the main prey of the rapacious hunter of the lake — Nile perch, *Lates niloticus*.

Although the Nile perch is present in the fossil record of Lake Victoria, it disappeared for millions of years, due, it is believed, to the formation of Uganda's **Owen Falls** on the north shore near Jinja, which prevented the fish from recolonizing the lake via the Nile. Other ichthyologists attribute the perch's disappearance to volcanic ash settling into the lake and raising the level of carbon dioxide. Sensitive fish like the Nile perch were unable to adapt, leaving the more tolerant species to flourish — minus one major predator.

Whatever the reason for its absence, there is no question that it was reintroduced in 1956. The effect was similar to putting a piranha into a goldfish pond. The fish is a voracious predator and can grow to more than 227 kilos (500 lbs). Within twenty years the Nile perch, with no natural enemies except the crocodile (which only occur in small numbers), had become master of the lake. The logic behind the perch's introduction to Victoria seemed to make sense — at the time. It was argued that the fish would effectively convert huge numbers of smaller fish species into a few large ones, thereby making the fisherman's lot an easier one. It is now understood (too late for Lake Victoria) that an ecosystem will support a greater weight of animals if there are many species rather than a few.

Even more tragic was the fact that no one bothered to ask the fishermen what they thought of the perch's introduction. The locals will not eat the fish if there is any other alternative; it is difficult to cook because of its large size; it is impossible to sun-dry and therefore preserve for any length of time; and the process of smoking the perch, which has experienced some success, makes serious demands on diminishing supplies of fire wood.

Nevertheless, they must continue to fish to survive, and today over eighty-five per cent of the total lake catch is Nile perch.

The population dynamics of the lake have still not returned to equilibrium. The fish is known to be a cannibal and perhaps it may turn on itself when its prey begins to run out. Meanwhile there is well-founded concern that the unique haplochromines and other cichlids face extinction.

Getting there

It is possible to reach the three major Tanzanian ports of Lake Victoria — Musoma, Mwanza, and Bukoba — by ferry from Kisumu in Kenya or Jinja in Uganda. From Musoma there is good tarmac to within a few kilometres of Mwanza and both Musoma and Mwanza can be reached from the Serengeti's western corridor. The road continues round the lake but, be prepared, it is no pleasure cruise. Stout shock-absorbers, four-wheel-drive and plenty of patience are essential for the trip. There is a train service to Mwanza from Tabora. More expensive, but more convenient, are Air Tanzania's scheduled flights to all three towns.

Where to stay

There is a reasonable selection of accommodation in Mwanza, the country's third-

---

Opposite: Grazing on the shores of Lake Victoria across from Mwanza, an important agricultural centre for maize, cassava, and cotton.

Above: Blue waters of Lake Victoria and the rocky shores of Mwanza, Tanzania's third-largest town.
Opposite: Bismarck's Rock and its gravity-defying boulder, off Mwanza's shore.

largest town. At the top end of the market is the Tanzania Tourist Board's New Mwanza Hotel, and Tilapia Hotel on the waterfront. The Shinyanga Guesthouse, Kishinapanda Guesthouse, Jafferies Hotel, Hotel Deluxe, and New Safari Lodge offer reasonable comfort. For the budget traveller the YMCA is dependable, along with camping at the Sukuma Museum.

Musoma, located on the eastern lake shore, offers limited options; the Embassy Lodge, Musambura Guesthouse, and the Mennonite Centre are some of the most popular. At Bukoba there is a choice of two hotels, the Coffee Tree Inn and the Lake. (See Listings for 'Accommodation').

Musoma

On the east side of **Lake Victoria**, as you approach it from the water, neglected groves of bananas and mangroves are visible. The land is fertile and the main crops are maize, millet, and cotton.

Starboard, as the ship pulls into port, is the old **boma** built by the Germans. For most travellers Musoma is nothing more than a stopping off point on their way from the Serengeti or Mwanza, Tanzania's most important port on Lake Victoria.

Mwanza: Lake-Shore Splendour

This panoramic town, built on **rocky hills** out onto a **narrow peninsula**, derives its energy and livelihood from the continuous motion of **Lake Victoria**. From the old **Indian Public Library** to the modern multi-storey **bank**, **Mwanza**'s fusion of African, Arab, Asian, and European cultures is always orientated towards the water.

The name Mwanza is derived from the Kisukuma phrase *nga nyanza*, meaning 'to the lake'; and it is to the water that a visitor must first head. Stroll down to the **ferry landing** and you'll see the area's most

famous landmark — **Bismarck's Rock** — a hill of stone rising from the lake crowned by a triangular boulder whose balance defies gravity. It is also along the waterfront that locals and visitors gather each evening to watch the last golden rays of the sun sink into the immense inland sea. In 1996 Mwanza was shrouded in grief after one of the passenger vessels that ply the lake capsized not far offshore with an estimated loss of almost a thousand lives.

Formerly a centre for **dhow building**, Mwanza has experienced an economic boost in recent years as the **agricultural centre** for the maize, cassava, and **cotton** grown by the **Sukuma**. (See 'The People: An Ethnic Puzzle', Part One).

In the rich, fertile soil surrounding the lake, cotton is planted then cultivated collectively. Villages draw up schedules and a family's field is harvested by young and old to feasting, music and dancing.

Nineteen kilometres (12 miles) from Mwanza is the **Sukuma Museum**, the first of Tanzania's **tribal museums**, which was established by a Québecois missionary. It is worth the trip out of town to see the displays of culture, tradition, and an excellent drum collection. Once a week tribal dancers perform the **Bugobogobo** and **Sukuma Snake Dance**. With gyrating and sinuous movements the dancers writhe with live snakes wrapped around their bodies in a symbolic choreography that is accompanied by the pulse of 200-year-old drums.

The museum also hosts examples of the traditional cone-shaped house with a thatched roof. The family and small livestock live in the inner circle and the outer ring is used for cooking and storage. Grouped together in the lee of a kopje for protection against the neighbouring **Nyamwezi**, with whom the Sukuma were often at war, the individual huts were enclosed by a circular corral of euphorbia and thorn hedge.

A second site worth visiting outside Mwanza is **Saa Nane Island**, a wildlife sanctuary where antelope and other tame herbivores roam free. You can reach the island from a **ferry** which calls at the **yacht club pier**. While the variety of animals is nothing spectacular, the view from the top of the island is worthwhile.

Rubondo Island National Park: The Floating Zoo

From the deck of the ferry a low-lying green island can be spotted off the port bow. This is Rubondo Island, designated a national park in 1977, in part due to the campaigning efforts of zoologist Bernhard Grzimek, who took a personal interest in the island's wooded wet-land ecosystem.

Ninety per cent of the 240-square-kilometre (93-square-mile) park is humid forest; the remainder ranges from coastal grassland to papyrus beds. A number of indigenous mammal species — hippo, bushbuck, monkey, genet and mongoose — share their protected habitat with introduced species that benefit from a controlled human population and Rubondo's relative inaccessibility.

Rhino, elephant, roan antelope, giraffe, suni, colobus monkey and chimpanzee have all been brought to the island and it is hoped that they will provide viable breeding populations that can be used as a source of animals for restocking other conservation areas.

Getting there
Rubondo is a long 300-kilometre (186-mile) drive west from Mwanza south around the Emin Pasha Gulf to Nkome. From there a boat takes two hours to reach the island. The other alternative is to take a car or bus from Mwanza to Mnganza via Sengerema, Geita, and Chato. The boat ride to the island from Mnganza is approximately half an hour. No cars are allowed on Rubondo. There is an airstrip at the park's headquarters in Kageye.

When to go
Best between November and February.

Where to stay
There are campsites on the island but campers must bring all their own equipment, cooking facilities and food. Two bandas are also available for hire. Accommodation at Biharamulo, on the mainland west of the island, is limited to a

Above: Dung beetles lay their eggs in balls of animal droppings which they then roll to safety.

guesthouse formerly used by hunting parties from Kenya. Guides are available.

Fees to pay

Fees are payable in foreign currency only and are subject to change. Information about the current fees charged for accommodation and entry to the national parks can be obtained from tour operators or the National Park Headquarters in Arusha.

Sightseeing

Game viewing on **Rubondo Island** is by boat or on foot, usually with an armed park ranger. Bird-watching excursions can also be arranged through the park warden.

With a little luck it may be possible to view one of Rubondo's indigenous and more unusual animals — the **sitatunga**. A member of the *Tragelaphines* (spiral-horned antelopes), this unique herbivore has taken to a largely aquatic existence, preferring to live in and among the papyrus and reed beds. As a result of its soggy habitat, the shaggy 125-kilo (275-lb) sitatunga has evolved elongated hooves that enable it to

support itself on sunken mats of vegetation. When threatened, perhaps by one of the island's many crocodiles, the sitatunga submerges until only its nostrils show above the water. The high water table of the island has given rise to a rich undergrowth where a number of **snake species** live, including pythons large enough to swallow a bushbuck, arboreal and deadly green mambas, and other poisonous snakes such as the cobra and viper.

While the snakes are to be avoided, the **bird life** is well worth seeking. The island serves as a breeding ground and stopover for fowl from East and Central Africa, Europe and South America.

More than 100 species live among the varied habitats provided by the island: open pools, marsh, forest, grassland, mangrove swamp and sandy beaches. With a keen eye and a little patience, ornithologists should be able to spot the fish eagle, martial eagle, goliath heron, sacred ibis and kingfisher.

The game reserve

Located south of Rubondo Island National

Park at the mouth of the **Emin Pasha Gulf** on the western shore of the inlet is the **Biharamulo Game Reserve** and, contiguous with it, the **Burigi Game Reserve**. Together these two reserves make up 3,500 square kilometres (1,351 square miles) of rarely visited — except by poachers — swamps and waterholes that provide year-round refreshment for almost thirty species of mammal including hippo, elephant, zebra, sable, roan antelope and the sitatunga.

Further north, along the borders of Uganda and Rwanda to the west of Lake Victoria, are the game reserves of **Ibanda** and **Rumanyika Orugundu**.

Recognized as protected areas by the Tanzanian government, these isolated areas await future development.

Bukoba

Considered by some to be the loveliest part of Tanzania, **Bukoba** sits on a lush green hillside overlooking the western shore of Lake Victoria. Located due north of **Rubondo** and **Biharamulo wildlife reserves**, the town is named after its original inhabitants, the **Bukoba**, who were absorbed by the **Wahaya** from **Uganda**.

The earliest European to take an interest in the area was Doctor Eduard Schnitzer (better known as **Emin Pasha**, later killed by Arab slave traders in the Congo).

Pasha helped to found Bukoba's **Robusta coffee industry** which is now the mainstay of the economy. Along with coffee, other crops grown include maize, beans, sweet potatoes and bananas — the area's main food staple.

In the village men can be seen strolling by, carrying fancy *bileles* (gourds) containing banana wine which is sipped through a *marwa* (grass straw). At home, families gather around the fire each evening to eat the roasted fruit, served in the traditional manner on banana leaves.

Lake Tanganyika: Exploring the Endless Depths

Lake Tanganyika is the longest freshwater lake in the world and the second deepest, outsized only by Russia's Lake Baikal. Plunging to murky depths of more than 1,433 metres (4,700 feet), Tanganyika stretches north to south 677 kilometres (420 miles) and averages fifty kilometres (31 miles) across. Its vast waters host one of the richest and most varied collections of fish — more than 250 different species.

The lake is not tidal but the fertile surface water constantly circulates and abundant plankton provide food for the denizens of its depths.

The continual movement, aided by stiff winds that blow off the surrounding mountains, inhibits the spread of bilharzia, the parasitic disease carried by shallow-water snails that is the debilitating scourge of Lake Victoria. Other types of mollusc, however, do exist on the shores and were collected by the explorer Speke in the nineteenth century. On examination back in England they showed distinctly marine-like features prompting the question: Was Tanganyika once connected with the sea? If so, to the east or west? The shells unleashed a storm of debate that continues today.

In years of heavy rain, such as 1962, the lake overflows into the Lukuga River which in turn feeds Congo's Lualaba, but in effect it is a vast landlocked sea. Much water is lost to evaporation and since 1962 Tanganyika has been dropping by forty-five centimetres (18 inches) a year, a fall of sixteen metres (50 feet). But with its depth and an area of 32,900 square kilometres (12,703 square miles) — larger than Belgium — it will be a long time before Tanganyika becomes a dry deep canyon.

Most of the lake water, so to speak, is dead, either too high in hydrogen sulphide or too low in oxygen to support life. No mixing of the lower relict water occurs, despite the ferocious storms that drive a foam-flecked six-metre (20-foot) swell across the lake.

Above: Playing in the waters of Lake Tanganyika, the longest freshwater lake in the world.

Only the upper 200 metres (656 feet) of water are active. The remaining 1,200 metres (3,936 feet) lie in isolation, devoid of life. Tanganyika, Malawi and, to a lesser extent, Kivu to the north, are the only lakes in the world that contain such dead 'fossil' water, which may be as old as 20 million years. By contrast the oceans, because of currents and up-wellings, have life forms that exist even in the deepest 11,000-metre (36,080-foot) trenches.

It may be this abyssal dead zone that contributes to Tanganyika's remarkably uniform temperature. From clear top to lightless bottom it only varies by 3°C. No one has been able to explain convincingly why this occurs. Tanganyika's unfathomable volume (it has only half the surface area of Lake Victoria, but contains seven times as much water), its great age and stability and, most of all, its isolation have made the lake an evolutionary showcase.

One measure of its isolation is the degree of endemism that its ecosystem contains. Ninety-eight per cent of Tanganyika's cichlids, which comprise two-thirds of all the lake's fish, are unique. Also endemic are all seven of its crabs, five out of thirteen bivalve molluscs, more than half its gastropod molluscs and eleven of its thirty-three copepod crustaceans. In short, it is one of the most biologically unique lacustrine habitats on earth.

Reaching the lake was a goal of the early explorers and a welcome relief after the rigours of the interior. Even so, Tanganyika provided little comfort for Burton and Speke, who were still exhausted and sick when they hired local dugout canoes for extortionate sums to explore its northern reaches. They were still hoping to find the source of the Nile, and it took a full month before they discovered that the Ruzizi River flowed *into* and not out of Tanganyika, and their search for the Nile continued. (See 'History: From the Cradle to Independence', Part One).

Fish and fishing

On moonless nights the local Ha people set out from villages along the eastern shore to catch *dagaa (Stolothrissa tanganyikae)* a small sardine-like fish. Dried on the beach, it is an important food staple and surpluses are exported throughout Tanzania.

At night the fish migrate upwards to feed off microscopic organisms near the surface, drawn to the lights the fishermen suspend from the bows of their boats.

At a given signal the men drum the side of the boat and the *dagaa* concentrate in a panic over their scoop nets which are quickly hoisted on board. Tonnes of fish are caught and there are nights when the lights from the boats look like a small village floating on the lake.

There are some forty families of freshwater fish in Tanzanian waters overall, and probably a thousand species. Of these Lake Tanganyika is known to have at least 250. They include the minute haplochromines; an evolutionary phenomenon that make the textbook example of adaptive evolution — Darwin's finches of the Galápagos Islands — look unimaginative by comparison.

Due to climatic and geological catastrophes that wiped out whole families of fish from the lake (including, perhaps, the Nile perch from Lake Victoria), haplochromines were left with an enormous number of niches to occupy in an environment with few underwater predators — one notable fish hunter being the endemic and poisonous Storm's water cobra.

As millions of years passed, the haplochromine ancestors evolved to produce hundreds of species that occupy particular and distinct places in the ecosystem. They are closely related, but the life styles they have adopted give each of them widely different physical features. There are species that eat other fish, egg-stealers, snail-eaters, weed-nibblers, plankton-sievers, bottom-dwellers and surface-swimmers of a bewildering variety of shapes and colours.

Kigoma: Tranquil Haven

Kigoma, a major town on the shores of Lake Tanganyika, can be reached by regularly scheduled Air Tanzania flights.

Kigoma is also the terminus of the Central Railway from Dar es Salaam. Trains usually depart from Dar twice a week and the journey takes approximately forty hours. The lake can also be reached by four-wheel-drive vehicle from Lake Victoria as well as from southern Lake Malawi. The bad state of the roads, however, makes this mode of travel time-consuming and back-breaking.

When to go
Lake Tanganyika is pleasant to visit at any time of the year.

Where to stay
Kigoma offers a variety of accommodation, from the top of the range Railway Hotel, with views overlooking the lake and landscaped gardens, to the budget Kigoma Community Centre. The Lake View Hotel, which despite its name offers no view of the lake, is a moderately-priced and clean alternative with a good restaurant attached.

Ten kilometres (six miles) south of Kigoma is the historic town of Ujiji and the Kudra Hotel. (See Listings for 'Accommodation'.)

Sightseeing
Most visitors to **Lake Tanganyika** arrive at the lake's major port — **Kigoma** — located at the end of the **Central Line** from **Dar es Salaam**. As the train draws into town the **harbour** can be seen on the right where either the old MV *Liemba* or her younger sister ship the MV *Mwongozo* are being loaded at the wharf.

Kigoma's deep harbour was developed by the Germans when Tanganyika was still German East Africa. With the outbreak of World War I, the lake was of vital strategic importance to them and, in a bid to control it, they had a warship carried piece by piece to Kigoma from Dar es Salaam where it was reassembled as the 1,300-ton *Graf von Götzen*. Yet before she even left the harbour her war was over.

Above: Except for the tin roofs, little has changed over the centuries in the remote villages that line the shores of Lake Tanganyika.

A direct hit by a bomb dropped from a Belgian aeroplane ensured that she never sailed. To prevent her falling into enemy hands towards the end of the East African Campaign she was greased and scuttled in the Gulf of Bangue.

In 1924 the warship was raised from the bottom by the British authorities, reconditioned, renamed the MV *Liemba* — a southern tribe — and entered service as a cargo and passenger vessel.

In 1970 she underwent a partial refit and her ancient engines were replaced with new diesels. Now the MV *Liemba* runs a weekly service from **Bujumbura**, the capital of **Burundi** at the northern tip of the lake, to **Kigoma**, then south to the town of **Mupulungu** in **Zambia**, officially taking four days to complete the trip.

Next to the historic harbour is the mock-Teutonic three-storey **railway station** built in 1914 with rusted red roof and louvred windows. In the hazy distance beyond the harbour are the cloud-hung **mountains** of the **Congo,** sixty-five kilometres (40 miles)

away across the slate-blue water. Kigoma itself is a quiet town with a **main street** that runs uphill from the railway station between mango trees and frangipani. On the left is the **market** and on the right **Alley's**, a good place for snacks and African music. Kigoma also boasts a **bank, hospital, airport, immigration office,** and the **Mahale Mountains Wildlife Research Office**. If you're planning a trip at **Mahale Mountains National Park**, stop in for latest information about camping, transportation, and fees.

In the shade of main street, locals sell pineapples, mangoes and heaps of sun-dried *dagaa* (that look like whitebait) which are measured out with an old 'Kimbo' tin. For most of the time Kigoma sleeps in the breeze off the lake, until the whistle of the MV *Liemba* or the arrival of the Dar es Salaam train rouses the inhabitants to activity.

Ujiji

Six kilometres (four miles) south of Kigoma lies **Ujiji**, one of Africa's oldest **market villages**. It is a bustling, colourful, lively commercial centre. The majority of the population is from the Ha tribe, although Arab influence is seen in the architecture. Structures bear a strong resemblance to coastal homes, nowhere more evident than in the **carved wooden doors**.

It was there that Burton and Speke refreshed themselves with milk, eggs, tomatoes and artichokes before taking to the waters of Tanganyika.

In 1871 Livingstone also made his way to Ujiji, at that time the terminus for caravans from the coast. There, near the lake shore, Stanley found him, and their meeting under a mango tree passed into history. (See 'History: From the Cradle to Independence', Part One.)

The mango tree has since died and the lake has receded 200 metres (218 yards), but the place where Stanley doffed his cap to the Doctor is named Livingstone Street. Nearby in the garden of the **cultural centre** is a **bronze plaque** donated by the Royal Geographical Society in 1927, commemorating the event.

Gombe Stream National Park: Primate's Playground

Although it is the smallest of Tanzania's national parks, Gombe's reputation is widespread thanks to the pioneering research of Dr Jane Goodall. Since 1960 Goodall and several colleagues have lived among the Gombe chimpanzees, making one of the most significant contributions to the study of primates. The results of Goodall's study are described in her book, *In the Shadow of Man*.

Years of familiarity with human researchers have given the chimpanzees remarkable tolerance, and thousands of observation hours have unlocked some of the secrets of their complex social behaviour. Chimpanzees show strong bonds between related individuals, particularly between mother and offspring,

with families living in loose-knit communities of up to fifty animals. Individuals interact continuously, spending hours grooming, playing, embracing and greeting one another enthusiastically. Primarily vegetarians, adults will cooperate occasionally to hunt such animals as monkeys and bush pigs. The chimpanzee also feeds on termites and ants, employing grass stalks as tools in a rare example of dexterity.

Getting there
Gombe Stream National Park is located twenty-four kilometres (15 miles) north of Kigoma. Travel to the park is by water only. Boat taxis run from Ujiji or Kigoma, taking between four and six hours. By speedboat the trip is shortened to forty minutes.

When to go
Gombe can be visited year-round.

Where to stay
It is possible to camp along the lake shore, but permission must be given from the warden because of the danger posed by baboons. There is also a hostel that can accommodate fifteen people. Facilities at the park are rugged and visitors should be self-sufficient. A hired guide is mandatory for trips away from the lake shore or station.

Fees to pay
Fees are payable in foreign currency only and are subject to change. Up-to-date information about the current fees charged for accommodation and entry to the national parks can be obtained from tour operators or the National Park Headquarters, PO Box 3134, Arusha.

Sightseeing
Protected from encroachment since 1943, **Gombe** was declared a **national park** in 1968. Although the area is small — five kilometres (three miles) wide and fifteen

Opposite: Gombe Stream National Park is a chimpanzee haven. Although primarily vegetarians, chimps will sometimes kill small animals for food.

kilometres (nine miles) long — the park contains some unusual **flora** for the western Tanzania region. During the Pleistocene age the **highland forests** of north-east Congo extended south along Lake Tanganyika in a continuous belt through Gombe and down into the Mahale Mountains south of Kigoma. Today Gombe and Mahale contain the only remnants of this **original forest**.

Although a mix of forest, woodlands and grass, Gombe is considered primarily a forest reserve. The majority of its mammals are primates rather than ungulates, and most of the primates are forest species. Likely to be sighted are the famous **chimpanzee**, **red colobus**, the colourful **red-tail** and **blue monkey** and **olive baboon**.

There are few herbivores in Gombe, partly because of the forest but mainly due to the high rainfall which causes grasses to grow tall and rank while washing nutrients from the soil. This makes the grass coarser and harder to digest as well as less nutritious than the savannah of central Tanzania. The most common hooved animals are bushbuck and bushpig. Occasionally the grey duiker can be spotted in the upper grasslands. Carnivores are also a rarity in the forests, making Gombe a haven for **walking safaris**.

Ornithologists with patience should be able to spot among the heavy foliage varieties such as the blue-breasted kingfisher and African broadbill. For a glimpse of Ross's turaco and a trumpeter hornbill, look in the fruit trees.

Along the lake shore sandpipers can sometimes be seen, but the lake is a more favourable habitat for the pied and giant kingfishers. Standing out among the birds of prey is the crowned eagle.

Mahale Mountains Park: Sheltered from the Storm

Like its northerly neighbour Gombe, the Mahale Mountains are home to some of the last remaining wild chimpanzees in Africa. There, in the isolated rainforest of Tanzania's second most recently established national park (1985), 1,000 *Pan troglodytes*

live in a mixed environment reserve covering 1,613 square kilometres (623 square miles).

The area is also known as Nkungwe — named after the park's massive mountain. At 2,460 metres (8,069 feet) it is the highest of the six prominent points that make up the mountain range which runs north-west to south-east down the Mahale promontory.

The park has two seasons; the dry season begins at the end of May and the wet season arrives with November. The latter brings heavy rains which can reach up to 250 centimetres (98 inches) a year.

Mahale's transitional mix of animals benefited greatly from the relocation of villages outside the park in 1975. Poaching and burning disappeared almost overnight and the virtually absent leopard and lion began to make a dramatic comeback.

Getting there
Whether you decide to drive, fly, or take the train to Kigoma, the rest of the journey to Mahale must be by boat. The MV *Liemba* and the MV *Mwongozo* depart from Kigoma and stop in Mugambo, where they load and unload. Passengers need to catch a boat to shore and from there hire a local craft for the remaining three-hour journey down the lake to Kasongo, the park's headquarters. The trip takes about nine hours.

When to go
Best months are May to October.

Where to stay
Camping is available and there is a guesthouse, but it provides little more than a roof and bare bunks. Visitors must be fully self-supporting and all the requirements for comfortable living should be taken.

Fees to pay
Fees are payable in foreign currency only and are subject to change. Up-to-date information about the current fees charged for accommodation and entry to the national parks can be obtained from tour operators, National Park Headquarters, PO Box 3134, Arusha, and the Mahale Mountains Wildlife Research Office in Kigoma.

Above: Boats on Lake Tanganyika are the only means of transportation to remote Mahale Mountains National Park.

Sightseeing

Mahale is remote and isolated — it can only be reached by **boat** from **Kigoma** — the south is tsetse fly infested; the north is cut off by the swamps of the **Malagarasi River**; and the mountains of the east make habitation difficult.

The park thrives on this inaccessibility and human encroachment is minimal.

There are no roads to spoil the natural beauty of the park and all game-viewing is done on foot. Left alone in this little-visited park, visitors can stroll through the forests, climb the Mahale Mountains, or lounge on Lake Tanganyika's sandy shores.

The park is a **unique ecological zone**; the meeting point for three different types of vegetation: **lowland forest** and **moist savannah** from the west and north, **miombo woodlands** and **dry savannah** from the east, and **open woodland** from the south. This varied terrain supports a host of plants and animals, the majority of which show closer affinities to western Africa than eastern Africa.

Animals of the relict northern montane forest include elephant, buffalo, leopard, bushpig, Sharpe's grysbok, bushbuck, blue duiker, brush-tailed porcupine, red-legged sun squirrel, and a wide variety of primates.

Other than the chimp there are olive baboon and black and white colobus monkeys.

In the south the miombo woodland plain supports healthy numbers of roan and sable antelope, giraffe, kudu, eland and lion.

The most remarkable creatures of the park are the **chimpanzees**, which have been the focus of a twenty-year study by Japanese biologists.

More than 100 have been identified and named individually. Be prepared to spend at least a week to ensure that you see and enjoy these fascinating primates.

The Southern Parks: Wild and Wonderful

Katavi National Park: Where the Adventurous Travel

To the south-east of Mahale Mountains National Park is Katavi National Park, located on a high, wide flood plain surrounding Lake Katavi. The park's main attractions are the lake's grassy plains to the north, palm-fringed Lake Chala in the south-east, and the Katuma River which connects the two lakes.

The 2,250-square-kilometre (869-square-mile) park was first gazetted as a protected area by the Germans. In 1974 it was granted national park status in order to conserve the flora and fauna that is centred on the lakes, river, and their adjacent swamps, grasslands, and black cotton pans known as *mbuga*.

Getting there

Katavi is one of the more difficult national parks to reach. Access is by very rough road from Kigoma via Uvinza, or cross-country from Mbeya through the Rukwa valley. Travel around this park is strictly for those of an adventurous spirit and requires a lot of time and sufficient petrol to get there and back. Do not expect to obtain fuel locally. The park also maintains an airstrip for charter planes.

When to go

July to October are the best months to visit Katavi.

Where to stay

Visitors must be self-sufficient and prepared to camp at sites arranged by park authorities if they wish to stay in Katavi overnight. Hotel and lodge accommodation are available at Mpanda, forty kilometres (25 miles) north of the park. (See Listings for 'Accommodation'.)

Fees to pay

Fees are paid in foreign currency only and are subject to change. Up-to-date information about the current fees charged for accommodation and entry to the national parks can be obtained from tour operators or the National Park Headquarters, PO Box 3134, Arusha.

Sightseeing

The water provides a welcome relief from the surrounding miombo and is home to crocodile, hippo and large flocks of pelican. The alternating **woodland, acacia bush country, lakes,** and **swamps** also encourage abundant **bird life,** and more than 400 species have been recorded. Ornithologists should be able to identify the go-away-bird, pale-billed hornbill, white-winged babbling starling and the Tanzania masked weaver.

In the short grasses and thickets lion, leopard, elephant, eland, sable and roan antelopes, southern reedbuck and topi abound. Katavi is also home to one of the largest herds of **buffalo.** As many as 1,600 of the ponderous herbivores are thought to roam the plains.

Ugalla River Game Reserve

Located approximately ninety kilometres (56 miles) north-east of Katavi National Park is the obscure and little-known Ugalla River Game Reserve. This 4,773-square-kilometre (1,843-mile) area can be approached from the south along roads which, according to maps, do exist, or from the north via Tabora, more than 160 kilometres (99 miles) away.

Its main attributes are the river valleys running through miombo woodland, an abundance of sable antelope, and its untouched atmosphere. For those planning a trip to Ugalla, self-sufficiency is the name of the game.

Uwanda Game Reserve: Dry and Dusty Shores

A scant thirty kilometres (19 miles) south-east from Katavi National Park is the seasonal Lake Rukwa.

Like an elongated hourglass in shape, the central 'waist' of marsh often dries out to form two lakes. In 1949 the lake dried up completely, leaving hippos, crocodiles, and fish to bake in the scorching Equatorial sun.

This temperamental alkaline lake is the central feature of the Uwanda Game Reserve, and its seasonal floodings and dryings have created wide shores of grass in the Rukwa Valley area that act as a mecca for grazers.

Getting there
Four-wheel-drive transport from Mbeya during the dry season is the easiest route to the Rukwa area. A secondary road also runs from the southern tip of Katavi National Park to the northern tip of the game reserve. Petrol is not available.

Where to stay
Adventurers planning to visit Uwanda should be completely self-sufficient. There is no lodging available in the park, so it is camping only.

Hotel accommodation is available at Sumbawanga, which lies forty kilometres (25 miles) to the east of the reserve. (See Listings for 'Accommodation'.)

When to go
The dry season, from July to October, is the best time to visit.

Sightseeing
The Rukwa Valley is awash in rich **grasslands**, and it is there that the extremely rare **puku** (*Kobu vardoni*), a spiral-horned antelope related to the Uganda kob, comes to browse.

More abundant are buffalo, eland, topi, zebra, hippo, elephant, reedbuck, impala, roan antelope, greater kudu and giraffe, which all flood into the Rukwa Valley during November at the start of the rains.

Fresh pools and newly hatched insect life — Rukwa is one of the main breeding zones for the **red locust** — also attract migrant birds. These foreign visitors, added to the indigenous varieties, make up more than 400 species around the lake.

There are two anomalous animals at Rukwa. Genetic mutation has thrown up **albino giraffes** and **zebras** with stripes that are broken into **black ovals and spots**. The colouration of the animals does not seem to be a serious disadvantage and they appear to live happily side-by-side with their conventional cousins.

Mbeya: Gateway to the Southern Highlands

Surrounded by rolling hills, mountain chains, volcanic lakes and sparkling waterfalls, Mbeya brings to mind images of Scotland rather than equatorial Africa. The town is the capital of the Southern Highlands, nestled in a gap at 1,700 metres (5,576 feet) between the Mbeya Mountains to the north and the Poroto Mountains to the south.

The town was founded in 1927 when gold was discovered in the neighbouring ranges and, during the 1930s, 'yellow-fever' brought a fleeting prosperity. Yet even nuggets weighing up to ninety-five ounces were not enough to sustain the workings and in 1956 the last field was abandoned to the eucalyptus and pine trees.

Construction of the Great North Road — connecting Zambia with Tanzania — saved Mbeya from becoming just another gold-rush ghost town.

The city's position was further enhanced with the arrival of the TANZAM line, giving Mbeya new life as a transport and communications centre.

Getting there
By rail from Dar es Salaam the trip takes approximately thirty-six hours, passing through some of Tanzania's most spectacular countryside. Mbeya can also be

Above: The vast majority of Tanzanians still rely on agriculture for their livelihood. Temperate climates, plentiful rainfall, and fertile soil in the Southern Highlands ensure the markets are always filled with fresh produce.

reached by road from Dar, where the road is good for most of its 853-kilometre (529-mile) length. Driving from the north-west — the town is 160 kilometres (99 miles) four-wheel-drive vehicle during the dry season. Mbeya is also served by scheduled Air Tanzania flights.

Where to stay

The Mbeya Hotel, opposite the football stadium, is popular with its comfortable colonial-style rooms. Other choices include the Holiday Inn, The Highlands and the clean and friendly Moravian Youth Hostel. (See Listings for 'Accommodation'.)

Sightseeing

Other than a **market**, **bank**, **post office**, **library**, **railroad station** and **several hotels**, Mbeya has little to interest tourists. The town is mainly used as a **stopping off point** for travellers passing through by rail, by road from Malawi, or arriving to explore the **Southern Highlands**.

The area was once the site of explosive volcanic activity and Mbeya is surrounded by **mountains**, **deep valleys**, **lakes** and **waterfalls**. The abundant rainfall makes the area suitable for growing **coffee** and **tea** and, in the rolling, lush hills, hiking is a fine way to spend the afternoon. The mountain streams are also renowned for their **fishing**.

In the Arabica coffee country to the west of the town is the famous **Mbozi meteorite**. Discovered in 1942, this vast iron monolith is the third largest in the world, weighing fifteen tons.

Poroto Mountains

The road south out of town toward **Lake Malawi** leads through the **Poroto Mountains**, site of the **Ngozi Crater Lake**. Considered the gem of the Porotos, the two-kilometre-wide lake appears black at the centre due to ash. Nothing lives in its waters except a few snakes swimming sinuously through the green, copper-tinged

Above: Colourful market in Mbeya, gateway to the Southern Highlands.
Overleaf: Lush tea estate at the head of Lake Malawi. In recent years production in Tanzania has increased, although coffee remains the most important cash crop.

surface. The local Safwa people believe that the still waters of Ngozi have magical properties.

To reach the lake follow a track off the main **Mbeya-Tukuyu road** through magnificent rain forest dripping with lichens, mosses and orchids until you reach the **forest edge**. A one-hour hike through the forest leads to the **rim** and a glorious view of the lake 200 metres (656 feet) below.

The Porotos have patches of forest and marshy depressions that are rewarding for the ornithologist. With its long tail and yellow shoulders the marsh widow is one of the more exhibitionist species found there. The African hobby, cuckoo falcon and green barbet are other feathered varieties that can be seen in the mountain forests.

On to Tukuyu

Located on the **western slope** of the **Porotos** along the main road to Lake Malawi lies the town of **Tukuyu**. At 1,545

metres (5,069 feet) above sea-level, the town is the wettest in Tanzania, gathering 256 centimetres (100 inches) a year.

Much of the rain that falls on the northern watershed of the mountains drains into the two great rivers of the south, the **Great Ruaha** and the **Rufiji**.

In the green hills near Tukuyu is a **natural land bridge** spanning the **Kiwira River**, formed when a molten lava flow from the erupting **Rungwe volcano** was interrupted by the rushing river waters. Three kilometres (two miles) up the deep gorge from the natural bridge is *Kijungu*, which means 'huge cooking pot'. There the Kiwira River flows into a seething cauldron or sump, before continuing down the gorge and under the bridge.

Kitulo Plateau

Heading south the Porotos gradually meld into the **Kipengere Range**. There, set in the middle of the mountains, are 30,000 hectares of hilly land known as the **Kitulo**

Above: Two-kilometre-wide Ngozi Crater Lake situated in the Poroto Mountains.

Plateau. Sloping from west to east, the plateau's highest points are the dome of **Chaluhangi** at 2,923 metres (9,587 feet) and 2,960-metre (9,709-foot) **Mtwori**.

Despite its location nine degrees south of the Equator, Kitulo experiences ninety-five days of frost a year. Lake Malawi provides most of the area's 140 centimetres (55 inches) of rain, which runs back down to the lake and the **Great Ruaha River**.

With the arrival of the rains in November, the burnt, brown grass of the plateau is transformed overnight into a sea of **wild flowers**. The first to bloom are the yellow and orange red-hot pokers (*Kniphofia*) and daisies (*Aster*), soon followed by lilies, aloes, delphiniums, irises, and the ubiquitous pink busy-lizzy. In December the orchids bloom.

Living among this colourful floral carpet are the **Wanji**, traditional cattle herders who have become acclimatized to the freezing night cold and blistering heat of the day.

The people of this area — between the Mbeya Mountains and Lake Malawi — bore the brunt of the slave raiders and the local population has still not recovered from the excesses of the trade. The name of the man who did so much to bring it to an end is remembered in the **Livingstone Mountains** which undulate south from the Kipengere Range to Malawi's north-eastern shores.

Lake Malawi: Exploring the Disappearing Shores

Slightly smaller and shallower than its northern cousin Tanganyika, Lake Malawi (also known as Lake Nyasa in Tanzania) is 500 kilometres (310 miles) from its northerly extent at Matema to its main outlet, the Shire River in the south. Shore to shore it averages forty-eight kilometres (30 miles) across and is 478 metres (1,568 feet) above sea-level.

Malawi is the most southerly of the Rift Valley's great lakes and is also the most biologically diverse. Although it has fewer fish families than Tanganyika it contains a high degree of endemism, a fact first hinted at by the fish specimens sent home to the British Museum by John Kirk, naturalist and one-time companion of Livingstone.

While the lake has a major outlet through the Shire which joins the Zambezi River, the colonization of the lake by Zambezi fish is only possible for those species that can swim up the Murchison Rapids located downstream from Malawi. Because of this biological isolation, the majority of fish are endemic.

The lake contains thirty per cent of the world's known cichlids and more than 400 species of haplochromine fish have been discovered during the last century. Many of the haplochromines are brightly coloured as a result of the lake's crystal-clear water. Colour and body pattern are important to the fish for recognizing one another, members of the opposite sex, and competitors. Lake Victoria, which is turbid by comparison, has fewer colourful species.

Getting there
The northern lake shores can only be approached by the 130-kilometre (81-mile) rough road from Mbeya, via Tukuyu, to the port town of Itungi.

Where to stay
There is a variety of accommodation available in Mbeya, including the Mbeya Hotel, the Holiday Inn, The Highlands, and the Moravian Youth Hostel. If you plan on staying along the lake shore, bring a tent.

Sightseeing
The northern Tanzanian shores of Lake Malawi are home to the **Nyakyusa** people. Joseph Thomson — Scottish adventurer, agent of the British South Africa Company, and discoverer of Lake Rukwa — met the tribe in 1879 on his way north to Lake Tanganyika.

He described their land as 'a perfect Arcadia', and enthused in a rather patronizing Victorian manner over the 'charmingly neat circular huts, with conical roofs, and walls hanging out all around, with the clay worked prettily into rounded bricks and daubed symmetrically with spots'.

The huts and villages are much the same today, traditionally organized according to age sets. Each homestead has its own banana grove, vegetable plot, and communal fields. The **Kisi**, another Lake Malawi tribe, make their home among the small bays at the foot of the **Livingstone Mountains**. They are famous throughout the country for the quality of their **pottery**, and samples of their work can be purchased in the lake towns and as far away as Dar es Salaam.

The immediate future of the Kisi is uncertain, however, due to rapidly rising lake levels. As a repository for several major rivers, Malawi receives millions of tons of silt, and every five years the lake level rises between two and five metres (six and 16 feet). **Itungi Port** has recently experienced flooding and, to the east, **Matema's** guesthouse, school and dispensary have all disappeared.

Iringa: Highland Haven

The serenity which pervades the highland town of Iringa belies the area's tempestuous past. The town's name is derived from the local word, *lilinga*, meaning fort. There is a fort, thirty-two kilometres (20 miles) away at Kalenga, close to the Little Ruaha River. It was built in 1894 by Hehe Chief Mkwawa as a stronghold against the Germans who were attempting to suppress his long-time insurgency. It was still unfinished in October of that year when the German troops attacked.

The thirteen-kilometre-wide (eight-mile) stockade was a formidable fortification, but its four-metre-high (13-foot) walls, central mound and lookout posts were not enough to hold off the Germans and a brutal defeat followed.

In part the military colonists were acting out of revenge. Five years earlier, in 1889, using spears and local weapons, Mkwawa's men ambushed a German contingent

Overleaf: Lake Malawi, the most southerly of the Rift Valley's greater lakes.

commanded by Lieutenant Zelewsky, killing nearly half of his 1,000 men and making off with 300 rifles, field guns, and tons of ammunition that kept the chief in bullets for the next three years.

Mkwawa survived the rout at Kalenga and fled with a few men to lend their support to the Bushiri rebellion, named after the chief's Arab ally (see 'History: From the Cradle to Independence', Part One). Even with the considerable reward of 5,000 rupees on his head, Mkwawa roamed free another four years, a constant thorn in the side of the German forces until they finally caught up with him in July 1898.

Rather than be taken alive, Mkwawa shot himself. His head was sent back to Germany, but in 1954 the skull was recovered and returned home. It is now the main exhibit of the Mkwawa Memorial Museum in Kalenga.

Overlooking Iringa are two hills. Lundamatwe, 'collection of skulls', was where the severed heads of enemy soldiers were left for the scavengers. The second hill, Tagamenda, means 'throw cloths'. There the clothes of the slain were laid out in the sun for mothers and wives to identify.

Getting there

Iringa can be approached by car from Mbeya in the south and from both Dar es Salaam and Dodoma in the north. Air Tanzania also maintains scheduled flights from Dar to Iringa.

Where to stay

At the top end of the hotel scale is the Isimila, located close to the railway/bus station. Other lodgings include the Sunset Motel, Railway Hotel, and Ruaha International Guesthouse. (See Listings for 'Accommodation'.)

Sightseeing

For many visitors Iringa is simply a jumping off point to **Ruaha National Park** to the west. But this bustling town of African and Muslim mix has many attributes of its own which are worthy of closer inspection.

Iringa is located halfway between Morogoro and Mbeya and is approached by a twisting, turning road up the escarpment. Situated on an easily defended **plateau**, the German-founded town is a blend of run-down Bavarian charm and rust-red corrugated iron roofing.

The highland altitude, 1,635 metres (5,363 feet), and plentiful rainfall make the area an important **farming** and **tobacco** centre. In the surrounding hills the local Hehe also grow beans, maize and groundnuts, and raise goats and cattle to supplement their income. To the south at Dabaga the country's well-known **chilli sauce** is made.

Isimila

The history of the Hehe's warring years comes to life at **Kalenga**, fifteen kilometres (nine miles) **west** from **Iringa** along the **Mloa road**. There the ruins of **Mkwawa's capital** can be found, along with his **mausoleum**, and a small **museum** featuring the famous warrior's head.

For truly ancient ruins, a trip to **Isimila** is mandatory. Located twenty-three kilometres (14 miles) west of Iringa, this **historical site** is among the most important in Africa. Making their home in these highlands more than 60,000 years ago, people of the **Acheulean age** have left a legacy of hand axes, stone picks, hammers and cleavers all associated with a large number of antelope and pig fossil bones that bear marks of butchery.

The partial skeleton of an ancestor of the modern hippo — Gorgops — also probably preyed upon by these Stone Age men, has been excavated as well.

In a **gully upstream** from the ruin site are several extremely fine **free-standing stone pillars**. Some of these natural abstract figures reach fifteen metres (49 feet) in height, fashioned from the surrounding rock by years of weathering.

Opposite: Busy street in Iringa, a town built on an escarpment in one of Tanzania's most fertile regions.

Ruaha National Park: The Rolling River Sets the Pace

Most visitors to Tanzania complete the northern game circuit, then take a minibus back to Nairobi or Dar, unaware that they have bypassed the country's most pristine and untouched wildlife areas. Vast tracts of land bearing enticing names like Selous, Ruaha, Ugalla and Rukwa, remain unexplored and unexploited — slices of original Africa as it existed millions of years ago.

The beauty and the burden of the southern parks lies in their inaccessibility. Bouncing for hours — or days — along dirt roads (when there is one) in a four-wheel-drive vehicle is the best way to get there. But be prepared, for most of the parks are ill-equipped for visitors. Food, water, camping equipment, and even fuel in some instances, must all be carried. And do not forget to take a compass.

Tanzania's second-largest national park is infested with the biting tsetse fly. The result has meant little disturbance from man and his cattle, and Ruaha has remained virtually unchanged through the centuries.

Ruaha is bordered to the north by the Kizigio and Rungwa River game reserves. Together the three total a protected area of 25,600 square kilometres (9,884 square miles). Originally the national park was a part of the Rungwa reserve, but in 1964 the land was partitioned and its status upgraded. The Ruaha National Park's name is taken from the Great Ruaha River that flows along its eastern border; the word Ruaha is a corruption of *Luvaha*, which means, quite simply, 'great'.

The river rises out of the Usunga flats to the north-east of Mbeya and far downstream, beyond the park's eastern boundary, is a reservoir at Mtera that provides most of the electrical power for Dodoma.

The Great Ruaha is also one of the main feeders for the Rufiji River that runs through the Selous. It has two sand river tributaries that, depending on the season, can range from braided trickles flowing through sand flats to torrential deluges.

Getting there

From Iringa it is 112 kilometres (70 miles) west to Msembe, the park's headquarters. The drive usually takes at least three hours. There are also airstrips at Msembe for charter flights. The Rungwa River Game Reserve can be entered from the west by Tabora. Travellers should make arrangements to take their own petrol. If you get stuck, check with park headquarters; they will sell fuel but only when available.

When to go

From January to March the rivers are in flood and up until June the rain encourages the growth of long grass that conceals the game. The best months to visit are between July and November when the animals are concentrated around the shrinking watercourses. During the wet season travel is next to impossible.

Where to stay

Run by the Fox family, Ruaha River Lodge with its reputation for good food, is beautifully situated around a kopje overlooking the river. Guests are housed in thatched stone bandas with their own bathrooms and verandahs. At Ruaha River Camp accommodation and camp sites are both available. A new tented camp fifty-five kilometres (34 miles) north-east of the park headquarters is operated by Wildlife Explorer Ltd. (See Listings for 'Accommodation'.)

Fees to pay

Fees are payable in foreign currency only and are subject to change. Up-to-date information about the current fees charged for accommodation and entry to the national parks can be obtained from tour operators or the National Park Headquarters, PO Box 3134, Arusha.

Sightseeing

The great Ruaha adventure begins at **Ibuguziwa**, eight kilometres (five miles) from the **park boundary** on the bank of the

Ruaha River. Here visitors check in before crossing the water by bridge or being hand pulled across on a **wooden ferry**. Safely landed on the opposite shore, the seldom-explored woodlands unfold before you. To the east acacia, baobabs and spiny *commiphora* are scattered among the dry bushland. To the mountainous west, forests cover the gentle plateau slopes that merge with Ruaha's typical miombo vegetation.

Superficially monotonous, the higher Ruaha **miombo woodland** actually provides a number of habitats where more than 1,600 species of plant and 400 varieties of bird have been identified. Those with a sharp eye should spot Dickinson's kestrel, violet-crested turaco, pale-billed hornbill, racquet-tailed roller, and perhaps even the elusive Eleonora's falcon.

The most common tree of the miombo woodland is the *Brachystegia* — fifteen species thrive in Tanzania. Distinguished by its open canopy, the tree grows to about ten metres (33 feet). It is adapted to the infertile soils that characterize the parts of East Africa (such as southern Tanzania) that lie in a single rainy season zone.

During the six-month dry season the mainly deciduous miombo sheds its leaves. As a prelude to the rainy season, **grass fires** often sweep through large tracts of land, painting the vegetation a Jackson Pollock vision of pale green, ochre, chestnut, bronze, yellow and black.

But the main showpiece is the **Great Ruaha River**. Crocodiles bask on sandbanks; hippos snort in the deeps; clawless otters slip into the shallows and skimmers in search of minnows carve up the water with their specialized lower bills.

Reedbuck, waterbuck and buffalo come down through the acacia trees to drink, watchful of lion, leopard, jackal, spotted hyena and hunting dog.

In the **grassland** borders of the river are greater and lesser kudu, eland, impala, Grant's gazelle, dik-dik, zebra, wart hog, mongoose, wild cat, porcupine and the rarely seen civet.

Eurasian migrant birds flock to Ruaha twice a year — October to November and March to April, on their outward and return journeys — to feed with the resident kingfishers, plovers, hornbills, green wood hoopoes, bee-eaters, sunbirds and egrets stabbing in the shallows.

Once noted for their size and heavy ivory, a disturbing trend found in Ruaha is the small but growing tuskless elephant population. In 1973 there were an estimated 60,000 tuskers and the riverbank acacias, which were subject to heavy elephant damage, were under threat of extinction. Today the trees are safe and the elephants in danger.

The population had been so heavily poached by mid-1990 only 3,000 pachyderms survived, widely scattered throughout the park. The handful of tuskless animals are not a target for the poachers and they will undoubtedly increase while their ivory-carrying relatives face an uncertain future.

Above: Elephants cause tremendous damage to trees, particularly river bank acacias.

The Selous: Grandest of the Wild Reserves

Tanzania contains one of the single largest remaining elephant populations in the world. Other contenders for the title include Gabon and Zaire; both have large herds but a proper census of elephant numbers is hampered by thick forest cover.

Indisputable is the fact that most of Tanzania's elephants live in one vast and remote tract of archetypical African wilderness, the Selous Game Reserve. It is an uninhabited area surpassing the size of Switzerland and is the largest reserve in Africa (as distinct from a national park). Selous is dominated by the Rufiji River and its tributaries, the Kilombero and Luwegu, a river system with the largest catchment area in East Africa.

More widely dispersed and difficult to see, the concentrations of wildlife in the Selous are second only to the Serengeti. The varied terrain of rolling savannah woodland, grassland plains, and rocky outcrops is cut by the sand streams of the Rufiji. Buffalo, crocodile, hippo and wild dog are numerous. In 1977 the elephant population stood at a magnificent 100,000. That number has been reduced now to 30,000, a grim reflection of poaching's inexorable toll.

The 50,000 square kilometres (19,305 square miles) of the reserve are actually part of the Selous' 75,000-square-kilometre (28,958-square-mile) ecosystem. It includes Mikumi National Park and other uninhabited areas to the north; the Kilombero Game Controlled Area to the west and other sparsely populated regions towards Kilwa to the east and Dar es Salaam to the north-east.

History

Caravans bringing slaves and ivory from the interior to the coast often passed through the Selous on their way to Kilwa. During the nineteenth century the village of Kisaki, on the northern border of the reserve, was a junction between two major trade routes. It is said that caravans containing more than 1,000 men regularly passed through during the dry season.

In 1905 the German colonial government began setting aside game reserves. A map dated 1912 indicates that the western Selous and most of the northern area between the Mgeta and Rufuji rivers were already designated and hunting was forbidden. During World War I the wildlife area was the scene of clashes between German and British forces. In 1915 the British used the island of Mafia as the first place in Africa to launch assembled planes for reconnaissance missions. Their greatest success was in finding the German battleship *Königsberg* hiding in the Rufiji delta.

The park derives its name from hunter-explorer Frederick Courteney Selous, born 31 December 1851, son of the London Stock Exchange chairman. He resisted pressures from his family to follow a professional career and landed on African shores during his twentieth year. There he roamed as far as Matabeleland and the Zambezi Valley in search of hunting grounds.

Selous was a keen naturalist and conservationist as well as hunter and wrote several books about his adventures which became best-sellers in Victorian England.

With the outbreak of World War I the great hunter, at the age of sixty-four, took up his gun once again. Captain Selous was killed while trying to encircle a retreating German detachment at Beho Beho in what is now known as the Selous Game Reserve.

In the 1930s and 1940s the Tanganyika government moved the local tribes away from the Selous in an effort to combat the area's endemic sleeping sickness. These formerly inhabited lands were then added to the reserve.

During the 1980s, oil exploration was carried out in the Selous without due consideration being given to the ecological impact. Extensive seismic lines were cut through previously untouched wilderness and today these cleared inroads are used by poachers.

Getting there

Two roads lead to the Selous from Dar es Salaam. The south-eastern access is a 250-kilometre (155-mile) drive through Kibiti,

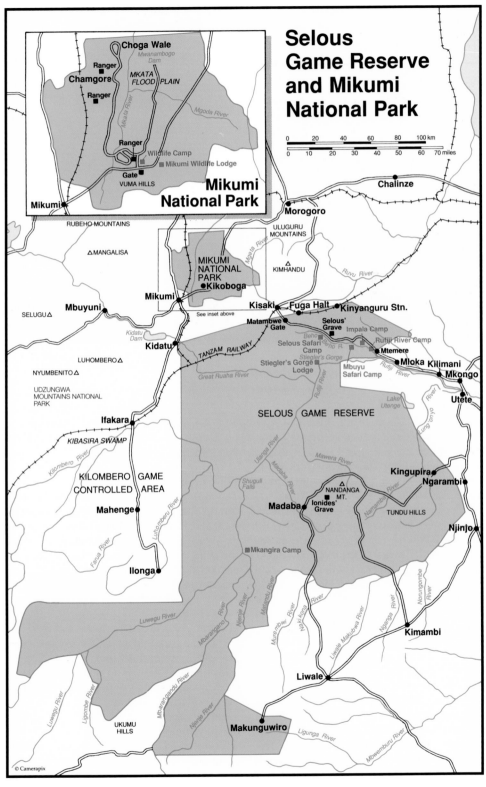

Selous Game Reserve and Mikumi National Park

0 20 40 60 80 100 km
0 10 20 30 40 50 60 70 miles

Mikumi National Park

Choga Wale
Ranger
Chamgore
Ranger
MWANAMBOGO DAM
MKATA FLOOD PLAIN
Mkata River
Mgoda River
Ranger
Wildlife Camp
Mikumi Wildlife Lodge
Gate
VUMA HILLS
Mikumi

RUBEHO MOUNTAINS

△MANGALISA

ULUGURU MOUNTAINS

Chalinze

Morogoro

MIKUMI NATIONAL PARK

△ KIMHANDU

Ruvu River

Mgeta River

Kikoboga

SELUGU △

Mbuyuni

Mikumi

Kidatu Dam

Kisaki Fuga Halt Kinyanguru Stn.

Matambwe Gate

Selous' Grave

Impala Camp

LUHOMBERO △

NYUMBENITO △

Kidatu

TANZAM RAILWAY

Beho Beho R.

Selous Safari Camp

Stiegler's Gorge

Rufiji River Camp

Mtemere

Mloka Kilimani

Mkongo

Stiegler's Gorge Lodge

Great Ruaha River

Mbuyu Safari Camp

Rufiji River

UDZUNGWA MOUNTAINS NATIONAL PARK

Ifakara

Lake Utenge

Lung'onyo River

Utete

KIBASIRA SWAMP

SELOUS GAME RESERVE

Kilombero River

KILOMBERO GAME CONTROLLED AREA

Ulanga River

Mawera River

Madaba River

Kingupira

Ngarambi

Mahenge

Luhombero River

Shuguli Falls

△ NANDANGA MT.

Namamba River

Madaba Ionides' Grave

TUNDU HILLS

Njinjo

Fanua River

Mkangira Camp

Ilonga

Luwegu River

Njenje River

Matandu River

Murembwi River

Nakikora River

Liwale Makubwe River

Nganga River

Norungombe River

Kimambi

Mbarangandu River

Liwale

Ligunga River

UKUMU HILLS

Luwegu River

Ligombe River

Njenje River

Makunguwiro

Mowembaru River

© Camerapix

227

Above: Ostrich, the largest bird in the world, is found throughout Africa, although it prefers savannah plains, dry thorn bush, and semi-desert country.

Mkongo, and Mloka to the Mtemere gate. Plan on seven to eight hours of driving time. The stretch from Dar to Kibiti is a tarmac road and the next thirty kilometres (19 miles) to Mkongo is along an all-weather dirt surface track. The remaining seventy-five kilometres (47 miles) can be impassable during the heavy rains between February and April.

The northern access from Dar is 350 kilometres (217 miles) to the Matambwe gate. The drive usually takes eight to nine hours. It is 190 kilometres (118 miles) on tarmac road to Morogoro, then a scenic route through the Uluguru Mountains along a very steep and rocky road.

A dry-season direct road from Mikumi National Park to the Selous has recently been under construction. The trip will probably take one full day.

Airstrips at Mtemere, Mbuyu, Beho Beho, and Stiegler's Gorge can be reached by light chartered aircraft. The TANZAM train passes through the northern edge of the park five times a week. The scenery along the line is superb and arrangements should be made with the camps in advance for passengers to be picked up from either Kinyanguru or Fuga Stations.

When to go

The most pleasant time to visit the Selous is during the cool season between the end of June and the end of October. There is also a dry spell in January and February. During the long rains between February and the end of May, the reserve is inaccessible and the tourist camps are closed.

Where to stay

There are four tented camps in the northern part of the park and all can be reached from Dar es Salaam by road, rail, or light aircraft. Selous Safari Camp is an old hunting camp on Beho Beho ridge with panoramic views over acacia woodlands. At nearby Lake Tagalala visitors can bathe in the hot springs flowing from Kipalapala Hill.

Stiegler's Gorge Camp is the largest, occupying high ground above a waterhole near the Rufiji and it is a short drive from

Above: The Klipspringer has hooves specially adapted to ensure a secure purchase on the rocky outcrops among which it lives.

there to the gorge's rapids. Rufiji River Camp is on a bank of the river just inside the eastern boundary of the reserve.

From there fishing trips and river safaris can be taken. Mbuyu Camp takes its name from the Swahili word for baobab, a tree that grows all around this site between lakes Nzerakera and Manze. Walking safaris can be taken from all the camps in the company of an armed guide. There are currently plans to offer camping facilities to visitors.

Fees to pay

Fees are payable in foreign currency only and are subject to change. Up-to-date information about the current fees charged for accommodation and national parks entry can be obtained from tour operators or the National Park Headquarters, PO Box 3134, Arusha.

Sightseeing

Opened in 1905 by the Germans as a hunting preserve, the Selous' unprecedented number of game attracted white hunters from Europe and America who for years tracked and shot countless trophies in the northern fringes around the Great Ruaha River.

It is rumoured that the Kaiser gave the hunting preserve to his wife in 1910 as a birthday present, though neither of them ever visited the area. This may be the reason why locals refer to the Selous as *shamba la bibi*, 'fields of the lady'. Today the indiscriminate killing has stopped and the Selous is the **largest protected wildlife area** in East Africa as well as one of the most pristine. In 1982 the United Nations declared it a **World Heritage Site**.

The main road

As few as 2,000 tourists visit the reserve's thousands of acres each year, entering the Selous through either the **Mtemere** or the **Matambwe Gates**. The reserve's **main road** stretches eighty-three kilometres (51 miles) between the two and the drive usually takes three hours. Along the way travellers

encounter all the different vegetational types the Selous has to offer and a wide variety of animal species.

Stiegler's Gorge

Forty kilometres (25 miles) from Matambwe is **Stiegler's Gorge**, one of the park's most striking features. Its 100-metre-deep (328-foot) by 100-metre-wide canyon channels the brown and turbulent confluence of the **Great Ruaha** and **Rufiji rivers**. Stiegler was a hunter who was killed by an elephant there in 1907.

The **tourist camp** at the gorge was originally built in 1977 for a team of scientists and engineers studying the feasibility of a hydroelectric scheme across the raging waters. Fortunately the idea was scrapped and a defunct cable car is one of the few remnants left from the grandiose plans.

After the **bottle-neck** of the **gorge** the Rufiji bellies out and continues its sluggish journey through the park to the Indian Ocean as a series of channels and small lakes. The lakes — **Tagalala, Manze, Nzerakera, Mzizima** and **Siwando** — are important sources of water for the animals and the variety of game there is impressive.

The hinterland around Lake Tagalala and **Beho Beho** area is some of the most beautiful. It can be reached from Matambwe by turning right after twelve kilometres (seven miles). This road leads to a **bridge** over the **Beho Beho River**, then continues through hilly woodland (a favourite retreat of the elephant and buffalo) until it reaches Beho Beho.

The old hunters found the buffalo the most dangerous of all the 'big five' — lion, leopard, buffalo, rhino, and elephant — and veteran single males were usually responsible for many injuries and deaths, as they can be — though not always — today. Old males leave the herds and take to a solitary life in the thick savannah. People on foot occasionally stumble on them and, in fright, the 800-kilo (1,760-lb) bull turns, head down, and charges instinctively. The Beho Beho region experienced heavy fighting during World War I and to the south-east of the **airstrip** are a number of **trenches**.

This is also the area where **Selous** met his end. To find his **grave** follow the road from Beho Beho back toward Matambwe. Two kilometres past the airstrip the road towards Mbuyu and Mtemere branches to the right. Another kilometre further the road turns to the right again. The simple stone marked by a cross reads: 'Captain FC Selous D S O 25th Royal Fusiliers. Killed in Action 4.1.1917'.

Lake Tagalala

Along the southern edge of the airstrip is the fourteen-kilometre (nine-mile) road to Lake Tagalala. Two kilometres before the tip of the lake is a **crystal-clear stream**. Turn right here and the road winds another kilometre to the **hot springs**, hidden in a ravine and surrounded by lush vegetation.

Lake Tagalala is connected to the Rufiji, and — like the river — its shape and size are constantly changing. Waterbuck, southern reedbuck and bushbuck are all common near the water's edge. The lion and small numbers of greater kudu frequent the long grassland and only come to drink when the dry season is at its highest.

Now sometimes found in the Beho-Beho vicinity, the sable antelope, with the unmistakable ridged scimitar horns which in the past made it the prime target of trophy hunters, is a member of the *Hippotragine* family of horse-like antelopes. The male is distinguished from the female by its black — opposed to chestnut — coat.

Rufiji River

Varying from forty-five metres (148 feet) to half a kilometre or wider during the rainy season, the Rufiji is the main artery of the Selous. Lined with *Borassus* palms, its chocolate-coloured waters bisect the park north from south, acting as an effective barrier to inhibit the spread of some animal

Opposite: Maji Moto hot springs in the Selous, perhaps the source of the legendary waters which Africans believed would protect them against German bullets during the 1905 Maji Maji Rebellion.

Above: Frederick C Selous, explorer, hunter, and naturalist, was killed in a German ambush during World War One. His remains lie buried in the largest protected area in East Africa — which is also named after him — the Selous Game Reserve.

species. Giraffes are confined to the northern parts of the park as they are unable to cross the moving waters.

Sailing or rafting down the river is a great way to view game, especially during the dry season (June to October) when the animals congregate along the sandy shores. Crocodiles, hippos and grazers can all be seen, along with other game forced out of the dry bush by the need for water.

Following the rising and falling river levels are birds such as the kingfisher, fish eagle and Egyptian goose. The reserve is home to more than 350 species of winged fowl; goliath heron, open-billed stork, hammerkop, secretary bird and sunbirds all feed and breed throughout the Selous.

Beneath the Selous waters

The **Kilombero Game Controlled Area** to the west is the haunt of two renowned East African freshwater fish, the tiger and the vundu. *Hydrocyon*, the tiger fish's Latin name, means water dog and it really is the Doberman of the deep. Fast, ferocious, and armed with blade-like teeth, it is a voracious predator. Many fishermen consider the larger southern species, *vittatus*, to be the finest freshwater fighting fish.

The vundu, *Heterobranchus longifilis*, is a catfish and makes up for its gentler nature by growing to enormous proportions. It regularly exceeds forty-five kilos (100 lbs) and is a representative of the claria family, fish that can breathe using the branchial organ. *Claria gariepinus*, the most common, utilizes this when it migrates from one landlocked pool to another by dragging itself short distances on its pectoral fins. Other catfish — silurids — give electric shocks or have barbed needle spines in their fins which are coated with an irritant mucus. When freshly caught the stiletto can be stabbed into the flesh of an unwary angler, an unpleasant experience — particularly when it is extracted.

Mikumi National Park: Perfectly Plain

North of the Selous, in the lee of the Uluguru Mountains, lies Mikumi, one of the most accessible and popular of Tanzania's national parks. Only 283 kilometres (175 miles) from Dar es Salaam, it was established in 1964 to protect the environment and resident animals from being hunted to extinction.

Because of the park's close location to Morogoro and Dar, Mikumi is an important educational centre where students go to learn about ecology and conservation matters. Associated with a residential teaching facility is an Animal Behaviour Research Unit that for years has been studying the yellow baboon.

The main feature of the national park is the Mikumi flood plain, along with the mountain ranges that border the park on two sides. Open grasslands dominate in the flood plain, eventually merging with the miombo woodland covering the lower hills.

Getting there

Mikumi National Park can be reached from Dar es Salaam along the Dar-Morogoro-Iringa road taking about four hours. The road bisects the park and the boundary is clearly marked.

Mikumi village, twenty kilometres (12 miles) from the park, is on a branch line between Kilosa and Kidatu of the main TANZAM/TAZARA railway.

When to go

The Ulugurus are not high enough to put Mikumi in a rainshadow and the park is affected by the monsoons. Northerly winds blow from the interior between October and March, bringing the short rains of November and December; while the cooler south-easterlies blow for the rest of the year, causing the long rains from March to May.

Some of the tracks become impassable during the wet season and drivers should check with park headquarters before setting off on safari.

Where to stay

The Mikumi Wildlife Lodge — with two suites, fifty double rooms and a pool — is the first choice for most travellers. The park also contains thirteen bandas with a restaurant and bar overlooking the Mkata flood plain near the park entrance.

There are also three camp sites in Mikumi. Fuel wood and toilets are provided but there is no water. Camping in special sites is allowed but prior arrangements must be made with the warden. (See Listings for 'Accommodation'.)

Fees to pay

Fees are payable in foreign currency only and are subject to change. Up-to-date information about the current fees charged for accommodation and entry to the national parks can be obtained from tour operators or the National Park Headquarters, PO Box 3134, Arusha.

Sightseeing

As you approach the park along the main **Iringa-Dar route**, the area to the north and west of the road is the **flood plain** of the **Mkata River**. The plain is made up of a combination of hardpan ridges and black cotton soil. The **hardpan** is an open area consisting of ridges made from impervious soils that drain into swamps or watercourses. The poor soil is unable to support much vegetation, although occasionally sparse tree populations — acacia, tamarind, or baobab — are able to find enough nutrients to survive.

Black cotton is a heavy clay that becomes a sticky mess once the rains arrive. The name originated from Sudan where cotton is grown in this type of soil. The flood plain is divided into three areas: **Kikoboga** and **Hippo Pools**; the **road** to **Chamgore** and **Choga Wale**; and the **road** to **Mwanambogo**.

Kikoboga and Hippo Pools

Lying at the southern end of the flood plain, the **Kikoboga** area contains several excellent drives including the **Kisingura Circuit** and the **Mkata Drive**. The yellow baboon is usually sighted there, feeding on grass, fruit,

Above: A lion's roar usually consists of long moaning grunts followed by a series of shorter ones. The whole process lasts between thirty to forty seconds and can be heard up to eight kilometres away.

and insects. Adults will also kill the young of impalas, reedbucks and other antelopes to round out their diet.

The **Hippo Pools** are five kilometres (three miles) north of the **main park entrance** and, as the name implies, is one place for hippo sightings as hippo tend to move about. To distinguish between the male and female, the male's neck is larger and the ears more upright. The female has a flatter head. Every hippo — like the zebra's stripes and giraffe's spots — has a different identifying pattern of wrinkles around its eyes. The pool waters are also attractive seasonally to open-billed storks which flock there to hunt for molluscs when they are in season.

Other animals commonly found in this area of the park are eland, elephant, Lichtenstein's hartebeest, buffalo, wildebeest, giraffe, zebra and elephant. The Mikumi elephants, noticeably smaller than elephants elsewhere, are mainly grazers and do not cause tree damage. Their destruction is limited to shaking the trunks of small trees called *Sclerocarya caffra* for their fruit. Other than a shake here and there the pachyderms feed almost exclusively on the tall grasses found along the swamp edges.

Lions are commonly found roaming the Mikumi plains for wildebeest and, like their Manyara counterparts, will take refuge in the branches of trees. They share the plains with black-bellied bustards and ground hornbills. Ground hornbills are like black turkeys with a call that resembles the sound of a distant lion. They often swagger around in pairs, stabbing at insects and reptiles with their red-wattled curving beaks.

A wild dog pack, rare elsewhere in Africa, may be seen at Mikumi. With their oversized ears, white-tipped tails, and blotched mustard, white, and black coats, it is easy to understand the origin of their scientific name, *Lycaon pictus* 'painted wolf'.

Above: Zebras are conspicuous in daylight, but at dawn and dusk — the usual predation hours — the stripes blend together, making them difficult to see.

Chamgore and Choga Wale

The road to **Chamgore and Choga Wale** leads past the Hippo Pools and north along the course of the **Mkata River**. The vegetation begins with woodland, followed by swampy areas, finally emerging into open grassland and two waterholes. The first, **Mkata**, is reached along a turn-off at marker 32. The second hole, **Chamgore** ('place of the python'), is one kilometre further north off the main track.

Inhabitants of the pools include the saddle-bill stork, hammerkop, malachite kingfisher, monitor lizard and python. Although the snake is non-venomous, it has a huge mouth and fangs and, with a well-timed blow, can knock down animals as large as an impala. The python then wraps its body, which can grow up to six metres (20 feet), around its prey and squeezes until the victim dies of asphyxiation.

It is best to be accompanied by a ranger for travel beyond the Chamgore Pool to the Choga Wale area and a four-wheel-drive vehicle is needed there, especially during the wet season when the road is always impossible and often impassable.

The pink jacaranda is one of the many beautiful trees found in this most northern section of the park. Its peeling bark is used by some of the locals as protection against witchcraft. There are several **picnic sites** in this area. **Choga Wale** is a small glade of *Hyphaene* palms and shady figs where lunch can be enjoyed uninterrupted. Another popular site is **Mbuyuni**, 'place of the baobab'. Look for the massive baobab with a gaping hole in its trunk. Also keep a watchful eye out for lions and leopards.

The road to Mwanambogo

There is a connecting dry-season road from Chamgore to **Mwanambogo** for those wishing to make a circuit around the park. Before setting out, however, check with headquarters. The trail is across black cotton soil and is often transformed into a bog.

The road to Mwanambogo is reached by taking the first **right** after the **main gate entrance**. The track leads north along the

Above: Travelling along the Rufiji River through the Selous Game Reserve, which was declared a World Heritage Site in 1982.
Opposite: Dinner for a week pulled from the Rufiji River.

eastern side of the flood plain to the **Mwanambogo Dam**. North of the dam the road is often impassable, so again, check with park headquarters before setting out.

The black-backed jackal is one of the more common carnivores seen en route to the dam. It is distinguished by its silver-streaked black saddle and yellowish-rust coloured flanks and legs. It is one of the few mammal species that mates for life.

Southern extension

In 1975 an extension reaching to the **TANZAM/TAZARA railway** and **Ruaha River** was added to the national park, making it contiguous with the **Selous Game Reserve**. Due to a shortage of funding, the area awaits future development.

The southern area's miombo woodland is filled with hot springs and populated by crocodiles who live along the river's edge. The area is home to the sable antelope and colobus monkey. The black and white primate is the most aboreal of all East African monkeys and rarely descends to the ground, preferring instead to swing through the canopy like an acrobat.

Udzungwa Mountains National Park

Many of Tanzania's smaller mountain ranges are remote and their unique and undisturbed habitats still await scientific investigation. A classic example is the Udzungwa Mountains, located just south of Mikumi National Park in the highlands overlooking Iringa. Within recent years four new species of bird — a weaver, a cisticola, the rufous-winged sunbird and a new partridge-like bird that is not closely related to any other bird in East Africa — have been discovered within these ranges, and two endemic species of primate — the Sanje crested mangabey and Iringa red colobus monkey.

Above: Greater Kudu, easily distinguished by its long spiral horns and the fringe of hair running from the chin to the neck, makes its home in the Selous.
Opposite: Crossing 120 metres (400 feet) above Stiegler's Gorge in the Selous. The gorge, carved by the Rufiji River, is named after a German adventurer killed by an elephant at the turn of the century.

Udzungwa's East African forest ranges from 250 metres (820 feet) to 2,576 metres (8,452 feet) and forms an important genetic plant pool containing species that grow nowhere else in the world. Gazetted in January 1992 and opened on 22 October that year, the 1,990-square-kilometre (768-square-mile) Udzungwa Mountains National Park will conserve these invaluable botanical treasures which might otherwise become extinct through logging.

Getting there
The park headquarters is at Mang'ula, sixty-five kilometres (40 miles) south of Mikumi on the Mikumi-Ifakara toad.

When to go
Between September and December is the best time to visit the Udzungwa Mountains.

Where to stay
Visitor facilities are under construction near the park headquarters. Enquiries should be to the warden in charge Udzungwa National Park, PO Box 62, Mikumi. There is accommodation at nearby Mikumi National Park and at Kidatu and Ifakara. (See Listings for Accommodation).

Sightseeing
Spectacular mountain scenery, waterfalls, rivers and grasslands await visitors to Udzungwa. Animals that make their home there include elephant, buffalo, lion, leopard, sable antelope, eland, waterbuck, duiker and bushbuck. The rolling countryside is also a bird-watcher's paradise, featuring hundreds of common species as well as those endemic unknowns still awaiting discovery.

The Heartland: Track to the Interior

Four times every week a passenger train pulling up to twenty carriages leaves Dar es Salaam on the 1,238-kilometre (770-mile) journey across the Tanzanian hinterland to Kigoma on the eastern shores of Lake Tanganyika. This is the country's oldest railway, the Central Line.

Probably the German colonists' most important contribution to Tanzania, the line was ostensibly intended to open up the country and improve communications, and this it did. But the real reason behind the line's construction was its use to deploy troops in a country notoriously difficult to cross and always on the brink of rebellion, if not actually fighting against German military rule.

Surveying for the line actually began in 1894, but while British rivals raced ahead with construction of a railway in Kenya, the Germans were side-tracked by insurgency, culminating in the Maji Maji Rebellion, and the project was put on ice for the next ten years. (See 'History: From the Cradle to Independence', Part One.)

Only when the rebellion had been firmly and finally crushed in late 1905 using troops brought in from Germany's Far Eastern territories, was the go-ahead given to start work by the new Colonial Council in Berlin. Indian labour — used so successfully on the railway from the Kenyan coast to Lake Victoria, the so-called 'Lunatic Line' — could not be enticed away from the British, and the Germans were obliged to use entirely African construction gangs.

Just outside Dar es Salaam they ran into their first technical problem. The plain of the Ruvu River was awash for much of the rainy season and when the waters subsided the clay and soft sandstone base required more bridges with deeper foundations than the surveyors had anticipated.

An even more fundamental problem was the lack of food. Local produce was not available in sufficient quantity to feed the Wanyamwezi work force and rice had to be shipped in from Bombay. Despite these difficulties, the one-metre-gauge railhead reached Morogoro by the end of 1907, a rate of sixty-six kilometres (41 miles) a year. At this turtle's pace Lake Tanganyika was sixteen years away, with the desolate miombo interior still to be carved through. To make matters worse, the route after Morogoro had not yet been chosen. The new German settlers of the Southern Highlands, growing coffee, tea and cotton on the fertile hills, wanted the line to run southwards through Iringa and Mbeya to boost their economy. But surveyors chose a more direct route via Dodoma, straight through the arid wastes of the Central Plateau.

As the land became more barren, track-laying took second place to the daily priority of getting food and water, and Sikh and Punjabi contractors were hired to haul provisions by donkey caravan from the northern highlands around Kilimanjaro.

Improvements in railway building technology came to the aid of the engineers. Innovations in plate-laying made the process cheaper and more efficient, and by the end of 1911 the line had overcome the wall of the Rift Valley at Saranda and put Tabora firmly on the railway map of East Africa.

The prosaically named Bismarckville, at the southern tip of Lake Tanganyika; Karema, located near the centre of the lake's eastern shore; and Kigoma to the north, had all been earmarked as the terminus of the line. With the introduction of the speedier technology and, perhaps conscious of the slow progress made so far, the authorities decided to head directly west for Kigoma and its deep-water harbour.

The last hurdle to cross was the Malagarasi River. Ingeniously, a pontoon carrying the bridge was built upstream of its intended site. When the river flooded the pontoon was guided into position, then secured as the waters subsided and the bridge was lowered into place.

Thanks to rapid progress in the later

Above: Sprawling suburbs of Dodoma, its famous landmark 'The Rock' in the background.

stages of construction the final spike of the Central Line — the 'spinal cord' of Tanganyika, as a later British governor was to describe it — was hammered into place at Kigoma on 1 February 1914, fourteen months ahead of schedule and just in time to see the outbreak of the First World War.

Towns on the track

Travel by train can be one of the most economical ways to tour Tanzania. From Dar es Salaam to Kigoma it takes a leisurely two nights and one full day, but sleeper cars are available. It is also an ideal place to meet the people of the country; Maasai herders rub shoulders with shopkeepers up and down the corridors and there is always time to strike up a conversation.

First Stop: Morogoro

Situated at the foot of the beautiful blue Uluguru Mountains, Morogoro is the first major town along the route heading west from Dar. The area boasts good trout fishing, particularly in the clear waters of the Mgeta River.

South-west of the town is Mikumi National Park and the Selous Game Reserve. Safari seekers often use the 100-bed Morogoro Hotel, operated by Bushtrekker, as a jumping-off point for these parks.

Morogoro can also be reached by an Air Tanzania flight or by the 193-kilometre (120-mile) tarmac from Dar es Salaam.

Dodoma: Future Capital?

With the arrival of the railway in 1910, Dodoma quickly flourished into an established station settlement. Prior to the tracks being laid, and with the exception of that massive rockpile 'The Rock', the *tembes* — rectangular, flat-roofed huts built around a kraal — of the local Gogo tribe, distinguished Dodoma from the surrounding miles of thin soil, monotonous miombo woodland, and granite outcrops.

The paucity of the area meant that the Gogo, whom Stanley found to be 'masters

Above: The Central Line took a decade to build, running the width of the country from Dar es Salaam to Kigoma across 1,248 kilometres (775 miles).
Opposite: Striped splendour of the vulturine guinea-fowl. This handsome bird with black and white and cobalt-blue feathers gets its name from its small head, which is reminiscent of a vulture.

in foxy-craft', were widely scattered over the plain, practising pastoralism and cultivation with sorghum, millet and maize. Waterholes were well maintained and, for a fee, could be relied upon by the slavers who passed during the dry season.

Idodomya means 'the place where it sank', 'it' being an elephant that got stuck in the mud of a Gogo watering hole. When the Germans drew the new Central Line on their maps the name became Dodoma.

The coming of the First World War saw the end of Dodoma. Not by bullets but by famine. Reckless appropriation of the village's grain supplies and cattle by both the Germans and British led to the death of 30,000 Tanzanians. Two words were coined by the stricken people during those years: *mutunya* and *kaputala*. *Mutunya*, meaning scramble, refers to the frenzy of the starving crowd whenever a supply train passed through. *Kaputala* refers to the shorts worn

by the British troops. It was these soldiers, according to the Gogo, who were responsible for the catastrophe.

At the beginning of the war a German administrator in Dodoma suggested that the small town should become the capital of German East Africa, but preoccupied authorities shelved the proposal.

Gradually Dodoma established itself as a communications centre based on its location at the crossroads of the country's main north-south and east-west roads. The town found itself in the international spotlight when it became the stopover for the record-breaking Cape-to-Cairo flights of the late 1920s and early 1930s. To further cement its new position, the town was chosen as Tanzania's relay station in the Pan-African telecommunications network.

As Dodoma continued to grow in importance, the plan to move the country's capital was raised again. But the scheme

Above: Dodoma's Islam Jamal Kher Mosque.

was still considered too ambitious and in 1959 it was vetoed by government officials. Finally in 1973, facing an independent and rosy socialist future under President Julius Nyerere, Dodoma became the leading centre of *ujamaa*, or villagization.

Getting there

Dodoma can be reached by the main Mbeya-Arusha tarmac or from Dar. Air Tanzania schedules regular flights from Tanzania's major towns and, of course, Dodoma is served by the Central Line.

Where to stay

The Dodoma Railway Hotel, built by the English during the 1940s, is one of the more popular spots. The Christian Centre of Tanzania offers clean accommodation for the budget traveller. Others include Central Province Hotel and Ujiji Guesthouse. (See Listings for 'Accommodation').

Sightseeing

The underlying concept of 'Dodoma, capital of Tanzania', was a town that catered to the needs and welfare of its inhabitants as well as to those of the country as a whole. Four settlements, each numbering 7,000 people, have been built around parkland and gardens in the shape of a flower. The buildings are constructed from local stone and wood and do not exceed four storeys.

Several light industries, such as ceramics and engineering, have already made the move to Dodoma. The rest of the country's businesses and many government offices, with the exception of the Revolutionary Party (CCM) headquarters, dragged their heels in Dar es Salaam, although some have relocated. One aspect not noted in the euphoria of planning the new capital was its critical deficiency of water resources.

Following World War Two dams were built and boreholes sunk to help stabilize the agricultural industry. Despite the poor soils of the area, an abundant water supply and ideal climatic conditions have turned Dodoma into the major viniculture centre between the Cape and North Africa.

The industry began in 1957 when Father

Above: Diamonds from the Williamson Diamond Mines at Shinyanga.

Ireneo Maggioni of the Bihawana Mission, perhaps in a bout of homesickness, planted three grape seedlings. They soon flourished and by the 1980s, 3,000 acres of vineyards were producing two harvests each year, amounting to over 5,000 tons of grapes destined to reach the table as Dodoma Red, White, or Rosé. New strains of French, Italian, German, and American vines are constantly being tried.

Tabora: Making Tracks to the West

The Central Line leaves Dodoma, then drops down to skirt the Bahi Swamp before climbing the escarpment of the Rift Valley at Saranda. For mile after mile the line follows the caravan route and trail used by the first explorers through the Itigi Thicket and into the open vastness of the *nyika* country.

Eventually there is respite from the endless tsetse-ridden bush as the train draws into Tabora station. Located 800 kilometres (496 miles) from the sea, Tabora was an infamous slave trading centre and the base Burton and Speke used during their Lake Tanganyika disappointments. (See 'History: From the Cradle to Independence', Part One).

Originally called Kazeh, Tabora was founded by the Arabs in 1820 as a caravan depot. It eventually became the hub of the slave routes that spread north to Speke's great lake and the country of Karagwe on its western shores, west to Lake Tanganyika, and south to the populous waterfront areas of Lake Malawi. Because it lay on the main route to the coast, it was only natural that other explorers, such as Livingstone and Stanley, should also pass that way.

Getting there
Most who pass that way today do so on the Central Line. Tabora is also the end of the railway line from Mwanza on Lake Victoria. Air Tanzania maintains regular scheduled flights to Tabora, and the town can be reached by rough road from Mwanza in the north and an even rougher road from Mbeya.

245

Above: Ripening grapes in a vineyard near Dodoma form one of two annual harvests. Barely palatable to sophisticated tastes, Dodoma wines are enjoyed in Tanzania and neighbouring countries.

Where to stay

The Railway Hotel offers adequate accommodation and reasonable meals and for budget travellers there's the YMCA or Moravian Guesthouse. The Tabora Hotel is another medium-priced option. (See Listings for 'Accommodation'.)

Sightseeing

The **house** where **Livingstone** and **Stanley** stayed after their famous meeting has been reconstructed on the original site six kilometres (four miles) from town at nearby **Kwihara**. There are Arab muskets on the walls and copies of Stanley's dispatches to the *New York Herald* blaring headlines that read 'Dr Livingstone Found', and 'The Famous Explorer in Good Health'.

The classical, rectangular-shaped *tembe*, with its faded brick-red walls and stamped earth floor, was built around a courtyard where small livestock was kept at night. Livingstone stayed there for five months, reading his Bible, catching up on his journal

and waiting for supplies and porters Stanley had promised to send him from Zanzibar. They eventually arrived and in August 1872 Livingstone left on his final journey.

The *tembe* now is partially shaded by the mango trees, providing pools of shadow in a climate hot by day and cool by night, receiving ninety centimetres (35 inches) of rain a year.

The aridity of the **Central Plateau**, at 1,202 metres (3,943 feet) above sea-level, is reflected in the name Tabora which derives from the local Nyamwezi word *matobolwa*, the dried sweet potato that is a traditional source of food during famine.

The **Nyamwezi** — People of the Moon — are the second-largest tribe in Tanzania and have a long tradition of trading in iron goods and salt and, when the opportunity presented itself, ivory and slaves. They also provided porters and guides for the onward journey to the inland seas.

During the latter half of the nineteenth century the tribe held sway over all the

Above: Replica of the *tembe* in Kwihara, near Tabora, that housed Burton, Speke, and Livingstone during their trek to the great lakes. The building is now a museum.

country to the west of Tabora between Lake Victoria, Lake Tanganyika, and Lake Rukwa in the south, led by only one chief — Mirambo. He united the democratically elected village leaders into a single powerful chiefdom and, with a regular army, subjugated neighbouring tribes and regularly attacked the Arabs. Stanley called Mirambo the Napoleon of Central Africa and on one occasion took time out from his exploring to fight with the Arabs of Tabora against the chief.

Mirambo's reign continued undiminished, despite Stanley's intervention, and the warrior and general also showed himself to be a shrewd diplomat when he wrote to the British consul of Zanzibar, Sir John Kirk, saying, 'This country is a hundred times more prosperous, ten-fold more peaceful, and a thousand-fold more safe than it was before I became chief of it. I wish to open it up, to learn of Europeans, to trade honestly with all, and to cultivate peaceful relationships with my neighbours.' His dream died with him in 1884

and his successor Isike failed to consolidate Mirambo's kingdom in the face of mounting hostility from the Arabs and their temporary allies, the newly arrived Germans. When Isike closed the caravan routes in 1892 the Germans attacked his fort. Repelled twice, the colonialists finally took the stronghold after two days of bloody hand-to-hand fighting.

As the walls were breached Isike took refuge in the powder magazine with his family and, seeing that the situation was hopeless, blew it up rather than be captured alive.

To prevent a recurrence of tribal autonomy the Germans built a grim **fortress on a hill** in Tabora which remains a landmark that can still be seen to this day. The Nyamwezi have abandoned their warlike ways and returned to trading and pastoralism, growing millet, sorghum, maize, cassava, and groundnuts for cash. They also keep bees and Tabora is well known for its fragrant honey. Despite their return to a peaceful coexistence, sometimes,

above the drone of the hives, comes the low rhythmic chant of Mirambo's feared war song, *Iron Breaks the Head*.

The final leg

From Tabora the Central Line heads due west to **Kigoma** — taken from the Swahili word *kikoma* meaning 'the end of the line' — down the gently dipping plateau that Stanley thought 'the finest country in eastern and central Africa'. To the north and south of the line are the small seasonal lakes **Masimba** and **Sagara**. Masimba is a lake on the **Malagarasi**, a river rising in the hills above Kigoma that defines the boundary of Tanzania and **Burundi** for some distance, before curving in a great arc to discharge into **Lake Tanganyika**. At **Uvinza** the line crosses the river near the **salt springs** used by the Vinza people for centuries. Pottery has been uncovered there dating from AD 500.

About forty hours out of Dar es Salaam the miombo scenery relents as the line descends to Kigoma and the glittering blue of Lake Tanganyika appears between rolling green hills.

Above: Kigoma railway station, terminus of the Central Line from Dar es Salaam.
Opposite: Hot and dry for most of the year, the area around Dodoma is more suited to grazing than agriculture.

PART THREE: SPECIAL FEATURES

Above: A crab searches for dinner in the crystal-clear waters of the Indian Ocean.
Opposite: For all its great length, the giraffe's neck has only seven vertebrae, the same as man.

Wildlife: An Inventory from the Ark

The popular image of wildlife is epitomized by the savannahs of East Africa. About a quarter of Africa's large mammals live on the plains of Tanzania, only one of the country's diverse habitats that make it nature's last natural stronghold.

The people of Tanzania recognize this fact — and that wildlife is possibly their country's greatest resource — and have made a strong commitment to its conservation.

The words of the Arusha Declaration specifically link Tanzania's future to the future of the animals: 'The survival of our wildlife is a matter of grave concern to all of us in Africa. These wild creatures amid the wild places they inhabit are not only important as a source of wonder and inspiration but are an integral part of our natural resources and of our future livelihood and well-being.'

To this end twenty-five per cent of the country is now protected by law, from the vast Selous Game Reserve to the tiny but equally unique national park at Gombe Stream.

In many of these parks and reserves, luxury lodges and permanent camps provide an ideal background from which to observe and delight in the remarkable spectrum of wildlife that abounds in Tanzania.

There are more than eighty major species — from the 'Big Five', the most cherished trophies of all among the old hunting fraternity, to the tiny dik-dik, so diminutive in stature that it stands shoulder to shoulder with a small dog.

The Big Five

Elephant

The adult African elephant weighs anywhere between 3.5 to 6.5 tonnes, needs between 136 and 300 kilos (300-660 lbs) of fodder a day and drinks between 200 and 300 litres (44-66 gallons) of water. They depend almost entirely on their trunk for scent and communication, for washing and cleaning, for carrying and clearing, and for drinking and eating.

Tusks — an elephant's upper incisors — are tools for lifting, carrying, and clearing. Today male tusks seldom exceed twenty kilos (44 lbs) each, though the heaviest on record weighed 103 kilos (227 lbs) and the longest, measured on the curve, was close to four metres (13 feet). They become visible at about sixteen months and grow throughout the animal's life.

An elephant's life span depends very much on its teeth, which are very highly adapted to its mode of living. As one is worn away the next moves down the jaw to push it out and replace it.

When the last tooth has come forward and is worn down, at an age between fifty and seventy years, the elephant will die of starvation.

Bush elephants average about six kilometres (four miles) an hour when walking, but can reach forty kilometres (25 miles) an hour when charging.

It takes close to two years from conception to birth, with the calf weighing plus or minus 100 kilos (220 lbs).

Elephants are highly sociable and move in herds that average between ten and twenty but have been known to exceed 1,000. Although their sight is poor, elephants have an excellent sense of smell and well-developed hearing, with a brain three times the weight of that of a human being — between 3.6 and five kilos (8-11 lbs).

Rhinoceros

Only the **black rhinoceros** makes its home in Tanzania. It is smaller than the white rhino, weighing around 907 to 1,364 kilos (1,995-3,000 lbs). The size of its horns varies between fifty to eighty-nine centimetres (20-35 inches) for the front horn and just under fifty-three centimetres (21 inches) for the rear horn.

With its relatively small feet, three toes on each hoof, and pointed prehensile upper

Above: Lions are sociable and rarely seen alone, living in prides made up of several adult males, females, and a majority of young.

lip, the black rhinoceros is a browser that originally ranged from sea-level to high savannah and montane forest.

Today, Ngorongoro and Selous are the only reserves in the country that contain an ever diminishing number of the creatures, which face possible extinction at the hands of professional poachers for whom the horn — made of compacted hair and keratin — is a highly profitable target.

Buffalo

The powerful **African buffalo** needs plenty of fodder to maintain its strength and stamina. Although the **West African forest** version is considerably smaller, often only half the weight, both races are voracious feeders, browsing and grazing on a variety of grasses, leaves, twigs, and young shoots for most of their fifteen to twenty years.

They are gregarious and frequently form herds with 500 to 2,000 members. En masse they are known to attack and kill large carnivores such as lion and leopard, which are their only natural enemies. Buffalo are

found at all altitudes in Tanzania, from sea-level to mountain forests above the 3,000-metre (9,840-foot) contour.

Lion

The lion is the largest of the three big cats, the male averaging 181 kilos (400 lbs) and the female 113 kilos (250 lbs). Their amber-coloured eyes, like those of the leopard, are different from the eyes of most cats — with circular rather than oval pupils.

Lions usually hunt communally, with lionesses running down their preferred prey — zebra, hartebeest, wildebeest and gazelles — at a top speed of around sixty-four kilometres (40 miles) an hour. Other hunting methods are to pounce on the victim's back, drag it to the ground and seize it by the throat, or suffocate it.

In an ordinary year a lion or lioness accounts for nineteen head of game at a weight of about 114 kilos (251 lbs) for each kill. They consume as much as twenty-five kilos (55 lbs) of meat in one meal. When present, males are usually the first to eat, females

253

Above: The largest of the spotted cats, this young leopard is well adapted to all but the driest African habitats.

second, and the young take what is left. In times of scarcity, many cubs die of starvation and vitamin deficiency.

Prides often total as many as thirty animals in the Serengeti, mostly females and young, and mark their range — up to 160 square kilometres (62 square miles) — by urination. The sound of the familiar roar, usually heard at night, carries as far as eight kilometres (five miles) and signals territorial ownership. The ability to roar is shared by the leopard, tiger and jaguar. So powerful is the roar it stirs the dust two metres (seven feet) away.

Leopard

The leopard is considerably smaller than the lion, weighing in between thirty and eighty-two kilos (66 and 180 lbs). Its sandy fur is covered with exquisite dark rosettes.

Leopard are largely nocturnal but are quite often around in the early morning or late afternoon when they feel safe. They are widely distributed, from mountain moorland to city suburbs — with the exception of grassland — but their secretive nature and varied diet enables them to survive unseen in most habitats.

An illustration of the leopard's ability to survive was their recorded presence in the 1970s on Zanzibar — the last place one would expect a Great Cat to thrive. In contrast, in open places like the Serengeti plains, where there are no trees to climb for refuge, leopard are few because of their vulnerability to the far larger lion.

Using cover, leopard normally stalk their kill. What they cannot eat immediately they haul up into branches, away from scavengers. In this way they monopolize the kill. Leopard kill anything from small rodents to large antelope. They even eat fish and will readily take to carrion.

They are usually solitary, but during mating move about in pairs. There are an average of two to three cubs in a litter. Leopard have the same vocal mechanism as the lion, and their roar, a grunting cough, sounds like a saw cutting rough wood.

Above: Two rare black rhino, their horns intact.

Other Cats

Cheetah

The cheetah, most slender of the three big cats, weighs between forty-three and sixty-three kilos (95 and 139 lbs). It rightly deserves its reputation as the fastest animal in the world, attaining speeds up to 113 kilometres (70 miles) an hour. Hunters of the plains, they rely on speed first and strength second when making a kill, a technique that culminates in a high speed sprint of up to 600 metres (656 yards).

To cope with the physical demands of sprinting, the cheetah has changed its physiology. The back and legs have lengthened to give a greater stride and weight has been lost at the expense of muscular strength.

This hardly matters since the prey is usually so out of breath that it is unable to put up any sort of fight. The cat has accordingly lost the retractile claws of other big cats that are used to hold and tear prey.

It prefers to kill by a bite to the throat after the prey has been knocked off its feet.

The conspicuous hunting technique of the cheetah, plus its relative weakness compared with other carnivores, means that kills are often stolen, even by smaller animals such as jackals.

Cheetah live and hunt alone or in pairs; at most in groups of six. Cubs are usually born in litters of two to four. They are born with their characteristic spots.

Serval

The serval has long legs, large oval ears, (used in locating and pinpointing prey), a medium build and weighs between thirteen and fifteen kilos (29 and 33 lbs). Its main source of food is the rodent, but this adaptable cat also eats lizards, fish, birds and small antelope.

It is found throughout Tanzania, from montane forest to lowland savannah, but prefers the environs of dry river beds. The serval is mainly nocturnal.

Litters usually number between two and four and the call of the kitten is a plaintive high-pitched 'how . . . how . . . how'. The young are born and reared in old porcupine and antbear burrows.

Caracal
The caracal's flat head, long legs, and powerful shoulders give it the proportions of a lynx. With hind legs longer than the forelegs, it has been known to kill prey as large as a reedbuck and few cats can emulate the caracal's sudden spring into the air to pull down a bird in mid-flight, sometimes as high as three metres (10 feet).

The soft thick coat has no distinct stripes but is spotted on the underside. The tail is shorter than any other African cat.

Civet
The civet, a long-legged, dog-like creature, is the largest of the *Viverridae* family, weighing between nine and twenty kilos (20 and 44 lbs). The long coarse body hair has a varied pattern of black spots.

Largely nocturnal and widely distributed, it is still sometimes seen by day, in both savannah and dense forest. It feeds on fruit, carrion, rodents, birds, eggs, lizards, small game, frogs, slugs, snails and insects. It has a low-pitched cough and growl.

Another species, the **two-spotted palm civet**, spends most of its life in trees or vines and mews like a cat.

Genets
The **small-spotted (or Neumann's) genet** is widespread throughout savannah country. Mainly solitary, it moves at night and is equally at home on the ground or in trees. So slender and flexible is the body of the genet that it can follow its head through any opening.

The **large spotted (or bush) genet**, longer than the more common small-spotted genet, lacks a dorsal crest, has shorter fur, and sports larger body spots. It favours woodland and forest habitats.

Genets spend their day in rock crevices, hollow trees, or dozing on a large branch. They return to the same place day after day, hunting mostly on the ground, only climbing trees to raid nests. Young are born two or three to a litter. Although a member of the *Viverridae* family, genet spit and growl like cats when angry or threatened. Normally quiet, their normal call is a clear, metallic note.

Common Sightings

Giraffe
Nature has given the giraffe, the world's tallest creature, several techniques to help it cope with life as the 'skyscraper of the bush'. It has a system of valves and canals that regulates and controls the massive increase in blood pressure in the head when the animal stoops to drink. Without such an aid the animal would black out.

Other adaptations that have evolved for this tree-browser include a forty-five-centimetre-long (18-inch) tongue and a prehensile upper lip. A giraffe's tongue is the longest in the world.

The giraffe measures anywhere from 4.6 to 5.5 metres (15 to 18 feet) from the tip of the toe to the top of the head, and weighs up to 1,272 kilos (2,798 lbs).

The young are already more than 1.5 metres (5 feet) at birth and tip the scales around sixty-eight kilos (150 lbs). They continue to grow for the first seven to ten of their twenty-five years. Both male and female are born with usually two short, bony 'horns' on their head, sometimes with a knob on the centre of the forehead.

Although *twiga*, the giraffe, is the national emblem, only the **Maasai giraffe** is found in Tanzania, and then just north of the Rufiji River; the **reticulated** and **Baringo** varieties are limited to the semi-arid regions of Kenya and Somalia. Giraffes run in a curious and fascinating loping gallop, which can produce speeds up to fifty-six kilometres (35 miles) an hour.

Opposite: Black rhino are usually solitary, especially the males, and only come together in pairs during the brief mating season.

Hippopotamus

The hippopotamus weighs up to four tonnes. Immersed in water, the third-largest land animal can hold its breath and stay submerged for up to six minutes. They mate and give birth under the water. Their skin is a uniform brownish-grey, lightening to pink around the eyes, muzzle, and throat.

These amphibians spend most of the day in water, sleeping and resting, coming up frequently to blow air and recharge their lungs. Around sundown — or even during the day if they do not feel threatened — the school (or sounder) leaves the water, adult bulls bringing up the rear, to feed within the limits of the 'home range', a pear-shaped area marked by well-defined pathways. Their search for grass and other vegetation amounts to around sixty kilos (132 lbs) of fodder every 24 hours for each animal. Day grazing may often be observed along the Rufiji River in the Selous.

The young are suckled at first on land. Hippo mothers are stern disciplinarians. Disobedient young are chastised, sometimes with a savage bite, and the youngster made to cower in submission. When a mother leaves the school at any time, other females take over as acting 'mothers'.

Hippos live nearly forty years and can have a beneficial effect on their environment by stirring up the water's bottom layers to spread nutrients for fish to feed on and providing large and frequent amounts of fertilizer through their dung. They also keep weed and papyrus beds clear.

Zebra

The zebra's vivid and eye-catching stripes are unique. No two animals are alike. Just as a fingerprint distinguishes one human from another, so the zebra's stripes mark each creature as a wholly distinct individual. Of the two species — **Grevy's** and **Burchell's** (or **common zebra**) — only the latter is present in Tanzania.

Zebra stallions fight ferociously for mates and dominance. These clashes are spectacular affairs with the rival stallions rearing and plunging, lashing out with both hind and forelegs, and neck wrestling. Occasionally, they will drop on their forelegs and slash savagely at each other's necks with bared teeth.

They are generally dependent on water, needing to drink daily. Their smell, sight, and hearing are acute and they can sustain high speeds over short distances.

Crocodile

The Nile crocodile, which grow to lengths upwards of five metres (16 feet) on the Grumeti River, for all its sinister mouthful of teeth, is unable to chew. To eat large prey, it clamps down on its victim and thrashes around in the water, rotating until a limb is wrenched off.

To swallow, it raises its head and lets the food fall to the back of its throat. Digestion is slow. Bodies recovered from dead crocs fifteen hours after a kill have been virtually unmarked.

Unable to thermostatically control their own temperature, they use external methods to maintain a constant body heat.

They will leave the water early in the morning to warm up in the sun, returning to the water to escape the excessive heat of high noon. When the day cools they will bask in the sun again until sundown, and retreat back to the water for the night.

Clutches of up to ninety eggs are laid about seventy to ninety centimetres (27 to 35 inches) beneath the lake or river bank. When ready to hatch, the young call their mother back to dig them out by grunting and chirruping inside their eggs. These 'crocklings' are easy prey for a host of hunters — from monitor lizards to raptors, wild cats and mongooses.

Mongoose

The **dwarf mongoose**, the smallest of Tanzania's several species, is active during the day, searching in packs of up to fifteen for grubs, insects, larvae, spiders, small rodents, reptiles, eggs and young birds as

Opposite: The male bull elephant loses the herd instinct as it gets older, often preferring solitude.

Above: Hippos are excellent swimmers, able to remain below the surface for as long as six minutes.

food. They attack live prey *en masse*, swooping down on victims with a savage growl. They are stockily built, with a short snout and speckled brown or reddish-brown coat. The dwarf mongoose lives in dry savannah woodlands — taking refuge in old termite hills, rock crevices, or hollow trees. They are nomadic creatures, showing little concern for their own safety and are frequently visible. They communicate with a wide vocabulary of bird-like chirps and whistles and are extremely sociable. Their groups are strongly territorial and are ruled by a dominant female. The biggest member of this family is the large **grey mongoose**, greyish-brown with a long and relatively slender tail ending in a black tuft. It is found in a variety of habitats, particularly along the edges of lakes and swamplands, woodlands and thick bush.

Another species, the **slender (black-tipped) mongoose**, is often mistaken for a ground squirrel when running because of the similar way it holds its tail up straight.

It is the most frequently seen of all mongooses, recognized by its coat of deep reddish-brown and long black-tipped tail. Active day and night, though basically a ground animal, it climbs trees to feed on rodents, reptiles, snakes, birds, eggs, insects, larvae and fruit. The slender mongoose has a litter of two to four young, born in hollow trees or holes in the ground.

The nocturnal **white-tailed mongoose** is a large, thickset animal with a shaggy grey coat — and white tail.They are the heaviest mongoose, favouring almost any kind of environment from wood, bush, and open plains, to locations where they add molluscs and crabs to their diet of small animals, frogs, rodents, reptiles and insects. When angry they communicate with a loud bark.

The **banded mongoose** is medium sized, with transverse dark-coloured bands along its greyish-brown body. It moves around in packs of up to several dozen and is never far from water. The banded mongoose is a highly social animal with groups often growing in size until they number between thirty and fifty gregarious creatures.

Above: The Cape buffalo, like a cow, must drink every day. They are also fond of wallowing in muddy shallow pools.

Hyrax

The nocturnal **tree hyrax** has remarkable soles to its feet, well adapted for climbing trees. They are kept continuously sticky by a substance secreted from a gland. Tree hyrax can be found at almost any altitude in almost any forest from sea-level to around 4,000 metres (13,120 feet).

It feeds throughout its ten years on a vegetarian diet of grass, berries, fruit, barks, lichens and leaves. This beguiling little creature is perhaps best known for its scream — delivered in the dead of night and sounding like the devil incarnate. The anguished cry is actually a territorial call.

The **rock hyrax** is lighter in colour and has feet which also enable it to move with agility in its chosen world of boulder and precipice. Its soles have elastic, rubber-like pads which provide a sure grip on all inclines in all conditions.

They are daytime creatures, living in large colonies, and may be seen sunning themselves on rocky hills or boulders in groups ranging from sixty to 100.

Hare

The **African hare**, with its big ears, grizzled black-and-buff body and long slender legs, is easily distinguishable and is widely distributed throughout East Africa. These solitary, nocturnal creatures with their large eyes are closely related to their European cousins. They are found in grassland, bush and sparse woodland.

Squirrel

The **striped ground squirrel** lives in burrows in the drier savannah and has an almost naked belly.

The **unstriped ground squirrel** is the same size and has the same habits. It is very sociable, a daytime creature, and lives in colonies — often with other species of rodents — excavating burrows that form warrens connected by tunnels spread over several square metres.

The rarely seen **scaly-tailed flying squirrel** belongs to a peculiar family of rodents, the *Anomaluridae* — the only living remnants of a family now extinct outside

Above: Jackals hunt in large packs for their prey which includes small antelopes.

Africa. Its gliding membrane — a flap of furred skin from wrist to ankle and from ankle to tail — forms a broad wind surface enabling the creature to 'plane' long distances. It can 'fly' up to ninety metres (295 feet), though it normally makes short flips — between fifteen to eighteen metres (49 to 59 feet).

Beneath this membrane, near the tail, scales enable it to establish a firm grip on a tree when it lands.

Wild dog

No longer as prolific in Tanzania as in former years, wild dogs live and hunt in packs, from as few as ten to as many as fifty. Numbers of ninety were at one time recorded. They can sustain a pace of forty-eight kilometres (30 miles) an hour for almost two kilometres.

When one is exhausted, another takes its place in the chase. The pack eats on the run, tearing the flesh off the luckless prey while it is in flight, often ripping out its entrails until it drops exhausted. A pack of twelve can consume a full-grown impala within ten minutes. They hunt at sun up and sundown, and a kill averages just under two kilos (four lbs) of flesh a day for each animal. They are social creatures taking great care of their young, feeding them with semi-digested meat that the adults regurgitate. The lame and sick which trail after the hunt are cared for too, and are made welcome at the feast. Colleagues will regurgitate for them also.

The young treat their seniors with deference. Those who do not are chastised with a snapping bite on the flank. This makes the youngster freeze, raise its head and whimper obedience.

To each other, wild dogs are gentle and persuasive, licking faces and muzzles, and crouching in deference whenever they want something.

A wild dog pack was once seen by a climbing party above the snow line of Kilimanjaro — but they have suffered a population crash in recent times due to canine distemper.

Above: Hyena pups await the return of their mother, upon whose milk they are entirely dependent for the first eight months of their lives.

Jackal

The **black-backed** (or **silver-backed**) **jackal** is the most common of the jackals, distinguished by its grizzled grey back and tawny underparts.

They are resourceful animals, hunting and scavenging in pairs or family groups. Their favourite prey includes small antelope, hares, rodents, guinea fowl and other ground birds, reptiles, eggs and insects.

The pack swoops down on a kill darting in and out among the feasting lion or cheetah, snatching titbits from under their noses. They are also prey themselves of lion, leopard and python and cubs are often taken by eagles.

The **golden jackal,** adaptable to changing cirumstances and environment, is most typical of the short grass plains.

The most elusive of the three, the **side-striped jackal,** gets its name from the indistinct light stripe along its flank and has a white tip to its tail.

Hyena

Hyena, for many years considered only as scavengers, are ruthless and successful hunters.

Spotted hyena usually hunt in large packs and their range of prey is varied and appetite indiscriminate. They cut down wildebeest, zebra and gazelle at speeds of up to sixty-four kilometres (40 miles) an hour.

These voracious killers follow pregnant females, snatching their newborn young as they are delivered. Their strong teeth and powerful jaws allow the hyena to crack bones easily. They are aided by an extraordinarily efficient digestion, which enables them to extract nutrients from waste that regularly includes other predators' dung, old dry bones and bits of leather.

Given the opportunity, spotted hyena will attack humans and, not infrequently, their own kind.

They have been seen eating brooms, old shoes and bicycle saddles. But live prey

Above: Chimpanzees are the most expressive of all animals, indulging in a variety of facial expressions and gestures.

forms about eighty per cent of their diet — making them more efficient hunters than lion which will often eat the hyena's leftovers. Hyenas bay, like dogs and wolves, but instead of throwing their heads back, they point their muzzles down. The spotted hyena prefers bush and wooded country, lush rolling grasslands, forest, and mountain slope. The **striped hyena**, a smaller animal, is found on the dry plains.

Marked by dark vertical stripes, the **aardwolf's** sandy-brown coat makes it look like a miniature striped hyena, to which it may be distantly related. Although some experts think the aardwolf is unique, many suggest it is a form of hyena which, through a changing diet over the centuries, has evolved into a family by itself. It lives entirely on termites.

Aardwolves move about by night, hiding during the daytime in old aardvark burrows in which they raise their young, usually three to a litter, often in small communities of nursing females.

Baboons and Monkeys

Of Tanzania's two baboon species, both of which occur inside and outside the parks and reserves except in dense forest areas, the stocky, heavily built **olive baboon** is more common than the slender, longer-legged **yellow baboon**. For both, the leopard is their most dreaded enemy.

They cover up to eighteen kilometres (11 miles) a day in a constant search for food — shoots, roots, seeds, bushes, flowers, insects and an occasional kill. They prey on small mammals — hares and young gazelles — whose defence is to 'freeze' to the ground. They will snatch up fledging birds.

Extremely social, their well-organized groups are known as troops and average between forty and eighty animals. They sleep, seek shelter and often feed in trees.

The permanent core of the troop is its adult females. Males come in from other troops and are thus always in a state of working on their relationships with each

Above: Baboons are found throughout East Africa, wherever perennial water and abundant forage can be found.

other. Baboons are fierce fighters, and predators regard them with respect. They are well-equipped for defence, with acute hearing and eyesight, and extremely strong teeth.

Youngsters, born black with red faces, are carried under the belly. Later, like young jockeys, they move to a 'horse-riding' position on the mother's back. These early months are an important introduction to the intricate rituals and behaviours of the troop's social structure.

Colobus

Black-and-white colobus monkeys differ from most other monkeys in two respects. They have only four digits on either hand — there is no thumb — and they spend virtually their entire lives above ground, in the highest levels of the forest.

Rarely do they come down to earth. Few creatures can equal their climbing ability or their plunging leap — as much as thirty metres (98 feet). They differ, too, from most other monkeys in their capacity to remain silent, often for hours on end.

Colobus live in troops of up to twenty-five members made up of several family groups and are the most specialized feeders of all monkeys — living on a selective diet of forest leaves. **Red colobus,** in larger groups, require a more varied diet.

Vervet

Another family of tree-top monkeys is the guenon group, daytime creatures confined to tropical forests. The one exception is the **black-faced vervet (or green) monkey** which has come down from the trees to live on the savannah. It uses the gallery forests and thick bush for refuge and sleep, but forages widely on the open ground in troops of between six to twenty (although groups of up to 100 have been observed).

They are mainly vegetarian, feeding on a diet of leaves, young shoots, bark, flowers, fruits, bulbs, roots and grass seeds for most of their twenty- to twenty-four-year life span. They augment their diet with insects, grubs, caterpillars, spiders, eggs, young

Above: The friendly bushbaby is a common tree-dweller throughout Tanzania's woodlands and forests.

ground birds like guinea fowl and francolin and, in rare instances, rodents or hares. Vervets have acute vision and excellent hearing but a poor sense of smell. They communicate with a wide range of facial expressions: lowering eyebrows, raising and jerking heads, and threatening with bared teeth and wide open mouth.

Patas

The patas monkey, the only primate that does not mix with other monkeys, is also known as the **red hussar**. Large, tall and long-legged, it lives almost exclusively on the ground and stands and walks on its hind legs. The patas, which weighs up to ten kilos (22 lbs), is known as the 'greyhound of the apes' and has been clocked at fifty-six kilometres (35 miles) an hour.

Sykes'

The Sykes' monkey, with its distinctive white throat and chest patch, is a member of the blue monkey races which are large and rather stout. They hold their thick long tails, with a slightly curved tip, higher than the body when walking.

Sykes' have narrow, elongated faces with a purplish-black tone and bristly tufts of hair on their foreheads, earning them the nickname of diadem. These monkeys are found wherever there are forests.

Bushbaby

The lesser galago, a nocturnal primate, is better known as the bushbaby. This endearing creature, small, slim-built with thick and woolly fur, has a conspicuous white stripe down its nose. It is widespread and common throughout Tanzania, secreting itself in coastal bush and acacia woodlands and forests.

The bushbaby is well-adapted to life in the trees, its tail acting as a counterweight, with the hind legs grasping the branches before leap-frogging from one to another. It sometimes drops to the ground where it walks upright, or in a crouch, leaping occasionally on its extremely powerful hind legs like a tiny kangaroo.

Above: Eland, the largest antelope, are stately and elegant residents of the Tanzanian plains.

Overleaf: Two young elephants spar in play along the shores of Lake Manyara. Adult males will tag along with family units for short periods to inspect females for their readiness to mate.

A bushbaby can jump an incredible three metres (10 feet). It has a large vocabulary — at least eight different calls, including a high-pitched alarm which it can keep up for an hour or more. Litters usually number two, born in a nest prepared by the mother. **Greater galagos** are noisier, less agile and are mainly fruit-eaters.

Potto

The potto is a little, bear-like animal without a tail — or at least only a rudimentary stump — rounded head, small ears, and unequal limbs.

Moving with a slow and deliberate gait, the potto, known in many an African vernacular as 'half-a-tail', lives exclusively in the top storeys of its forest home — rarely, if ever, coming down to earth. The curious, lethargic animal is easily located at night by shining a powerful torch into its reflective, always astonished eyes.

Grazers and Browsers

Eland

The eland, heavyweight of Tanzania's fragile pastures, weighs close to a tonne. But it can leap, virtually from a standing position, to a height of more than two metres (seven feet).

Averaging 1.7 metres (six feet) at the shoulder, they are the largest of the antelopes.

Their twisted horns are around seventy-six centimetres (30 inches) long — the record length being more than one metre (39 inches).

These horns are important for feeding, for grasping branches and breaking them loose with a shake of the head and powerful neck.

For all their size and weight, with their powerful chest hidden behind the large and pendulous dewlap, eland are graceful

267

creatures, well-proportioned and elegantly symmetrical. Old bulls live solitary lives away from the herds which, in Mikumi and Mkomazi, may be over 70 strong. Their life span is 15 to 20 years.

Kudu
Weighing between 272 and 317 kilos (598-697 lbs), **greater kudu** can easily clear two metres (seven feet) at a jump despite their impressive weight. They are distinguished by magnificent spiralled horns averaging around 1.3 metres (four feet) long, with the record length a fraction under 1.8 metres (six feet).

Their acute hearing is accentuated by an ability to turn their large rounded ears in almost any direction. These large, slender, and elegant antelopes, grey in colour with six to eight prominent vertical white stripes on either flank, raise their tail when alarmed — the white underside serving as a warning. Kudu live out their twelve to fifteen years in small herds or families of four to five, although herds of thirty have been seen.

The **lesser kudu**, a smaller, more graceful version of the greater, displays more stripes — between eleven and fifteen — down the flank. They prefer much drier country and can go without water for a long time.

Sitatunga
The swamp-dwelling sitatunga, or marshbuck, is unique among antelopes and easily distinguished. Its two-toed, elongated hooves spread widely to dissipate its weight, enabling it to move about on mats of floating weeds and appear to walk on water.

When alarmed, it sinks into the water with only the tip of its nostrils showing. Sitatunga also swim adeptly.

They are mainly night antelopes, browsing on leaves, twigs, fruits, and tender grass. They live alone or in pairs or sometimes in occasional herds of up to fifteen.

They bark when alarmed and communicate by bleating. The only place they can be seen easily in Tanzania is Rubondo Island National Park.

Waterbuck
Waterbuck have scent glands that emit an unpleasant musky smell so powerful that, long after they have left, it serves as a telltale indication of their previous presence.

Their majestic horns are unmistakable and average around seventy centimetres (27 inches) long. The record length is a fraction over one metre (39 inches).

With a long, shaggy brown to greyish-brown coat, an elliptical white ring around each buttock distinguishes the **common waterbuck** from the **Defassa waterbuck** which has entirely white buttocks. Waterbuck are grazers, found in woodlands, flood plains and clearings, but usually close to water.

Oryx
The handsome oryx wield their long horns with dexterity in the savage cut and thrust of the wild, sometimes impaling their victims with such force the horns pass clean through the body. Horns average about seventy centimetres (27 inches), with a record length of more than a metre (39 inches). When seen in profile, the oryx appears to have just one horn, giving rise to the legend that it may have been the model for the mythical unicorn.

They are usually found in groups of ten or twelve and live out their twelve to fifteen years on a varied died of grass, leaves, shoots, wild melons, succulent roots, tubers, and bulbs. These grazers go long periods without water.

Unlike most other antelopes they do not jump often — although they can do so with prodigious power when needed — preferring instead to creep under obstacles rather than leap over them.

Topi
The topi, familiar sentinel in the Serengeti, is prime flesh for all the predators which follow the migration. It is large and robust, and its shoulders are noticeably higher than its rump, giving it the familiar hartebeest look. They have an overall reddish-brown to purplish-red appearance with distinct dark patches on the face, upper forehead, legs, hips and thighs.

Above: After killing, the leopard will drag its quarry into a tree, safe from fellow predators.

Jousting males, each of which has its own territory, drop to their knees and clash horns. Rutting males mark out their territory with dung heaps and by rubbing facial and foot glands on the ground. They then take guard on the nearest high ground, usually an old termite mound.

Topi are pure grazers, going without water for a long time if the grass is green and succulent. They also eat grasses disdained by other antelope. They are swift runners, making off with a bounding gait.

Hartebeest

Topi behaviour also characterizes the hartebeest. Males keep watch from knolls or high ground after defining their territory and winning the courtship battle for a harem.

But for a good part of their twelve to fifteen years, hartebeest bulls are celibate. Losers form bachelor herds and old bulls are cast out to live a solitary existence until they die.

The most common, **Coke's hartebeest**, is around 1.2 metres (four feet) high at the shoulder, and weighs between sixty-two and ninety kilos (136 and 198 lbs).

Lichtenstein's hartebeest is distinguished by the chestnut brown patch behind the foreleg. Sandy-fawn in colour, the hump-shouldered hartebeest appear out of proportion with their long heads and massive brows giving them a doltish look. Hartebeest bulls are placid, except when rutting, and snort when alarmed.

Wildebeest

The wildebeest is the star of the world's greatest animal spectacle — the annual migration from the Serengeti to Kenya's Maasai Mara.

More than a million of these strange-looking creatures, joined by zebra and topi, trek seasonally, when the grasslands of the Serengeti have dried up, to the lusher feeding in the Maasai Mara. The young are born a reddish-brown and can stand within minutes of birth. They take on their mature colour after two months. The wildebeest habit of migrating in single-file formation makes them unique among plains game.

Above: Two male impala use speed and agility to escape danger. Rams lead herds that number up to 150 females and young.

Extremely gregarious, each herd is headed by one bull who trots around his group in a peculiar, head-high, rocking gait, forcing his females and their young into a tight mass. Wildebeest bulls defend their territory even on the move, making a continuous cacophony of low, moaning grunts and explosive snorts.

They scatter during the rains and, in the dry season, cover up to fifty kilometres (31 miles) a day to find water. Their diet is almost entirely grass.

Roan and sable antelope

The **roan antelope,** like the sable, has ridged, scimitar-curved horns, present in both sexes. The females' horns are smaller.

The roan depends almost entirely on grass throughout its fifteen-year life span, living in herds of up to twenty animals. Rutting males joust with rivals by going down on their knees and making sweeping movements with their horns.

The **sable antelope** is one of the most beautiful of the larger antelopes, the male's satin-like coat appearing almost pure black, the female's a dark reddish-brown.

Gazelle

Both grazers and browsers, **Grant's gazelle** can endure extreme heat and exist without water for long periods during their ten- to twelve-year life span.

They are an active species, rarely seeking shade, often seen as a shimmering outline on the plain during the unremitting heat of the day. Grant's form herds varying in size from six to thirty, usually with one male in charge of a dozen does. Their call is an alarmed grunt or bleat.

Thomson's gazelle are their smaller look-alikes and are often found together on the Serengeti plains. The only certain way of telling them apart is by the white markings on the buttocks of the Grant's that reach above the tail; in Thomson's they end below the root of the tail.

Thomson's gazelle are prey to almost every predator but they have no audible alarm call. Instead, they signal danger by rippling and flexing the muscles in their flanks. They can leap incredibly high in a stiff-legged, standing-still jump known as 'stotting' or 'pronking'. Females, which have smaller horns, breed all year-round, sometimes giving birth to two fawns in twelve months. Both young and adult have the ability to 'freeze' in the prone position — even the chin extending horizontally along the ground — when threatened.

Impala
The impala, emblem of the East African Wildlife Society, is also regular prey for almost every large predator, yet continues to maintain itself in large populations.

One reason is its agility when threatened. Taking off in a series of soaring bounds, spectacularly beautiful to watch, they can jump obstacles towering three metres (10 feet) above the ground or leap ditches up to ten metres (33 feet) wide, changing direction upon each landing, to disconcert predators.

Set above a profile of deceptively simple beauty, the distinctive lyre-shaped horns of the male average just over thirty centimetres (12 inches), with a record length of around a metre (39 inches). They are active both day and night, browsing throughout their twelve years on leaves, bushes, short grass and fruit. They drink dew and in some, but not all areas, can survive without visible sources of water. Impala range over acacia savannah and light woodlands but are absent from Ngorongoro Crater.

Bushbuck
The bushbuck's dappled white markings are a perfect example of natural camouflage. Blending into rock and bush, this shy, mainly nocturnal creature of forest and thicket flits elusively in and out of cover. Bushbuck need their camouflage to avoid their principal enemy, the leopard.

When cornered or wounded they defend themselves and their young with considerable courage. Their short bushy tails, which are white underneath, are raised on the run to serve as a warning beacon for others.

They are mainly nocturnal, spending most of their twelve to fifteen years alone or in small groups, browsing on leaves, shoots, acacia pods, tubers and roots, only eating the first flush of young grass. They communicate with a loud bark — similar to that of the baboon — and also in a range of grunts.

Reedbuck
Though essentially a day creature, the **bohor reedbuck** is an elusive antelope, shy and easily startled. It is normally seen at sun up and sundown. These small, graceful creatures lie in reed beds or tall grasses during the day, shaping the stems around them into a shelter.

When alarmed they go down onto the ground in a squatting position — only bolting at the last moment. They run with a peculiar 'rocking-horse' gait.

The short horns of the reedbuck — hunted by all the large predators — provide little defence. They average less than thirty centimetres (one foot); the record length is under forty-five centimetres (18 inches).

Although they are sometimes solitary, reedbuck normally move around in pairs or small family groups, with young males forming bachelor herds of no more than three to four.

Dik-dik
Dik-dik are gentle, greyish wraiths occasionally seen darting through thickets in shy and elusive flight. Their locations are easily identified by the middens which they establish — up to a metre in diameter — to mark the boundaries of their territory.

Kirk's dik-dik, with their hindquarters taller than their front shoulders and forward sloping back, look permanently startled. They are the most common and roam dry and arid lands even where the trees are very scattered — as long as there is enough undergrowth for refuge.

Dik-dik are extremely territorial, and rarely wander far, preferring to remain in one small district and always moving about on the same pathways. Normally they live in pairs and occasionally form small family groups.

Dik-diks feed throughout their five to ten

years of life on leaves, shoots, fruit, roots and tubers. They can go without water indefinitely. In flight, they run in a series of zig-zag bounds. Their alarm call is a shrill whistle, a bit like a bird call — or a 'zik-zik' cry — hence their name.

Klipspringer

The klipspringer, measuring around fifty-one to fifty-six centimetres (20 to 22 inches) high from hoof to shoulder and weighing between eleven and eighteen kilos (24 and 40 lbs), is a phenomenal jumper. It bounces on the tips of its rubbery hooves as it walks, making its exceptionally long legs look even longer — the tiptoe effect accentuating the impression.

Unlike the coat of any other African antelope, the klipspringer's olive-yellow coat, speckled with grey, is stiff and brittle, serving as a cushion to ward off the shocks of hitting rock walls when they jump.

Klipspringers live only on rocky hills and, like most other antelope, mark their territories with a secretion from their scent glands. They graze on herbs and shrubs and drink water when it is available, but can draw enough liquid from their food.

Oribi

The oribi is another of Tanzania's beautiful small antelopes, with a long slender neck and silky coat.

With a colour that varies from pale fawn grey to bright reddish-brown, oribi are distinguished by the bare, black glandular patches below their large, oval-shaped ears. Their short tails, which have a black tip, are raised when running.

Oribi are almost exclusively grazers, spending the day in long grass or light bush. They live in pairs or small parties and when alarmed give shrill loud whistles or sneezes before leaping straight up in the air in a stiff-legged jump then bounding away. Some experts suggest that in this way they scan a larger area of bush for signs of predators.

Steinbok

The little steinbok (or steenbok) often eludes its predators by darting down an old aardvark burrow which, in more placid times, the females may also use to raise their young.

Steinbok are slim and slender creatures with a black crescent patch between their horns and a smaller one on the nose. Their belly and buttocks are pure white and the coat sometimes greyish with a light, silvery sheen.

They live alone, pairing only during the mating season. Steinbok are both browsers and grazers, embracing a wide range of food and having the ability to survive without water.

Gerenuk

The gerenuk spends a great deal of its life on its hind legs, searching for the lusher leaves found high up on acacia thorns and other desert shrubs on which it survives.

This unique antelope was only discovered as recently as 1878. Its name derives from the Somali language meaning 'giraffe-necked'. Using its rear legs to stand in a vertical posture while feeding, the antelope's neck has evolved through the millennia to become longer and longer.

Gerenuk are the antelope of the desert, surviving without water, drawing all the liquid they need from their vegetarian diet. During extreme drought, however, one animal has been observed to drink the urine of another.

These elegant creatures are also fascinating when they run. They are extremely swift, and bring their long necks down in line with their slender backs, making them appear to have shrunk to about half their height.

Suni

No taller than thirty-one centimetres (one foot) and only eight kilos (18 lbs) in weight, the suni is rarely seen. It moves mostly at sun up and sundown. But it

Opposite: The giraffe's unique loping gait is due in part to its enormous weight, up to 1,272 kilos (2,798 lbs), and high centre of gravity.

Above: The unusual-looking, long-necked gerenuk stands on its hind legs when browsing. This unique antelope is specially adapted to desert life, and can go for long periods without water.

leaves one telltale clue to its presence — a strong, musky scent which lingers, like that of the waterbuck, long after it has left a location. Suni are mainly browsers, favouring leaves, young shoots, roots, and a limited amount of grass. They, too, can live almost entirely without water and can be found throughout Tanzania wherever there are forests.

Their specific Latin name, *moschatus*, derives from the large gland below their eyes which gives off the strong musky odour.

Duiker

The **bush (or grey) duiker** stands around sixty-one centimetres (two feet) from hoof to shoulder and weighs between eleven and thirteen kilos (24 and 29 lbs). Duiker are widespread throughout the country, but vary locally in body size, horns, colour, and thickness of coat. In mountain regions the duiker is unusually shaggy.

The bush duiker are the most universal — ranging from sea-level desert to snow line, although almost never in bamboo or dense forest. They are also the most adaptable of the duiker and have survived where others have become extinct. They are often found on farms — even in small vegetable gardens.

Forest duikers, including **Harvey's,** are red in colour and move in characteristically hunched posture, with their head close to the ground. It enables them to move more easily through thick and often tangled undergrowth, using regular, well-marked trails and passages. When alarmed, all duiker plunge into thick cover; hence their name, given to them by the early Afrikaans settlers, from the Dutch word meaning 'diver'.

Abbott's duiker is endemic to Tanzania's mountains. Identified by its dark brown coat, it is the second-largest of duikers. The smallest, **Ader's duiker**, is not found on the mainland, but only on Zanzibar.

Birdlife: Flocking to Tanzanian Shores

Of the world's estimated 8,600 bird species, sub-Saharan Africa boasts about 1,750, of which East Africa can claim 1,294 — and Tanzania just over 1,000 species. It is truly an ornithologist's paradise outdone only by some Latin American countries where dense cover can make spotting difficult.

The 'twitchers' of Tanzania, on the other hand, stand a good chance of seeing at least sixty per cent of all African avifauna, and to see more than 100 species in a day's outing is not uncommon.

Tanzania — with its diverse geography, shifting pattern of rainfall and dynamic ecology — provides environments that support a vast number of species, some of which are found nowhere else in the world. Even in the last decade three entirely new species have been found in the southern Udzungwa Mountains, and more await discovery.

Add to the list the migrants that winter in East Africa from their summer breeding ground in the northern hemisphere, and the year-round diversity of the country's bird life is staggering.

Waterbirds

Tanzania's Rift Valley lakes support an immense number of waterbirds and many other species abound in the surrounding grasslands and acacia woodlands.

More than 400 species — greater than the total bird species of the British Isles — have been recorded at Lake Manyara alone. There you will see the black **greater cormorant** resting on rocks or tree trunks in the water.

Cormorants dive and swim beneath the water for their prey, bringing it to the surface where it is tossed in the air, caught, and swallowed. Afterwards they stretch out their wings to dry in the sun.

The **African darter** is similar though it has a much longer neck — which takes on an 's' shape at rest — enabling the bird to dart its bill forward like an arrow and pierce its prey. Other large waterbirds present, either standing at the water's edge or wading in the shallows fishing, are different species of **heron, ibis,** and **stork**.

The most outstanding is the **goliath heron**, largest of all the herons. The smaller **black-headed heron** (which also feeds on insects and rats) is easily recognized by its grey, white, and black colour.

Even smaller is the **squacco heron**, a thickset, biscuit-coloured bird with white wings.

When searching for food, this characteristically stealthy heron stands stock still, neck held back as it waits for prey to come within distance, then it strikes in a flash. Some herons move their heads from side to side when fishing, enabling them to get a proper fix on the target.

Ibis are readily identified by their down-curved bills. The loud shriek of the **hadada ibis** can be heard just around sundown and sun up — and during the night when the moon is bright. A sociable bird, its olive-brown wing feathers frequently reflect a bright metallic-green.

The **sacred ibis** is seen more often. Flocks gather on waste ground around towns as well as lakes and they are found in lagoons and on estuaries. They are easily identified by their white feathers, black bare head and neck, and long down-curved bill.

The ancient Egyptians worshipped them as the embodiment of the god of wisdom. On many murals and tombs, the moon deity Thoth was shown with the head of an ibis that has been extinct in Egypt for more than a century.

Ducks and geese

Freshwater and mildly alkaline lakes such as Manyara also play host to a great many ducks, some resident, others migrant. Because all their flight feathers moult at once, ducks and geese are unable to fly for some weeks after the breeding season — and are extremely vulnerable to predators.

The biggest, a tree duck somewhat misleadingly known as the **spurwing goose**, has a dark-red bill, glossy metallic black upper parts, and white belly. The much smaller **white-faced whistling duck**, also a tree variety, has a distinctive clear whistling call — as its name implies — and is easily spotted by its white face, reddish plumage, and barred flanks.

The **Egyptian goose**, with its predominately brown plumage, white shoulders, and honking call, is very common in Tanzania. It is another bird that was worshipped by the Egyptians, and many tomb murals depict the sacred bird.

Although of similar size, the **knob-billed goose** by comparison is almost silent. It is readily identifiable by its black and white plumage and, during the breeding season, the male develops a distinctive knob at the base of its bill.

One of the most beautiful of the large African birds — which is also the national symbol of Uganda — is the **crowned crane**. It is easily recognized by its straw-coloured crest and black crown.

Their ceremonial dance is fascinating to watch. Two birds spread their wings and bow formally to each other, followed by a sudden leap high into the air and a running dash around each other. Then the sequence starts all over again.

Birds which rely on water for their food supply find the trees bordering Tanzania's watercourses ideal. One such bird is the **hammerkop**, sole species of its family, which is wide ranging in tropical Africa. Its conspicuous long, backward-pointing crest gave rise to its name.

The hammerkop's nest is an astonishing work of sticks and vegetation, lined with mud or dung, usually wedged in the fork of a tree near a river or swamp. The nest is vast — approaching one metre in diameter (39 inches) — and has a side entrance leading to an enclosed chamber.

Hammerkops will return to an old nest and add to it year after year eventually causing the huge edifice to collapse under its own weight. They live off frogs, tadpoles, and small fish.

Birds of prey

Three birds of prey are common on the Rift lake shores; the **fish eagle** with its striking black-and-white colouring — white head,

chest, back and tail, chestnut belly, and black wings — being the most frequently seen, usually perched on the limb of a tall tree along the shoreline.

It will take off with astonishing suddeness to swoop down over the surface where, talons outstretched, it grasps wriggling prey with consummate ease. Its haunting cry is one of the most dramatic and familiar of the lakes and rivers. It is also found in estuaries and lagoons — in fact, wherever there is permanant water.

Another inshore predator seen as it darts and flashes among the reeds and papyrus is the diminutive but spectacular **malachite kingfisher**. It lives extensively off tree frogs and fish.

The exquisite colouring — cobalt-blue crown barred with black, bright ultramarine blue back, and reddish underparts — make the malachite kingfisher truly beautiful in contrast with its almost dull black-and-white brother, the **pied kingfisher**. This bird, best seen in characteristic hovering flight over creeks and estuaries, spots its prey, then plunges headlong into the water with its eyes closed. It surfaces immediately, with or without the fish, usually scoring a low success rate of about one in every ten attempts.

The **grey-headed gull** is found almost exclusively on the lakes — easily recognized by its grey head and generally white and pale grey colours marked by a red bill and legs.

Another familiar lake resident is the **red-knobbed coot**, a plain slate-black bird distinguished by the red knob on its forehead. It lives off weeds and grasses just beneath the surface, performing a valuable environmental function in keeping the water free of weeds.

The **African jacana** appears to walk on water. In fact, its widely-splayed feet and long toes enable it to walk — as well as feed — on water-lilies and water grasses.

Alkaline lakes

Lake Natron is the ultimate alkaline lake, so rich in dissolved sodium carbonate that the water is frequently viscous to the touch. But the algae that lives there where nothing else can is the sole food source for flamingos.

Above: Kori bustard, one of Tanzania's largest flying birds, measures around 100 centimetres (40 inches). The ornamental plumes around its head, nape, and long neck are used in remarkable breeding displays.

They build domed nests of mud for their single egg and have made Natron their biggest breeding ground on the continent.

Of the world's 6.5 million **flamingos**, the **lesser** is most numerous; about four million of them living in the alkaline lakes of the East African Rift Valley. The **greater flamingo**, outnumbered almost 100:1, is readily distinguished by height. The male reaches an impressive 1.4 metres (4.5 feet), while the lesser flamingo grows to a metre (three feet).

Both types are pink with red legs and webbed feet and have the familiar long sinuous neck and unique bill adapted for their food needs. The inside of the mouth is of combined scales edged with stiff hair which serve as an efficient filter. Flamingos suck in water, suspended with fine particles of diatomite and algae, and force it out again by using the tongue like a piston — leaving the food behind to be swallowed.

An additional filter system in the greater

flamingo allows it to feed on molluscs and crustacea as well, while the diet of the lesser flamingo is restricted almost exclusively to diatomite and algae. The amount they eat is staggering, estimated at 66,040 tonnes a year for a million birds. The filter is so efficient that little if any alkaline water — which could prove fatal — is swallowed. Flamingos drink at springs and freshwater inlets.

On less alkaline lakes the **white pelican,** almost entirely white with black flight feathers, is often seen with another species, the **pink-backed pelican**, distinguished by its smaller size, pale grey plumage, and a head crest.

They mingle with a black-and-white wader who, with a straight long bill and extraordinary vermilion-red legs, is instantly recognizable as the **black-winged stilt**. This is the only other bird apart from the flamingo whose legs are longer in proportion to its body. When parents are disturbed they create a diversion by walking away from the nest dragging an open wing on the ground as if it were damaged.

Several species of stork are frequently seen on Tanzania's lakes and waterways. The distinctive **yellow-billed stork** sports black and delicately hued pink-white plumage, red legs, and down-curved orange bill. It catches fish and frogs with astonishing speed as it stands in the water, its open bill half submerged.

The ugly, unmistakable **marabou stork**, perhaps the most common stork in Africa, is often associated with rubbish tips because of its scavenging habits. It is known to hunt flamingos by stampeding a flock and picking up stragglers.

Migrant **waders** and **plovers** are often seen in the thousands at Manyara. One of the most common is the **ruff** which breeds in Russia. Their breeding plumage is spectacular and elegant but they are seen in their rather dull non-breeding plumage when they winter in Africa.

The resident **blacksmith plover** is obvious from its white crown and distinctive black, white, and grey plumage. It is commonly found on land near water where short grass and muddy shores are present, but can also be seen on cultivated fields.

It is normally silent but becomes extremely noisy when breeding or flying fearlessly at any enemy. Its characteristic metallic cry — something like a hammer hitting an anvil — lends the bird its unusual name.

Coastal areas

During the northern winter sizeable numbers of wading birds can be seen along the coast running in and out with the tide and foraging for food along the water's edge while other birds probe the rock pools. They are mostly waders and plovers that have flown long distances deep into Africa to escape the chilly north.

Africa south of the Sahara is estimated to support as many as 3,750 billion migrants a year. East Africa as a whole receives 159 species, twenty-nine of which are waders or shore birds. Some of the remaining species include **warblers**, **shrikes**, **ducks**, **falcons**, and **gulls**.

European visitors often find the migrant waders difficult to identify because summer and winter plumage differ considerably. Winter plumage tends to be drab while elaborate and colourful summer plumage is donned for the mating season. Identification is further complicated between April and May when some waders change into their summer plumage as they ready themselves for the flight back to their northern breeding grounds.

Although the **greenshank**, a sizeable wader with a slightly up-curved bill, is common to all Tanzania's wetlands, the largest numbers are found at the coast. The **little stint**, the smallest of the wintering shorebirds, arrives early in August from its breeding grounds in Russia, making its way along the eastern Mediterranean.

The **sanderling**, a small dumpy bird

Opposite: Clockwise from top left: Sacred ibis, secretary bird, red and yellow barbet, superb starling, golden weaver, blacksmith plover.

Above: The haunting cry of the African fish eagle is commonly heard near Tanzanian waters.

from eastern Greenland, Siberia and Arctic America, always seems in a hurry, running at breakneck speed as it feeds along the tide's edge.

Other favoured wet habitats at the coast include creeks, tidal inlets, estuaries, and salt pans. Creeks are often lined with mangroves that form dense swamps.

Among the visiting birds is the **great white egret**, a member of the heron family that is distinguished from its close relatives, the **yellow-billed egret** and **little egret**, by its size and facial skin.

Another bird with all-white plumage, the **African spoonbill**, has bare red legs and face. It takes its name from its long, spatulate bill.

With its large head and big yellow eyes, the **water thick-knee**, widespread along the creeks and islands of the coast, is an unusual looking bird. The large eyes help it to see at night when it is active. The thickly wooded coastline also attracts many birds. When indigenous trees are in fruit, raucous brayings and grunts give away the presence of the **silvery-cheeked hornbill** — better seen, perhaps, on Kilimanjaro and Mount

Meru — one of a distinctive group of birds with an unusually large down-curved bill, often adorned with a curious growth on the upper mandible that is filled with spongy bone tissue.

Bee-eaters, slim, attractive birds with long bills and brilliant plumage, are plentiful inland and often along certain parts of the coast, especially during migrations when it is not uncommon to see three species in one tree.

Although the birds have a high immunity to bee venom, they use special eating techniques. Once caught, the bee is taken to a perch, where the bird changes its grip to hold it near the end of its abdomen, where the sting is. The bee's head is then knocked against a branch until all the venom is discharged and the bee is ready to swallow.

The **white-fronted bee-eater**, like other family members, is a fearless bird, readily identified by its brilliant plumage. It breeds in colonies often numbering hundreds. Tunnels are dug almost horizontally into the walls of cliffs, often extending as far as three metres (10 feet). The end is expanded into an oval nesting chamber.

Common along the course of a coastal river or stream, in trees, bushes and reeds, is the ubiquitous **golden palm weaver**, an entirely yellow bird with a bright orange head and black eyes. Its look-alike, the **golden weaver**, has a chestnut head and pale red eyes.

Woodland birds

The **secretary bird**, sole member of its family, is found only in Africa. It is usually seen in pairs from sea-level to 3,000 metres (10,000 feet). This terrestrial bird of prey stands almost one metre (three feet) high and has a wingspan of more than two metres (seven feet). The bird is unmistakable with its grey and black plumage, long legs, black 'plus-fours' and conspicuous crest which can be raised like a halo.

Its life is spent on the ground, looking for insects, rats and snakes. It kills the latter by pounding them on the ground with sledgehammer blows of the feet. To avoid poisonous bites the bird performs like an acrobat, somersaulting and contorting with wings outstretched.

Found anywhere between 400 and 4,600 metres (1,300-15,000 feet), one of the most frequently seen birds of prey in Tanzania is the **augur buzzard**, usually sighted atop a vantage point where it sits for long periods scanning the area below for a meal of rodents, reptiles and insects. It is recognized by its slaty-grey upper parts and entirely white underparts, although about ten per cent are melanistic, with dark or black pigment granules in their feathers. Once in flight you can be absolutely sure it is the augur from its chestnut-coloured tail.

Not long ago the **helmeted guinea-fowl** could be seen in flocks numbering as many as 2,000. In recent years, however, they have been hunted extensively for the pot. They are generally black, though freckled thickly all over with white, and sport a bony crest or horn on their crown. The birds awake at first light with a vociferous dawn chorus, then make their leisurely way to water, eating insects, seeds and roots as they go.

Another plentiful game bird is the **yellow-necked spurfowl** which frequents open bush country, particularly along the edges of forest and woodland. It is about the size of a domestic fowl and has an olive-brown back, cream striations, and dark-brown underparts, with a conspicuous yellow throat. It is not found at Mikumi or the Selous, however, where its niche is taken by the **red-necked spurfowl.**

There are sixteen species of **pigeon** in Tanzania, of which the **speckled pigeon** is the largest. Extremely widespread, it is found between 500 and 3,000 metres (1,600-10,000 feet) in acacia woodlands, on cliffs, and sometimes in houses. It is easy to identify by its brownish back and wings, grey underparts, and marked 'dominoes' round each eye.

The **owl** has developed a number of features as a consequence of its nocturnal habits which make it a highly efficient hunter. The large, round eyes are designed to gather as much light as possible, and the two orbs overlap almost completely, creating binocular vision that enables the hunter to judge distances accurately.

The owl can turn its head almost completely round to scan all directions. Its feathers are velvety soft with furry edges to act as sound-deadening devices and the flight feathers are specially adapted for silent movement. With their extremely acute hearing, owls can pinpoint the origin and direction of any sound. The **Verreaux's eagle owl**, common to woodland, is conspicuously large. When its eyes are closed the upper lids are noticeably pink.

Such attractive families as bee-eaters, hoopoes, and hornbills are also distant kin to the roller, one of Africa's most beautiful birds. The **lilac-breasted roller**, perhaps the most eye-catching of all, is tawny-brown on top, rich lilac on the throat and breast, with the remaining plumage in shades of blue.

When courting, these birds perform stunning aerobatics, carrying out somersaults and rolls which have earned them their name. They can be seen perched in trees and bushes searching for grasshoppers on the ground or on any vantage points, from which to spy for lizards and insects.

The prominent down-curved bill with a

large casque is the most noticeable feature of **hornbills**. Some authorities think the casque acts as a resonance chamber for the bird's call.

The plumage of the largest member of the family, the **ground hornbill**, is generally black and the face and throat red in the male and blue in the female. It is often seen in open savannah country in family parties of two to eight. Hornbills quarter their territory on foot, searching for fruit and berries, insects, small mammals, reptiles, and even birds. They nest in hollow trees and occasionally in small cliff caves.

The hornbill family has another fascinating distinction; when breeding the female **red-billed hornbill** finds a suitable hole or hollow in a tree and then walls herself in with mud, dung, and saliva regurgitated by the male in the form of pellets. The female pats these into the entrance hole until the opening is reduced to a narrow vertical slit and she can no longer leave the nest. Now she settles down to lay three to six eggs, the male continuing to feed her through the small opening.

During incubation the wings and tail feathers of the female moult. As the eggs hatch and the chicks grow, the male works hard to feed the vociferous and demanding family until the female acquires new feathers and breaks out of her prison where the young are half-grown.

The chicks replaster the damaged exit as soon as the mother has left. Now both parents feed the hungry brood until the young are fully grown and ready to break out.

The **Nubian woodpecker** is a short-legged bird with strong feet which — along with its stiff, wedge-shaped tail — enables it to climb trees easily. The bird's long tongue, with its mucus coating, is flicked out to lick sap from trees, or to spear large insects. The strong, chisel-like bill is used for tapping rapid blows into wood for larvae and excavating nest holes.

The **flycatcher** family is made up of medium-sized birds that generally perch on branches and make erratic sorties to catch insects on the wing.

The male **paradise flycatcher**, with its glossy-black chest, neck, and head; blue eye-ring and bill; black flight feathers, and long bronze tail must be the most colourful. In some areas, particularly the coast, it is more common in its white phase when the tail, back, and wings are colourless. Cobwebs are used to build its nest, a small cup made of twigs, grass and lichen in the fork of a tree.

Another attractive member of the family is the **white-eyed slaty flycatcher**. As it lands it is a blend of grey, with a conspicuous white eye-ring.

Less common than the **superb starling**, the **blue-eared glossy starling** glitters with a metallic iridescent green sheen in bright sunshine, but in certain light can appear bluish, violet, or even golden. The yellow-orange eye is characteristic.

Semi-arid lands, bush, and scrub
Despite their seemingly inhospitable aspects, arid areas are home to an abundance of bird life.

The pale chanting **goshawk**, found in dry-bush country of the north, acquired the name because of its melodious call repeated for hours on end during the early breeding season.

The chant is also made on the wing when the pair display by soaring together in circles sixty to ninety metres (200-300 feet) above the ground.

It is pale-grey with bright reddish-orange legs, finely-barred belly, and a white rump. Unlike other hawks, the bird spends much time on the ground, walking with ease and even running to pursue prey such as lizards, frogs, small snakes, grasshoppers and other insects.

Bustards, with their strong legs adapted to terrestrial habitats, are well suited to desert life. The **kori bustard**, the biggest member of the family, is easily identified by its large size and broad wings. Though laboured, its flight is powerful and rapid.

The ornamental plumes of loose feathers on the head, nape, and long neck are used in breeding displays remarkable to witness. When threatened they hide by crouching low. These omnivorous birds take both animal and vegetable matter.

The **spotted thick-knee** — the dry country counterpart of the **water thick-knee** — has the same large eyes indicative of a nocturnal lifestyle.

Thick-knees are habitually watchful, spending the day standing or sitting motionless in shade. Their appearance enables them to 'disappear' into their surroundings and when approached they will flatten themselves on the ground with head and neck outstretched. At night they become active and noisy, especially during the breeding season.

The **sandgrouse** family has a closer affinity to **pigeons** than to any other family. They resemble pigeons in size, but their colouring matches the arid area in which they live, making it possible for them to nest out in the open, generally near a bush. Their diet is entirely vegetarian, consisting mainly of grasses and seeds.

Because they are living in hot, arid lands and eat grain, sandgrouse need to drink at least once and sometimes twice a day. Although when the young are hatched they can feed themselves almost immediately, they must rely on the parents for their water supply.

Flights to water at dawn or sundown often cover up to eighty kilometres (50 miles). These naturally gregarious birds gather in large numbers before flying and are joined by more on the way, producing flocks in the hundreds or even thousands.

They cruise at around sixty-five to eighty kilometres (40-50 miles) an hour on a journey that takes an hour. When they reach the water they quench their thirst within twenty or thirty seconds and are ready to leave immediately.

Males with young chicks to satisfy have a special trick up their feathers; they crouch down in the water and thoroughly soak their belly feathers. They then make a slower journey back to the nest area.

Once home, the male stands upright with his feathers fluffed out and the chicks crouch beneath him drawing the water from his plumage with their beaks. These belly feathers can hold three times as much water as those of other birds and maintain their structure in spite of regular wetting and sucking. The feathers in the female are not so effectively developed.

One of the most common and most photographed birds in East Africa is the **superb starling**, notable for its metallic greenish-blue back, black head, and narrow white band across the breast separating the upper parts from the bright chestnut belly.

Travelling through wooded grassland below 1,400 metres (4,500 feet), the **white-headed buffalo weaver** is often seen, although it does not appear to associate with the buffalo, despite its name.

The bird's nest, an untidy retort-like structure hung from the branch of a thorn tree, is made of thorn twigs for protection and lined with grass or feathers.

There are eighty-nine members of the **weaver** family in East Africa out of a world total of 142. All share the ability to weave nests that are completely enclosed.

Taking a long piece of grass, which they usually place at the tip of a branch, weavers hold one end down with a claw and then, with the beak, work the other end in, out, and over, until a suspended ring is formed.

Now more and more strands are woven in, with the bird standing in the middle of the ring, meticulously working in each piece of grass. The end is finally pulled through and the loose pieces tucked away making a hollow ball.

The elaborate hanging nest of the **vitelline masked weaver**, which is entered from the bottom, contains a partition to prevent eggs from falling out. It is suspended from the end of a slim branch — another safety device against monkeys, snakes, and other predators.

Some weavers build even more elaborate nests with long entrance tunnels hanging vertically to the side. Additional protective measures include building nests close to the homes of stinging insects, large birds, or even people.

A common bird seen in dry country is the **white-browed sparrow weaver**, whose rather loose and untidy nests can readily be seen on surrounding acacia trees. Another member of the family, the **red-naped widowbird**, has an entirely black body with a scarlet crown and nape. The female is much less colourful, being nondescript tawny and buff. After the breeding season, the male moults and loses his handsome tail feathers and colouring. The new feathers are like those of the female and the once attractive male returns to dull mediocrity.

Holub's golden weaver, golden yellow in colour, is usually found in pairs or occasionally small parties. The female places heavy demands on the male, who may have to build up to six large, rough, and loosely woven nests before she expresses satisfaction. Sometimes she will refuse all offerings of a home.

Two exceptions to laws protecting birds are the **quelea** and the **mousebird**, agricultural pests that damage grain and fruit.

The **red-billed quelea**, a member of the weaver family, is entirely colonial in habit, often found in concentrations of over a million. In spite of immense slaughter and large-scale efforts to control them, the crop plague continues.

The **speckled mousebird** is a member of a small family peculiar to Africa. Its body is no bigger than that of a sparrow, but its long tail, made up of ten stiff, graduated feathers, gives it an overall length of thirty-two centimetres (12 inches). The head is topped by a marked crest.

Mousebirds are usually seen in small parties. They have extremely strong feet with sharp claws and the outer toes move forwards or backwards, enabling them to perch, climb, or cling with dexterity.

Grasslands

It is in many, but not all, of Tanzania's grassland areas, that you see the majestic **ostrich**. It measures two to two-and-a-half metres (seven-eight feet) high from the tip of its two-toed claw to the crest of its bald head. It is the largest living bird and although flightless, has powerful legs which enable it to bound up to 1.5 metres (five feet). Its lethal kick is said to bend an iron bar.

It can maintain fifty kilometres (31 miles) an hour for up to thirty minutes. On the run, however, it can seem to vanish abruptly from view for it has the ability to stop in full stride and drop suddenly into a squatting position, extending its neck along the ground. Females are shabby brown with pale edgings to their feathers but the males are more resplendent with vivid black and white plumes on their wings and tail. The adult male stands 2.4 metres (eight feet) and weighs more than 130 kilos (286 lbs).

Eggs average fifteen to sixteen centimetres (six inches) long and weigh up to 1.4 kilos (three lbs). One ostrich egg is equal to two or three dozen domestic eggs and there can be thirty in a nest. Chicks can run almost as soon as they hatch and after only a month can reach a speed of fifty-six kilometres (35 miles) an hour.

Ostrich have tough gullets and voracious appetites and have been known to swallow iron objects including coins, nails and horseshoes.

The **cattle egret** is one of the few bird species that benefits from mankind. The introduction of domestic cattle and the opening up of new grassland has enabled it to expand explosively. In the last sixty years it has migrated from Africa and colonized the West Indies, the Americas and Australia.

Grasslands are also the hunting ground for Africa's big game and attendant scavengers. High above them, hungry birds search for the remains of dead animals.

The majority of these birds — vultures — remain aloft virtually all day, circling slowly and gliding on the rising thermals. Using their keen eyesight they will quickly spot a corpse and plane down to be joined by others. They gorge heavily, feeding to repletion, the distended crop and gizzard being able to hold over 1.5 kilos (3.3 lbs) of food. Thus bloated, the birds find it extremely difficult to take off and have to retire to a secluded spot on the ground to digest their meal.

The largest African vulture, the **lappet-faced vulture**, has a massive bill and bald pinkish head. It is seen most frequently in the national parks. **Ruppell's griffon vulture**, common in some areas, is somewhat smaller. Its dark brown plumage with creamy white edges gives it a spotted appearance.

A predator in its own right is the **black-shouldered kite**, a member of the **hawk**

Above: Conspicuous tuft of straw-coloured feathers on its head makes the crowned crane easy to identify.

family. It is thickset, pale grey above, white below, with black shoulders, a square white tail, and striking red eyes. They combine to make it a beautiful bird of prey with a slow graceful flight. Its food consists of large insects and small mammals, and a plentiful supply may attract these birds in large numbers.

The **black kite**, one of the most familiar and common of the family, is often seen near human habitation in Tanzania up to 3,000 metres (10,000 feet). It is recognizable by its dark brown plumage and markedly forked tail.

Kites have a useful role scavenging for offal and dead creatures and are frequently seen in the mornings searching the highways for animals killed by traffic.

Although **plovers** are usually associated with habitats near the sea, lakes, rivers, mudflats and swamps, the **crowned plover** is a resident and wanderer in grassland up to 3,000 metres (10,000 feet) above sea-level. A handsome bird notable for its black head with a white ring on the crown

(reminiscent of an English schoolboy's cap) it has a white abdomen, pale greyish-brown back, red legs, and a red bill with black tip. Like all plovers it builds its nest in a shallow indentation, quite often unlined, on the ground. Both parents incubate and care for the young, which are ready to leave the nest immediately after their down feathers are dry.

The marking of the chicks provides excellent camouflage. When warned by a parent, they crouch down as the adult bird diverts attention by spreading one of its wings as if injured.

Ground-living **larks** are usually softly coloured birds, but their exquisite song, serving as both courtship and territorial defence, more than compensates. They normally sing from a high perch and prefer open country. An early morning drive through bushland will often reveal a bird on every suitable spot singing its heart out. The **red-winged bush lark** is typical and is frequently seen on the tops of small bushes.

On the open grasslands larks and **pipits**

predominate. Although somewhat alike in appearance, the two families are not closely related. The pipit family consists of graceful, slender birds with an upright stance.

Oxpeckers, known as tick-birds, belong to the **starling** family. The **red-billed oxpecker** provides a good example of typical behaviour, walking about on an animal in the manner of a woodpecker. Its structural peculiarities, especially the stiffened tail and the sharp, curved claws, enable it to move about without difficulty.

It feeds on bloated ticks, but flies, scar tissue, blood and living tissue and the discharge from open wounds on the 'hosts' are also taken. The damage this causes to the hide of domestic animals makes the bird unpopular with cattle breeders.

Garden birds

The unmistakable **African hoopoe** is strikingly beautiful. Its main body plumage is bright pinkish-cinnamon with wings and tail having alternate black and white bars. The erectile crest feathers are again pinkish with black tips, and the black bill has a slightly downward curve.

They nest in a hole, either in a tree, rock, or building. Pairs are often seen on lawns hunting for large insects, larvae, worms, and lizards. Their monotonous call of 'hoop, hoop, hoop' is low and penetrating.

Looking rather like **thrushes** to whom they are related, the **babblers** move around in bushes or on the ground in noisy parties.

The **robin chat**, reminiscent of the **English robin**, has a reddish-orange throat and chest, well-marked white eye-stripe, and a grey belly. It is an excellent mimic of other bird calls and often gives a full concert repertoire. As with other birds, its natural song seems to have territorial and advertising functions. Robin chats, which are rather shy, feed mainly on the ground, but can be relatively tame in gardens.

It is often the unwitting host to a **red-chested cuckoo**, often referred to as the 'rain bird' by locals because its distinct three-note call (Rain Will Come) is most noticeable around the time of the rains. During nest building the chat is kept under close observation by the female cuckoo.

The moment the nest is left unattended the cuckoo sneaks in and deposits her egg, sometimes removing one belonging to the robin chat. The cuckoo egg hatches first and the new chick ejects any other object in the nest — including the eggs or the young of the robin chat.

Host parents, seemingly unaware about their own offspring, feed the large, demanding interloper for the next seventeen to twenty days until it leaves the nest. Even then the foster parents continue to feed the growing cuckoo until it is independent — about another four weeks.

Perhaps the most spectacular of Tanzania's brilliantly coloured **starlings** is the male **violet-backed starling**, which has an iridescent purple back and head.

Sunbirds occupy a similar niche in the Third World to that filled by hummingbirds in the New World. Both groups have long curved beaks, brilliant plumage, and take nectar from flowers, thus helping in their pollination. But the two families have only superficial structural similarities.

Sunbirds are a distinct family with slender, pointed, down-curved bills. The males in most species have brilliant iridescent plumage while the females are generally drab. As they move from blossom to blossom, frequently calling in their sharp metallic voices, the sunbird's flight is rapid and erratic. Besides taking nectar from flowers they eat a large quantity of small insects. Their nests are closed, with a side opening, generally made of grass or fibres and bound together with spiders' webs.

The **waxbill** family is made up of small to tiny seed-eaters, including the **red-billed firefinch**. Because of its tameness and liking for human habitations, the firefinch is perhaps the most familiar bird in Africa. It likes to explore gardens and verandahs with a companion. The female is dull brown with a tinge of red on the tail, but male plumage is entirely pinkish-red with whitish spots on the breast.

Aptly christened an 'animated plum', this waxbill will visit the lawn, picking up minute seeds and small insects, and readily uses birdbaths.

Flora: An International Bouquet

One absorbing facet of Tanzania's indigenous forests is the wide-ranging diversity found within their shady environs. Where forests in Europe and North America have no more than twenty-five species, Tanzania's forests frequently have over fifty, with some of the Eastern Arc Mountain forests hosting many more.

Most contain a mixture of indigenous and non-indigenous trees as logged areas have been replaced with faster growing exotics (indigenous trees taking 200 years to mature).

Besides trees, there are numerous species of shrubs, herbs, grasses, seedlings, ferns, mosses, orchids, lianas, fungi and lichen — a mix determined by the micro-climate that exists beneath the foliate canopy.

On the coast, **mangrove swamps** flourish around the delta of the Rufiji and Kilwa islands in particular. They have great commercial value, for mangrove timber is used as building poles, charcoal, and the bark for leather tanning.

They also play a critical ecological role, filtering the organically rich material carried out to sea by the inland rivers, thus serving as important breeding grounds for various forms of marine life.

Trees
Also found in abundance on the coast is the ubiquitous **coconut**, whose original home remains a mystery. Some authorities believe it hails from Polynesia, while others maintain that it came from South America, then journeyed westwards thousands of years ago drifting in ocean currents across the Pacific to reach the shores of Africa.

Besides providing valuable food and drink through its nut, the coconut palm provides almost everything people need for survival and shelter. The fibre of the husk makes ropes and mats and is used as stuffing for mattresses, the shell of the nut is turned into charcoal, the leaves are used for roofing and weaving baskets and the trunk is used for building houses. The major economic product is the dried flesh of the nut, known as copra, which is processed to yield coconut oil for cooking and coconut meal, a valuable high-protein livestock food.

The indigenous **doum palm** is the only member of this family that grows branches — the long slender stems divide regularly into two, giving the tree its distinctive appearance as it grows to a height of more than fifteen metres (49 feet).

Its three-cornered orangey-brown fruit — the skin of which is edible but not very tasty — is often eaten by elephants, who then disperse its seeds. Traditionally the fruit is used to make buttons and necklaces and the leaves for weaving baskets and mats.

Another palm, widespread throughout Tanzania wherever there is a high water table — and particularly in the hot areas where it thrives alongside streams and swamps — is the **wild date palm**.

Although edible, its fruit is disappointing to taste, but the commercially cultivated variety has a bigger, fleshier and more palatable fruit.

One of the most successful of the East African plant families is the **acacia**. Tanzania has more than forty indigenous species, including the **flat-topped red thorn**, which grows in many parts of the Rift Valley. Its heavy, durable hardwood is used for building bridges, fence posts, pulley blocks and rough farm buildings.

One of the most beautiful of the acacias, found beside streams and lakes throughout the Rift, is the distinctive **fever tree**. With its widespread, flat-topped crown, the tree is easily recognized by its yellow bark. Because of its association with watercourses — where mosquitoes breed abundantly — early travellers who camped in its shade linked the tree with their bouts of malarial fever and thus gave it its common name.

Besides creating shade and beauty, acacia trees serve many functions such as food for goats, material for fencing posts and wood for fuel. They also anchor soil on river banks, adding nitrogen to the earth as they drop their nutrient-rich leaves at the beginning of the rainy season. Because of its resin content, acacia hardwood timber is also a lasting building material and useful for carving and tanning leather. One species yields high-quality gum used in industry.

The **baobab**, with its 'upside-down' look, figures in local legends and African superstitions. It is found in many parts of Tanzania, notably Tarangire National Park below 1,300 metres (4,000 feet). The baobab grows to a diameter of five to seven metres (16 to 23 feet) and can live for many centuries, higher than it is wide.

The rotund, glossy trunk sprouts a crown of thick branches that look more like roots since they are usually bare of leaves. The hollowed-out trunk can store water or is sometimes used for making canoes. The bark fibre will produce ropes and baskets, the leaves and fruit-pulp are used medicinally, and the seeds and leaves are edible.

A familiar plantation tree around Moshi and Mbeya is the exotic **blue gum eucalyptus**. It is fast-growing, loose-rooted and reaches heights of more than 100 metres (330 feet). The blue gum was first introduced to provide firewood for the steam locomotives of the early railways.

Another Australian exotic, the **bottle-brush tree**, owes its name — and beauty — to the many red, sometimes white, flowers draped around its stem like a bottlebrush. The round, button-like decorative fruits of this ornamental tree make it a popular choice for parks and gardens.

The **kapok** (or **silk-cotton tree**) is an exotic from Brazil and reaches close to twenty-five metres (80 feet). It is often confused with its **bombax** look-alike. The seed of the fruit is protected by a cushion of fine cotton-like materal which can be used to stuff cushions, mattresses and toys. Its smooth, green trunk is covered with spines and its flowers, which vary in colour from vivid red to pink, have five petals.

The **Australian flame tree** is glorious when it bursts into fiery colour, rising more than thirty-three metres (100 feet) high.

The magnificent and spectacular **flamboyant** is a native of Madagascar and was first discovered in 1824. Since then it has been introduced to tropical areas all over the world, including the parks and gardens of Dar es Salaam. In Zanzibar it is known as the 'Zanzibar Christmas tree' in full flower each late December.

One of the most memorable and striking of all trees is the **Nandi flame tree**, also known as the **African tulip tree**. It is a deciduous tree that is spectacular when in bloom. Its large orange-red flowers with gold margins, set off against dark green heavy foliage, appear after the start of the rainy season. Buds are filled with water. If punctured, the water spurts out, earning it the nickname of the 'Fountain Tree'.

Imported from the West African jungle, where it was discovered in 1757, the tree was thought to possess supernatural powers — the flowers were used in voodoo ceremonies by witch doctors and the wood for making tribal drums.

The delicate, bell-shaped flowers of the **jacaranda**, an exotic from Brazil, open soon after the 'short rains' between October and November when Tanzanian towns are strewn with a carpet of blue-violet. At its best at higher altitudes it does not grow well at the coast.

Prunus, the quick-growing, deciduous Himalayan bird cherry tree, blossoms twice a year at the beginning of the short and long rains. Its delicate pink flowers are seen in gardens and along residential streets.

A beautiful tree with plentiful clusters of yellow, pea-shaped flowers, the **Pride of Bolivia,** or the **Tipu tree**, is an attractive sight along roads and in parks.

Shrubs

There are more than 200 species of **Acalypha** shrubs, all tropical, with varied foliage ranging from deep-pink, red and brown to various shades of green. They grow more than two metres (seven feet) high and make attractive hedges and border plants.

Opposite: Clockwise from top left: Frangipani, yellow alamanda, bombax, *Impatiens kilimanjari*, moorland thistle, canna.

Despite its name and pretty pink flowers, the **mock azalea**, which grows in the dry parts of the country, is highly lethal. It has a milky sap that is toxic and used as arrow poison.

Yesterday, today and tomorrow, an evergreen from Brazil, takes its name from its dark purple-blue blossoms which change to mauve, cream, and white as they age.

Candle bush, an indigenous shrub growing wild in grassland, scrub and at the edge of forests, is often seen along country roads during the flowering season when its bright yellow petals form dense clusters of upright spikes like a candelabra.

The fast-growing **moonflower**, or **devil's trumpet**, a soft-wood shrub, bears sweet-scented white flowers. But beware, the fragrance conceals the kiss of death. The flower of this common garden plant is extremely poisonous.

From Guatemala, **snow on the mountain** is an easy-to-grow deciduous plant reminiscent of a miniature poinsettia with tiny cream bracts, sometimes tinted rose, completely covering the one- to three-metre-high (three- to 10-foot) compact bush.

As characteristic of Christmas in the tropics as holly is in the northern latitudes, **poinsettia** is widely used for decoration and to illustrate cards and calendars.

Hibiscus, also known as the **Chinese rose**, which originated from China and is probably the world's best-known tropical flower. It is now cultivated throughout the tropics where it produces a host of beautifully coloured flowers, all with prominent yellow stamens and red stigmas.

Christ thorn, which was imported from Madagascar, is perhaps the best-known member of the euphorbias. With its formidable thorns it makes an excellent hedge, growing to about two metres (seven feet) high. It can also be clipped back to edge flowerbeds or allowed to grow into a large, attractive bush covered with red flowers.

There are many species of the butterfly-attractive **lantana** which grow into decorative and attractive shrubs, but one has prickly square stems and is regarded as a dangerous weed. Its small pinkish-purple flowers are quite pretty, but when the fruit — in the form of black berries — is dispersed by birds, the shrub colonizes large tracts.

The cultivated varieties do not proliferate in the same manner and with their orange, yellow or white flowers, they make a colourful addition to any garden.

Found along the coast and in upcountry Tanzania, the **frangipani** or **temple tree**, with its nostalgic fragrance, is perhaps the loveliest of the exotic shrubs of East Africa. It takes its name from the sixteenth-century perfume developed from its flowers by Frangipani, a Roman nobleman.

The white variety, **Plumeria**, a native of the West Indies, is named after the Frenchman who was a pioneer of West Indian botany. The pink-flowered frangipani that comes from Central America now has a wide range of allied colours.

The **fire bush**, an evergreen shrub from Colombia, is also known as **oranges and lemons**. It carries a great profusion of bright orange-yellow flowers.

Yellow bells, also known as **yellow elder**, which was introduced from tropical America, is an attractive ornamental shrub found in many gardens because of its decorative yellow, bell-shaped flowers.

Cape honeysuckle, as its name suggests, originates from South Africa. In full sun and dry conditions it produces a wonderful show of orange-red spikes of flowers in terminal clusters. Because of its climbing habit, it makes an excellent hedge.

Thevetia (yellow oleander) comes from tropical America and has shiny, elongated leaves that are reminiscent of the **oleander**. The attractive lemon-yellow blossoms are in flower most of the year and have a sweet and delicate fragrance. But the plant contains a glycoside in its milky sap and is poisonous.

Climbers

Gloriosa virescens is an extremely attractive lily-like climbing plant that is native to tropical Africa and Asia. Its ostentatious red and yellow flowers are solitary and begin to appear with the advent of the rains. The small plant climbs with long tendrils growing from the tips of its leaves.

If any plant is a symbol of colourful

gardens, it has to be the **bougainvillea**. Found everywhere in Tanzania, this thorny shrub climbs to the top of the tallest tree by its long, sharp spines and is usually seen as a hedge or a garden shrub.

There are scores of different forms and colours of this commonly cultivated plant, creating a fantastic mosaic of colours ranging from deep magenta-purple, through crimson and soft-pink, to brick-red and bronzy-gold, even white. Contrary to popular belief these colours do not come from the flowers but the three large and colourful bracts. The true flowers are quite inconspicuous. The shrub is a native of Brazil, and was first brought to Africa by an eighteenth-century French navigator, Louis de Bougainville, who discovered specimens in Rio de Janeiro.

Golden shower, a native of Brazil and perhaps the best-known of the begonia family, grows freely and blooms in gorgeous clusters of tubular, orange-coloured flowers. They can be seen everywhere — on roofs, hedges, pergolas and even trees. It flowers most of the year and is drought resistant.

Succulents

Sisal, a native of Mexico, is grown commercially on large plantations around Tanga and Morogo. It has elongated, blue-green leaves with sharp spikes at their tips. The name derives from the port in Mexico from which it was originally exported.

Coarse, yellow-white fibre is produced from the leaves when they are crushed. These are made pliable by beating and brushing, and when dry are used in the manufacture of twine, rope, nets, hammocks, and carpets.

Aloes, African members of the lily family, are often grown in gardens as ornamental plants and are found in the wild in a variety of rocky habitats. They are known for their high degree of speciation. New varieties turn up with regularity. Tanzania has many species which flower after the rain.

The juice of the spiny, sharp-pointed leaves has long been used medicinally to relieve burns, insect bites, and other inflammations, and the plant is grown commercially for use in beauty preparations such as suntan lotions.

The **candelabra tree**, a succulent cactus-like tree euphorbia growing as high as fifteen metres (49 feet) in savannah country, sometimes on termite mounds, is extremely common in parts of the Rift Valley. From the short, thick trunk a number of spiny branches spread in a candelabra fashion.

The **prickly pear** often reaches five metres (16 feet). It is a member of the cactus family and its 'leaves' are really stems and branches punctuated with spines and bristles. The yellow to orange flowers turn into edible pear-shaped fruits — after careful removal of the spines.

Above: Unmistakable red-hot poker, with its large, candle-like spikes of tubular red, orange or yellow flowers, is commonly seen at 3,000 metres (10,000 feet) on Mount Kilimanjaro.

Vegetation: An East African Greenhouse

Eastern Africa, including Ethiopia, Somalia, Uganda, Kenya, Rwanda, Burundi, Zambia, Tanzania and Malawi, is bounded in the north and east by the Red Sea and the Indian Ocean. Its western border is marked by the scarps of the Ethiopian massif, the western arm of the Rift Valley, and lakes Mobutu, Edward, Kivu, and Tanganyika. In the south the Zambezi River, the eastern shore of Lake Malawi, and the Ruvuma River also form boundaries.

Though these physical features serve as demarcators, ecologically they are incomplete. Between Lake Mobutu and the Ethiopian highlands no barrier separates Eastern Africa from the vast flatlands of Sudan that extend into West Africa. In the south-west there is no distinct physical or zoological break between Zambia, the Congo, or Angola.

Biologists once looked for stable habitats in Africa. They believed every area had a 'climax' habitat — the mythical point where nature 'balanced'. But it has become more apparent that no such condition exists, except in a few extremes — such as Afro-Alpine zones or swamp forests.

Now evidence points to constant and considerable ecological change. Given Eastern Africa's geological and climatic diversity, with change so persistent, it is best to describe habitats in general terms only. There are thirteen major categories, most of which are found in Tanzania, the only African country to have part of five biogeographical zones.

Lowland rainforest

Lowland rainforests require year-round rainfall of at least 1,100 millimetres (43 inches) and occur no higher than 1,200 metres (4,000 feet) above sea level. Typical inhabitants are *Afzelia* and *Trachylobum* with *Brachylaena* in the drier areas. They are relatively rare in East Africa, forming less than one per cent of the habitats of the region. In Tanzania they only occur in small patches along the coast and on the lower eastern slopes of the Usambara Mountains.

These rainforests have canopies up to sixty metres (200 feet) high, sometimes with secondary and tertiary canopies at the middle and lower levels. Botanically they are the richest habitats; the Usumbaras alone contain more than 2,000 plant species.

Lowland dry forest

These rare forests occur below 1,200 metres (4,000 feet) and receive as little as 760 millimetres (30 inches) of rain annually.

Swamp forest

Swamp forests form a tiny but distinct lowland habitat. Perhaps the largest in Eastern Africa is Sango Bay on the western shore of Lake Victoria. Plants are adapted to having their 'feet' in water. Among these, the most characteristic are the two palms — *Phoenix reclinata* and *Raphia*. Found in many 'gallery' forests — narrow ribbons along river banks — in otherwise unforested country, these draw moisture from the rivers instead of relying upon rainfall.

Montane forest

All forests between the 1,200-metre contour and the tree line at 3,000 metres (10,000 feet) are montane in nature. With cooler temperatures and lower evaporation rates, these elevated forests exist on as little as 635 millimetres (25 inches) of rainfall a year.

Montane forests show great variety. Those in wet regions are richer in species. While those at higher altitudes generally have fewer. In several places — the eastern Usambaras being one — the lowland rainforests merge with montane forests in an unbroken swathe — a feature likely to have once been far more widespread when the ancient rainforest stretched from West Africa to the East African coast.

Today montane forests are overwhelmingly associated with mountains, a result of human settlement. People prefer lower, warmer levels and settle the flatlands and plateaux in preference to high ground and steep slopes.

Above: Rubber plantation thrives in the tropical climate of Pemba, Tanzania's second-largest island.

Montane forests are characteristic of all the larger mountains of Tanzania: Gelai, Kilimanjaro, Oldeani, Meru, Rungwe, the Crater Highlands, Pare, Usambara, Poroto, Uluguru, Livingstone, and Mahale. Relict tufts of forest occur on many lesser hills.

Bamboo zone

In the higher montane forests, at altitudes dominated by *Podocarpus* or cedar (*Juniperus procera*), extensive alpine bamboo is common up to the edge of the tree line at 3,000 metres (10,000 feet).

Though technically a grass, bamboo has the physical properties of forest, growing nine metres (30 feet) high — although individual plants only live for some twenty-five to thirty years before flowering and dying. Bamboo therefore is characterized by patches at different stages of the cycle.

Heath zone

Above the tree line, between 3,000 metres (10,000 feet) and 3,500 metres (11,500 feet), Eastern Africa's mountains support giant heath vegetation. Characteristic is heather and *Philippia* up to five metres (16 feet) high. Drawing moisture from mists and clouds, even where rainfall is limited, it is a sodden and cold habitat losing little to evaporation. Both heather and *Philippia* are festooned with 'old man's beard' and other lichens.

Afro-Alpine moorland

Between the heath and the snow line at around 5,000 metres (16,400 feet) lie the most unusual habitats. Tropical in location only, they are in many ways reminiscent of the sub-Arctic tundra. While subject to the same intense cold at night, daylight hours are spent exposed to the intense Equatorial sunshine.

Kilimanjaro shows this vegetation at its most developed, along with Mount Kenya, the Ruwenzoris on the Congo and Uganda border and, most extensive, on Ethiopia's Bale Mountains. Vegetation in these Afro-Alpine habitats is generally wet, tussocky grassland interspersed with giant senecios, lobelias, and groundsels (See 'Mount Kilimanjaro: Roof of Africa', Part Two).

Above: Brilliant flamboyant, common throughout East Africa.

Woodland

Woodland lacks an interlocking, closed canopy. Trees are sufficiently open for grasses and other sun-loving plants to grow beneath. By far the largest woodlands in Eastern Africa are in the miombo belt of southern Tanzania, Zambia, and parts of western Malawi. The vegetation grows on the infertile soils of old Africa that existed before the rifting and volcanism that created much of the region's relatively high fertility and spectacularly varied scenery. Most trees are deciduous and shed their leaves during the six-month dry season.

This miombo belt is in Eastern Africa's southern, single rainy season zone.

Savannah or wooded grassland

This is the archetypal vegetation of East Africa. In some areas the predominant trees may be *Combretae*, in others *Acaciae* or an African ebony, *Diospyros*. A wide variety of grasses are associated with this most general of habitats, varying with rainfall, soils, altitude and usage. Its salient features are trees, grass and distant horizons. Many savannah plants are adapted to fire. In the miombo woodlands where grasses commonly grow two metres (seven feet) high and sometimes to four metres (13 feet), extensive fires are yearly events.

Thicket and bushland

Cheek by jowl with savannahs are dense thickets and bushland, where low trees and shrubs shade out grasses. As a result fires cannot take hold and the undergrowth is rich in succulents. Visibility is seldom greater than fifty paces, often much less.

Common on hill sides and in rocky places, such habitats are most extensive around the drier edges of the savannah zones. Thickets are widespread along the landward side of the coastal forest belt and also occur in central Tanzania, a notable example being the Itigi Thicket on the Central Line between Dodoma and Tabora, an area dreaded by early explorers of the interior.

Semidesert

All areas receiving between 127 millimetres (five inches) and 250 millimetres (10 inches)

Above: Feathery Spanish moss — or 'Old Man's Beard' — drapes itself around a tree.

of rain a year fall into the semidesert category. It is dominated by short acacia shrubs and *Commiphorae*. This vegetation characterizes the Horn of Africa, of which Somalia is the greater part. Harsh and arid, it is the land of frankincense and myrrh. There are no true year-round semi-arid zones in Tanzania.

Desert

All areas that receive less than 127 millimetres (five inches) of rain a year, or none at all for several years, qualify as true desert. In this most hostile environment plants lie dormant as seeds, only germinating when conditions are right. Then they grow rapidly in order to ensure survival for the next batch of seeds. Poor wildlife habitats, they are used only briefly during their irregular green flushes. In Eastern Africa the only real deserts are the small Chalbi Desert of northern Kenya and parts of northernmost Somalia.

Grassland

Grasslands occur widely in Eastern Africa in any of the areas occupied by the vegetation categories other than desert. But most exist through the influence of man or other animals. The plains of the Maasai Steppe and the Serengeti are a case in point. The growth of thicket and woodland there is only held in check by the high concentration of grazers; any radical change in human activity or animal numbers could see the balance swing back to the perennials.

Tastes of Tanzania

The cuisine of Tanzania can largely be divided into the food of the coast — and the rest.

Coastal food reflects the racial mix of indigenous Africans overlaid by hundreds of years of Arabic, Asian and ultimately Swahili cooking traditions. Rather like a pot that has been simmering for a long time before the herbs and spices are added.

The staple foods of the interior are ubiquitous and nourishing (if not a little bland) and comprise vegetables and cereals such as **maize**, **cassava**, savoury **bananas**, **rice**, **spinach**, **beans** and **peas**. Combined in a number of ways and lightly spiced they are the basic accompaniment to meat or fish.

High in carbohydrates, fibre, protein and vitamins, the food of Tanzania, and East Africa as a whole, is almost completely unadulterated, unprocessed and healthy.

Maize is perhaps the most readily available cereal and is eaten either roasted whole over charcoal — served as a snack food from braziers at the side of the road — or in the home and restaurant as *posho* or *ugali*. The making of *ugali* in rural areas is the preserve of women and is highly labour intensive. Whole maize is turned into flour by women wielding large wooden pestles with which they pound at the kernels in a mortar.

The flour is then slowly cooked with water to produce a heavy grey porridge that is given taste by adding meat or vegetable stew, curried fish, or roasted goat. Using the right hand, the ugali is moulded into a small ball to scoop up gravy and is eaten in one mouthful. In the towns 'instant *ugali*' mix can be bought but, like most convenience foods, the taste and quality is not as good as the real thing.

Maize is a significant proportion of most people's diet, as can be seen by the maize stalks growing on every available plot of land, including road verges.

Among the pastoralists, especially the Maasai, **meat**, **blood** and **milk** from their herds and flocks, supplement a diet so rich in cholesterol and protein it would probably kill a sedentary Westerner in a year. But their active existence — they walk miles every day herding their cattle and goats — prevents them from suffering from the so-called 'affluent diseases' of the heart. After all, how often do you ever see a fat Maasai?

Cattle are only slaughtered for a celebration, when the beef is boiled, portions being reserved for certain age and sex groups, the *wazee* (elders) getting the choicest pieces.

Throughout the country *ndayu* (roasted, young goat) is a popular delicacy, usually served at parties, weddings, anniversaries and birthdays.

Traditionally, the fare of most Africans is built around a breakfast of sweet, milky tea and bread or *mandazi* followed by a lunch and dinner of *ugali*, spinach, *kande*, *kisamuru* (cassava leaves), stew and roast meat.

Although *kande* is often only simple beans and maize, additional vegetables and meat may be added to enhance the flavour. The ingredients follow local tradition. Doughnut-like *mandazi* go well with tea and can be lifesavers on safari.

Most urban Tanzanians come from a rural background and cultivate a smallholding or well-tended vegetable garden that grows most of their produce. Even in Dar es Salaam *biringani* (eggplant), *mchicha* (a leafy green vegetable), *nyanya chungu* (literally translated as 'bitter tomatoes'), some *bamia* (okra or ladies' fingers) and a patch of **pumpkin** are found in virtually every garden — at the expense of flowerbeds and lawns.

With Tanzania's many rivers and lakes, and the 800-kilometre (500-mile) coastline, fish dishes are widespread. The lack of refrigeration in rural areas and transportation difficulties mean that the tasty *tilapia* and *dagaa* — the super-abundant fish similar to whitebait — have to be sun-dried. Boiled in water with coriander, black pepper, chillies, onions and tomatoes, it makes an excellent fish soup. In southern Tanzania, near Lake Malawi, fish is prepared with banana to create the local dish *imbalagha*.

Nile perch is equally tasty but must be consumed quickly as it cannot be effectively sun-dried due to its large size. Perch is a fine fish — sweet, firm and so versatile that it can be adapted to any kind of cooking, Oriental, Mediterranean or European. It is usually served in huge slabs steamed with herbs and butter, or with fresh slivers of green onion and ginger.

Inland, Africans bake or roast the firm white fish, but generally prefer their staples of maize and vegetables served with either fowl or goat, beef or game. Bananas also figure in the local diet. Near Kilimanjaro a mixture of meat soup and the yellow fruit are combined in a sauce known as *mtori*.

River dwellers enjoy the small **catfish** that live in muddy streams. They are smoked, baked and sold on long kebabs, tied nose to tail like German sausages.

North, south, east, or west, the *chapati* is sure to be found. It resembles a large, thin pancake. This flour favourite is used as a utensil, scoop, and sopper of sauces. You can roll it, rip it, or fold it around your food. The plain wholesome flavour complements any meal.

The coast and islands

For fish dishes and varied cuisine the coast cannot be beaten. The choice is vast: **sea perch**, **parrotfish**, **red snapper**, **rock cod**, **kingfish**, giant **crayfish**, jumbo-size **crabs**, **lobsters**, **prawns**, **oysters** and many more.

Asians delicately steam **sea perch** with scallions and ginger, while the Swahili simmer their fish in all manner of spices and flavours — lime and ginger, garlic and coconut milk, tomatoes and onions. They cook **parrotfish** with seaweed and oranges.

A complement to any dish is *pilau*. This tasty concoction is a mixture of rice simmered with such delightful spices as cinnamon, ginger and garlic. The type of meat that the pilau is served with dictates the combination of spices.

Try **tuna** steaks steamed in ginger; **jack fish** baked with limes and garlic; whole **bass** in coconut sauce; **lobster** served in its shell; **chillied smoked octopus** served up in cones of newspaper at the night food stalls of Jamituri Gardens, washed down with fresh pressed **sugar cane juice**. Other delicacies include cubes of **goat** marinaded in garlic and chilli sauce cooked over charcoal and served as **kebabs**, or **lamb curry** with a glass of **Safari beer** on the side. The choice is yours.

Makonde Treasures

Makonde carving is surely Tanzania's greatest art form. It originated with the Makonde people of the southern Tanzania highlands who migrated north from Mozambique. For centuries their figures, carved out of ebony, have played a central role in their ceremonies and even formed their beliefs concerning the origin of man.

According to Makonde legend: 'In the beginning, there was a being, not yet a man, who lived alone in a wild place and was lonely. One day he took a piece of wood and shaped it with a tool into a figure.

'He placed the figure in the sun by his dwelling. Night fell, and when the sun rose again the figure was a woman and she became his wife. They conceived and a child was born, but after three days it died. "Let us move from the river to a higher place where the reed beds grow," said the wife. And this they did.

'Again they conceived and a child was born; but after three days it, too, died. Again she said, "Let us move to yet higher ground where the thick bush grows."

'And once more they moved. A third time they conceived and a child was born. The child lived and he was the first Makonde.'

The importance of the woman is also reflected in the matrilineal structure of their society. Early carvings were based on the mother figure and only later included themes such as life, love, good and evil.

Great Uhuru Railway: An Engineering Marvel

It began as a walk across 1,870 kilometres (1,160 miles) of tough terrain and ended as the showpiece of African railways. That is the history of the now famous Great Uhuru Railway. In between came five years of hard work, technical skill and brilliant engineering which melded together to create the TANZAM or TAZARA railway.

In contrast with Tanzania's Central Line, which crosses flat plateau and infrequent rivers, a railway serving the south from Dar es Salaam to Mbeya and on to Zambia, was a considerable engineering feat.

In addition to the Great Ruaha River several major tributaries of the Kilombero had to be crossed before the ravines and valleys of the Southern Highlands. Nevertheless, with optimism running high, the scheme was officially endorsed.

The motives were not only economic. At the time of Tanzania's independence, landlocked Zambia was dependent upon the ports of South Africa for exporting its principal commodity, copper ore. Socialist Tanzania's new railway could change all that by providing access to the Indian Ocean, and the potential to inflict damage on apartheid South Africa's economy gave President Nyerere another good reason to begin a project both the Germans and British had failed to realize.

Finding no help from Western sources, Nyerere turned to China, a country that could provide extensive (though antiquated) railway engineering expertise and a ready donor of foreign aid to a nation which was embracing a communist social system (See 'History: From the Cradle to Independence', Part One). The loan agreement was signed and after Chinese surveyors spent nine months walking the route from the coast to Kapiri Mposhi in Zambia's copper belt, construction began in 1970. It was the biggest railway project undertaken since the Second World War. Twenty-five thousand Chinese and 50,000 African workers laid 310,000 tonnes of steel rail over 300 bridges, through twenty-three tunnels, past 147 stations, using 330,000 tonnes of cement in the process.

They finished the job ahead of schedule in 1975 and, including locomotives and rolling stock, the bill for the Great Uhuru Railway came to a colossal US$230 million.

The railway crosses some of the most scenically attractive and technically difficult landscapes in East Africa. The train departs Dar es Salaam five times a week, climbing from the coastal strip to run between Mikumi National Park and Selous Game Reserve. Herds of game can be seen from the carriages before they enter the Kilombero Valley to edge around the Kibasira Swamp.

Within the next ninety-seven kilometres (60 miles), between Mlimba and Makambako, the underpowered Chinese diesel engine struggles up the steep 1,220-metre (4,000-foot) climb into the heart of the Southern Highlands, where it crosses the most dramatic feature of the line, the dizzying heights of the Mpanga River bridge.

Dropping away to the south are the Kipengere Mountains, dominated by volcanic Rungwe at 2,901 metres (9,515 feet); to the north, the wide expanse of the Usangu Flats. Finally, after 853 kilometres (529 miles) from Dar es Salaam, Mbeya is reached. From there it is a short ride to the border at Tunduma.

Completion of the line coincided with the oil crisis of the early 1970s. The railway received only the most essential maintenance and fuel was a persistent problem. China's loan has since been rescheduled and the system is now in better shape.

With the changing political scenario in southern Africa in the 1990s, landlocked Zambia no longer had to depend on the northern rail link for economic survival and TAZARA faced competition from the alternative southern rail routes and an ever-increasing threat from road-hauliers. Track rehabilitation goes ahead, funded by the Austrian government and the US$33 million first phase is expected to be completed by the year 2000. Phase two, funded from TAZARA's own resources, is also underway.

Climbing and Trekking Advisory

The rush of excitement brought on by the thought of tackling one of Africa's highest peaks can cause day-to-day practicalities of high-altitude living to be overlooked.

The following information is essentially an outline for the non-mountaineer and includes preparations to be considered *before* boarding the plane to Tanzania. It does not claim to be exhaustive.

Anyone who is reasonably fit and can adjust to high altitudes can climb Mount Kilimanjaro. Each year over 60,000 people reach Gillman's peak, the 'top' of the mountain that is actually 120 metres (394 feet) below the true summit at 5,896 metres (19,340 feet). Climbers range from school children to pensioners.

However, if you are not used to trekking, walk and exercise regularly to prepare yourself for Tanzania's mountains.

Despite preparations you will still feel the effects of cold and altitude, ranging between uncomfortable and fatal. Several layers of thin clothing should be worn rather than one or two thick garments, so that the body can be kept at a comfortable temperature by shedding or putting on clothing when necessary.

Forty per cent of the body's heat is lost through the head — so wear a hat — it will keep your feet warm when two pairs of socks may not! A high-rated sleeping bag with a hood on an insulated mat will cut down heat loss at night.

It has been calculated that active climbing requires about 5,000 calories per day, an impossible amount of food to consume in the same period, so most people who tackle the mountain lose some weight. Nevertheless, try to eat a large quantity of food — preferably carbohydrates for breakfast and protein in the evenings — to combat fatigue.

Altitude can suppress appetite, so eating may become a chore. More important than eating large quantities of food is taking sufficient liquid to prevent dehydration. Even at relatively low altitudes cold produces a low humidity that causes loss of fluid from exposed surfaces. Two litres a day can be lost with ease, adding to the headache that many climbers will experience. To combat dehydration four litres of liquid should be taken at regular intervals.

Reduced oxygen in the air — hypoxia — has three physiological effects on the body, accompanied by an obvious shortness of breath above 3,500 metres (11,480 feet). A chemical is released into the bloodstream that enables more dissolved oxygen to be used by the muscles, the red blood cell count gradually increases (to a maximum after six weeks) and the heart and lungs increase their rate of activity.

This process of acclimatization is the body's reaction to low oxygen and takes time. As much as possible your rate of ascent should be guided by your breathing. An extra night should be spent acclimatizing for every three days of climbing.

The consequences of a rapid ascent can be extremely uncomfortable, not to say fatal. In addition to the normal headache — relieved by aspirin — the symptoms of Acute Mountain Sickness (AMS) include nausea, vomiting, fatigue, insomnia, and swelling of the hands and face. These can be reduced or prevented by descent, resting an extra night, or slower ascent.

A small proportion of climbers may go on to develop High Altitude Pulmonary Oedema (HAPE), or High Altitude Cerebral Oedema (HACE), both potentially fatal. Put crudely, the conditions are waterlogged lungs and waterlogged brain. (Due to the long, slow climb on Kilimanjaro these conditions are not as frequent as on Mount Kenya).

The only 'cure' for HAPE — characterized by a persistent cough and bloody spittle — and HACE — hallucinations, severe headaches and lack of coordination — is rapid and immediate descent, even if this means walking at night.

It is advisable to select well-worn boots

Above: Crossing the highland desert of Mount Kilimanjaro. In this zone nights are below 0°C and daytime temperatures may reach as high as 40°C.

and attend to blisters quickly by covering them with bandages. Wear a sun block with a protection factor of at least six and apply regularly if sweating; ultraviolet radiation at high altitudes, coupled with the reflection of the sun off the snow, can cause unexpectedly fierce and painful sunburn.

Ultraviolet is also responsible for another preventable mountain ailment, the burning of the eye surface known as sun-blindness. This intensely painful and debilitating ailment can be easily avoided by wearing goggles or sunglasses with side-shields.

Do not let these real but largely avoidable hazards put you off climbing Kilimanjaro. Even if you do not reach either of the peaks, the personal satisfaction and challenge of simply being on Africa's highest mountain will be rewarding enough.

What to take

Trekking demands strong, comfortable boots with good soles, although at low altitudes tennis shoes or running shoes are adequate. Higher up good boots are essential and in snow or ice these should be large enough to allow for one or two layers of heavy woollen or cotton — never nylon — socks. Take several pairs. Wearing light shoes or sneakers after the day's walk will help to relax your feet.

Loose fitting trousers, hiking shorts or, for women, wraparound skirts are ideal. It is better to wear two light layers of clothing than a single thick one. At very high altitudes wear thermal underwear.

Your pack should be as small as possible, light, and easy to open. The following gear is recommended: Two pairs of woollen or corduroy trousers or skirts; two warm sweaters; three drip-dry shirts or T-shirts; ski or thermal underwear; at least six pairs of woollen socks; a pair of walking shoes; an extra pair of sandals; light casual shoes or sneakers; woollen hat; gloves or mittens; strong, warm sleeping bag with hood; a thin sheet of foam rubber for a mattress; padded anorak or parka; waterproof cagoule, preferably Goretex; sunglasses;

Above: Last chance for water before the assault on Kibo begins.
Overleaf: Tropical winter wonderland: the permanent ice fields of Mount Kilimanjaro account for approximately one-fifth of all the natural ice in Africa.

toilet gear; towels; medical kit; water bottle; and a light day pack. It is better to carry too many clothes than not enough. Drip-dry fabrics are best. Your medical kit should include pain killers (for high-altitude headaches); mild sleeping pills (for high-altitude insomnia); streptomycin (for diarrhoea); septram (for bacillary dysentery); tinidozole (for amoebic dysentery); throat lozenges and cough drops; ophthalmic ointment; one broad spectrum antibiotic; alcohol (for massaging feet to prevent blisters); blister pads; bandages and elastic plasters; antiseptic and cotton; a good sun block and a transparent lip salve.

In addition to these you should carry food, a torch, candles, lighter, pocket knife, scissors, spare shoelaces, string, safety pins, toilet paper, and plastic bags to protect food, wrap up wet or dirty clothes and carry your litter.

Do not assume that you will be able to buy any of this equipment in Tanzania. You can certainly buy your tent and photographic equipment more cheaply at home. It is also wise to carry high-energy food such as nuts, chocolate and dried fruit. You may be tempted to take whisky, brandy, or vodka for a warming night-cap. But be forewarned that altitude depresses the appetite for alcohol as well as food.

Cooking and eating utensils are normally provided by the trekking agency and are carried by the porters.

Lock your bag against theft or accidental loss. And make sure you have plenty of small currency notes for minor expenses along the way.

Water is likely to be contaminated below 2,900 metres (9,500 feet), so do not drink from streams no matter how clear or sparkling they look. Chlorine is not effective against amoebic cysts. All water should be well boiled or treated with iodine: add four drops per litre and leave for twenty minutes before drinking.

THE IMPALA HOTEL
and
CLASSIC TOURS & SAFARIS

Sheer comfort, pure luxury

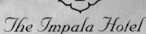

The Impala Hotel

Located in a garden setting surrounded by colourful flowers and natural landscape, Arusha's Impala Hotel is an ideal base for businessmen, convention participants and tourists. With 109 well-furnished rooms, two junior suites, 16 executive suites, four deluxe suites and two presidential suites, the Impala Hotels offers gracious living at its best.

Great safaris, unlimited adventure

And from the comfort of the Impala Hotel our sister company can whisk you to anywhere in Tanzania. The country's number one safari operator has a fleet of spacious and durable safari vehicles equipped for your comfort and pleasure; from the Serengeti in the north-west to the Selous Game Reserve in the far south-east; from the breathtaking heights of snow- capped Kilimanjaro to the turquoise lakes of the Great Rift Valley.

CLASSIC Tours & Safaris

For further information contact: PO Box 7302 Arusha, Tanzania
Tel: 255-57-2398, 2962, 7083, 8448-51 • Hot lines: 255-57-3453, 3782 • Direct Lines: 7197, 7394
Telex: 42132 TOURS TZ • Fax: 255-57-8220, 8680
E-mail: impala@cybernet.co.tz/E-mail: impala@eoltz.com

THE IMPALA HOTEL and CLASSIC TOURS & SAFARIS

In a different world we make a world of difference

PART FOUR: BUSINESS TANZANIA

The Economy

Among professional economists the consensus would be that President Julius Nyerere's embrace of African socialist economics throughout the late 1960s and 1970s brought the country to its current position — a troubled financial state.

In the early 1980s the United Nations listed Tanzania as the second-poorest country in the world. Only Bangladesh was poorer. Now Tanzania's ranking is better — in the bottom twenty-five — but an overall look at the country's economy leads one to believe this is partly due to other developing countries falling even further behind.

It would be easy to say that the situation is wholly Tanzania's 'fault'. But countries do not exist in isolation and external influences have had a strong hand to play in the fortunes of Tanzania.

Nyerere's track record should not be judged too harshly and his aims — broadly to lift his people out of ignorance, poverty and disease, encapsulated in the Arusha Declaration of 1967 — have experienced a measure of success.

He inherited a post-colonial legacy of serious underdevelopment. The ravages of the East Africa campaign of 1914-18 — the only active African theatre of war during the First World War — fought almost entirely within what was to become Tanzania, left the people starving and the economy in tatters.

The war only served to compound the effects of a German administration that had never been able to win significant financial backing for development from the fatherland. German East Africa was not only expected to be self-sufficient but, as a territory, preferably make a contribution to the German economy. It was not to be.

At the close of the war Britain was left with a Trust Territory mandated under the terms of the League of Nations. Tanganyika Territory, as it was officially known, was the poor relation of Britain's East African empire. White settlers were not attracted to the country as they were to Kenya, with its policy of active white settlement, and the country's ample resources remained largely untapped.

The effects of the Great Depression hit Tanganyika as hard as any other country under colonial rule, the only crumb of comfort being that it perhaps had less to lose. Nevertheless the small economic growth that had been enjoyed under the British came to a standstill and was not to recover until sisal and cotton became a commodity in demand during the Second World War.

The economy blossomed in the war years as Tanzania's products were sold around the world to make uniforms. Fortunately the war ended, but unfortunately with peace came another period of stagnation. British attentions were elsewhere and the country's natural resources — with the exception of sisal — were seriously neglected.

At independence in 1961 Nyerere was dealt few cards with which to play the economy. It was not a winning hand.

By 1970, 1,200 *ujamaa* villages comprising eleven million people — almost half the population — had been registered under a scheme where collective production and self-reliance were the watchwords. Western business practices and trading links were abandoned. The country's principal trading partners — Britain, Kenya, and Japan — no longer monopolized imports and Tanzania began dealing with the European Community, the United States, and most significantly — China.

On the twentieth anniversary of independence Nyerere made a speech in which he tacitly admitted that twenty years of agrarian collectivism — the linchpin of his *ujamaa* socialist plan — had not worked. (See "History: From the Cradle to Independence", Part One.)

The model of *ujamaa* was based on the Chinese Communist system of a village-based economy. Their political bonding was strengthened when China built Tanzania the Great Uhuru Railway — still being paid for — when other (Western) backers had declined to help either financially or materially. (See "Great Uhuru Railway", Part Three.) Large aid donors like the United States may well have been reluctant to give assistance to a country that was avowedly socialist. The United States was not alone in its attitude and Tanzania received virtually no Western aid during the decade after independence.

Nyerere's cause was not helped by world events, particularly in the 1970s. The OPEC oil crisis raised the fuel bill to the point where oil and petrol were in serious short supply and some railways ceased to run. In Dar es Salaam during 1977 no petrol could be sold between Thursday evening and Monday morning.

Drought and partial famine hit the country several times during this period and the export of traditional cash crops — coffee, tea, cotton, cashew nuts and sisal — was seriously diminished.

In 1977 the East African Community acrimoniously collapsed. This trading coalition between socialist Tanzania, capitalist Kenya, and militaristic Uganda began strong during its initial days of the '60s, but differing political outlooks made the mismatched union a volatile affair. With the dissolution Kenya seized most of the community's assets and in response Nyerere closed the border. Only then was the financial contribution to the Tanzanian tourist economy from Kenya fully appreciated.

Perhaps the most serious setback of all was the war with Uganda, which cost the country an estimated US$500 million and brought about near bankruptcy. (See "History: From the Cradle to Independence", Part One.) Despite verbal international support for Tanzania's actions against Amin's regime, the country did not receive a single dollar of financial assistance.

For a country that began from a base of absolute poverty and which has few, if any economic buffers, the financial shocks of the 1970s were almost terminal.

Faced with popular discontent over the fundamentals of *ujamaa*, which included forced relocation of some villages and a deteriorating economic situation, Nyerere was forced to modify his policies and adopt a more liberal economic approach, culminating in the Economic Recovery Programme of 1985.

Popular with the International Monetary Fund and other donors, the ERP was seen by many as a relaxation of staunchly socialist economic policies. Soon the aid money and loans began to flow. By the late 1980s the country was the second-largest recipient per person of non-military aid in the world. The ERP was largely responsible for pragmatic measures to boost productivity and stimulate the private sector, such as devaluing the shilling, relaxing import restrictions, and enabling businesses to obtain foreign exchange. The effect of these initiatives on economic recovery since 1985 has been dramatic, not least the contribution the tourist industry has made to the treasury. (Tanzanian tourism is set to explode as Kenya approaches its saturation point.)

There have been hiccups. In 1987 the cotton crop doubled from the previous year to 400,000 bales, but the agricultural and transport infrastructure was in such disarray after years of neglect that the crop could not be exported to the markets.

Additionally, a cautious path must be taken between the hard-liners and the out-and-out capitalists, and there have been few united solutions to the problem of the economy.

Nevertheless, Tanzania remains true to its socialist principles and is a loud voice among the countries which believe that the IMF and the World Bank should take greater account of the social implications of large long-term loans, itself saddled with a vast national debt.

The future is uncertain but, with Tanzania's abundant natural resources — gemstones, gold, gypsum, kaolin, fossil fuels and wildlife — the prospects are better than ever before.

As one recent external survey concludes: "With proper planning and thoughtful development, the country has enormous potential."

Agriculture

Throughout Tanzania's history, agriculture has been the mainstay of the economy. It contributes fifty per cent to the Gross Domestic Product, employs about eighty per cent of the population and earns the country three-quarters of its total foreign exchange.

Many problems face this crucial segment of the economy; the most important being the downward spiral in world commodity prices coupled with a crumbling infrastructure. Years of neglect have led to dilapidated plantations; obsolete processing equipment; a lack of storage; and inadequate roads, trucks and spare parts to move the crops when a market is available.

Tanzania's main crops are coffee, cotton, sisal, tea, tobacco, cloves (Zanzibar), cashew nuts and pyrethrum. Recently, poor world demand and distribution problems have converted farmers to subsistence crops: maize, cassava, bananas and plantains.

A revival of the agricultural industry has been given top priority under the Economic Recovery Plan, and by 1988 the government claimed that supplies of fertilizers, hoes, machetes and pesticides were sufficient to meet demand.

Sisal, one of the country's former foreign currency producers, has once again met with renewed interest in the world market and Tanzania is well placed to benefit. In 1987 the country witnessed the first reversal in production decline since the early 1970s, following the nationalization of many of the big estates.

The growing of cashew nuts, one of the few commodities that saw a price increase during the late 1980s, is also recovering and production levels continue to rise.

Tobacco is also on the upswing, but still falls short of production a decade ago. Overall, however, domestic food production has continued to increase.

Industry

Beset by an acute shortage of raw materials, spare parts, and expensive and unreliable power, water, and transport, Tanzania's industrial sector has many difficulties to surmount in the coming years. The state-owned companies — textile mills, flour mills, breweries, canning factories and other manufacturing industries — operate at less than fifty per cent of their capacity.

Through the ERP programme, agricultural industries — farm equipment and tyre manufacturers — have posted impressive increases, but the improvement has been slow to reach the rest of the sector.

During the late 1980s Tanzania's overall industrial contribution to the economy continued to increase and today accounts for about eight per cent of the GDP.

Mining

Minerals account for less than one per cent of the Gross Domestic Product, of which about eighty per cent is derived from the Mwadui diamond mines in the Shinyanga region. Efforts are being intensified to extract more benefit from Tanzania's considerable reserves of varied gemstones, gold, gypsum, kaolin and fossil fuels, although mining has yet to attract any large-scale investment.

International companies are exploring on- and offshore for oil and natural gas. Substantial gas reserves, which are said to be of great economical value, have been discovered near Songo Songo Island, 190 kilometres (118 miles) south of Dar es Salaam.

Marine
This is another area of potential development that is not being fully utilized. The country's numerous lakes, rivers and the Indian Ocean provide ample fish to generate much needed foreign exchange, but to date, only a few individual small-scale industries, along with the Tanzania Fisheries Corporation (TAFICO), export prawns and lobsters.

Tourism
Many economists argue that tourism could become the leading sector in the Tanzanian economy. Great efforts have been made to protect the natural beauty and wildlife of the country, but little has been done to develop tourism. The shilling's depreciation and an expansion of hotel accommodation in the northern game parks has enabled tourism revenue to rise since the 1980s, but Tanzania's potential to attract visitors remains largely untapped.

The marketing and promotion of tourism — the responsibility of the state-owned Tanzania Tourism Board (TTB) — is being urgently promoted and its development encouraged. The board own fifteen hotels and lodges in the north and along the coast. TTB is in the process of negotiating with international and local organizations to construct more hotels and lodges.

Transport
Transportation has topped the priority list for funding from the recent influx of aid, due to its importance in getting agricultural exports moving. After a virtual seven-year freeze on the importation of commercial vehicles, Tanzania received 1,530 lorries in 1986 and 1,040 in 1987.

A five-year government programme to upgrade core routes in agricultural areas has drawn considerable interest from potential donors. The United States recently made its first major cash contribution (US$12 million) to the government to be used for transportation improvement.

Extensive repairs to the railways are also in progress, with a Canadian and British consulting team completing a US$960,000 development study in 1988.

Workforce
According to 1996 estimates, the total population of Tanzania is 29 million. The mainland has 28.2-million people, while Zanzibar has 801,000 million. The size of the labour force is currently estimated at about ten million, out of which one million are registered employees (wage and salary earners).

Investment

Tanzania is endowed with a wide range of resources offering considerable economic potential. The country has extensive areas of arable land and unique tourist attractions. Its locational advantage within the countries of the Southern African Development Coordination Conference (SADCC), Preferential Trade Area (PTA), and East Africa, all provide additional opportunities for economic expansion.

However, economic performance and growth have not been commensurate with the available economic potential, in part because of foreign exchange constraints and slow growth in domestic and foreign investments.

In response, on 19 June 1990, the Tanzanian government established the National Investment (Promotion and Protection) Act. The strategy of this policy is to create an environment that will attract and promote both local and foreign investments of public and private ownership. Through new legislation the government hopes to address the problems of economic dependence and under-development, to promote rapid economic growth and to increase employment opportunities, while ensuring an improved standard of living for the people of Tanzania.

The principal objectives of the National Investment Act are as follows:
- Maximum mobilization and utilization of domestic capacity, including cooperation with other developing countries
- Maximization of external resource inflows from industrialized countries to supplement national efforts.

The specific economic objectives the government hopes to further through local and foreign investment are as follows:
- Maximum utilization of the nation's natural and other resources
- Maximize foreign resource inflows through export-oriented activities to complement domestic resources
- Encourage non-debt-creating foreign investment
- Achievement of identifiable and substantial foreign exchange savings through efficient import substitution activities
- Increase food production
- Provision of services or the production of goods which improve linkages among various economic sectors
- Promotion of balanced and equitable growth throughout the country
- Enhancement of economic cooperation and development within Eastern and Southern African Sub-region.

Investment Promotion Centre

To oversee and regulate this ambitious new investment policy, the Tanzanian government has established the Investment Promotion Centre. The IPC acts as both a promotional agency as well as a focal point in the country for mobilizing local and foreign investors. As a "one-stop" centre it should facilitate the speedy acquisition of all the necessary permits, land leases, licenses, bank clearances and other infrastructural services necessary to businesses. Some of the other services offered by this invaluable organization include:

- The collection, compilation and dissemination of information on investment opportunities in Tanzania
- Assist, where appropriate, in the identification of local partners for foreign investors
- Identify and advise potential investors on possible areas of investment and provide them with available feasibility reports and market studies
- Organize promotional activities such as seminars and exhibitions, both in Tanzania and abroad, in order to stimulate local and foreign investments
- Liaise with Tanzania Missions abroad in order to publicize Tanzania's investment prospects overseas and to disseminate information on investment opportunities in Tanzania
- Act as a link between local inventors and possible investors or manufacturers
- Liaise with the similar institution in Zanzibar.

Local and Foreign Investors

During the post-independence period, private local and foreign investment have played important roles in the development of the economy, including participation in jointly-owned enterprises.

With the exception of a few economic activities reserved for the public sector, local and foreign investors will have, as far as possible, equal access to all other priority investment areas and will enjoy comparable incentives under the new Investment Promotion Act. In line with the overall development objectives of the country, this policy is expected to stimulate local and foreign investors individually or in partnership, either with the government or with other private investors.

The government welcomes local and foreign investors in the following areas:

- Agriculture and livestock development
- Tourism
- Natural resources
- Mining and petroleum development
- Construction
- Transport
- Transit trade
- Computers and other high technologies.

This list is not necessarily exhaustive and may be amended as appropriate by the government as advised by the IPC.

In order to accord appropriate preference to local investors, the following areas have been exclusively reserved for Tanzanian citizens:

- Retail or wholesale trade
- Product brokerage
- Business representation for foreign companies
- Operation of public relations businesses
- Operation of taxis
- Barber shops, hairdressing and beauty salons
- Butcheries
- Ice-cream making and parlours.

Foreign investors are also excluded from undertaking the following listed activities when their employed capital remains less than US$250,000:

- Travel agencies
- Car hire services
- Bakeries, confectioneries and food processing for the local market
- Tailoring of garments for the domestic market
- Manufacture of leather goods for the domestic market
- Building repair and decoration units
- Manufacture of house and office furniture for the domestic market.

Public Investment

Investments large enough to qualify for the application of incentive packages under the National Investment Act which are in the following areas of major economic importance will normally be reserved for public investment or joint public and private enterprises:

- Iron and steel production
- Machine tool manufacture
- Chemical fertilizer and pesticide production
- Airlines.

The following areas of strategic importance are reserved exclusively for investment by the public sector, although special licenses may be granted:

- The manufacture, marketing and distribution of armaments and explosives of all types
- The generation and distribution of electricity in urban areas or through the national grid
- The provision of public water for domestic and industrial purposes
- The building and operation of all railways
- Radio and television broadcasting
- Postal and telecommunications services (but not necessarily the production of equipment and accessories)
- Insurance and assurance services
- Banks.

Incentives

Investment Priorities

The Tanzanian government recognizes that the basic economic problems facing the country are a result of overall economic and technological underdevelopment. To enhance the nation's efforts in addressing the core causes of underdevelopment, both local and foreign investment are accorded top priority where:

"Products, commodities, or services produced will improve the balance of payments position by significantly increasing the foreign exchange earnings through exports or reducing Tanzania's reliance on imports.

"Such investments will improve the technological capabilities, including managerial skills, with adequate and appropriate safeguards against environmental degradation."

The government has also designated certain areas in Tanzania as special growth centres for development purposes. In addition to the global incentives offered investors under the National Investment Act, approved enterprises located in a growth centre will qualify for an extra incentive package. In order to hasten the development of Dodoma as the proposed new capital of the country, Dodoma Municipality is the first Designated Special Growth Area.

Guarantees to Investors

The government recognizes the importance that investors attach to the protection of investments and to both fair and stable opportunities and predictable treatment. In this light, it undertakes to maintain a legal framework that gives due guarantee of protection to investments in Tanzania, whether of domestic or foreign origin. Contractual and property rights are protected under the Tanzania legal system and fundamental principles on which the Constitution of the United Republic of Tanzania is based. In accordance with the Tanzania Constitution, each person has the right to receive from society the protection of life, freedom and lawfully acquired property, as confirmed by the following sections of the Constitution:

(1) *Notwithstanding the provisions of any other law to the contrary, every person shall have the right to own private property and to receive protection of lawfully acquired property.*

(2) *Without prejudice to provisions of clause (1) of this article, it is hereby prohibited to expropriate or acquire for the purpose of nationalization or any other purpose, private property lawfully acquired without due process of a law providing for payment of full and fair compensation.*

In addition, Tanzania, according to the National Investment Act, will join the International Centre for Settlement of Investment Disputes (ICSID), the Multilateral Investment Guarantee Agency (MIGA), as well as other relevant international agencies, for the purpose of consolidating guarantees and confidence to private investors.

Getting Started

Company Registration

All documents, forms and information regarding establishment of a local or foreign-owned company can be obtained through the Investment Promotion Centre, PO Box 938, Dar es Salaam, Tanzania.

Partnership

Private investment is welcome whether domestic or foreign in origin. Joint ventures between local and foreign investors (public and private) are also encouraged. The Tanzania government does not impose any pre-determined proportion of equity holding between local and foreign investors. Accordingly, the extent of a local investor's participation in foreign funded projects is determined through negotiations between relevant investors. The government, in particular, encourages joint ventures between the following groups:

- Foreign investors and local cooperative or parastatal organizations
- Foreign investors and local private investors
- Domestic private investors and local parastatals and or cooperative organizations.

Foreign Exchange Benefits

The government will continue to expand on the current foreign exchange incentives, including:

- Maintenance of foreign exchange retention schemes to be used by exporters of goods from Tanzania to pay for the importation of approved inputs
- Preferential allocation of foreign exchange funds to manufacturers of exports and import substituting items
- The servicing of term loans and dividends through export retention funds.

Land

Land is owned by the government and can be leased on a short, medium or long-term basis. In certain cases, land under lease may be sub-leased. Village land is not available for commercial activities, except by the village itself, or for joint ventures with the Village Government or the village's Cooperative Society. Similarly, village land may be sub-leased by the village for small or medium scale, private or public economic activities. It should be emphasized that there are extensive areas of arable land outside designated village land that are still available for lease by private or public investors.

Finance

The government of Tanzania attaches great importance to the creation of an appropriate domestic banking environment that offers a broad range of financial services expected by, and normally available to, competitive investors. Towards this objective they have commissioned a major study of the financial system in the country. The findings of the study should pave the way for corrective measures to be implemented regarding the current monetary and banking system, in order to provide competitive and efficient specialized services such as the financing of foreign trade as well as investment promotion and analysis. Bureaux de change now exist in many places.

The following is a list of current facilities:

- Bank of Tanzania
- Standard Chartered Bank
- National Bank of Commerce
- People's Bank of Zanzibar
- Tanzania Investment Bank
- Cooperative and Rural Development Bank
- Tanzania Housing Bank
- Tanganyika Development Finance Company Limited
- Post Office Saving Bank
- National Insurance Corporation Limited
- National Provident Fund
- Karadha Company Limited
- National Development Credit Agency
- Government Employees Provident Fund
- Public Trustee Reserve Fund
- East African Development Bank.

Taxation

The government recognizes the importance of effective incentives in mobilizing appropriate local and foreign investments. According to the National Investment Act the following categories of incentives will be made available:

Corporate Taxation
In the case of initial investments there will be a tax holiday applicable on profits for up to the first five years of production. Thereafter, the corporate tax applied will be fifty per cent on taxable profits from non-residents' investment projects; forty-five per cent on taxable profits from residents' investment projects.

Taxation of Cooperative Societies
Incentives will also be extended to investing cooperative societies registered under the Cooperative Societies Act of 1982. They will qualify for a tax holiday in the same manner as corporate investors. However, after the tax holiday, taxation rates applicable on their approved investments will be 22.5 per cent.

Personal Income Taxation
Sole proprietors whose investments have been approved by the IPC will enjoy a similar tax holiday for the first five years of production. However, the tax rates applicable after the initial five-year tax holiday shall remain as specified in the Income Tax Act of 1973 which makes provisions for the charge, assessment and collection of income tax.

Under the Income Tax Act individual rates of tax are based on a progressive scale with a maximum marginal rate of tax at fifty per cent on a monthly income of 20,000 Tanzania shillings or more.

Dividends
The current rate of twenty per cent for non-residents and ten per cent for residents shall be reduced to ten per cent and five per cent respectively. Dividends shall be governed by the Companies Act of 1972, which regulates the distribution of profit and cash flow of certain boards and corporations, and makes special provisions relating to companies.

Royalties
To encourage innovation and transfer of appropriate technology, withholding tax rates on royalties on imported technology shall be reduced from thirty per cent to twenty per cent on the gross amount payable, while an incentive arrangement applicable for domestic-based technology will be worked out.

Interest
In cognisance of the current international move to reduce the burden of foreign debts and the massive transfer of resources externally, the government encourages investment in equity rather than loan capital. In this regard, so as to minimize the incurrence of foreign debts, the Withholding Tax rates on interest payable on foreign loans shall remain at twenty per cent.

Tax on Expatriate Salaries
All expatriate are required to pay tax on income earned in Tanzania, with the exception of those who come under special agreements with the Government.

Indirect Taxation
Indirect taxes in Tanzania include customs duties, sales tax and excise duty. These taxes on imported items are in line with those imposed by many developing countries and would generally not exceed sixty per cent in each case on most imported items of interest to investors. However, in order to encourage investments in the priority areas the government has introduced numerous concessions, providing either for customs duty-free imports, or for the refund of duty and sales tax on certain imported goods and, in some instances, for the refund of domestic sales tax and excise duty.

Capital Gains Tax
Capital Gains Tax is chargeable on capital gains arising from the sale of real property. The rate of tax varies from twenty per cent on a gain of 500,000 Tanzanian shillings, to thirty per cent on gains exceeding 1,000,000.

Comprehensive information about tax issues can be obtained from the Commissioner of Income Tax, PO Box 9131, Dar es Salaam, Tanzania; or the Commissioner of Customs and Sales Tax, PO Box 9053, Dar es Salaam, Tanzania.

PART FIVE: FACTS AT YOUR FINGERTIPS

Visas and immigration requirements
Visa requirements are reciprocal, in that visas are required by citizens of countrieswhich require visas from Tanzanian citizens. As these are liable to change visa information should be obtained from the relevant Tanzanian Diplomatic Mission.

Health requirements
Visitors from countries infested with cholera and yellow fever must display international certificates of vaccination against these diseases. Mosquito control has reduced the risk of malaria, but it is advisable for visitors to begin taking a prophylactic two weeks before their date of arrival.

International flights
Among airlines serving Tanzania are Aeroflot, Air Botswana, Air France, Air Tanzania, Air Zimbabwe, British Airways, EgyptAir, Ethiopian Airlines, Gulf Air, Kenya Airways, KLM, Lufthansa, Royal Swazi, Swissair and Zambia Airways. There are frequent services to Dar es Salaam and a limited number to Kilimanjaro International Airport. Dar es Salaam Airport is sixteen kilometres (10 miles) from the centre of the city.

Air fares
The usual range of fares is available: business and economy class; excursion fares, bookable anytime for stays of between fourteen and forty-five days; and Advance Purchase Excursion (APEX) fares bookable one calendar month in advance. The price of the cheaper APEX fare varies according to the season, with June to September and December to January considered the 'high' seasons. You can make stopovers en route with all fares except APEX. Reductions are available for children.

Departure tax
As of January 1992, the airport departure tax was US$20, payable in hard currency. Traveller's cheques are not acceptable.

Customs
Besides personal effects, a visitor may import duty-free spirits (including liqueurs) or wine up to one litre; perfume and toilet water up to half a litre; tobacco (up to 200 cigarettes or 50 cigars or 250 grammes of tobacco) tax free but must only be possessed by individuals over sixteen years of age.

Arrival by rail
The sole point of entry into Tanzania by rail is from Kapiri Mposhi in Zambia on the TANZAM/TAZARA Railway. The line travels from the Zambian mining town to the border towns of Nakonde/Tunduma before passing through Mbeya en route to Dar es Salaam.

There are usually two trains a week running in each direction. The schedules are unreliable due to the poor condition of the line and should be confirmed prior to travel. First, second and third class (not recommended) cars are offered. Dining is only rarely available. Expect full immigration and customs checks when crossing the border.

Arrival by water
Tanzania can be reached by way of Lake Tanganyika, Lake Victoria and the Indian Ocean.

The MV *Liemba*, one of the world's oldest operating steamships, runs scheduled services from Burundi and Zambia across Lake Tanganyika to Kigoma once a week. Delays can be up to twenty-four hours. First, second and third class (not recommended) compartments are available. Meals may be purchased on board.

On Lake Victoria, the MV *Victoria*. Services the ports of Bukoba and Mwanza. Smaller ferries service the other lake ports carrying cargo and passengers.

Dar es Salaam, Tanga, Mtwara, and Zanzibar are served by various ocean-going freighters and passenger liners. There are also two leisure cruise ships in operation from the Kenya port of Mombasa to Zanzibar and Dar es Salaam.

Arrival by road
All vehicles entering Tanzania must be in possession of a *Carnet de Passage*. All vehicles not registered in Tanzania should carry an approved nationality plate. The overland route from Kenya via the main border posts — Nairobi to Arusha via Namanga; Mombasa to Dar es Salaam via Lunga Lunga — are in good order: the routes from Uganda and Rwanda are not. Entering Tanzania by road, you can expect full immigration and customs checks. A US$60 fee is required for all foreign vehicles to be temporarily imported.

Driving
Driving in Tanzania is on the left-hand side and traffic signs are international. Visitors may drive in Tanzania using a valid international driver's licence provided they register with the Driving Licence Issuing Authority upon arrival.

Car hire
There are car hire companies in Dar es Salaam and the larger towns that offer a small range of vehicles from two-door cars to four-wheel drive vehicles. Some offer a flat weekly rate but most charge a

daily rate, plus mileage, insurance and petrol. Drivers can also be hired. Payment in foreign currency is usually required.

Road services
Tanzania has almost 40,000 kilometres (24,800 miles) of road. Between 3,000 to 4,000 kilometres (1,860 to 2,480 miles) have been tarred, but some deteriorate. The road is good between Dar es Salaam and Moshi. By March 1990 an attempt at restoring and resealing old roads and building new ones was under way. The first 100 kilometres (62 miles) of a new road between Arusha and Dodoma was completed in April 1990. The road to Zambia is very good for most of its length. Elsewhere, heavy rains have turned long stretches of secondary roads into a sometimes impossible challenge.

Domestic air services
Air Tanzania operates regional and domestic flights from Dar es Salaam to Arusha and Moshi (Kilimanjaro Airport), Dodoma, Mwanza, Kigoma, Songea, Mafia, Iringa, Bukoba, Tabora, Tanga, Mtwara/Lindi, Zanzibar and Pemba several times weekly. Light aircraft can be chartered from Dar es Salaam and Arusha.

Public transport
Buses and taxis of varying reliablity and cost are available in most towns. Price is open to negotiation. Often vehicles will only depart when they are full. Payment is in Tanzanian currency.

Trains are cheap, slow and subject to delay. Do not rely upon the timetables. Book your reservations in advance. First, second and third class travel is available; first differs from second only in the number of beds in a compartment, usually two instead of six. Third class is best avoided.

Climate
There are minimal temperature changes throughout the year. Coastal areas are hot and humid, with an average day temperature of 30°C (86°F). Sea breezes make the climate very pleasant from June to September. Two periods of monsoon winds bring most of the country's rain. The 'long rains' are from March to May, the 'short rains' are between October and December. The hottest months are between October and February. The central plateau, 1,200 metres above sea-level, has hot days and cool nights. The hilly country between the coast and Kilimanjaro has a pleasant climate from January to September.

Currency
The Tanzanian shilling is issued in coins valued 1 shilling, 5 shillings, 10 shillings and 20 shillings. Notes are issued in 10, 20, 50, 100, 200, 500 and 1,000 shilling denominations.

Currency regulations
There is no limit to the importation of foreign currency provided it is declared upon arrival

through a currency declaration form. The National Bank of Commerce (Bank of Tanzania) performs all central banking functions, including issuing currency and exchange control. Branches can be found throughout the country.

All offers of foreign currency exchange are against the law and should be avoided. Tanzanian currency cannot be imported or exported and any surplus, up to a maximum of 4,000 shillings, should be reconverted against your currency declaration form and bank exchange receipts before departure. Visitors to Zanzibar are required to pay for any services in foreign currency.

Banks
Branches of the National Bank of Commerce or their authorized dealers can be found in all large towns and most operate a bureau de change. Hours of business: Monday-Friday, 08.30-12.30; Saturday, 08.30-11.30. Standard Chartered Bank, Stanbic Bank and Kenya Commercial Bank have offices in Dar es Salaam.

Credit cards
Major credit cards are accepted at the larger hotels around the country. Otherwise, apart from an extremely few shops and restaurants in Dar es Salaam and Arusha, their use is limited.

Government
The President of the Union Government of the Republic of Tanzania is elected by universal suffrage. Executive power resides with him and the ruling political party, the Chama Cha Mapinduzi (CCM), or the Revolutionary Party of Tanzania. The CCM was formed in 1977 when the Tanganyika African National Union (TANU) merged with Zanzibar's Afro-Shirazi Party (ASP). Elections are held every five years for the president and the National Assembly, which consists of 297 members.

Tanzania's first president, Julius K Nyerere, was chairman of the Revolutionary Party until October 1992, when elections for the chairmanship took place. The president is also second vice president of the union.

In December 1995 Benjamin Mkapa was elected president after the party was returned to power in a multi-party general election.

Language
The official languages are Kiswahili and English, although there are more than 120 tribal tongues. Kiswahili is the lingua franca throughout the country and English the language of business and legislation.

Religion
There is freedom of worship in Tanzania. Approximately thirty-two per cent of the population adheres to traditional beliefs. Christians account for thirty-three per cent and Muslims, mainly Sunni, make up the other thirty-five per cent, with a small minority of Hindus.

Time

Tanzania is three hours ahead of Greenwich Mean Time.

Daylight

The sunrise and sunset start at around 06.30 and 18.45 respectively — ensuring an almost constant twelve hours of daylight.

Business hours

Government offices remain open from 08.00 to 15.00, Monday to Friday, and 08.00 to 12.30 on Saturday. They remain closed on Sunday. Shops are open 08.30 to 18.00 from Monday to Friday with a lunch break from 12.30 to 14.00, and 08.30 to 12.30 on Saturday. Some shops open on Sunday mornings. Banking hours are from 08.30 to 12.30 Monday to Friday, and 08.30 to 11.30 on Saturday.

Security

Tanzania is well policed but honesty cannot be taken for granted. Take the usual precautions to safeguard yourself and your belongings: don't leave valuables or money in hotel rooms, and deposit anything of great value with a bank. In Dar es Salaam avoid walking out of the city centre after dark, especially near the beach front.

Communications

The post is well organized and you should have no problem with expected letters turning up. The same is true for telegrams. If you need to make an international call, however, try to do it from a private home or large hotel (although a twenty-five per cent surcharge is usually added by the hotel). The Extelecomms telephones are located off Samora Machel Avenue on Bridge Street. There are a very limited number of international lines for public use. Be prepared to wait.

Media

All major mass media institutions are owned by the government and ruling party. Radio Tanzania is the principal link throughout the country, serving about sixty per cent of the population. Broadcasts are in Kiswahili and English from the mainland between 05.00 and 24.00. Zanzibar has its own radio station, operating only in Kiswahili for the local population and part of the coast.

Television is still in its infancy and a viable mainland station is not envisaged before the year 2000. Zanzibar does have a colour facility, which broadcasts educational programmes to about 6,000 sets, many of them located at community centres.

The national newspapers are the *Daily News* and the *Sunday News*, both published in English.

The daily *Uhuru* and Sunday paper *Mzalendo* appear in Kiswahili. Foreign periodicals such as *Time*, *Newsweek* and the *Economist* are available sporadically, and at a price. There are also a small number of regional and denominational publications.

Energy

The local electricity supply is 230 volts, 50 cycles AC. Some hotels can supply adaptors. American visitors should bring a small step-down voltage converter.

Medical services

Medical services are undeveloped and only Dar es Salaam and a few other major centres have anything that would be considered adequate by Western standards. Appendicitis in a rural area would qualify as a very serious emergency indeed.

Medical insurance

Medical insurance should be purchased before you leave and should preferably include emergency air evacuation coverage.

Chemists/pharmacies

Medical supplies are limited in Tanzania. Visitors should carry an adequate supply of all medicines they may need with them. Most chemists are open 08.30 to 12.30 and 14.00 to 18.00 Monday to Friday; 08.30 to 12.30 on Saturday; and remain closed on Sunday.

Liquor

Licensing hours are liberal. Local spirits and wines as well as imported brands are available. Beer is price controlled and, as with most African varieties, is cheap and of a very good standard.

Tipping

In the better restaurants and hotels a service charge is included in the tariff. If you should want to tip someone who has been especially helpful, ten per cent is reasonable. Otherwise, do as you see fit — remembering that while not to tip can result in poor service, too large a tip can make it difficult for the next customer.

Clubs

The social and sporting clubs in Tanzania are limited. These include Gymkhana Club with golf course, tennis and squash courts, the regional yacht clubs and Lions Club. Visitors are usually welcomed, a temporary membership fee is sometimes charged.

English	Kiswahili	English	Kiswahili	English	Kiswahili
Hello	Jambo	Miss	Bibi	Four	Ine
How are you?	Habari	I	Mimi	Five	Tano
I am well		You	Wewe	Six	Sita
(good, fine, etc.)	Mzuri	He, She	Yeye	Seven	Saba
Thank you	Asante	We	Sisi	Eight	Nane
(very much)	(sana)	They	Wao	Nine	Tisa
Goodbye	Kwaheri	What?	Nini?	Ten	Kumi
Hotel	Hoteli	Who?	Nani?	Eleven	Kumi na moja
Room	Chumba	Where? (Place)	Mahali gani?	Twelve	Kumi na mbili
Bed	Kitanda	Where? (Direction)	Wapi?	Thirteen	Kumi na tatu
Food	Chakula	When?	Lini?	Twenty	Ishirini
Coffee	Kahawa	How?	Vipi?	Twenty-one	Ishirini na
Beer	Bia	Why?	Kwanini?		moja
Cold	Baridi	Which?	Ipi?	Twenty-two	Ishirini na
Hot	Moto	To eat	Kula		mbili
Tea	Chai	To drink	Kunywa	Twenty-three	Ishirini na tatu
Meat	Nyama	To sleep	Kulala	Thirty	Thelathini
Fish	Samaki	To bathe	Kuoga	Forty	Arobaini
Bread	Mkate	To come	Kuja	Fifty	Hamsini
Butter	Siagi	To go	Kwenda	One hundred	Mia moja
Sugar	Sukari	To stop	Kusimama	One thousand	Elfu moja
Salt	Chumvi	To buy	Kununua		
Bad	Mbaya	To sell	Kuuza		
Today	Leo	Street/road	Barabara		
Tomorrow	Kesho	Airport	Uwanja wa	Where is the hotel?	Hoteli iko
Now	Sasa		Ndege		wapi?
Quickly	Haraka	Shop	Duka	Good morning	Habari ya
Slowly	Pole-pole	Money	Pesa		asubuhi
Hospital	Hospitali	Cent	Senti	Good afternoon	Habari ya
Police	Polici	One	Moja		mchana
Mr	Bwana	Two	Mbili	Good evening	Habari ya
Mrs	Mama	Three	Tatu		jioni

Please come in	Karibu ndani tafadhali	Turn left	Geuka kushoto
		Go straight	Nenda moja kwa moja
Please sit down	Keti tafadhali	Please stop here	Simama hapa tafadhali
You're welcome	Una karibishwa	How much?	Ngapi?
Where do you come from?	Unatoka wapi?	Wait a minute	Ngoja kidogo
I come from . . .	Nime toka . . .	I have to get change	Ni badilishe
What is your name?	Jina lako nani?		pesa kwanza
My name is . . .	Jina langu ni . . .	Excuse me	Samahani
Do you understand	Unafahamu	Where is the toilet?	Wapi choo?
Swahili?	Kiswahili?	In the back	Upande wa nyuma
Yes	Ndiyo	Where may I get	Naweza kupata
No	Hapana	Something to drink?	Wapi kinywaji?
Only a little	Kidogo tu	One cup of coffee	Kikombe kimoja
I want to learn more	Nataka kujifunza zaidi		cha kahawa
		How much does this cost?	Bei gani?
How do you find	Waonaje	That's quite expensive	Waweza kupunguza
Tanzania?	Tanzania?	Fine	Sawa
I like it here	Hapa napenda	I will buy it	Nita nunua
The weather is hot,	Hewa hapa ni		
isn't it?	joto, sivyo?		
Yes, a little	Ndiyo, kidogo		
Where are you going?	Unakwenda wapi?		
I am going to . . .	Nakwenda . . .		
Turn right	Geuka kulia		

In Brief

Tanzania National Parks

The game parks of Tanzania have been set aside by the government as wildlife and botanical sanctuaries that enjoy a high degree of protection and management. They serve a conservational, educational and recreational purpose for Tanzanians and overseas visitors and form the mainstay of the country's tourist industry.

Twenty-five per cent of Tanzania is gazetted as reserves of one sort or another, making conservation a major element in land use.

National Parks
These are declared by an act of Parliament after approval by ministry and district/regional authorities under the powers of the Wildlife Conservation Act. They are chosen and recognized by their outstanding flora, fauna and landscape, and for their aesthetic and economic value. The establishment of a national park is a conscious decision to preserve an area for future generations.

Conservation Areas
Ngorongoro Conservation Area, Tanzania's sole conservation area, was specially designated to accommodate the needs of the Maasai who were not allowed to graze their cattle in what was then Serengeti National Park. Now they are allowed to practice pastoralism but not settle. Agriculture was introduced in 1993.

Game Reserves
Tanzania has more than twenty game reserves, including the world's largest — Selous. Some exploitation of their natural resources is permitted — such as licensed fishing and logging, and professional hunting between the months of July and December — but only park staff are allowed to reside within the boundaries. Five game reserves have been declared national projects, which increases their status and protection.

Game Controlled Areas
There are about fifty of these areas totalling more than 120,000 square kilometres (46,300 square miles). Within these unmanaged areas unauthorized hunting is prohibited, but poaching and hunting for food still occurs.

Forest Reserves
These cover ten to fifteen per cent of the country and within them nearly half of the timber species are protected by law.

Biosphere Reserves
In 1989 there were 271 designated biosphere reserves throughout the world, with three in Tanzania.

These are protected environments that contain unique landforms, landscapes, and systems of land use. Their management is undertaken by the host government, with different ministries responsible for each different land use. Funds for specific research projects and scientific and administrative training are provided through UNESCO. Tanzania's biosphere reserves are Lake Manyara National Park, Serengeti National Park, and Ngorongoro Conservation Area.

World Heritage Sites
These areas are either unique culturally — the Pyramids, the Acropolis, the Taj Mahal — or naturally like the Great Barrier Reef. Today more than 100 sites exist worldwide, all protected under international law. Ngorongoro Conservation Area, Selous Game Reserve, and Serengeti National Park are Tanzania's World Heritage Sites.

National Parks

Arusha National Park
Size: 137 sq km
Geographical location: Area surrounding and including Mount Meru
Altitude: 1,525-4,565m
Vegetation: Dense forest or thicket made up of olive, Nuxia congesta and pencil cedar. Bamboo forests are also found at higher elevations. The park contains good examples of vegetational zonation.
Fauna: Black and white colobus monkey, giraffe, waterbuck, leopard, declining numbers of elephant and hippo. The Momela lakes support healthy numbers of flamingo species, wildfowl, and over-wintering Eurasian migrant birds.
Visitor facilities: Camp sites, mountain huts and two tourist lodges.

Gombe Stream National Park
Size: 52 sq km
Geographical location: Eastern shore of Lake Tanganyika, about 24 km north of Kigoma
Altitude: 750-1,500m
Vegetation: Miombo woodland on lower slopes of the escarpment, merging into gallery forest and upland grassland.
Fauna: Gombe was established mainly to protect the chimpanzee. Other primates include baboon, red colobus monkey, and blue monkey. Leopard, bushbuck, and waterbuck are also present in the park. There are several rare bird species, notably the palm-nut vulture and the very localized Forbes' plover.
Visitor facilities: Guesthouse and camp sites.

Katavi National Park

Size: 2,253 sq km
Geographical location: North-west of Rukwa and directly east of Lake Tanganyika
Altitude: 900m
Vegetation: Miombo woodland and much grassy floodplain.
Fauna: Lion, leopard, elephant, zebra, eland, buffalo, sable and roan antelope, and topi. Over 400 species of bird have been recorded in the area.
Visitor facilities: Camp sites are located within the park, hotel and lodge accommodation is available 40 km away at Mpanda.

Lake Manyara National Park

Size: 325 sq km, of which approximately one-third is land, the remainder being part of Lake Manyara
Geographical location: 120 km south-west of Arusha
Altitude: 960-1,478m
Vegetation: A northern ground water forest fed by springs from the Rift Valley escarpment gives way to yellow fever trees, alkaline grasslands, and eventually coarse sedges at the lake shore and streams. There are baobabs on the valley walls.
Fauna: Hippo, elephant and buffalo are plentiful, and lions laze in the park's acacia trees. There are also giraffe, zebra, impala, bushbuck, and leopard. The park is a preserve for herds of wildebeest during the dry season.

The lake and feeder streams often support large flocks of waterbirds including pelican, yellow-billed stork, and white-necked cormorant. There are several species of cobra and the Nile monitor lizard is present.
Visitor facilities: A first-class hotel, camp sites, a hostel, and self-help bandas.

Mahale Mountain National Park

Size: 1,613 sq km
Geographical location: On the eastern shore of Lake Tanganyika about 150 km south of Kigoma
Altitude: 780-2,462m
Vegetation: Lowland forest, montane forest mixed with bamboo, and 75 per cent tall miombo woodland trees.
Fauna: Many primates — notably chimpanzee — brush-tailed porcupine, blue duiker, lion, wart hog, sable antelope, and Lichtenstein's hartebeest are some of the 55 recorded mammal species.
Visitor facilities: Ngare Sero Luxury Tented Camp, camp sites and a guesthouse are available.

Mikumi National Park

Size: 3,230 sq km
Geographical location: 280 km west of Dar es Salaam
Altitude: 500-1,257m
Vegetation: Miombo woodland on the Mkata River flood plain. The remainder is thorn acacia, ebony shrub, baobab and riverine thicket broken by *Borassus* palm.
Fauna: Mammals include yellow baboon, vervet monkey, Sykes monkey, lion, elephant, rhino, giraffe, zebra, eland, buffalo, greater kudu, bushbuck, waterbuck, and Lichtenstein's

hartebeest. There is abundant and varied bird life that has both northern representatives — superb starling and straw-tailed whydah — and a southern species — Dickinson's kestrel.
Visitor facilities: Camp with bandas, luxury lodge and camp sites.

Mount Kilimanjaro National Park

Size: 755 sq km, surrounded by a forest reserve
Geographical location: Upper levels of Mount Kilimanjaro including corridors in the forest belt
Altitude: 1,830-5,896m
Vegetation: Kilimanjaro shows textbook vegetational zonation: lowland forest, heather moorland, montane desert, and arctic summit.
Fauna: Blue monkey, black and white colobus, leopard, elephant, bushbuck, eland, buffalo, and the rare Abbott's duiker. Unusual birds include the infrequent lammergeier, Hunter's cisticola, and the scarlet-tufted malachite sunbird. The Kilimanjaro swallowtail is a butterfly that occurs on the mountain with a very restricted distribution.
Visitor facilities: About 67,000 people climb Kilimanjaro each year and accommodation on the mountain is very good.

Ruaha National Park

Size: 12,950 sq km
Geographical location: West of Iringa in the Southern Highlands
Altitude: 750-1,830m
Vegetation: The park contains treeless grasslands and swamps as well as miombo woodland and evergreen forests growing over undulating plateaux to the north of the Great Ruaha River.
Fauna: Mammals include lion, leopard, cheetah, elephant, buffalo, greater kudu and lesser kudu, as well as the most southerly population of Grant's gazelle. More than 370 species of bird have been spotted.
Visitor facilities: A lodge, a luxury camp, bandas, and camp sites are all available.

Rubondo Island National Park

Size: 240 sq km
Geographical location: An island in south-west Lake Victoria
Altitude: Approximately 1,130m
Vegetation: Ninety per cent moist evergreen forest with some woodland and open grassland.
Fauna: Indigenous species include bushbuck, sitatunga, hippo, vervet monkey, and marsh mongoose. Introduced species include chimpanzee, elephant, roan antelope, suni, and black and white colobus monkey.
Visitor facilities: Bandas and camp sites.

Serengeti National Park

Size: 14,763 sq km
Geographical location: 200 km west of Arusha: the northern boundary abuts the Kenya border, and Lake Victoria in the west.
Altitude: 950-1,850m
Vegetation: Undulating open grassland plains with an extensive block of acacia woodland savannah in the centre.

Fauna: Unrivalled herds of plains game, which migrate between seasonal water supplies, include 1.3 million wildebeest, zebra, Thomson's gazelle, eland, and spotted hyena. Non-migrants are lion, hunting dog, cheetah, black rhino, elephant in the north, giraffe, buffalo, topi, numerous rodents and bats, golden and side-striped jackal, mongoose, and otter. There are over 496 birds on record, including 53 raptors species.

Visitor facilities: Seronera, Serena, Serengeti Sopa and Lobo luxury lodges, Grumeti River Camp and nine campsites.

Tarangire National Park
Size: 2,600 sq km
Geographical location: South-east of Lake Manyara, 114 km from Arusha
Altitude: 1,100-1,500m
Vegetation: Tarangire has 9 different vegetation zones on and around the Tarangire River. Baobabs are a dominant tree.
Fauna: Plains game is abundant in the dry season. Mammals include lion, leopard, cheetah, elephant, zebra, lesser kudu, eland, and buffalo.
Visitor facilities: Three luxury lodges, one luxury tented lodge and three camp sites.

Udzungwa Mountains National Park
Size: Approximately 1,990 sq km
Geographical location: Iringa District (headquarters 65 km south of Mikumi)
Altitude: 300-2,800m
Vegetation: Widely varied forest types.
Fauna: Primates (including two endemic forms), bushpig, buffalo, elephant, hyrax, squirrel, and numerous threatened and endemic birds.
Visitor facilities: None.

Conservation Areas

Ngorongoro Conservation Area
Size: 8,280 sq km
Geographical location: South-east of Serengeti National Park, 180 km from Arusha
Altitude: 1,500-3,600m
Vegetation: Montane and highland forests grassy open plains, swamps, bush country and acacia woodland.
Fauna: Large population of ungulates in the crater and high numbers of predators, particularly lion. Elsewhere in the NCA are giraffe, impala and elephants.
Birdlife includes ostrich, kori bustard, Verreaux's eagle, Egyptian vulture, rosy-breasted longclaw, and lesser flamingo.
Visitor facilities: Three luxury lodges on the crater rim and three beyond it. Campsites throughout the NCA.

Game Reserves

Biharamulo Game Reserve
Size: 1,300 sq km
Geographical location: Adjacent to the south-west shore of Lake Victoria
Altitude: 1,250-2,000m
Vegetation: The northern limit of *Brachystegia* — miombo woodland. Also riverine and savannah woodland.
Fauna: Mammals include hippo, elephant, zebra, sable and roan antelope, sitatunga, topi, and a small isolated population of red colobus monkey.
Visitor facilities: A guesthouse.

Burigi Game Reserve
Size: 2,200 sq km
Geographical location: On the shores of Lake Burigi in Kagera Province next to Biharamulo Game Reserve
Altitude: About 1,000-1,500m
Vegetation: Central swamp surrounded by riverine forest and papyrus beds with some relict forest.
Fauna: Twenty-eight species of mammal including giraffe, impala, eland, hippopotamus, and lake-shore populations of waterbuck.
Visitor facilities: None.

Maswa Game Reserve
Size: 2,200 sq km
Geographical location: Adjacent to the Serengeti's southern border
Altitude: 950-1,850m
Vegetation: Classical East African woodland savannah with grassland plains in the north.
Fauna: Extensive migrants including wildebeest at the end of May, followed by Thomson's and Grant's gazelles between July and August. Resident mammals are giraffe, hartebeest, roan antelope, eland, wart hog, buffalo, hyena, and jackal.
Visitor facilities: None.

Mkomazi Game Reserve
Size: 2,500 sq km
Geographical location: On the Kenya/Tanzania border south-east of Mount Kilimanjaro and contiguous with Tsavo National Park.
Altitude: 630-1,630m
Vegetation: Open plains with thorn bush.
Fauna: Elephant, lion, leopard, giraffe, lesser kudu, and prolific bird life.
Visitor facilities: A banda is located within the reserve's boundaries.

Rungwa Game Reserve
Size: 9,000 sq km
Geographical location: Central Tanzania adjacent to Ruaha National Park
Altitude: 1,350-2,350m
Vegetation: Mainly miombo woodland savannah.
Fauna: Large numbers of greater kudu as well as elephant, black rhino, sable and roan antelope, lion, leopard, cheetah, zebra, lesser kudu, and bushbuck.

Visitor facilities: Guesthouse, Ruaha National Park facilities.

Saadani Game Reserve
Size: 300 sq km
Geographical location: Near Saadani town on the coast, directly west of Zanzibar
Altitude: Sea-level to 50m
Vegetation: Coastal savannah, grassland, and thickets within 20 km of untouched coastline.
Fauna: Bohor reedbuck, duiker, lion, leopard and Coke's hartebeest.
Visitor facilities: None.

Selous Game Reserve
Size: 50,000 sq km around the Rufiji and Great Ruaha rivers
Geographical location: South-east Tanzania, south of Mikumi National Park
Altitude: 100-1,200m
Vegetation: One-third wooded grassland dominated by *Terminalia spinosa*, the remainder being deciduous miombo, some dense thicket, and riverine and ground water forest.
Fauna: Most representatives of East African wildlife, including 200,000 buffalo, 30,000 elephant, 100,000 impala, 80,000 wildebeest, and the country's largest populations of crocodile and hippopotamus. Birds are equally abundant.
Visitor facilities: Five tented camps.

Ugalla River Game Reserve
Size: 4,773 sq km
Geographical location: South-west of Tabora and north-east of Katavi National Park
Altitude: 1,400m
Vegetation: Flood plain grasslands, termite-mound woodland, *Borassus* palm woodland, and *Brachystegia* miombo.
Fauna: Open vegetation makes game viewing of sable and roan antelope, greater kudu, buffalo, elephant, and topi relatively easy.
Visitor facilities: None.

Umba River Game Reserve
Size: 1,500 sq km
Geographical location: On the Kenya/Tanzania border, north-west of Tanga
Altitude: 630-1,630m
Vegetation: Thornbush scrub, coastal savannah, and thickets.
Fauna: Unusual animals include oryx, gerenuk, and lesser kudu.
Visitor facilities: None.

Uwanda Game Reserve
Size: 5,000 sq km
Geographical location: Encompasses the northern section of Lake Rukwa directly east of Lake Tanganyika
Altitude: 1,200m
Vegetation: Complex flood plain vegetation.
Fauna: The puku is a notable inhabitant of Uwanda, only one of two areas where it is found in Tanzania. Other mammals include zebra, topi, buffalo, and elephant.
Visitor facilities: None.

Forest Reserves

Usambara Mountains
Size: 6,213 sq km
Geographical location: Runs parallel with the north-eastern border with Kenya, 100 km from Tanga
Altitude: 1,000-2,286m
Vegetation: One of the richest plant and animal communities in Africa in terms of variety and endemic wildlife. Over 250 forest tree species have been recorded.
Fauna: Fifty-five mammal species recorded including lion, leopard, marsh mongoose, civet, 7 species of insectivores, 11 species of bat, 18 species of rodent, bushpig, buffalo and Harvey's duiker. Several species of bird are unique to the mountains and are listed as threatened. Other rarities are the southern banded snake eagle, Fischer's turaco, and green tinkerbird.
Visitor facilities: None.

Jozani Forest Reserve
Zanzibar
Size: 196 hectares
Geographical location: Near Pete in the south, adjoining 1,500 acres of natural forest, the last red colobus monkey sanctuary in the world.
Altitude: Sea level
Vegetation: Lush tropical including Alexandrian laurel, screwpine, eucalyptus, palms and figs.
Fauna: The Zanzibar red colobus monkey
Visitors facilities: None except elsewhere on the island.

Wildlife Profile

Eastern Africa's open plains, including Tanzania's, support some of the last great herds of wildlife left in the world. They hold a greater number and diversity of species than any other continent.

There are almost 100 species of grazers (ungulates) whereas the whole of Asia can claim only seventy, South and Central America only sixteen, Europe only thirteen and North America only eleven. (Swahili names in brackets):

Mammals

Spectacled elephant shrew, *Elephantulus rufescens*: Widely distributed. Lake Manyara, Mikumi, Serengeti.

Giant white-toothed shrew, *Crocidura occidentalis*: Widely distributed. Can be seen around swamps and in damp woodlands. Lake Manyara, Arusha, Serengeti.

Ant bear or **Aardvark**, *Orycteropus afer*: Widely distributed. Nocturnal and rarely seen. Found in areas where termite hills appear. Lake Manyara, Mikumi, Arusha, Ruaha, Serengeti.

African elephant, *Loxodonta africana* (Tembo or Ndovu): Widely distributed. Rainforests, secondary forests, highland forests, open woodlands, savannah, dry bush and swamps. Most national parks, but not Gombe.

Bush hyrax, *Heterohyrax brucei* (Pimbi): Widely distributed. Cliffs, rocky hills and stony mountain slopes. All national parks.

Tree hyrax, *Dendrohyrax arboreus* (Perere): Widely distributed. Forests. Nocturnal. More often heard than seen. Lake Manyara, Ngorongoro Crater, Arusha, Ruaha, Serengeti, Tarangire.

Black rhinoceros, *Diceros bicornis* (Kifaru): Widely distributed but few of them remaining. Bush, savannah, light forests, highland forest and high altitude moorlands. Mikumi, Serengeti, Ngorongoro Crater, Rungwa, Selous.

Burchell's or **Common zebra**, *Equus burchelli* (Punda milia): Widely distributed in grasslands, open savannah, and grassy flats surrounded by bush. Most parks except Gombe and Kilimanjaro.

Buffalo, *Syncerus caffer* (Nyati or Mbogo): Widely distributed. Rainforests, secondary forests, highland forests, open woodlands, savannah, bush, and swamps. Large numbers in Serengeti, Ngorongoro Crater, Manyara, Ruaha, Mikumi, Selous, Rukwa and Mount Meru.

Wildebeest or **Gnu**, *Connochaetes taurinus* (Nyumbu): Widely distributed. Grassland, savannah and open woodlands. Their mass migrations to and from the Serengeti are impressive. Mikumi, Ngorongoro, Manyara, Serengeti.

Coke's hartebeest, *Alcelaphus buselaphus cokii* (Kongoni): Widely distributed. Grasslands and open grassy savannah. Lake Manyara, Katavi, Ngorongoro Crater, Serengeti, Tarangire.

Lichtenstein's hartebeest, *Alcelaphus lichtensteinii*: Prefers open plains, bush, and wooded grasslands. Mikumi and Selous.

Jackson's Hartebeest, *Alcelaphus jacksoni*: South west of Lake Victoria.

Topi, *Damaliscus korrigum jimela* (Nyamera): Grasslands and open savannah. Serengeti, Katavi.

Harvey's or **Red duiker**, *Cephalophus harveyi* (Funo): Widely distributed in forests, bush, and high grass jungles. Being secretive in their habits, duikers are seldom encountered. Lake Manyara, Mikumi, Arusha, Serengeti.

Abbott's duiker, *Cephalophus spadix*: Mount Kilimanjaro National Park.

Ader's duiker (Zanzibar duiker), *Cephalophus adersi*: Partly nocturnal and found only on the island of Zanzibar.

Blue duiker, *Cephalophus monticola*: Widely distributed in forests, gallery forest and bushlands. Lake Manyara, Arusha, Serengeti.

Bush duiker, *Sylvicapra grimmia*: Woodland, scrub and bush country.

Suni, *Nesotragus moschatus* (Paa): Locally in highland forests, coastal forests and dense bushlands. Lake Manyara, Arusha, Serengeti.

Steinbok, *Raphicerus campestris* (Dondoro): Widely distributed. Grasslands, with a certain amount of scattered bush. Serengeti, Tarangire.

Klipspringer, *Oreotragus oreotragus* (Mbuzi mawe): Widely distributed but confined to rocky hills and mountain ranges. Lake Manyara, Arusha, Ruaha.

Oribi, *Ourebia ourebia* (Taya): Widely distributed. Grasslands, open savannah woodlands, hilly country, and scrubby bush. Serengeti.

Kirk's dik-dik, *Rhynchotragus kirkii* (Dikidiki or Suguya): Widely distributed in dry bush country. Lake Manyara, Ruaha, Serengeti, Tarangire, Arusha.

Waterbuck, *Kobus ellipsiprymnus* (Nkulu): widely distributed Savannah, bush and gallery forests along watercourses. Lake Manyara, Mikumi, Ngorongoro Crater, Arusha, Ruaha, Serengeti, Tarangire.

Bohor reedbuck, *Redunca redunca* (Tohe): Widely distributed in grassy areas with patches of bush, and reedbeds. Never far from water. Lake Manyara, Mikumi, Ngorongoro Crater, Arusha, Ruaha, Serengeti, Tarangire, Saadani.

Gerenuk, *Litocranius walleri*: North from the Pare Mountains into northern Tanzania.

Impala, *Aepyceros melampus* (Swala pala or Swara pala): Widely distributed in Tanzania with the exception of Ngorongoro Crater.

Thomson's gazelle, *Gazella thomsonii* (Swala tomi): Grasslands; savannah. Serengeti, Ngorongoro Crater, Manyara.

Grant's gazelle, *Gazella granti* (Swala granti): Grasslands, open savannah and dry bush. Widely distributed.

Fringe-eared oryx, *Oryx beisa callotis* (Choroa): Dry bush country and grasslands. Serengeti, Tarangire.

Sable antelope, *Hippotragus niger* (Palahala or Mbarapi): Savannah with patches of bush and open meadow, especially of the miombo forest type. Mikumi, Ruaha, Selous.

Roan antelope, *Hippotragus equinus* (Korongo): Savannah interspersed with grassy patches, rolling uplands with bush, and open forest. Katavi, Ruaha.

Eland, *Taurotragus oryx* (Pofu or Mbunja): Widely distributed though numbers much reduced in densely settled areas. Grasslands, savannah and mountain moorlands. Serengeti, Ngorongoro, Selous, Mikumi and Mkomazi.

Bushbuck, *Tragelaphus scriptus* (Mbawala or Pongo): Widely distributed wherever bush and undergrowth offer good cover. Common on Rubondo Island. Lake Manyara, Mikumi, Ngorongoro Crater, Arusha, Ruaha, Serengeti, Tarangire.

Greater Kudu, *Tragelaphus strepsiceros* (Tandala mkubwa): Dense savannah, especially of the miombo forest type, rocky hills covered with forests, and thorn thicket belts of dense bush along rivers. Mikumi, Ruaha, Selous.

Lesser Kudu, *Strepsiceros imberbis* (Tandala ndogo): Arid bush country and coastal bush. Serengeti, Tarangire.

Sitatunga, *Tragelaphus spekei* (Nzohe): Swamps. Rarely seen. Rubondo.

Puku, *Adenota ardonii*: Mixed grass and woodlands and flood plains in Southern Tanzania. Rukwa Valley.

Common Giraffe, *Giraffa camelopardalis* (Twiga): Open acacia woodland and scrub and coastal forest.

Maasai giraffe, *Giraffa camelopardalis tippelskirchi* (Twiga): Dry thorn country, acacia grasslands, savannah, bushlands and highland forest. Northern Serengeti, Manyara, Arusha, Ruaha and many other parks.

Bushpig, *Potamochoerus porcus* (Nguru wemwitu): Widely distributed but rarely seen. Forests, gallery forests, and bushy savannah. Crepuscular and nocturnal. Arusha, Serengeti, Ngorongoro, Selous, Gombe, Mikumi.

Wart hog, *Phacochoerus aethiopicus aeliani* (Ngiri): Widely distributed. Savannah and bushy grasslands. Lake Manyara, Mikumi, Ngorongoro Crater, Arusha, Ruaha, Serengeti, Tarangire.

Hippopotamus, *Hippopotamus amphibius* (Kiboko): Widely distributed. Rivers, lakes, and swamps. Lake Manyara, Mikumi, Ngorongoro Crater, Arusha, Ruaha, Serengeti.

CARNIVORES
Lion, *Panthera leo* (Simba): Still widely distributed. Grasslands, savannah, open woodlands, bush and semidesert. Lake Manyara, Mikumi, Ngorongoro Crater, Ruaha, Serengeti, Tarangire, Selous, Mkomazi, Katavi.

Leopard, *Panthera pardus* (Chui): Widely distributed. Forests of every type, savannah, bush, grasslands, semidesert and rocky mountain areas. Usually secretive and rarely seen. Lake Manyara, Mikumi, Ngorongoro Crater, Arusha,

Ruaha, Serengeti, Tarangire.

African wild cat, *Felis sylvestris lybica* (Paka pori): Widely distributed. Nocturnal. Ngorongoro Crater, Ruaha, Serengeti, Tarangire, Mikumi, Selous, Mkomazi.

Cheetah, *Acinonyx jubatus* (Duma): Widely distributed in grasslands and open savannah. Mikumi, Ngorongoro Crater, Ruaha, Serengeti, Tarangire.

Serval, *Leptailurus serval* (Mondo): Widely distributed but rarely seen. Dry bush country and savannah. Shy, solitary and mainly nocturnal. Mikumi, Ngorongoro Crater, Arusha, Ruaha, Serengeti, Tarangire.

Spotted hyena, *Crocuta crocuta* (Fisi): Widely distributed. Mainly nocturnal, but sometimes encountered in daytime. Lake Manyara, Mikumi, Ngorongoro Crater, Arusha, Ruaha, Serengeti, Tarangire.

Striped hyena, *Hyaena hyaena* (Fisi): Nocturnal and rarely seen. Serengeti.

Aardwolf, *Proteles cristatus* (Fisi ndogo): Looks like a small striped hyena; sometimes encountered in daytime. Ngorongoro Crater, Mikumi, Serengeti, Mkomazi.

Spotted-necked otter, *Lutra maculicollis* (Fisi maji): Widely distributed. Rivers, lake shores, papyrus marshes, reed beds and quiet backwaters. Especially common around Lake Victoria.

Clawless otter, *Aonyx capensis* (Fisi maji): Found in rivers, streams and swamps up to 3,000 metres (9,843 feet). Lake Manyara, Serengeti.

Honey badger, *Mellivora ratel* (Nyegere): Nocturnal. Can be seen regularly near several lodges and do-it-yourself camps. Lake Manyara, Ngorongoro Crater, Ruaha, Serengeti, Tarangire, Mikumi.

Grey or **golden jackal**, *Canis aureus* (Mbweha): Grasslands and savannah. Serengeti, Tarangire.

Black-backed jackal, *Canis mesomelas* (Mbweha): Widely distributed. Savannah and grasslands. Ruaha, Manyara, Serengeti, Ngorongoro, Tarangire, Mikumi, Selous.

Side-striped jackal, *Canis adustus* (Mbweha): Nocturnal, rarely seen. Serengeti, Ngorongoro.

Wild dog, *Lycaon pictus* (Mbwa mwitu): Widely distributed though much reduced in numbers. Bush, light forest, savannah and grasslands. Serengeti, Ngorongoro Crater, Mikumi, Selous, Tarangire.

Bat-eared fox, *Otocyon megalotis* (Mbwela masikia): Widely distributed. Grasslands and open woodlands. Lake Manyara, Mikumi, Ngorongoro Crater, Serengeti, Ruaha.

White-tailed mongoose, *Ichneumia albicauda* (Nguchiro): Widely distributed. Nocturnal. Often seen in car lights. Serengeti, Tarangire, Ruaha.

Black-tipped mongoose, *Herpestes sanguineus* (Nguchiro): Widely distributed. Diurnal. Often seen crossing the road. Lake Manyara, Arusha, Serengeti, Mikumi.

Dwarf mongoose, *Helogale undulata* (Nguchiro): Widely distributed. Diurnal and gregarious. Often seen on termite hills. Lake Manyara, Ruaha, Serengeti, Tarangire, Mikumi.

Banded mongoose, *Mungos mungo* (Nguchiro): Grasslands. Diurnal and gregarious. Often seen in Mikumi. Lake Manyara, Ngorongoro Crater, Serengeti, Tarangire.

Genet, *Genetta genetta* (Kanu): Widely distributed. Nocturnal. Have become very tame at several lodges. Lake Manyara, Mikumi, Ngorongoro Crater, Arusha, Ruaha, Serengeti, Tarangire, Gombe.

Zorilla, *Ictonyx striatus* (Kicheche): Widely distributed though rarely seen. Nocturnal. Lake Manyara, Arusha, Serengeti.

African civet, *Civettictis civetta* (Fungo): Widely distributed though rarely seen. Nocturnal and shy. Zanzibar, Ngorongoro Crater, Arusha, Ruaha, Serengeti, Tarangire, Lake Manyara, Gombe, Mahale.

PRIMATES

Thick-tailed galago, *Galago crassicaudatus* (Komba): Widely distributed. Gallery highland forests and bamboo thickets. Nocturnal. Can often be heard wailing and screaming.

Senegal yellow-legged galago or Lesser bush baby, *Galago senegalensis* (Komba): Found in savannah and woodlands. Zanzibar, Lake Manyara, Mikumi, Arusha, Ruaha, Serengeti, Tarangire.

Olive baboon, *Papio anubis* (Nyani): Savannah, gallery forests, bush, rocky mountains. Throughout Tanzania, including Lake Manyara, Arusha, Ngorongoro Crater, Serengeti, Tarangire.

Yellow baboon, *Papio cynocephalus* (Nyani): An important study of the yellow baboon was undertaken at Mikumi. Mikumi, Ruaha, Serengeti, Selous.

Black and white colobus monkey, *Colobus abyssinicus* (Mbega): Inhabits forest areas. Mount Meru, Kilimanjaro, Mahale, Arusha, Serengeti.

Black-faced vervet monkey, *Cercopithecus aethiops* (Tumbili): Commonly found in woodland along streams, rivers and lakes. Lake Manyara, Mikumi, Ngorongoro Crater, Arusha, Ruaha, Tarangire, Serengeti.

Blue Monkey, *Ceropithecus mitis*: Ngorongoro, Manyara, Gombe, Mahale, Arusha, Kilimanjaro.

Patas monkey, *Erythrocebus patas:* In bush and savannah country in northern Tanzania.

Red-tailed monkey, *Ceropithecus nictitans:* Evergreen and gallery forests. Zanzibar, Gombe, Mahale.

Sykes' monkey, *Ceropithecus mitis* (Kima): Favours dense and extensive forests. Very variable in colour. Zanzibar, Lake Manyara.

Potto, *Perodicticus potto:* Confined to rain forests.

Chimpanzee, *Pan troglodytes:* East of Lake Tanganyika south to the Mahale Mountains.

Bird Life Profile

From glacial mountain to savannah plain, semidesert to tropical rainforest, Tanzania's botanical versatility supports more than 1,000 bird species. Some of the more common or spectacular birds are:

Maasai Ostrich, *Struthio camelus massaicus:* Grasslands and open savannah.

Pelicans: Pink-backed pelican, *Pelecanus rufescens:* White, greyish on wings, head and belly, tinged pinkish on back and rump. Inland lakes. White pelican, *Pelecanus onocrotalus:* Somewhat larger, white, tinged with pink during breeding season.

Cormorants: Long-tailed or Red Cormorant, *Phalacrocorax africanus* and White-necked cormorant, *Phalacrocorax carbo:* Common on Lake Manyara and Rufiji River. Darter, *Anhinga rufa:* Related to cormorants. Widespread on lakes and rivers. Long, thin neck.

Herons: Black-headed heron, *Ardea melanocephala:* Common and widely distributed. Lake shores, river banks, and swamps; often quite far from water. Goliath heron, *Ardea goliath:* Largest African heron. Never far from water. Lake Manyara, Tarangire and Serengeti. Night heron, *Nycticorax nycticorax:* Lakes, rivers, and marshes.

Egrets: Yellow-billed egret, *Egretta intermedius:* Swamps, rivers, and lakes. Locally numerous. Little egret, *Egretta garzetta:* Smaller with black bill. Cattle egret, *Bubulcus ibis:* Widely distributed, usually in flocks, often accompanying game or domestic stock. Feeds on insects disturbed by grazing animals.

Storks: Saddle-billed stork, *Ephippiorhynchus senegalensis:* Swamps, marshes, and reedy lake shores. Singly or in couples. Seen fairly regularly at Lake Manyara, Ngorongoro, Mikumi, Selous and Rubondo Island. Yellow-billed stork — or wood ibis — *Ibis ibis:* Widely distributed. Flat shores and sandbanks of shallow lakes and rivers. Often in small parties. Open-billed stork, *Anastomus lamelligerus:* Lakes, marshes, and large lagoons. Sometimes in large flocks. Marabou stork, *Leptoptilus crumeniferus:* Widely distributed. Open savannah, often in big flocks. A stork with the habits of a vulture. Hammerkop, *Scopus umbretta:* Rivers, pools, and shallow lake shores. Vast spherical nest can be seen in riverine forests. Abdim's stork, *Sphenorynchus abdimii:* Visits East Africa from Sudan, often in large flocks. White

stork, *Ciconia ciconia:* A winter visitor.

African spoonbill, *Platalea alba:* Shallow lakes, lagoons and dams. Can be seen in Rift Valley lakes.

Ibises: Sacred ibis, *Threskiornis aethiopicus:* Widely distributed. Lakes, rivers and marshes. Often in flocks. **Hadada ibis,** *Hagedashia hagedash:* Well-watered and well-wooded areas. Usually single or in pairs and a common visitor to urban gardens.

Flamingos: Lesser flamingo, *Phoeniconaias minor:* Dark red bill, tipped black. Common at Lakes Natron, Ngorongoro and the Momella lakes of Arusha. **Greater flamingo,** *Phoenicopterus ruber:* Pink and black bill. Recorded breeding at Lake Natron. Often in close association with smaller species.

Geese: Egyptian goose, *Alopochen aegyptiacus:* Common and widely distributed. Lakes, ponds, dams, rivers and marshes. In pairs and family parties. Outside breeding season also in flocks. **Spurwing goose,** *Plectropterus gambensis:* Lakes and rivers, often in big flocks. **Knob-billed goose,** *Sarkidiornis melanotos:* In small flocks on lakes, pools and wooded swamps. Can be seen at lakes Manyara, Mikumi, Momella, and at Ngorongoro.

Ducks: African pochard, *Aythya erythrophthalma:* Common on lakes, often in flocks of fifty or more. **Yellow-billed duck,** *Anas undulata:* Open waters, reedy ponds and rivers. Gregarious. **Red-billed duck,** *Anas erythrorhyncha:* Common in swamps, reedy pools and inlets of lakes. **Hottentot teal,** *Anas punctata:* Shallow saline and freshwater pools with mud banks, shallow grassy coves. **Cape Wigeon,** *Anas capensis:* Large and small sheets of saline water and marshes. **White-faced tree-duck:** *Dendrocygna viduata:* River flats, swamps, saltwater lagoons, estuaries, pools and rivers. Often in large flocks. **Fulvous tree-duck,** *Dendrocygna bicolor:* Inland lakes and marshes.

Secretary bird, *Sagittarius serpentarius:* Often seen in grasslands, savannah, and light bush. Forages on ground.

Vultures: Animal carcasses very quickly attract vultures of several species, especially **hooded vultures,** *Necrosyrtes monachus;* **white-backed vultures,** *Pseudogyps africanus;* the **Palm-nut vulture** or **Vulturine fish eagle,** *Gypohierax angloensis* and **Ruppell's griffon vultures,** *Gyps ruppellii.* They all give way to the large **lappet-faced vulture,** *Torgos tracheliotus.* The **Egyptian vulture,** *Neophron percnopterus,* uses stones to break ostrich eggs.

Lammergeier or **bearded vulture,** *Gypaetus barbatus:* Rather scarce, but can be seen around Mount Meru and Gol Kopjes in the Serengeti.

Kites and buzzards: Black-shouldered kite, *Elanus caeruleus:* Savannah, dry grasslands, and cultivated areas. **Black (yellow-billed) kite,** *Milvus migrans:* A subspecies of the European black kite. Common in savannah, along lakes, rivers and also in towns. **Augur buzzard,** *Buteo rufofuscus:* Very common in mountains, open savannah and cultivated areas.

Eagles: Verreaux's eagle, *Aquila verreauxii:* Rocky hills, mountains and gorges. Kopjes of Serengeti and the escarpment of Lake Manyara are breeding areas. **Tawny eagle,** *Aquila rapax:* Widely distributed. Common in open savannah, cultivated areas, bush, and semideserts. **Martial eagle,** *Polemaetus bellicosus:* Widely distributed. Woodlands, savannah and thornbush. **Long-crested hawk eagle,** *Lophoaetus occipitalis:* Fairly common in riverine forests, bush, wooded and cultivated areas. Can often be seen perched on telegraph poles. **Bateleur eagle,** *Terathopius ecaudatus:* Fairly common in open savannah and thornbush country. Flight is swift and rocking. **African fish eagle,** *Cuncuma vocifer:* Common along rivers, lakes, estuaries and seashore. Loud, haunting call. **Southern banded snake eagle:** *Circaetus cinerascens,* Usambara mountains.

Falcons: Many different species can be seen. **Peregrine,** *Falco peregrinus:* A small race of the well-known cosmopolitan species. **African hobby,** *Falco cuvieri:* A distinct species. Savannah and thornbush country. **Lanner,** *Falco biarmicus:* Seen fairly often in savannah and in dry country, usually near rocks. The shrike-sized **pigmy falcon,** *Poliohierax semitorquatus:* Thornbush and semidesert areas. Smallest of African raptors.

Hawks: There are several species of goshawks and sparrowhawks. **African goshawk,** *Accipeter tachiro.* **Gabar goshawk,** *Micronisus gabar.* **Pale chanting goshawk,** *Melierax poliopterus:* Often seen in acacia and bush country.

Guinea-fowl: Helmeted guinea-fowl, *Numida mitrata:* Widely distributed. Often seen in big flocks. **Vulturine guinea-fowl,** *Acryllium vulturinum.* Dry bush. Maasailand.

Francolins: Yellow-necked spurfowl, *Francolinus leucoscepus:* Widespread and common in dry open bush and grasslands in the vicinity of cultivated areas. **Hildebrandt's francolin,** *Francolinus hildebrandti:* uncommon species. Calls mainly at dawn or dusk. It frequents well-wooded hill country, scrub covered hillsides and sometimes on hillsides where the only cover is a little grass and rock. **Kirk's francolin,** *Francolinus rovuma.*

Coots and crakes: Black crake, *Limnocorax flavirostra:* Common and often seen. Marshes, swamps, river banks and lake shores. Will walk around on a hippo's back. **Red-knobbed coot,** *Fulica cristata:* Lakes, dams and swamps. Seen on the Great Ruaha river. **Purple gallinule,** *Porphyrio porphyrio:* Swamps and papyrus marshes. Can often be seen at Rubondo Island.

Crowned crane, *Balearica regulorum:* Widely distributed. Swamps, lake shores and grasslands. In pairs, small parties, or flocks.

Bustards: Kori bustard, *Ardeotis kori:* Open savannah, thornbush and grasslands. Serengeti, Ngorongoro. **Black-bellied bustard,** *Lissotis* *melanogaster*: Fairly common in open grasslands and cultivated areas. **White-bellied bustard,** *Eupodotis senegalensis*. **Hartlaub's bustard,** *Lissotis hartlaubii*.

Stone curlews: *Burhinus* spp: Of the three species of stone curlews, one is found near water, the others in dry scrub, bush, and open woodlands.

Jacana, or **lily-trotter,** *Actophilornis africanus*: Walks on floating vegetation. Common throughout Lake Victoria.

Plovers and related species: **Crowned plover,** *Stephanibyx coronatus*: Not bound to the vicinity of water. Very common on grasslands, especially in short grassy areas. **Blacksmith plover,** *Hoplopterus armatus*: Common near rivers, swamps and lakes. **Forbes' plover,** *Charidrius mongolus*: Often seen at Gombe Stream. **Senegal plover,** *Stephanibyx lugubris*. **Long-toed lapwing,** *Hemiparra crassirostris*. **Spurwinged plover,** *Hoplopterus spinosus*: Along rivers and lakes, usually seen around Rift Valley lakes. **Wattled plover,** *Afribyx senegallus*: Swamps and damp areas with short grass. Of the smaller species, **Kittlitz's plover,** *Charadrius pecuarius*, and the **three-banded plover,** *Charadrius tricollaris*, are widely distributed on sand banks and mud flats along lakes, rivers, and dams. **Black-winged stilt,** *Himantopus himantopus*: Marshes and salt lakes. Very common at Lake Manyara and Momella lakes. **Avocet,** *Recurvirostra avocetta*: Mud flats, estuaries, and lagoons.

Coursers: Several species on grasslands and dry bush country. **Temminck's courser,** *Cursorius temminckii*: Can often be seen on recently burnt ground. **Heuglin's courser,** *Hemerodromus cinctus*.

Gulls: **Grey-headed gull,** *Larus cirrhocephalus*: Most common gull on East African inland waters. **Sooty gull,** *Larus hemprichii*: Occurs on the coast.

Sandgrouse: Several species. **Yellow-throated sandgrouse,** *Eremialector gutturalis*: One of the most common and widely distributed. At Serengeti and in many other places it can be seen coming to water holes in large flocks. **Black-faced sandgrouse,** *Eremialector decoratus*. **Chestnut-bellied sandgrouse,** *Pterocles exustus*.

Pigeons and doves: Numerous in species and numbers. **Speckled pigeon,** *Columba guinea*: One of the most handsome. **Ring-necked dove,** *Streptopelia capicola*: Widely distributed. Very common in savannah, bush, and cultivated areas. **Namaqua dove,** *Oena capensis*: Dry bush and semidesert areas. The smallest African dove. **Red-eyed dove,** *Streptopelia semitorquarta*: Common in semi-desert bush, forest margins and wooded areas, cultivation and gardens.

Cuckoos: Well represented in East Africa. **Red-chested cuckoo,** *Cuculus solitarius*: Calls "tit-tit-whoo". **White-browed coucal,** or **water-bottle bird,** *Centropus superciliosus*: Skulks in dense bush, especially near rivers and in reed beds. Has a bubbling call, like water being poured out of a bottle. **Emerald cuckoo,** *Chrysococcyx cupreus*; **Didric cuckoo,** *Chrysococcyx caprius*; and **Klaas' cuckoo,** *Chrysococcyx klaas*: Distinguished by the metallic colouration of their upperparts.

Turacos: **Green red-winged turaco,** *Touraco shalowi*: Coastal highland and mountain forests. **Fischer's turaco:** Short crest, hindneck crimson. **Grey turacos** or "go-away" birds are partial to savannah and dry bush. **White-bellied go-away bird,** *Corythaixoides leucogaster*: Common in the Serengeti. **Livingstone's Turaco,** *Turaco livingstonii*: Common in wooded country, mountain and riverine forest in eastern and southern Tanzania.

Rollers: Represented by several species. **Lilac-breasted roller,** *Coracias caudata*: Commonly seen in savannah and bush country. **Broad-billed roller,** *Eurystomus glaucurus*: Forests, savannah, riverine forests and mountain areas, going up into the bamboo zone. **Rufous-crowned roller,** *Coracias naevia*. **Raquet-tailed roller,** *Coracias caudata*.

Bee-eaters, *Melittophagus*: **Little bee-eater,** *Melittophagus pusillus*: Widely distributed. **White-fronted bee-eater,** *Melittophagus bullockoides*: Often seen in the Lake Manyara region. **Cinnamon-chested bee-eater,** *Melittophagus oreobates*: Highland forests. **Carmine bee-eater,** *Merops nubicus*: Common in coastal areas from November to April. The migrant **Southern carmine bee-eater,** *Merops nubicoides* and the winter-visiting **European bee-eater,** *Merops apiaster*.

Kingfishers: Some kingfishers are always found close to water. **Giant kingfisher,** *Megaceryle maxima,* and **Pied kingfisher,** *Ceryle rudis*: Large rivers and lakes. **Malachite kingfisher,** *Corythornis cristata*: Along streams, rivers and lake shores fringed with reeds, papyrus and other dense vegetation. Very pretty **Chestnut-bellied kingfisher,** *Halcyon leucocephala*: Seen far away from water. **Brown-hooded kingfisher,** *Halcyon albiventris*, and **Striped kingfisher,** *Halcyon chelicuti*: Mainly birds of savannah and woodlands.

Hornbills: *Tockus erythrorhynchus*, and others: Widely distributed. Savannah and bush country. Large forest hornbills, such as **Trumpeter hornbills,** *Bycanistes bucinator,* and the **Silvery-cheeked hornbill,** *Bycanistes brevis*: Coastal, riverine, and mountain forests. **Ground hornbill,** *Bucorvus leadbeateri*: Grasslands and savannah. Forages on the ground. **Pale-billed hornbill,** *T. Pallidirostris*: In dry bush and wooded areas.

Hoopoes and wood-hoopoes: The **African hoopoes,** *Upupa* spp: A race of the European species. **Wood-hoopoes** are long-tailed, iridescent green, black, or blue in colour. **Green wood-hoopoe** or **kakelaar,** *Phoeniculus purpureus*: Woodlands and riverine forests. Usually seen in small, noisy flocks. **African scimitarbill,** *Rhinopomastus minor* and *R cyanomelas*. Bush, woodlands and savannah.

Nightjars: Some have distinctive calls, but when seen flitting at night, or sitting on a road in car lights, the many different species are not easy to distinguish from each other.

Owls: African marsh owl, *Asio capensis:* Quite frequently flushed out of high grass. **Verreaux's eagle owl,** *Bubo lacteus:* Often discovered sitting on an acacia tree in riverine forest or savannah country. **Mackinder's owl,** *B. poensis:* uncommon species. Usually found in the highlands, rocky cliffs and escarpments often near water. **African Scop's owl,** *Otus scops.* **White-faced Scop's owl,** *Otus leucotis.* **Spotted eagle owl,** *Bubo africanus.* **Pel's fishing owl.**

Mousebirds: Speckled mousebird, *Colius striatus:* Common and widespread along forest edges, bushy savannah, thick scrub, and cultivated areas. **Blue-naped mousebird,** *Colius macrourus:* Dry bush. **Red-faced mousebird,** *Colius indicus.*

Trogons: Narina's trogon, *Apoloderma narina:* Highland and mountain forests. One of the most beautiful East African birds. Mount Meru.

Barbets: Many species. **Red-and-yellow barbet,** *Trachyphonus erythrocephalus:* Often seen perched on termite hills in dry bush country. One of the most striking. **D'Arnaud's barbet,** *Trachyphonus darnaudii:* Less colourful but worth watching for its interesting mating behaviour. Male and female sing and posture together, bobbing, bowing, and wagging their tail feathers. **Green tinkerbird,** *Viridibucco simplex.*

Honey guides: Greater or **black-throated honey guide,** *Indicator indicator:* So named because they guide humans or honey badgers to bees' nests.

Woodpeckers: Many species. One of the most common and widely distributed is the **Nubian woodpecker,** *Campethera nubica:* All types of savannah country.

Swifts: Various species. Seen practically everywhere, from the streets of Dar es Salaam (**Little Swift,** *Apus affinis*) to the crags of Mount Meru (**Alpine Swift,** *Apus melba*).

Starlings: Many varieties including **Superb starling,** *Spreo superbus:* Very tame around lodges and picnic sites. **Golden-breasted starling,** *Cosmopsarus regius.* **White-winged babbling starling,** *Neocichla gutturalis:* Found in small groups. Uncommon ground feeders. Inhibits woodland especially where trees are well spaced and large.

Sunbirds: Small, often colourful birds that dip their beaks into flowers. Not to be mistaken for hummingbirds. **Scarlet-chested sunbird,** *Chalcomitra senegalensis:* Very striking and often seen. **Scarlet-tufted malachite sunbird,** *Nectarinia johnstoni:* Mt Kilimanjaro region.

Weaver birds: Make beautifully woven nests, often arranged in such large colonies. Yellow or yellow and black. **White-browed sparrow weaver,** *Plocepasser mahali:* One of the most common and widespread. Brown and white plumage. **Red-billed buffalo weaver,** *Bubalornis albirostris:* Male is black. The enormously long-tailed **whydahs** and **widow-birds** are related to the weavers. **Pin-tailed whydah,** *Vidua macroura:* Black and white. At mating time widow-birds perform interesting courtship dances, **Straw-tailed whydah,** *Vidua fischeri.* **Tanzania masked weaver,** *Poceus intermedius:* Common and widespread. Usually found in acacia woodlands, savannah and in the vicinity of swamps and wet areas.

Finches: There are many small and colourful species, especially **cordon bleu,** *Uraeginthus bengalus;* **fire-finch,** *Lagonostica rubricata;* and **purple grenadier,** *Granatina ianthinogaster.*

No traveller in East Africa can miss the black and white **fiscal shrike,** *Lanius collaris.* The shrike family as a whole is very well represented, but many species are shy and less easily seen than the fiscal and its close relations.

Game watchers will soon become aware of two oxpeckers: the **red-billed;** *Buphagus erythrorhynchus,* and the **yellow-billed;** *Buphagus africanus.* They climb around on rhino, buffalo, giraffe and other animals in search of ticks.

Reptile and Amphibian Profile

Nile Crocodile, *Crocodylus niloticus:* Widely distributed in rivers, lakes, and swamps, but much reduced through shooting and trapping. One of their last great sanctuaries is Rubondo Island National Park. The long-nosed crocodile is also common in Lake Tanganyika.

Lizards: Monitor lizards can attain lengths of two metres (seven feet) or even more. **Nile Monitor,** *Varanus niloticus:* Mainly found along rivers. Known to dig up crocodile nests and eat the eggs. **Spotted Monitor,** *Varanus occelatus:* Dry bush and savannah country, at a considerable distance from any water. **Small geckos** have established themselves in human habitations. The adhesive pads on their toes allow them to run up and down walls and even to walk on ceilings. **Rock agama,** or **rainbow lizard,** *Agama agama:* Very beautiful. Can be seen around many of the kopjes of the Serengeti. Males are blue with red heads. Their colours become intense or fade according to their emotional agitation.

Chameleons are represented by a number of species, some of which are armed with horns.

Turtles are common in streams, rivers and the sea.

Tortoises — especially the **leopard tortoise,** *Testudo pardalis* — can often be found in grasslands and savannah.

Snakes: Visitors are usually surprised at the apparent lack of snakes. However, these reptiles are shy and secretive, and some have predominantly nocturnal habits. Only on rare occasions will the tourist travelling by car glimpse a snake as it slithers across the road.

In the country, moving about on foot, you soon realize that snakes are not uncommon. Most venomous species tend to avoid humans, warned of their approach by the ground's vibration.

Black mamba, *Dendroaspis polylepis*: Has a sinister reputation for attacking without provocation, but this usually happens when it finds itself cut off from its hiding place. **Puff adder**, *Bitis arietans*: Widespread and numerous. The most dangerous of Tanzania's snakes. Relying on its wonderful camouflage, it usually does not take evasive action but remains motionless. A person walking through scrub or high grass can easily put their foot within striking distance. **Black-necked** or **spitting cobra**, *Naja nigricollis*: When cornered accidentally it ejaculates its venom, aiming, if possible, at the face of its enemy. **Green tree snake** or **boomslang**, *Dispholidus typus*: May be seen slithering along a branch. It carries its poison fangs so far back in its jaws that to be bitten a human would have to put a finger into its mouth. **Rock python**, *Python sebae*: Widely distributed and quite common although seldom seen. A truly magnificent snake that often attains five metres (16 feet) in length. There are records of pythons measuring more than eleven metres (36 feet). It asphyxiates its victims, and is not poisonous.

Amphibians: East Africa contains its fair share of **caecilians**, **toads**, and **frogs**. There are no newts or salamanders. Frogs are numerous, ranging from tiny **tree frogs** with adhesive pads on their toes, to the huge **bullfrog**, *Pyxicephalus adspersus*, up to twenty-five centimetres (10 inches) in length and able to dig itself into the earth, vanishing within twenty minutes. **Clawed frog**, *Xenopus laevus*: Rarely leaves the water. Has a flattened body, small forelimbs, large hind-limbs and carries sharp, black claws on the first, second and third toe. Males make rattling calls that can be heard for a considerable distance.

Caecilians: The legless, worm-shaped **caecilians** spend most of their time burrowed in the ground, under stones and fallen leaves, or in rotten tree trunks and termite hills. They are rarely seen.

Insect and Arachnid Profile

Most tourists who come to East Africa to collect insects are searching for **butterflies**, **moths**, or **beetles**. For those who know where to look, more than 600 species of butterfly can be found, from the coast to the dry highlands to the relict forests. Only a very few common species are found throughout the entire country.

Along the coastal belt there are several interesting species. *Euphaedra neophron*, a purplish-brown butterfly, is usually seen in the forests and around the cashew nut and coconut plantations; also *Papilio ophidicephalus*, a magnificent black and yellow butterfly whose long tail has a brilliant blue and red patch at its base.

On the inland plains and the grasslands of the Rift Valley, where there is often not enough rain to allow trees to grow, a special group of butterflies has evolved that thrives off dry vegetation — *Colotis*. These white butterflies, with brilliant red or orange tips, are some of the country's most common. So are the blue and yellow pansies, *Precis* spp, which can be seen settled on their territories of dry earth among the grass.

The Eastern Arc Mountains, particularly the Usambaras and Udzungwas, contain the same richness of fauna as the great rainforests of the Congo Basin and attract a similar butterfly population.

The best butterfly areas are also good for **moths**, particularly during the rains. The first night of the wet season is the most productive. It is advisable to use an ordinary pressure lamp and a white sheet for collecting, or the moths will be badly damaged by large beetles.

If it starts raining, or is raining in a normally dry area, any light will produce magical results. Great clouds of moths, along with millions of termites, always appear in the wet weather.

The best areas for **beetles** are the same as for butterflies. During the first nights of the rains the road through the Serengeti often swarms with **dung-beetles**, *Scarabaeidae*.

Spectacular manifestation of insect life are **termite hills.** Up to three metres (10 feet) in height, they're often crowned by a series of turrets containing air shafts or one single hollow tower that resembles a miniature factory chimney.

Termites, often referred to as 'white ants' are related to cockroaches. They may have been the first creatures on Earth to establish a social organization. Deep in the termite castle lies the strongly cemented royal cell where the gigantic queen spends her life tended by an army of workers and well-armed soldiers, producing eggs at a rate of about one every two seconds.

During the wet weather, columns of **soldier ants**, also known as 'safari ants' or *siafu*, march in thick black bands through bush and forest. These bands are formed by a two-way stream of bush ants and are guarded on both flanks by aggressive, large-pincered 'soldiers'.

If you look closely where the column fans out, you'll see a wholesale massacre of spiders, cockroaches, crickets, caterpillars, even of frogs.

An **arthropod** not classified among the insects is the **giant millipede**, popularly known as the 'Tanganyika Train'. This glossy black creature with reddish-brown legs grows up to thirty centimetres (12 inches) in length and is perfectly harmless. However, the big **centipedes** that lurk under tree trunks and fallen leaves have a venomous bite.

There are **scorpions** in Tanzania, most of them are small with disagreeable but harmless stings. In dry bush country, they can be up to twenty centimetres (eight inches) long and little yellow ones that are as dangerous as they look. Scorpions are related to **spiders**. Most are harmless with the exception of the uncommon relation of the black widow, *Latrodectes*. Its bite is venomous though not necessarily fatal.

Wildlife Checklist

MAMMALS

INSECTIVORES
(Insectivora)
East African Hedgehog
Ruwenzori Golden
  Mole
Spectacled Elephant
  Shrew
Yellow-Rumped
  Elephant Shrew
Otter Shrew
Giant White-Toothed
  Shrew

BATS
(Chiroptera)
Banana Bat
Angola Free-Tailed Bat
Flat-Headed Free-
  Tailed Bat
Giant Free-Tailed Bat
White-Bellied Free-
  Tailed Bat
Epauletted Fruit Bat
Hammer-Headed Fruit
  Bat
Straw-Coloured Fruit
  Bat
Hollow-Faced Bat
Lander's Horseshoe
  Bat
Giant Leaf-Nosed Bat
Lesser Leaf-Nosed Bat
Long-Eared Leaf-
  Nosed Bat
African Mouse-Eared Bat
Mouse-Tailed Bat
White-Bellied Tomb Bat
False Vampire Bat
Yellow-Bellied Bat
Yellow-Winged Bat

GREAT APES,
GALAGOS,
MONKEYS,
& POTTOS
(Primates)
Olive Baboon
Yellow Baboon
Chimpanzee
Greater Galago
Lesser Galago
Blue Monkey
Black and White
  Colobus
Red Colobus
Patas Monkey
Red-Tailed Monkey
Sykes' Monkey

Black-Faced Vervet
  Monkey
Potto

PANGOLIN
(Pholidota)
Lesser Ground
  Pangolin

CARNIVORES
(Carnivora)
Aardwolf
Honey Badger
Caracal
African Wild Cat
Golden Cat
Cheetah
African Civet
African Palm Civet
Bat-Eared Fox
Large-Spotted Genet
Small-Spotted Genet
Spotted Hyena
Striped Hyena
Black-Backed Jackal
Golden Jackal
Side-Striped Jackal
Leopard
Lion
Banded Mongoose
Black-Tipped
  Mongoose
Dwarf Mongoose
Large Grey Mongoose
Marsh Mongoose
White-Tailed
  Mongoose
Clawless Otter
Spotted-Necked Otter
Serval
Wild Dog
Zorilla

AARDVARK
(Tubulidentata)
Aardvark

HYRAXES
(Hyracoidea)
Rock Hyrax
Tree Hyrax

ELEPHANT
(Elephantidae)
African Elephant

ODD-TOED
UNGULATES
(Perissodactyla)
Black Rhinoceros
Burchell's Zebra

EVEN-TOED
UNGULATES
(Artiodactyla)
Roan Antelope
Sable Antelope
African Buffalo
Bushbuck
Bush Pig
Kirk's Dik-Dik
Ader's Duiker
Blue Duiker
Bush Duiker
Harvey's Duiker
Yellow-Backed Duiker
Eland
Grant's Gazelle
Thomson's Gazelle
Common Giraffe
Masaai Giraffe
Coke's Hartebeest
Hunter's Hartebeest
Jackson's Hartebeest
Lichtenstein's
  Hartebeest
Hippopotamus
Impala
Klipspringer
Greater Kudu
Lesser Kudu
Oribi
Fringe-Eared Oryx
Bohor Reedbuck
Sitatunga
Steinbok
Suni
Topi
Wart Hog
Common Waterbuck
Wildebeest
Gerenuk

HARES
(Lepus)
African Hare
Spring Hare

RODENTS
(Rodentia)
Rock Hare
African Dormouse
Cane Rat
Crested Rat
Giant Rat
Mole Rat
Naked Mole Rat
Porcupine
Bush Squirrel
Giant Forest Squirrel
Striped Ground
  Squirrel
Unstriped Ground
  Squirrel

BIRDS

OSTRICH
(Struthionidae)
Ostrich

GREBE
(Podicipidae)
Little Grebe

PELICANS
(Pelecanidae)
Pink-Backed Pelican
White Pelican

CORMORANTS
(Phalacrocoracidae)
Long-Tailed
  Cormorant
White-Necked
  Cormorant

DARTER
(Anhingidae)
African Darter

EGRETS & HERONS
(Ardeidae)
Yellow-Billed Egret
Little Egret
Cattle Egret
Black-Headed Heron
Goliath Heron
Grey Heron
Night Heron
Squacco Heron

HAMMERKOP
(Scopidae)
Hammerkop

STORKS
(Ciconiidae)
Abdim's Stork
Marabou Stork
Open-Billed Stork
Saddle-Bill Stork
White Stork
Yellow-Billed Stork

IBISES &
SPOONBILLS
(Threskiornithidae)
Hadada Ibis
Sacred Ibis
African Spoonbill

FLAMINGOS
(Phoenicopteridae)
Greater Flamingo
Lesser Flamingo

SECRETARY BIRD
(Sagittariidae)
Secretary Bird

VULTURES
(Accipitridae)
Egyptian Vulture
Hooded Vulture
Lammergeier
Nubian Vulture
Palm-Nut Vulture
Ruppel's Vulture
White-Backed Vulture
White-Headed Vulture

BIRDS OF PREY
(Accipitridae)
Augur Buzzard
African Fish Eagle
Bateleur Eagle
Ayres' Hawk Eagle
Crowned Hawk Eagle
Long-Crested Eagle
Martial Eagle
Tawny Eagle
Verreaux's Eagle
Wahlberg's Eagle
Southern Banded
Snake Eagle
African Goshawk
Pale Chanting
Goshawk
Gabar Goshawk
Montagu's Harrier
African Marsh Harrier
European Marsh
Harrier
Pallid Harrier
Harrier Hawk
Great Sparrow Hawk
Little Sparrow Hawk
African Black Kite
European Black Kite
Black-Shouldered Kite

FALCONS
(Falconidae)
Peregrine Falcon
Lanner Falcon
Pygmy Falcon
African Hobby
European Hobby
European Kestrel
Lesser Kestrel
Dickinson's Kestrel

FRANCOLINS, QUAILS & SPURFOWL
(Phasianidae)
Crested Francolin
Kirk's Francolin
Hildebrandt's
Francolin
Red-Necked Spurfowl

Yellow-Necked
Spurfowl

GEESE
(Anatidae)
Egyptian Goose
Knob-Billed Goose
Spurwing Goose

DUCKS
(Anatidae)
African Pochard
Yellow-Billed Duck
Red-Billed Duck
White-faced Tree-Duck
Falvous Tree-Duck
Hottentot Teal
Cape Wigeon

GUINEAFOWL
(Numididae)
Crested Guineafowl
Helmeted Guineafowl
Vulturine Guineafowl

CRANE
(Gruidae)
Crowned Crane

COOTS & CRAKES
(Rallidae)
Red-Knobbed Coot
African Crake
Black Crake
Purple Gallinule

BUSTARDS
(Otididae)
Black-Bellied Bustard
White-bellied Bustard
Hartlaub's Bustard
Jackson's Bustard
Kori Bustard

JACANA
(Jacanidae)
African Jacana

PLOVERS & ALLIES
(Charadriidae)
Blacksmith Plover
Crowned Plover
Kittlitz's Plover
Senegal Plover
Three-Banded Plover
Wattled Plover
Black-Winged Stilt
Long-toed Lapwing

COURSERS
(Glareolidae)
Temminck's Courser
Heuglin's Courser

GULL
(Laridae)
Grey-Headed Gull
Sooty Gull

SANDGROUSE
(Pteroclididae)
Black-Faced
Sandgrouse
Chestnut-Bellied
Sandgrouse
Yellow-Throated
Sandgrouse

DOVES & PIGEONS
(Columbidae)
Laughing Dove
Namaqua Dove
Emerald Spotted Dove
Red-Eyed Dove
Ring-Necked Dove
Tambourine Dove
Green Pigeon
Speckled Pigeon

COUCALS, CUCKOOS & TURACOS
(Cuculidae)
White-Browed Coucal
Red-Chested Cuckoo
White-Bellied Go-
Away Bird
Hartlaub's Turaco
Livingstone's Turaco
Schalow's Turaco
Ross's Turaco

OWLS
(Strigiformes)
African Marsh Owl
Spotted Eagle Owl
Verreaux's Eagle Owl
Pel's Fishing Owl
African Scops Owl
White-Faced Scops
Owl
Pearl-Spotted Owlet
Mackinder's Owl

SWIFTS
(Apodidae)
Horus Swift
Little Swift
Mottled Swift
Palm Swift
White-Rumped Swift
Alpine Swift

MOUSEBIRDS
(Coliidae)
Blue-Naped Mousebird
Red-Faced Mousebird
Speckled Mousebird

TROGONS
(Trogonidae)
Narina's Trogon

KINGFISHERS
(Halcyonidae)
Chestnut-Bellied

Kingfisher
Giant Kingfisher
Half-Collared
Kingfisher
Malachite Kingfisher
Pied Kingfisher
Pygmy Kingfisher
Striped Kingfisher
Brown-hooded
Kingfisher

BEE-EATERS
(Meropidae)
Boehm's Bee-Eater
European Bee-Eater
Little Bee-Eater
Madagascar Bee-Eater
Southern Carmine Bee-
Eater
Swallow-Tailed Bee-
Eater
White-Throated Bee-
Eater

ROLLERS
(Coraciidae)
Broad-Billed Roller
European Roller
Lilac-Breasted Roller
Racquet-Tailed Roller
Rufous-Crowned
Roller

HOOPOES
(Upupidae)
African Hoopoe
European Hoopoe

SCIMITARBILLS & WOOD-HOOPOES
(Phoeniculidae)
African Scimitarbill
Green Wood-Hoopoe
Violet Wood-Hoopoe

HORNBILLS
(Bucerotidae)
Crowned Hornbill
Grey Hornbill
Red-Billed Hornbill
Yellow-Billed Hornbill
Pale-Billed Hornbill
Trumpeter Hornbill
Silvery-Cheeked
Hornbill
Ground Hornbill

BARBETS
(Capitonidae)
D'Arnaud's Barbet
Red and Yellow Barbet
Red-Fronted Barbet
Golden-Rumped
Tinkerbird
Red-Fronted
Tinkerbird
Green Tinkerbird

WOODPECKERS
(Picidae)
Bearded Woodpecker
Cardinal Woodpecker
Grey Woodpecker
Little-Spotted
  Woodpecker
Nubian Woodpecker

LARKS
(Alaudidae)
Fawn-Coloured Lark
Flappet Lark
Rufous-Naped Lark
Fischer's Sparrow Lark
Short-Tailed Lark

MARTINS &
SWALLOWS
(Hirundinidae)
African Rock Martin
Banded Martin
Angola Swallow
European Swallow
Mosque Swallow
Red-Rumped Swallow
Striped Swallow
Wire-Tailed Swallow

LONGCLAWS, PIPITS
& WAGTAILS
(Motacillidae)
Yellow-Throated
  Longclaw
Golden Pipit
Long-Billed Pipit
African Pied Wagtail

BULBUL
(Pycnonotidae)
Yellow-Vented Bulbul

SHRIKES
(Laniidae)
Slate-Coloured Boubou
Tropical Boubou
Black-Headed Gonolek
Fiscal Shrike
White-Crowned Shrike
Black-Headed Tchagra

THRUSHES & ALLIES
(Turdidae)
Anteater Chat
Robin Chat
White-Browed Robin
  Chat
Stone Chat
White-Starred Bush
  Robin
Olive Thrush
Capped Wheatear

WARBLERS
(Sylviidae)
Black-Breasted Apalis
Grey-Backed
  Camaroptera
Hunter's Cisticola
Rattling Cisticola
Crombec
Tawny-Flanked Prinia

FLYCATCHERS
(Muscicapidae)
Silverbird
Blue Flycatcher
Paradise Flycatcher
White-Eyed Slaty
  Flycatcher
Chin-Spot Puffback

TITS
(Paridae)
African Penduline Tit
Black Tit
Grey Tit
Cinnamon-Breasted Tit
White-Breasted Tit

SUNBIRDS
(Nectariniidae)
Amethyst Sunbird
Beautiful Sunbird
Bronze Sunbird
Collared Sunbird
Eastern Double-
  Collared Sunbird
Golden-
  Winged Sunbird

Malachite Sunbird
Mariqua Sunbird
Red-Chested Sunbird
Scarlet-Chested
  Sunbird
Tacazze Sunbird
Variable Sunbird

WHITE-EYE
(Zosteropidae)
Yellow White-Eye

BUNTINGS, CANARIES
& FINCHES
(Fringillidae)
Golden-Breasted
  Bunting
Brimstone Canary
Yellow-Fronted Canary
Locust Finch
Quail Finch
Streaky Seed-Eater
Yellow-Rumped Seed-
  Eater

WAXBILLS & ALLIES
(Estrildidae)
Red-Cheeked Cordon
  Bleu
Red-Billed Firefinch
Purple Grenadier
Bronze Mannikin
Green-Winged Pytilia
Cut-Throat
Common Waxbill
Yellow-Bellied Waxbill
Paradise Whydah
Pin-Tailed Whydah
Straw-Tailed Whydah

WEAVERS & ALLIES
(Ploceidae)
Black-Winged Bishop
Red Bishop
West Nile Red Bishop
Yellow Bishop
Cardinal Quelea
Red-Billed Quelea
Black-Headed Weaver
Red-Billed Buffalo

Weaver
White-Headed Buffalo
  Weaver
Chestnut Weaver
Taveta Golden Weaver
Masked Weaver
Vitelline Masked Weaver
Golden Palm Weaver
Red-Headed Weaver
Baglafecht Weaver
White-Browed Sparrow
  Weaver
Spectacled Weaver
Speke's Weaver
Grey-Capped Social
  Weaver
Jackson's Widow-Bird
Red-Collared
  Widow-Bird
White-Winged Widow-
  Bird

STARLINGS
(Sturnidae)
Blue-Eared Starling
Golden-Breasted
  Starling
Hilderbrandt's Starling
Ruppell's Long-Tailed
  Starling
Red-Billed Starling
Superb Starling
Violet-Backed Starling
Wattled Starling
White-Winged Babbling
  Starling

CROWS
(Corvidae)
Indian House Crow
Pied Crow
Fan-Tailed Raven
White-Naped Raven
Cape Rook

OXPECKERS
(Buophagus)
Red-Billed Oxpecker
Yellow-Billed Oxpecker

Demographic Profile

Population
According to 1996 estimates the population of Tanzania stands at 29 million. This figure includes the 801,000 inhabitants of Zanzibar and Pemba islands as well as 30,000 unassimilated Asians. The country's annual growth rate is one of the continent's highest at 3.2 per cent.

Death rates
The infant mortality rate was estimated for the most recent population census data in 1978 to be 137 per 1,000 live births. Of the 1,000 children born, 231 were estimated to die before their fifth birthday. More than half of all deaths in Tanzania are of children under five years old.

Language
Each one of Tanzania's 120 tribes features their own customs, traditions, and language, so in 1963 Swahili was made the lingua franca, a Bantu based language with a strong Arabic influence which is widely understood throughout the country. Until 1967 English maintained joint status as an official language. It remains today the language of higher education and is also used in business and international circles.

Religion
Freedom of worship exists in Tanzania. Thirty-two per cent of the country's inhabitants follow their traditional beliefs, thirty-three per cent are Christians, thirty-five per cent are Muslim, and a very small minority adhere to Hinduism.

Gazetteer

(Second line indicates kilometre distance between major towns)

ARUSHA
Arusha Region.
Dar es Salaam 647, Dodoma 687, Kigoma 1,216, Morogoro 625, Moshi 85, Mwanza 855, Namanga 72, Singida 386, Tabora 730, Tanga 439.
Pop: 200,000. Alt: 1,390m (4,560ft). Post Office. Hospital Tel: 3351. Police Tel: 3561. Petrol. Hotel. Airport.

BUKOBA
West Lake Region.
Dar es Salaam 1,763, Kigoma 558, Musoma 658, Mwanza 420, Nzega 501, Tabora 616.
Pop: 60,000. Alt: 1,000m (3,280ft). Post Office. Hospital Tel: 351. Police Tel: 357/444. Petrol. Hotel. Airport.

DAR ES SALAAM
Dar es Salaam Region.
Arusha 647, Dodoma 479, Iringa 501, Kigoma 1,539, Lindi 449, Mbeya 851, Morogoro 196, Moshi 562, Mwanza 1,178, Ndola 1,896, Tabora 1,053, Tanga 354.
Pop: 2 million. Alt: sea-level. Post Office. Hospital Tel: 30081/74324/23895. Police Tel: 21266/27063/29596/62061. Petrol. Hotel. Airport.

DODOMA
Dodoma Region.
Dar es Salaam 479, Arusha 687, Iringa 251, Morogoro 283, Singida 230.
Pop: 200,000. Alt: 1,115m (3,658ft). Post Office. Hospital Tel: 21851. Police Tel: 21721. Petrol. Hotel. Airport.

IRINGA
Iringa Region.
Dar es Salaam 501, Dodoma 251, Mbeya 350, Morogoro 305, Songea 491.
Pop: 90,000. Alt: 1,582m (5,190ft). Post Office. Hospital Tel: 2041. Police Tel: 2046. Petrol. Hotel. Airstrip.

KIGOMA
Kigoma Region.
Dar es Salaam 1,539, Arusha 1,216, Moshi 1,301, Mpanda 340, Mwanza 1,237, Nzega 601, Tabora 716.
Pop: 100,000. Alt: 773m (2,536ft). Post Office. Hospital Tel: 533. Police Tel: 6. Petrol. Hotel. Airstrip.

LINDI
Lindi Region.
Dar es Salaam 449, Mtwara 106, Nangurukuru 169, Songea 601.
Pop: 100,000. Alt: sea-level. Post Office. Hospital Tel: 2027. Police Tel: 2505. Petrol. Hotel. Airport.

MBEYA
Mbeya Region.
Dar es Salaam 851, Iringa 350, Mpanda 169, Songea 509, Tunduma 109.
Pop: 200,000. Alt: 1,744m (5,721ft). Post Office. Hospital Tel: 3571/3502. Police Tel: 3505. Petrol. Hotel. Airport.

MOROGORO
Morogoro Region.
Dar es Salaam 196, Arusha 625, Dodoma 283, Iringa 305, Moshi 540, Tanga 332.
Pop: 120,000. Alt: 521m (1,708ft). Post Office. Hospital Tel: 2645. Police Tel: 2111. Petrol. Hotel. Airport.

MOSHI
Kilimanjaro Region.
Dar es Salaam 562, Arusha 85, Dodoma 772, Kigoma 1,301, Morogoro 540, Mwanza 940, Namanga 157, Singida 471, Tanga 354.
Pop: 100,000. Alt: 831m (2,726ft). Post Office. Hospital Tel: 2325/2741. Police Tel: 4511. Petrol. Hotel. Airport.

MTWARA
Mtwara Region.
Dar es Salaam 555, Lindi 106, Songea 689, Nangurukuru 275.
Pop: 110,000. Alt: sea-level. Post Office. Hospital Tel: 2226. Police Tel: 2221. Petrol. Hotel. Airport.

MUSOMA
Mara Region.
Dar es Salaam 1,416, Bukoba 658, Mwanza 238, Nzega 478, Shinyanga 401, Tabora 593.
Pop: 63,000. Alt: 1,134m (3,720ft). Post Office. Hospital Tel: 111. Police Tel: 117. Petrol. Hotel. Airport.

MWANZA
Mwanza Region.
Dar es Salaam 1,178, Arusha 885, Bukoba 420, Kigoma 1,237, Moshi 940, Musoma 238, Nzega 240, Tabora 355.
Pop: 250,000. Alt: 1,134m (3,720ft). Post Office. Hospital Tel: 3066. Police Tel: 40805. Petrol. Hotel. Airport.

SONGEA
Ruvuma Region.
Dar es Salaam 992, Iringa 491, Lindi 601, Mbeya 509, Mtwara 689, Tundura 266.
Pop: 120,000. Alt: 1,400m (4,590ft). Post Office. Hospital Tel: 240. Police Tel: 223. Petrol. Hotel. Airport.

TABORA
Tabora Region.
Dar es Salaam 1,053, Arusha 730, Bukoba 616, Kigoma 716, Musoma 593, Mwanza 355, Rungwa 272, Singida 344.
Pop: 100,000. Alt: 1,202m (3,943ft). Post Office. Hospital Tel: 2122. Police Tel: 2206. Petrol. Hotel. Airport.

TANGA
Tanga Region.
Dar es Salaam 354, Arusha 439, Lungalunga 72, Morogoro 332, Moshi 280.
Pop: 210,000. Alt: sea-level. Post Office. Hospital Tel: 2381. Police Tel: 40602. Petrol. Hotel. Airport.

ZANZIBAR
Zanzibar Region.
Arusha 772, Bagamoyo 43, Dodoma 554, Iringa 576, Kigoma 1,614, Lindi 524, Mbeya 926, Morogoro 271, Moshi 687, Mwanza 1,253, Ndola 1,971, Tabora 1,128, Tanga 125.
Pop: 160,000. Alt: sea-level. Post Office. Hospital Tel: 31071. Police Tel: 30246/30771. Petrol. Hotel. Airport.

National Museums and Historical Sites

Catholic Mission, Bagamoyo
Region: Coast
Features: Erected in 1868 by the fathers of the Holy Ghost, this house of worship was the first to be built in East Africa. It was in this chapel that Livingstone's body lay before being taken to Zanzibar en route to Westminster Abbey. Within the church is a small museum containing relics of the slave trade and displays about the early European explorers Burton, Speke and Stanley.

Old Prison, Bagamoyo
Region: Coast
Features: During the trading heyday of the nineteenth century, slaves were held in the back courtyard, then herded blindfolded through an underground tunnel to waiting dhows. Today this historic building is the local police station.

National Museum, Dar es Salaam
Region: Dar es Salaam
Features: Established in 1940, this museum contains archaeological collections displaying some of the most important fossil hominid finds excavated, notably the partial skull of *Zinjanthropus* (Nutcracker man), unearthed by Mary Leakey at Olduvai Gorge. The museum also contains displays of handicrafts, witchcraft paraphernalia, and traditional dancing instruments.

Village Museum, Dar es Salaam
Region: Dar es Salaam
Features: These authentically constructed dwellings display a variety of Tanzania's distinct architectural styles and locally made handicrafts and features traditional dance performances.

Ujiji
Region: Dodoma
Features: Lakeside Ujiji is one of Africa's oldest and most vibrant market villages and it was there that the famous words "Dr Livingstone, I presume", were spoken by the explorer and journalist, Henry Morton Stanley. Although the original mango tree where Stanley doffed his cap is now gone, the event is commemorated by a bronze plaque located in the garden of the Ujiji Cultural Centre.

Sukuma Museum, Mwanza
Region: Mwanza
Features: The first of Tanzania's tribal museums, Sukuma Museum (also referred to as Bujora Museum), offers information about the local Sukuma tribe. The museum also boasts an excellent drum collection and features traditional dance performances including the spectacular Bugobogobo and the Sukuma Snake Dance.

Amboni Caves and Hot Springs, Tanga
Region: Tanga
Features: During the 1950s and '60s, many tourists visited the Tanga Hot Springs — which were reputed to hold curative powers. The arrival of the 1980s saw the springs fall into a state of neglect. The Amboni Caves are noted for their beautiful stalactites, stalagmites and animal paintings.

Tongoni Ruins, Tanga
Region: Tanga
Features: Comprising more than forty tombs dating back to the tenth century, the Tongoni Ruins contain the largest concentration of ancient burial sites found along the East African coast.

Arab Fort, Zanzibar
Region: Town/West
Features: Surrounded by towering stone walls, the Arab Fort was built by the Portuguese in 1700.

Beit el Ajaib (House of Wonders), Zanzibar
Region: Town/West
Features: Constructed in 1883 by Sultan Barghash, this four-storey structure is the tallest in Zanzibar.

Jozani Forest, near Pete, Zanzibar
Region: South
Features: This 484-acre reserve is the only sanctuary of the Zanzibar red colobus monkey.

Kidichi Persian Baths, Zanzibar
Region: Town/West
Features: Constructed at the beginning of the nineteenth century by Sultan Sayyid Said for his Persian wife, these remarkably preserved domed bathhouses are built on the island's highest point at 153 metres (504 feet).

Livingstone's House, Zanzibar
Region: Town/West
Features: The famous missionary/explorer used this site between January and March of 1866, to gather his essential supplies before setting out on his final expedition.

Mangapwani Slave Caves, near Bumbwini, Zanzibar
Region: North
Features: After the abolition of slavery in the late 1800s, these underground caves were used to hold slaves captive until the dhows could slip past the British blockade under the cover of night.

Maruhubi Palace Ruins, Zanzibar
Region: Town/West
Features: Only a few rooms and arches remain of this nineteenth-century palace built by Sultan Sayyid Barghash to house his harem.

National Museum, Zanzibar
Region: Town/West
Features: Exhibits of local wildlife, dhow construction, traditional carving and relics from the era of the Sultans and early explorers are all on display at this quaint museum.

Old Slave Market/Cathedral Church of Christ, Zanzibar
Region: Town/West
Features: Originally the site of the afternoon slave market, the location today is marked by the first Anglican cathedral to be built in East Africa. Inside the church, constructed in 1897, the altar occupies the spot where the whipping block used to be.

People's Palace, Zanzibar
Region: Town/West
Features: This historic building was once the home of the Sultan and his royal family.

Shirazi Mosque, near Kizimkazi, Zanzibar
Region: South
Features: This ancient mosque, dating back to AD 1107, was the first to be built on the East African coast.

PUBLIC HOLIDAYS		VARIABLE DATES
1 January	New Year's Day	
12 January	Zanzibar Revolution Day	Good Friday
5 February	Founding of the Chama Cha Mapinduzi Party (CCM)	Easter Monday
26 April	Union Day	Idd-ul-Fitr (end of Ramadan)
1 May	International Worker's Day	
7 July	Peasant's Day	Islamic New Year
9 December	Tanzania Independence and Republic Day	The Prophet's Birthday
25 December	Christmas Day	

Listings

Dialling Codes

Arusha	57
Chake Chake	54
Dar es Salaam	51
Dodoma	61
Iringa	64
Kilimanjaro Airport	575
Mbeya	65
Mkoani	54
Morogoro	56
Moshi	55
Mtwara	59
Mwanza	68
Tabora	62
Tanga	53
Wete	54
Zanzibar	54

Airlines

Arusha
Air France
c/o Abercrombie and Kent
Novotel Mt Meru
PO Box 427
Tel/Fax: 8988

Precisionair
AICC Building
PO Box 1636
Tel: 6903/2836/7319

Dar es Salaam
Aeroflot
Eminaz Mansion
Samora Avenue
PO Box 2758
Tel: 113332

Air Botswana
c/o Emsilies
PO Box 6684
Tel: 35065/6

Air India
Bibi Titi Street
PO Box 1709
Tel: 117036/41

Air Tanzania
ATC House
Ohio Street
PO Box 543
Tel: 110245/48
Fax: 113114

Air Zaire
IPS Building
Samora Avenue
PO Box 2554
Tel: 20836/25988

Air Zimbabwe
Kilimanjaro Hotel
Tel: 23526/21747

Alliance Air
Bibi Titi Street
PO Box 76404
Tel: 117044/7

Alitalia
AMI Building
Samora Avenue
PO Box 9281
Tel: 23621/24318

British Airways
Sheraton Hotel
PO Box 2439
Tel: 113820/2/116756/30204
Fax: 112629

EgyptAir
Matasalamat Bldg
Samora Avenue
PO Box 1350
Tel: 113333

Ethiopian Airlines
TDFL Building
Ohio Street
PO Box 3187
Tel: 20863/20933
Telex: 42101

Gulf Air
PO Box 9794
Tel: 22112/22814

Kenya Airways
Peugeot House
PO Box 3804
Tel: 119376-7

KLM Royal Dutch Airlines
Peugeot House
PO Box 3804
Tel: 113336/7

Lufthansa
Upanga Road
PO Box 1993
Tel: 46813/38844

PIA
IPS Building
Samora Avenue
PO Box 928
Tel: 31263/46292

Precisionair
PO Box 70770
Tel: 30800

Royal Swazi
TDFL Building
PO Box 22636
Tel: 51-11357
Fax: 51-113182

Swissair
Luther House
Sokoine Drive
PO Box 2109
Tel: 118870-2
Telex: 41644

South African Airways
PO Box 76044
Tel: 117044-8
Fax: 116715

Zambia Airways
IPS Building
Azikiwe Street
PO Box 21276
Tel: 29071/2/24316

Nairobi
Air Malawi
(Kenya office)
PO Box 42676
Tel: 333683/240965
Fax: 340212

Zanzibar
Air Tanzania
PO Box 773
Tel: 32441/30213

Gulf Air
PO Box 3179
Tel: 33379/33221

Kenya Airways
PO Box 3840
Tel: 32041-3

Precision Air
PO Box 1511
Tel: 30029/16

Air Charter Companies

Arusha
Corsair Novotel
Mt Meru Hotel
PO Box 2752
Tel: 57-2480
Fax: 57-4287

Fleet Air
PO Box 432
Tel: 7612
Fax: 7612
Telex: 42067

Dar es Salaam
Aviazur Ltd
PO Box 70999
Tel: 51-843075

Dar Air Charters
Old Terminal 1
PO Box 18104
Tel: 844158

General Aviation Services
PO Box 18166
Tel: 51-843313
Fax: 51-843313

Nahalo Air Safaris Ltd
PO Box 20066
Tel: 843201-2/0811 320812
Fax: 116711
E-mail: noble@twiga.com

Tanzania Air Services
Sheraton Hotel
PO Box 364
Tel: 113151/112416
Fax: 112946

Dodoma
Mission Aviation Fellowship
Air Charter Msalato
PO Box 491
Tel: 21535/20224

Zanzibar
Air Zanzibar
PO Box 1784
Tel: 32512/33098
Fax: 32512

Coastal Travel
Air Charter
PO Box 992
Tel: 33112
Fax: 33112

Island Air Services
PO Box 907
Tel: 31228/32550
Fax: 32546

Skyland Safaris and Travel
PO Box 518
Tel: 32652/31744

Sky Tours
PO Box 4040
Tel: 33689
Fax: 33089

ZAN Air
PO Box 2113
Tel: 33768
Fax: 33670

Airports

Dar es Salaam International Airport
PO Box 543
Tel: 844610

Dodoma Airport
Dodoma
Tel: 21938/21465

Kigoma Airport
Kigoma
Tel: 165

Kilimanjaro International Airport
Moshi
Tel: 2223

Mtwara Airport
Mtwara
Tel: 2177/2475

Mwanza Airport
Mwanza
Tel: 2741

Tabora Airport
Tabora
Tel: 2042

Tanga Airport
Tanga
Tel: 2991/3006

Zanzibar Airport
Zanzibar
Tel: 32001/32872

Accommodation

Arusha
Arusha Duluti
PO Box 376
Tel: 2699

Dik Dik Hotel
PO Box 1499
Usa River
Tel/Fax: 8110

Hotel Equator
PO Box 3002
Tel: 8410-2
Fax: 4379
Telex: 42034

Hotel Seventy-
Seven
Moshi Road
PO Box 1184
Tel: 3800
Telex: 42055

Hotel Tanzanite
Usa River
PO Box 3063
Tel: 8455

Impala Hotel
(Kijenge Area)
PO Box 7302
Tel: 8448-51/2398/
7083
Fax: 8220/8680

Kirurumu Luxury
Tented Lodge
PO Box 2047
Tel: 7011/7541
Fax: 8226

Masai Campsite
PO Box 6130
Tel: 8299

Momella Lodge
PO Box 418
Tel: 3038/3798

Mountain
Village Lodge
PO Box 376
Tel: 2699/2799/
8967
Fax: 8749
Telex: 42107

Mount Meru
Game Lodge
Moshi Road
PO Box 659
Tel: 7179

Novotel
Mount Meru
Moshi Road
PO Box 877
Tel: 2711/8804/
4292
Fax: 8303/8503

New Arusha Hotel
PO Box 88
Tel: 8541/3
Telex: 42034

New Safari Hotel
PO Box 303
Tel: 8545
Telex: 42038

Ngarasero
Mountain Lodge
Usa River
PO Box 425
Tel: 3629

Ol Donyo
Orok Lodge
PO Box 535
Tel: 7020
Telex: 42047

Bagamoyo
Bagamoyo
Beach Hotel
PO Box 250
Tel: 83

Bodego
Beach Hotel
PO Box 261
Tel: 22

Gogo Hotel
Bagamoyo Road
PO Box 21114
Tel: 68410/67785

Traveller's Lodge
PO Box 275
Tel: 77

Dar es Salaam
Amani Beach Club
PO Box 1547
Tel: 600020/601721
Fax: 602131

Bahari Beach Hotel
PO Box 9312
Tel: 647051
Fax: 647052

Baobab Village
PO Box 250
Tel: 602012
Telex: 41268

Dar es Salaam
Sheraton
Ohio Street
PO Box 791
Tel: 51-112416
Fax: 51-113981

The Haven
at Kunduchi
PO Box 23272
Tel: 811-323443
Fax: 811-320525

Hotel Agip
PO Box 529
Tel: 117075/6
Fax: 117079

Hotel Embassy
Garden Avenue
PO Box 3152
Tel: 111181/117086
Fax: 112634

Hotel Karibu
PO Box 20200
Tel: 67940/68458
Fax: 68254

Hotel Mawenzi
Maktaba Street
PO Box 3222
Tel: 27761
Telex: 41384

Keys Hotels
Uhuru Street
PO Box 5330
Tel: 52250

Kilimanjaro Hotel
Kirukoni Front
PO Box 9574
Tel: 11088/8
Fax: 113304

Kunduchi
Beach Hotel
PO Box 9313
Tel: 47622/3
Telex: 41061

Mafia Island Lodge
PO Box 2485
Dar es Salaam

Mahale Mountains
Tented Camp
PO Box 1658
Telex: 41782

Motel Afrique
Kaluta Street
PO Box 2572
Tel: 31034

Motel Agip
City Drive
PO Box 529
Tel: 35711
Telex: 41276

Mount
Usambara Hotel
PO Box 22770
Tel: 181309

New Africa Hotel
PO Box 9314
Tel: 117132/050/1
Fax: 116731/112495

Oyster Bay Hotel
Toure Drive
PO Box 2261
Tel: 668062/4
Fax: 668631

Palm Beach Hotel
Upanga Road
PO Box 1520
Tel: 38437/28892

Queen of
Sheba Hotel
PO Box 63080
Tel: 71780

Silversands Hotel
PO Box 60097
Tel: 47427/8

Starlight
PO Box 3199
Tel: 119387/8/9

Twiga Hotel
Independence
Avenue
PO Box 1194
Tel: 22561
Telex: 41114

WhiteSands Hotel
PO Box 3030
Tel: 51-113678/
116483
Fax: 51-118483/
39885

Vatican City Hotel
Sinza Block D
PO Box 45110
Tel: 48447

Dodoma
Dodoma Hotel
PO Box 239
Tel: 22992

Iringa
Isimila Hotel
PO Box 216
Tel: 64-2605

Karatu
Ndutu Safari Lodge
PO Box 1501
Tel: 25 Karatu
Telex: 42041

Kigoma
Aqua Lodge
PO Box 34
Tel: 695-2408
Fax: 695-3707

Railway Hotel
Tel: 900 ext
Kigoma 64

Lake Tanganyika
Beach Hotel
PO Box 9
Tel: 695-2694/3633

Mahale
Mountain's
Tented Camp
PO Box 1373

Manyara
Kirurumu
Tented Lodge
Hoopoe
Adventure Tours
PO Box 2047
Arusha
Tel: 7011/7541

Lake Manyara
Hotel
PO Box 3100
Arusha
Tel: Mto wa mbu 10

Maji Moto
Luxury Tented
Camp
PO Box 217
Arusha
Tel: 6079/7931/
7880
Fax: 0576475
Telex: 42110

Lake Manyara
Serena
PO Box 2551
Arusha
Tel: 57-8175
Fax: 8282

Mbeya
Mount
Livingstone Hotel
PO Box 1401
Tel: 3331-4

Rift Valley Hotel
PO Box 1631
Tel: 4429/4351

Mikumi
Mikumi
Wildlife Camp
PO Box 2261
Dar es Salaam
Tel: (51) 668062/4
Fax: (51) 668631

New Mikumi
Wildlife Lodge
PO Box 6550
Dar es Salaam
Tel (51) 75399/
74159
Fax: (51) 75398

Morogoro
Morogoro Hotel
PO Box 1144
Tel: 3270/2

Savoy Hotel
PO Box 35
Tel: 2345

Sofia Hotel
PO Box 557
Tel: 4847/8

Moshi
Hotel Capricorn
PO Box 938
Marangu
Tel: 51309
Fax: 51309

Hotel Newcastle
PO Box 2000
Tel: 50853

Keys Hotel
PO Box 933
Tel: 50075/52250
Fax: 50073
Telex: 43159

Kibo Hotel
PO Box 102,
Marangu
Tel/Fax: 51308/
52687

Kilimanjaro
View Hotel
PO Box 6467
Tel/Fax: 50335

Marangu Hotel
PO Box 40
Tel: 51307
Fax: 50639

Moshi Hotel
PO Box 1819
Tel: 52439/55248/

Moshi View Hotel
PO Box 13
Tel: 50993
Fax: 50994

New Kindoroko
Hotel
PO Box 1341
Tel: 54054/52988
Fax: 54062

Mwanza
Jafferies Hotel
PO Box 647
Tel: 42075/41393

New Mwanza Hotel
PO Box 25
Tel: 500551/088/
40620/2
Telex: 46284

Ngorongoro
Gibbs' Farm
(Ngorongoro
Safari Lodge)
PO Box 2, Karatu
Tel: 4040
Fax: Arusha 8310

Ndutu Safari Lodge
PO Box 6084, Karatu
Tel: 6702/8310
Fax: Arusha 8310

Ngorongoro
Crater Lodge
PO Box 751,
Arusha
Tel: 8187/3303/
3530

Ngorongoro
Serena
Safari Lodge
AICC Building
Ngorongoro wing
PO Box 2551
Arusha
Tel: 57-6304/8175
Fax: 57-4058

Ngorongoro
Sopa Lodge
PO Box 1823
Arusha
Tel: 57-6886/6896
Fax: 57-8245

Ngorongoro
Wildlife Lodge
PO Box 3100
Arusha
Tel: 8622
Arusha 4604

Ruaha
Ruaha River Lodge
PO Box 10270
Dar es Salaam
Tel: 327706
Fax: 327706

Ruaha River Camp
PO Box 3052
Dar es Salaam

Selous
Beho Beho
Safari Camp
PO Box 2261
Dar es Salaam
Tel: (51) 668062/4
Fax: (51) 668631

Mbuyu Safari
Camp
PO Box 2341
Dar es Salaam
Tel: 24897
Fax: 75862

Selous Safari Camp
PO Box 1192
Dar es Salaam

Stiegler's
Gorge Camp
PO Box 9320
Dar es Salaam

Rufiji River Camp
PO Box 13824
Dar es Salaam
Tel: 71610/75164
Fax: 75165

Sand River's Camp
PO Box 70192
Dar es Salaam

Serengeti
Grumeti
River Camp
PO Box 2174
Tel: 6079/7931/
7880

Kijireshi
Tented Camp
Western Corridor
Serengeti
PO Box 190
Tel: 40139/41068
Telex: 46213

Lobo
Wildlife Lodge
PO Box 3100
Tel: Radio Call
Arusha 4419

Serengeti
Safari Lodge
Uhuru Road
PO Box 3100
Arusha
Tel: 2960/2404/
2858/3173
Telex: 42037

Serengeti
Sopa Lodge
PO Box 1823
Arusha
Tel: 57-6886/6896
Fax: 57-8245

Seronera
Wildlife Lodge
PO Box 3100
Arusha
Tel: Radio Call
Arusha 4643

Serena
Kirawira Camp
PO Box 2551
Arusha
Tel: 57-6304/4159
Fax: 57-4155/8185

Tanga
Baobab
Beach Hotel
PO Box 180
Tel: 40162
Fax: 40162
Telex: 45132

Mkonge Hotel
Hospital Road
Ras Kazone
PO Box 1544
Tel: 44542/6

Tarangire
Oliver's Camp
PO Box 425
Arusha
Tel: 3108
Fax: 8548

Tarangire
Safari Lodge
PO Box 1182
Tel: 3090/3625
Telex: 42038

Tarangire
Sopa Lodge
PO Box 1823
Arusha
Tel: 57-6886/6896
Fax: 57-8245

Tukuyu
Rift Valley Hotel
PO Box 7
Tel: 3756

Zanzibar
Africa
House Hotel
PO Box 216
Tel: 30709

Baghani
House Hotel
PO Box 609
Tel: 811-321058
Fax: 33030

Bwawani Hotel
PO Box 670
Tel: 30200/30760
Telex: 57157

Changuu
Island Resort
(Prison Island)
PO Box 216
Tel: 32344
Telex: 57144

Clove Hotel
PO Box 1117
Tel: 31785
Telex: 57018

East Coast Beach
Bungalows
PO Box 216
Tel: 32344
Telex: 57144

Emerson's
Guesthouse
PO Box 4044
Tel: 30609/32153

Hotel International
PO Box 3784
Tel: 33182
Fax: 54-30052

High Hill Hotel
PO Box 907
Tel: 30000/32550

Karafuu Hotel
PO Box 71
Tel: 811-325157
Fax: 811-325670

Lail-Noor
Guest House
PO Box 132
Tel: 31086

Maruhubi Hotel
PO Box 216
Tel: 30341/32344
Telex: 57144

Mawimbi
Club Village
PO Box 4281
Tel: 31163

Mazson's Hotel
PO Box 3367
Tel: 54-33694/
33062
Fax: 54-33695

Mbweni
Ruins Hotel
PO Box 2542
Tel: 31832
Fax: 30536

Oyster Hotel
PO Box 4199
Tel: 31560

Pyramid Hotel
PO Box 254
Tel: 33000/30045
Fax: 33000

Ras Nungwe
Beach Resort
PO Box 1784
Tel: 33767
Fax: 33098

Sau Inn Hotel
PO Box 1656
Tel: 32215

Shangani Hotel
PO Box 4222
Tel: 33688/33524
Fax: 33688

Spice Inn Hotel
PO Box 1029
Tel: 30728/9

Uwanjani Hotel
PO Box 516
Tel: 32804/5/6
Telex: 56132

Zanzibar Hotel
PO Box 216
Tel: 30708/9

Zanzibar
Reef Hotel
PO Box 2586
Mazizini
Tel: 473034/471771

Zanzibar
Serena Inn
PO Box 3716
Tel: 33051

Zanzibar Village
PO Box 2529
Tel: 0811-320987

Banks

Arusha
Bank of Tanzania
PO Box 3043
Tel: 3414

National Bank
of Commerce
PO Box 1256
Tel: 7085

Clock Tower
Branch
Tel: 2093

Mount Meru
Branch
Tel: 3484

Uhuru Road
Branch
Tel: 2732

Dar es Salaam
Bank of Tanzania
PO Box 2939
10 Mirambo Street
Tel: 21291
Telex: 41024

National Bank
of Commerce
NBC House
Sokoine Drive
PO Box 1255
Tel: 28671
Telex: 41201/41018

Airport Branch
Tel: 42266

Kichwele Branch
Tel: 23499

Mnazi Road
Branch
Tel: 25370

Morogoro Road
Branch
Tel: 23182

Pugu Road Branch
Tel: 64832

Temeke Branch
Tel: 50142

Twiga Branch
Tel: 36083

Kenya Commercial
Bank (Tanzania)
Limited
PO Box 804
Tel: 115388
Fax: 115391

Stanbic Bank
Tanzania Ltd
PO Box 72647
Tel: 112195/8
Fax: 113742

Standard
Chartered Bank
Tanzania Ltd
Sukari House
PO Box 9011

Dodoma
National Bank
of Commerce
PO Box 888
Tel: 22191

Kuu Street Branch
Tel: 21619

Mazengo Branch
Tel: 22454

Karatu
National Bank
of Commerce
PO Box 1600
Tel: 24

Mafia
National Bank
of Commerce
PO Box 200
Tel: 23

Mbeya
Bank of Tanzania
PO Box 1203
Tel: 2433

National Bank
of Commerce
PO Box 418
Tel: 3361

Karume Avenue
Branch
Tel: 2245

Mbalizi Road
Branch
Tel: 2547

Mbulu
National Bank
of Commerce
PO Box 33
Tel: 64

Monduli
National Bank
of Commerce
PO Box 2
Tel: 32

Moshi
Bank of Tanzania
Arusha Road
Tel: 4389

National Bank
of Commerce
PO Box 3022
Tel: 2520

Boma Road
Branch
Tel: 2042

Kibo Branch
Tel: 2804

Mawenzi Branch
Tel: 4401

Mwanza
Bank of Tanzania
PO Box 1362
Tel: 40071

National Bank
of Commerce
PO Box 1580
Tel: 40483

Kenyatta Road
Branch
Tel: 40115

Nyerere Road
Branch
Tel: 40600

Regional Drive
Branch
Tel: 2446

Tanga
Bank of Tanzania
Independence
Avenue
Tel: 40709

National Bank
of Commerce
PO Box 5039
Tel: 40052

Bank Street
Branch
Tel: 2149

Madaraka Branch
Tel: 40434/2287

Market Street
Branch
Tel: 2363

Zanzibar
Bank of Tanzania
PO Box 568
Tel: 30803

Greenland
Bank Ltd
Tel: 0182-780607

National Bank
of Commerce
PO Box 157
Tel: 32507

People's Bank
of Zanzibar
PO Box 1173
Tel: 11138/9

Bars/ Nightclubs

Dar es Salaam
Bandari Grill
PO Box 9314
Tel: 29611
Telex: 81049

Las Vegas Casino
Ali Hassan
Mwinyi Road
Tel: 116512

Princess Bar
Libya Street
PO Box 15198
Tel: 21628

Safari Resort
PO Box 25172
Tel: 48499

Shirikisho Bar
Ukwani Street
Kawe
PO Box 60011
Tel: 47768

Simba Grill
PO Box 9574
Tel: 21281
Telex: 41021

Business Associations and Societies

Arusha
Arusha Chamber
of Commerce and
Agriculture
PO Box 141
Tel: 3721

Arusha
Co-op Union
PO Box 7073
Tel: 6515

Tanzania
Association of
Agricultural
Employers
50 Haile Selassie Rd
PO Box 97
Tel: 2017

Tanzania
Coffee Growers
Association
PO Box 102
Tel: 7308

Tanzania Farmers
Association
School Road
PO Box 3010
Tel: 3191

Dar es Salaam
Association
of Business
Consultants
PO Box 3361
Tel: 28336

Association of
Commercial
Enterprises
29 Morogoro Road
PO Box 392
Tel: 21558

Association
of Tanzania
Employers
AMI Building
Samora Avenue
PO Box 2971
Tel: 22981/23152

Automobile
Association
of Tanzania
Cargen House
Azikiwe Street
PO Box 3004
Tel: 27727
Fax: 112363

Commonwealth
Trade Union
Council of East
Africa
Uhuru Street
PO Box 8031
Tel: 31220

Dar es Salaam
Merchants Chamber
Market Street
PO Box 12
Tel: 22267

Dar es Salaam
Regional
Multi-Purpose
Co-op Union
Lumumba Street
PO Box 71170
Tel: 30497

Dar es Salaam
Transport
Co-op Society
PO Box 15260
Tel: 24352

Institution of
Engineers of
Tanzania
PO Box 2938
Tel: 29236
Fax: 36585
Telex: 41924

Insurance Brokers
of East Africa
Samora Avenue
PO Box 1947
Tel: 29134

Law Reform
Commission of
Tanzania
Maktaba Street
PO Box 35801
Tel: 36859

Tanzania
Association of
Accountants
THB Building
Sokoine Drive
PO Box 459
Tel: 36493

Tanzania
Association of
Chambers of
Commerce
Kelvin House
Samora Avenue
PO Box 41
Tel: 21893
Telex: 41628

Tanzania Boy
Scouts Association
Malik Road
PO Box 945
Tel: 22707

Tanzania
Christian Medical
Association
Saint Alban's
Church
Upanga Road
PO Box 9433
Tel: 27720

Tanzania Council
of Koran Reading
4 Sukuma Street
PO Box 15433
Tel: 36703

Tanzania Diabetes
Association
PO Box 65201

Tanzania Drivers
Association
Sokoine Drive
Station
PO Box 15210
Tel: 21742

Tanzania Law
Society
Makunganya Street
PO Box 2148
Tel: 21907

Tanzania Leprosy
Association
Ocean Road
Hospital
PO Box 5478
Tel: 31926

Tanzania Machines
Co-op Society
Morogoro Road
PO Box 5890
Tel: 37245

Tanzania
Mechanical
Engineers Co-op
Chang'ombe Road
PO Box 40057
Tel: 63922

Tanzania Red
Cross Society
Upanga Road
PO Box 1133
Tel: 20464

Tanzania Society
for the Blind
598 United
Nations Road
Makunganya Street
PO Box 2254
Tel: 26139

Tanzania
Society for the
Preservation and
Care of Animals
Morogoro Road
PO Box 1844
Tel: 20534

Tanzania Stars
Co-op Society
Makunganya Street
PO Box 1756
Tel: 35192

Tanzania Tea
Growers
Association
Luther House
Sokoine Drive
PO Box 2177
Tel: 22033

Dodoma
Railway
African Union
5th Avenue
Private Bag
Tel: 20250

Mbeya
Agricultural
Sector Support
Programme
Co-operative
Forest Area
PO Box 678
Tel: 2978

Mbeya Area
Consumer
Co-op Society
Soko Motor Street
PO Box 218
Tel: 2597

Mbeya
Co-op Union
Sisimba Street
PO Box 174
Tel: 3476

Morogoro
Morogoro Farmers
Co-op Society
Korogwe Road
PO Box 608
Tel: 3996

Moshi
Association
of Business
Consultants
Kawawa Street
PO Box 691
Tel: 2097

Kilimanjaro
Society for Child
Welfare
PO Box 267

Moshi and District
Consumers
Co-op Society
Kawawa Street
PO Box 606
Tel: 4806

Tanzania Sugar
Manufacturers
Association
PO Box 93
Tel: 2331

Musoma
Associated
Builders
PO Box 133
Tel: 240

Mwanza
Associated Builders
Post Street
Tel: 3105

Mwanza Uzahishaji
Co-op Society
Airport Road
PO Box 1422
Tel: 2913

Bus
Companies

Arusha
Imam Bus
and Transport
Wapare Street
PO Box 7061
Tel: 3886

Dar es Salaam
National Bus
Service
(Kamata)
Msimbazi Street/
Pugu Road
PO Box 9302
Tel: 27631/26095

Nyota Bus Service
Narung'ombe St
PO Box 25053
Tel: 38298

Usambara Line
Transport Bus
Service
6 Mkunguni Street
PO Box 5838
Tel: 37058

Moshi
Upare Bus Service
Old Moshi Road
PO Box 644
Tel: 4377

Mwanza
African Bus Service
Custom Road
PO Box 932
Tel: 41524

Amin Mungu
Safari Bus
Plot No 157
Lumumba Street
PO Box 1972
Tel: 2068

Pamba Quick
Bus Services
Rwagasore Street
PO Box 1613
Tel: 41348

Car Hire

Arusha
Hertz
PO Box 3063
Tel: 8459

Ker and Downey
Safaris
PO Box 2782
Tel: 7755/7700
Telex: 42013

K's Enterprises
Kaloleni
PO Box 1318
Tel: 6465

Dar es Salaam
Across
Tanzania Safaris
Makunganya St
PO Box 219961
Tel: 23121

Avis
Ghana Avenue
PO Box 6385
Tel: 30505/34562
(Airport: 843162)
Fax: 112979/37442

Bugoni Super
Auto Garage
PO Box 25087
Tel: 63708

Europcar Inter Rent
2 Nelson Mandela
Express Way
PO Box 208
Tel: 0811-786000/
325990
Fax: 0811-326770

Evergreen
PO Box 1476
Tel: 183345/7
Fax: 183348

Hertz
PO Box 20517
Tel: 25753/25237

Hima
PO Box 10879
Tel: 29085/29687
Fax: 111083

Jeka Sokoine Drive
PO Box 22333
Tel: 118517
Fax: 118517

Kara Motors
Car Hire
Morogoro Road
PO Box 64
Tel: 33549

Leisure Tours
and Holidays
Upanga Road
PO Box 6100
Tel: 32251/35982/
27494

Mil Tours
and Safaris
PO Box 19604
Tel: 22114

Trans African
Guides
Indira Gandhi St
PO Box 853
Tel: 34805

White Cabs
Zanaki Street
PO Box 2107
Tel: 23078/30454/
33450
Telex: 41181

Yellow Cabs
Upanga Road
PO Box 6100
Tel: 35981

Mwanza
Khalfan Traders
69 Kaluta Street
Tel: 41072

Masumi's Tours
and Safaris
110 Nkomo Street
PO Box 1884
Tel: 41109

Cinemas

Arusha
Elite Cinema
Jacaranda Street
PO Box 3180
Tel: 3458

Dar es Salaam
Drive-In-Cinema
Old Bagamoyo Rd
PO Box 1525
Tel: 67035

Empire Cinema
Azikiwe Street
PO Box 272
Tel: 20539

Empress Cinema
Samora Avenue
PO Box 9023
Tel: 22395

Odeon Cinema
Zaramo Street
PO Box 577
Tel: 22302

Starlight
Cinema Kisutu
PO Box 3199
Tel: 23845

The New Chox
Nkrumah Street
PO Box 472
Tel: 25331

Moshi
ABC Cinema
Rengua Road
PO Box 785
Tel: 4765

Zanzibar
Empire Cinema
Mkunazini
PO Box 95
Tel: 32265

Clubs

Bukoba
Tanzania Red
Cross Club
Uganda Road
PO Box 860
Tel: 735

Dar es Salaam
Bank Staff Club
PO Box 2939
Tel: 50519

Dar es Salaam
Gymkhana Club
PO Box 286
Tel: 20519/38439

Dar es Salaam
Yacht Club
Leopard Cove
PO Box 1280
Tel: 41814

Fitness Centre
(Health Club)
PO Box 2615
Tel: 67646

Lions Club
PO Box 1620
Tel: 21407

Pearl Club
Upanga Road
PO Box 5350
Tel: 37810/38757

Railway Club
Gerezani
PO Box 475
Tel: 21522

Rotary International
District 920
PO Box 1533
Tel: 64043

Selander
Bridge Club
Bagamoyo Road
PO Box 2124
Tel: 20741

Tanzania
International
Organization of
Good Templers
Kurasini-Shomo
la Udongo
PO Box 6051
Tel: 50169

Mbeya
Mbeya Club
Lupaway Road
PO Box 135
Tel: 3264

Morogoro
Morogoro
Ceramic Club
PO Box 1107
Tel: 4891

Moshi
Moshi Club
Tel: 2022

Mwanza
Mwanza Club
PO Box 246
Tel: 2777

Mwanza
Yacht Club
Usagara Walk
PO Box 760
Tel: 2729

Tanga
Tanga Club
Independence
Avenue
PO Box 5565
Tel: 40924

Tanga Yacht Club
Ras Kazone
PO Box 346
Tel: 40933

Cultural Centres, Libraries and Museums

Arusha
Arusha Declaration
Museum
Kaloleni Road
PO Box 7423
Tel: 3683

Arusha Library
PO Box 1273
Tel: 2642

National Natural
History Museum
Boma Road
PO Box 7423
Tel: 7540

Dar es Salaam
Goethe Institute
German Cultural
Centre
IPS Building
Azikiwe Street
PO Box 9510
Tel: 22227

National Central
Library
UWT Street
PO Box 9283
Tel: 261212

National Museum
of Tanzania
Shaban Robert St
Nyumba ya Sanaa
PO Box 511
Tel: 22030

Village Museum
A H Mwinyi Rd
PO Box 511
Tel: 72850

Other Areas
Bukoba Library
Barongo Road
PO Box 321
Bukoba
Tel: 460

Institute of
Kiswahili and
Foreign Languages
Kidutani SLP 882
Zanzibar
Tel: 30724

Kibaha Library
Kibaha
Tel: 2069

Mara Library
Jamathkhana St
PO Box 874
Musoma
Tel: 183

Mbeya Library
PO Box 842
Mbeya
Tel: 2589

Morogoro Library
Morogoro
Tel: 2160

Moshi Library
Kibo Road
PO Box 863
Moshi
Tel: 2432

Mtwara Library
Uhuru Street
PO Box 37
Mtwara
Tel: 2400

Mwanza Library
Station Road
PO Box 1363
Mwanza
Tel: 2314

Tabora Regional
Library
Lumumba Street
PO Box 432
Tabora
Tel: 2008

Tanga Library
Independence
Avenue
PO Box 5000
Tanga
Tel: 3127

Foreign Diplomatic Missions

Dar es Salaam
Algeria
34 A H Mwinyi Rd
PO Box 2963
Tel: 117619

Belgium
NIC Investment
House
7th Floor - Wing A
Samora Avenue
PO Box 9210
Tel: 112688/113466
Telex: 41094

Bulgaria
Mikocheni
A H Mwinyi Rd
Tel: 72140

Canada
Pan African
Insurance Building
Samora Avenue
PO Box 1022
Tel: 51-112831/5

China
2 Kajificheni Close
Dar es Salaam
Tel: 667586/212

Denmark
Ghana Avenue
PO Box 9171
Tel: 113887/8

Egypt
24 Garden Avenue
PO Box 1668
Tel: 113591/117622
Telex: 41173

Finland
Mirambo St/
Garden Avenue
PO Box 2455
Tel: 119170

France
A H Mwinyi Rd
PO Box 2349
Tel: 666021/3
Telex: 41006

Germany
New NIC Building
10th Floor
Samora Avenue
PO Box 9541
Tel: 117409/13

India
NIC Investment
House
11th Floor —
Wing A
Samora Avenue
PO Box 2684
Tel: 117175/6

Indonesia
299 A H Mwinyi Rd
Tel: 119119/118133

Iran
31 A H Mwinyi Rd
PO Box 5802
Tel: 117623/112255

Ireland
Msasani Rd
Tel: 666211/348

Italy
316 Upanga Road
PO Box 2106
Tel: 115935/6
Telex: 41062

Japan
1018 A H Mwinyi
Road
PO Box 2577
Tel: 115827/9

Kenya
NIC Investment
House
Samora Avenue
PO Box 3152
Tel: 112811/955/8
Fax: 113098

Korea
420, United
Nations Rd
Tel: 115925/118512

Malawi
NIC House
PO Box 7616
Dar es Salaam
Tel: 113238/241
Fax: 113360

Mozambique
25 Garden avenue
Tel: 116502

Netherlands
New ATC Building
Ohio Street
PO Box 9534
Tel:118566/8

Nigeria
Ali Hassan
Mwinyi Road
PO Box 9214
Tel: 666000/1

Norway
Mirambo St/
Garden Avenue
PO Box 2646
Tel: 118807/113366

Pakistan
149 Malik Rd
Tel: 117630

Russia
A H Mwinyi Rd
PO Box 1905
Tel: 666005/6

Rwanda
32 A H Mwinyi Rd
PO Box 2918
Tel: 117631/115889

South Africa
Mwaya Rd
Tel: 600484/5

Spain
99B Kinondoni Rd
PO Box 842
Tel: 666018/9

Sudan
64 A H Mwinyi Rd
Tel: 117641/115811

Sweden
Extelecomms
Building
Mirambo St/
Garden Avenue
PO Box 9274
(Embassy)
PO Box 9303
(SIDA)
Tel: 111235
Telex: 4113

Switzerland
Kinondoni Rd
Tel: 666008/9

Syria
276 Ali Khan Rd
Tel: 117656/118782

Uganda
Samora Avenue
PO Box 6237
Tel: 117646/7

United Kingdom
Hifadhi House
Azikiwe Street/
Samora Avenue
PO Box 9200
Tel: 112953/117659
Telex: 41004

United States
of America
36 Laibon Street/
Bagamoyo Road
PO Box 9123
Tel: 666010/5
Telex: 41250

Yemen
135 United
Nations Road
Tel: 117650/110615

Zambia
Ohio St/Sokoine
Drive
Tel: 118481/2

Zimbabwe
NIC Life Building
Sokoine Drive
Tel: 116789

Hospitals

Arusha
Arusha Provincial
Hospital
PO Box 3092
Tel: 3351

Mount Meru
Hospital
Tel: 3354

Dar es Salaam
Aga Khan Hospital
Ocean Road
PO Box 2289
Tel: 30081

Kigarama Hospital
Regent Estate
PO Box 65300
Tel: 74324

Shree Hindu
Mandal Hospital
Chusi Street

PO Box 581
Tel: 23895/6/
25451/30831

Other Areas
Bagamoyo District
Hospital
Bagomoyo
Tel: 8

Dodoma Provincial
Hospital
PO Box 904
Dodoma
Tel: 21851

Iringa Hospital
Iringa
Tel: 2041

Kigoma
Government
Hospital
Kigoma
Tel: 533

Kondoa District
Hospital
Kondoa
Tel: 8

Lindi Province
Hospital
Lindi
Tel: 2027

Mafia Hospital
PO Box 51
Mafia Island
Tel: 5

Mbeya Provincial
Hospital
PO Box 419
Mbeya
Tel: 3571/3502

Mbulu District
Hospital
Mbulu
Tel: 40

Monduli District
Hospital
Monduli
Tel: 10

Morogoro Hospital
Morogoro
Tel: 2645

KCMC Hospital
Moshi
Tel: 2741

Moshi/
Kilimanjaro
Hospital
Moshi
Tel: 2325

Mpwapwa District
Hospital
Mpwapwa
Tel: 8

Mtwara
Provincial
Hospital
Mtwara
Tel: 2226

Musoma
Provincial
Hospital
PO Box 21
Musoma
Tel: 111

Hindu Union
Hospital
Balewa Road
PO Box 192
Mwanza
Tel: 2090/42070

Sumve Hospital
PO Box Mantare
Ngudu
Tel: 64

Chake Chake
Hospital
Chake Chake
Pemba Island
Tel: 2311

Mkoani Hospital
Pemba Island
PO Box 201
Chake
Tel: Mkoani 6075/
6011

Wete Hospital
Wete
Pemba Island
Tel: 4001

Songea District
Hospital
Songea
Tel: 240

Tabora
Provincial
Hospital
Tabora
Tel: 2122

Tanga Provincial
Hospital
PO Box 5019
Tanga
Tel: 2381

V I Lenin Hospital
PO Box 672
Zanzibar
Tel: 31071

Media

Shihata (State
News Agency)
PO Box 4755
Dar es Salaam
Tel: 29311/38752
Telex: 41080/41147

Newspapers
Business Times
PO Box 71439
Dar es Salaam
Tel: 21731/4
Telex: 41996

Daily and
Sunday News
PO Box 9033
Dar es Salaam
Tel: 29881/25318
Telex: 41072

The Express
PO Box 20588
Dar es Salaam
Tel: 33013/34253
Fax: 37029
Telex: 41147

People's Daily
Bureau
130 Lugalord Road
PO Box 2682
Dar es Salaam
Tel: 33619

Uhuru Newspapers
(*Mzalendo*)
13 Pugu Road
PO Box 9221
Dar es Salaam
Tel: 64341

Magazines
Government Gazette
PO Box 261
Zanzibar

Foreign Trade
News Bulletin
PO Box 9503
Dar es Salaam
Tel: 22775
Telex: 41689

Family Mirror
PO Box 6804
Dar es Salaam
Tel: 37750

The African Review
PO Box 35042
Dar es Salaam
Tel: 49192

Radio
Radio Tanzania
Pugu Road
PO Box 9191
Dar es Salaam
Tel: 63342/38011
Telex: 41201

Voice of
Tanzania-
Zanzibar
PO Box 1178
Zanzibar
Tel: 31088
Telex: 57207

Television
Zanzibar
Television
PO Box 314
Zanzibar
Tel: 32816
Telex: 57200

International
News Services
(Dar es Salaam)
Asia and Africa
Today
Tel: 67641

Associated Press
PO Box 2665
Tel: 23226
Telex: 41542

Inter-Press Service
PO Box 257
Tel: 29311
Telex: 41080

Korean Central
News Agency
Tel: 23598

Moscow TV
and Radio
Tel: 26648

Reuters
PO Box 770
Tel: 36747/25314/
6

TASS
Plot 2112/5-7
Sea View
Tel: 24329

Xinhua News
Agency
72 Upanga Road
PO Box 2682
Tel: 23967
Telex: 41563

Religious Missions

East Africa Union
Mission of Seventh
Day Adventists
Utimbaru Mission
PO Box 15
Tarime
Tel: Radio call
Nairobi 2231

East Africa Yearly
Friends Mission
Station Magumu
PO Box 196
Musoma
Tel: Radio call
Nairobi 2456

Mission Aviation
Fellowship Church
Mission Air
Charter
Msalato
PO Box 491
Dodoma
Tel: 21535/20224

Mission to Seamen
Kilwa Road
PO Box 1179
Dar es Salaam
Tel: 20887/25736

Mission to
the Needy
Uhuru Street
PO Box 7545
Dar es Salaam
Tel: 38273

Missionaries
of Charity
PO Box 1916
Tabora
Tel: 2561

Missionaries
of Charity
Mburahati
PO Box 25086
Dar es Salaam
Tel: 48083

St Joseph's
Mission School
Bridge Street
PO Box 9052
Dar es Salaam
Tel: 20537

Sea Sports and Tour Operators

Zanzibar
Adventure Afloat
PO Box 4056
Tel: 31832/30536

Indian Ocean
Divers
PO Box 2370
Tel: 33860
Fax: 33860

Matemwe
Bungalows
PO Box 3275
Tel: 2554/31342

Mawimbi
Village Club
PO Box 4281
Tel: 31163

Mtoni Marine
Centre
PO Box 992
Tel: 32540
Fax: 32540

One Ocean
Dive Centre
PO Box 608
Tel: 33686
Fax: 31242

Tamarind
Beach Hotel
PO Box 2206
Tel: 33060

Uroa Bay Hotel
PO Box 3389
Tel: 32552
Fax: 33504

Zanzibar Dive
Adventures
PO Box 2282
Tel: 32503
Fax: 32503

Shipping

Zanzibar
The African
Shipping
PO Box 3231
Tel: 330312
Fax: 33032

Azam Marine
PO Box 74
Tel: 33013/02
Fax: 33013

Sea Express
Service
PO Box 4096
Tel: 33013/02
Fax: 33013

Zanzibar Sea
Ferry Ltd
PO Box 2222
Tel: 33725
Fax: 33725

Tanzanian Missions Abroad

Angola
CP 1333
Luanda
Tel: 335205/030/
33686

Belgium
363 Avenue Louise
1050 Brussels
Tel: 6476479/44/
6406500

Burundi
Patrice Lumumba
Avenue
BP 1653
Bujumbura
Tel: 24634/30

Canada
50 Range Road
Ottawa, Ontario
KIN 8 J4
Tel: (613) 2321500/
9

China
53 San Li Tun
Dongliujie
Beijing
Tel: 521408/491/
719

Egypt
9 Abdel Hamid
Loufty Street
Dokki
Cairo
Tel: 704155/286

Ethiopia
PO Box 1077
Addis Ababa
Tel: 448155/6/7

France
70 Boulevard
Pereire Nord
75017 Paris
Tel: 47762177

Germany
Theaterplatz 26
5300 Bonn 2
Tel: (0228) 353477/
356095/6

Guinea
BP 179 Donka
Conakry
Tel: 461332

India
27 Golf Links
New Delhi 110-003
Tel: 694351/2

Italy
Via Giambattista
Visco 9-00196
Rome
Tel: (06) 3610898/
3610901/3611904

Japan
21-9 Kamiyoga
4 Chome
Setagaya-ku
Tokyo 158
Tel: (03) 4254531/3

Kenya
PO Box 47790
Nairobi
Tel: 331056

Mozambique
Ujamaa House
Avenida Marites
Da Machava 852
PO Box 4515
Maputo
Tel: 744025/6/7

Netherlands
Amalistraat No 1
2514 JC The Hague
Tel: (070) 653800/1

Nigeria
8 Agoro Odiyan St
Victoria Island
PO Box 6417
Lagos
Tel: 613594/604

Russia
Pyatnitskaya
Ulitsa 33
Moscow
Tel: 2318146/5431

Rwanda
Rue De Commerce
BP 669
Kigali
Tel: 6074

Saudi Arabia
PO Box 94320
Riyadh
11693
Tel: (45) 42859

Sudan
PO Box 6080
Khartoum
Tel: 78407/9

Sweden
Oxtorgsgatan 2-4
PO Box 7255
103-89 Stockholm
Tel: (08) 244870

Switzerland
47 Avenue Blanc
1202 Geneva
Tel: 318929/20

Uganda
6 Kagera Road
PO Box 5750
Kampala
Tel: 256272

United Kingdom
43 Hertford Street
London W17 8DE
Tel: (071) 499-8951

United States
of America
2139 R Street NW
Washington,
DC 20008
Tel: (202) 9396125

205 East 42nd
Street
13th Floor
New York,
NY 10017
Tel: (212) 9729160

Zaire
142 Boulevard
du 30 Juin
BP 1612
Kinshasa
Tel: 32117

Zambia
Ujamaa House
Plot No 5200
United Nations
Avenue
PO Box 31219
Lusaka
Tel: 211422/665

Zimbabwe
Ujamaa House
23 Baines Avenue
PO Box 4841
Harare
Tel: 721870/
724534/173

Tanzanian Tourist Offices Abroad

Germany
6 Frankfurt/Main
Tel: (0611) 280154
Telex: 413158

Italy
Palazzo Africa
Largo Africa
1 - Milano
Tel: 432870/464421
Telex: 331360

Saudi Arabia
Salahudin Building
Suite 103
PO Box 1349
Manama Bahrain

Sweden
PO Box 7627
10394 Stockholm
Tel: (08) 216700/
216770
Telex: 17187
Tantours

United Kingdom
43 Hertford Street
London W1Y 7TF
Tel: (071) 407-0566
Telex: 262504

United States
of America
201 East
42nd Street
8th Floor
New York,
NY 10017
Tel: (212) 986-7124
Telex: 68320

Tanzanian Tourist Offices

Director of
Operations and
Marketing
Tanzanian Tourist
Corporation
PO Box 2485
Dar es Salaam
Tel: 27671-5/26680
Telex: 41061

Central
Reservations
Serengeti Safari
Lodges
PO Box 3100
Arusha
Tel: 3842
Telex: 42037

State Travel
Service
PO Box 1369
Arusha
Tel: 3300/3113/
3114/3152
Telex: 42138

State Travel
Service
PO Box 5023
Dar es Salaam
Tel: 29291-8
Telex: 41508

Travel, Tour, and Safari Operators

Arusha
Abercrombie
and Kent
PO Box 427
Tel: (057) 7803
Fax: (057) 7003
Telex: 42005

Adventure Tours
and Safaris
PO Box 1014
Tel: 6015

African
Gametrackers
PO Box 535
Tel: 3779

African Trails
PO Box 2130
Tel/Fax: 4406

African
Wildlife Tours
PO Box 767
Tel: 2913/7791

AICC Tours
PO Box 3081
Tel: 3181 ext. 23

Arumeru Tours
and Safaris
PO Box 730
Tel: 7637/2780

Blue Bird Tours
PO Box 1054
Tel: 3934

Bobby Tours
PO Box 716
Tel: 3490

Bushmen
Company
(hunting safaris)
Dodoma Road
PO Box 235
Tel: 6210

Bushbuck Safaris
PO Box 1700
Tel: 7473/7779
Fax: 2954

Chasse D'Afrique
PO Box 384
Tel: 2241

Classic Tours
and Safaris
PO Box 7302
Tel: 7197

Cordial Tours
Tel: 6495
Fax: 8866

Disneyland Tours
and Safaris
PO Box 279
Tel: 6340

Dorobo Tours
and Safaris
PO Box 2534
Tel: 3699

Eagle Tours
and Safaris
PO Box 343
Tel: 2909

Executive
Travel Services
AICC Building
Kilimanjaro Block
PO Box 7462
Tel: 2472/3181
ext. 2279
Telex: 42136

Euro-Tan Safaris
PO Box 1028
Tel: 8777/3747
Fax: 8221

Fauna Safari Club
PO Box 15019
Tel: 4487/8660/2
Fax: 4162

Flamingo Tours
PO Box 2660
Tel: 6976/6152
Telex: 42003

Flight Services
International
PO Box 7155
Tel: 2018

Flycatcher Safaris
PO Box 591
Tel: 3622

Gibbs Farm Safaris
PO Box 2, Karatu
Tel: Arusha 8930/
6702
Fax: 8310

Himat Transport
and Tours
PO Box 7008
Tel: 2242

Hoopoe Tours
India Street
PO Box 2047
Tel: 7011
Fax: 8226

Jas Tours
and Safaris
PO Box 76
Tel: 7381

Jeff's Tours
and Safaris
PO Box 1469
Tel: 6980/7541

K and S Enterprise
PO Box 1318
Tel: 6465

Ker and Downey
Safaris
PO Box 41822
Tel: 556164/466
Fax: 552378/556183

Kingfisher Safaris
PO Box 701
Tel: 2123

King Safari Club
PO Box 7201
Tel: 3958

King Tours and
Hunting Safaris
PO Box 7000
Tel: 3688

KLO
International Hotel
PO Box 6165
Tel: 3181 ext. 121

Laitolya Tours
and Safaris
PO Box 7319
Tel: 2422/2984

Leopard Tours
PO Box 1638
Tel: 7906/8422/3
Fax: 8219/4131

Let's Go Marve
Holidays
ARCU Building
Uhuru Road
PO Box 2660
Tel: 3613

Lions Safaris
International
PO Box 999
Tel: 6422

Moon
Adventure Safaris
PO Box 12023
Tel: 8017

New
Victoria Tours
PO Box 644
Tel: 2735

Ngaresero
Mt Lodge
PO Box 425
Tel: 3629

Nyota Trans Tours
PO Box 2759
Tel: 2276

Ostrich Tours
and Safaris
PO Box 12752
Tel: 4140

Ranger Safaris
AICC Building
PO Box 9
Tel: 3074/3023
Telex: 42063

Roy Safaris
PO Box 50
Tel: 2115/8010
Fax: 8892

Sable Safaris
PO Box 7145
Tel: 6711

Scan-Tan Tours
PO Box 1054
Tel: 6978

Sengo Safaris
PO Box 180
Tel: 6982

Serengeti
Select Safaris
School Road
PO Box 1182
Tel: 7182

Shallom Tours
and Safaris
PO Box 217
Tel: 3181

Shidolya Tours
PO Box 1436
Tel: 8506/2813
Fax: 8242/4160

Simba Safaris
PO Box 1207
Tel: 3509/3600
Telex: 42095

Sokwe
PO Box 3052
Arusha
Tel: 057-8182
Fax: 057-8182

State Travel
Service
PO Box 1369

Star Tours
Uhuru Road
PO Box 1099
Tel: 2553

State Travel
Services
PO Box 1369
Tel: 3300/3113/
3152
Fax: 8209
Telex: 42138

Sunny Safaris
PO Box 7267
Tel: 3181

Tanzania Guides
PO Box 2031
Tel: 3625

Tanzania Serengeti
Adventure
PO Box 1742
Tel: 6769

Tanzania Wildlife
Corporation
37 India Street
PO Box 1144
Tel: 3501

Tanzanite
Wildlife Tours
PO Box 1277
Tel: 2239

Tareto
PO Box 17586
Tel: 31713

Tarimo Tours
PO Box 6125
Tel: 3181

Tarus Tours
and Safaris
PO Box 1254
Tel: 2388

Tracks Travel
PO Box 142
Tel: 3145

Transafrican
Safaris
PO Box 468
Tel: 6305

Tropical Tours
PO Box 727

Universal Tours
PO Box 1264

U T C
PO Box 2211
Tel: 7931
Fax: 6475
Telex: 42110

Wapa Tours
and Safaris
PO Box 6165
Tel: 3181

Wildersun Safaris
and Tours
Jael Maeda Road
PO Box 930
Tel: 6471/3880

Wildtrack Safaris
PO Box 1059
Tel: 3547

W J Travel Service
New Arusha Hotel
PO Box 88
Tel: 6444

Dar es Salaam
Across
Tanzania Safaris
PO Box 21996

African
Expeditions
Mindu Street
PO Box 1857
Tel: 34574/38985

All African
Travel Agents
PO Box 1947
Tel: 20886

Ami
Samora Avenue
PO Box 9041
Tel: 115777/9

Azania Tours
and Travel
UWT Street
PO Box 3707
Tel: 36959

Bahari Enterprises
and Safaris
PO Box 15384
Tel: 63422/29

Bon Voyage
Travels
Zanaki St
Tel: 33080/25951

Coastal Travels
Upanga Road
PO Box 3052
Tel: 37479/37480

Cordial Tours
(hunting safaris)
Jamhuri Street
PO Box 1679
Tel: 38070
Fax: 116685

Delvims Travel
International
Sukari House
Tel: 119797

East African
Holidays
PO Box 2895
Tel: 25989

Easy Travels Ltd
Kilimanjaro Hotel
Tel: 23526/21747

Fauna Safari Club
PO Box 77590
Tel: 30551/29
Fax: 116454

Flag Tours
and Safaris
PO Box 16046
Tel: 37075

Gerald Posanisi
Safaris
(hunting safaris)
PO Box 45640
Tel: 47435

Gogo Safaris
Mkwepu Street
PO Box 21114
Tel: 0811/321552

Hippo Tours
and Safaris
Kilimanjaro Hotel
PO Box 13824
Tel: 71610/75164
Fax: 75165
E-mail:-
hippo@twiga.com

Hit Holidays
Bibi Titi Street
PO Box 1287
Tel: 0811/324552

Holiday Africa
Tours and Safaris
Ohio Street
PO Box 2132
Tel: 11357/8

Hotel Tours and
Management
PO Box 5350
Tel: 31957/32671

Iramba Tours
PO Box 21856
Tel: 44482

Kara Motors
PO Box 64
Tel: 33549

Kearsley
Kearsley House
Indira Gandhi St
PO Box 801
Tel: 115183/4
Telex: 42126

Leisure Tours
and Safaris
PO Box 6100
Tel: 32251

Mill Tours
and Safaris
PO Box 19604
Tel: 22114

Molenveld
Travel Agency
Samora Avenue
Tel: 0811/324609

Multi Travel
and Tours
Zanaki Street
PO Box 6940
Tel: 30501/22147

Panorama Tours
PO Box 7534
Tel: 31200/35663

Parklands Tours
PO Box 19630
Tel: 68586

Parkways Tours
and Safaris
PO Box 6549
Tel: 6731

Pwani Tours
and Safaris
Kaluta Street/
Morogoro Road
PO Box 50007
Tel: 22433/32261

Reza Travels
and Tours
Jamhuri St
Tel: 334458/34814

Safari Travels
Samora Avenue
PO Box 9442
Tel: 28422/28737/
28765

Savannah Tours
PO Box 4382
Tel: 0811-326782/
38088

Skylink Travel
and Tours
Ohio Street
Tel: 115381/30110

State Travel Service
PO Box 5033
Tel: 112747/110038

Sunshine
Safari Tours
PO Box 5575
Tel: 22700

Sykes Travel
Agents
Indira Gandhi
Street
PO Box 1947
Tel: 110552/115542
Telex: 41046

Takims Holidays,
Tours and Safaris
PO Box 20350
Tel: 25691/2/3
Telex: 41351
Arusha branch tel:
3174

Tankar Limited
PO Box 5286
Tel: 31091

Tanzania Tourist
Corporation
PO Box 2485
Tel: 27672-5

Tourcare Tanzania
PO Box 22878
Tel: 112752/4
Fax: 119411

Trans African
Guides
PO Box 853
Tel: 30912

Valji and Allibhai
Bridge Street
PO Box 786
Tel: 20522/26537/
37561

Walji Travels
PO Box 434
Tel: 111157
Telex: 41180

Iringa
Iringa Safaris
and Tours
PO Box 107

Karatu
Gibbs Farm Safaris
PO Box 2
Tel: Karatu 25
Telex: 42041

Marangu
Kibo Hotel
PO Box 102
Tel: 4

Morogoro
Vulture
Hunting Safaris
PO Box 3180
Tel: 2234

Moshi
Emslies Tours
Old Moshi Road
PO Box 29
Tel: 2701/4742

Fortes Safaris
Lumumba Street
PO Box 422
Tel: 41764

Fourways
Travel Services
Station Road
PO Box 990
Tel: 2620

Kilimanjaro
Guide Tours
PO Box 210
Tel: 50120
Fax: 51220

Mauly Tours
and Safaris
Rombo Avenue
PO Box 1315
Tel: 2787

M J Safaris
PO Box 9593
Tel/Fax: 51241

Shah Tours
and Travel
PO Box 1821
Tel: 52998
Fax: 51449

Trans Kibo Travels
PO Box 558
Tel/Fax: 52017/
51241

Zara Travel
Agency
PO Box 1990
Tel: 4240

Mwanza
Masumi's Garage
PO Box 1884
Tel: 2890

Tanga
Khanbhai Tanzania
Safaris
PO Box 169
Tel: 40350

Zanzibar
Asumi Tours
and Travel
PO Box 2758
Tel: 30298
Fax: 30298

Centre
Island Tours
PO Box 3445
Tel: 33845
Fax: 33845

Chema Brother
PO Box 1865
Tel: 33385
Fax: 33642/33385

Dolphin Island
Tours and Travel
Agency (DITTA)
PO Box 138
Tel: 33386

Equator Tours
and Safaris
PO Box 2096
Tel: 33799
Fax: 33882

Fazea Tours
PO Box 1224
Tel: 33326/30638
Fax: 33326

Fernades Tours
PO Box 547
Tel: 30666
Fax: 33102

Fisherman Tours
PO Box 3509
Tel: 31859/33060

Jasfa Tours
and Safaris
PO Box 4203
Tel: 31560
Fax: 32387

Kikuba Tours
PO Box 1887
Tel: 33416/33292
Fax: 33020

Maha Tours
PO Box 1511
Tel: 30029
Fax: 30016

Maya Tours
PO Box 3508
Tel: 30986
Fax: 33202

Madeira Tours
PO Box 251
Tel: 30406
Fax: 30406

Modesty Tours
PO Box 2331
Tel: 32999
Fax: 33080

Mreh Tours
PO Box 3769
Tel: 33476
Fax: 30344

Mystique Tours
PO Box 3409
Tel: 31615

Orient Expeditions
PO Box 4253
Tel: 30813
Fax: 30344

Rainbow Tours
and Safaris
PO Box 2173
Tel: 33469
Fax: 33469

S and M Company
PO Box 3175
Tel: 33475
Fax: 33475

Salama Tours,
Travel and Cargo
PO Box 3179
Tel: 32824/33772/3

Sama Tours
and Safaris
PO Box 2276
Tel: 33543
Fax: 33543

Serene Tours
PO Box 326
Tel: 31816
Fax: 31859

Spot Tours
PO Box 2210
Tel: 33923
Fax: 33925

Stone Town Safaris
PO Box 2209
Tel: 30423
Fax: 30423

Triple M Tours
PO Box 139
Tel: 33073

United Travel
Agency (UTA)
PO Box 122
Tel: 30874/32258

World Wide Travel
and Tourism
PO Box 180
Tel: 30993/32041
Fax: 30990

Zanzibar
SeventyTours
PO Box 3268
Tel: 30705
Fax: 30705

Zanzibar Travel
and Tourism
Agency
PO Box 4064
Tel: 31930
Fax: 33138

Zanzibar Tourist
Corporation (ZTC)
PO Box 216
Tel: 32344
Fax: 33430

Zanzique Tours
PO Box 154
Tel: 31033
Fax: 31033

Zenith Tours
PO Box 3643
Tel: 32320/33973
Fax: 32320

Taxis

Dar es Salaam
Jamhuri Taxi
and Tours
Jamhuri Street
PO Box 20998
Tel: 31543

Purshotam Taxi
4 Bridge Street
PO Box 2205
Tel: 21916

White Cabs
PO Box 2107
Tel: 23078/30454/
33450

Moshi
Azizi Taxi
Market Road
PO Box 1972
Tel: 2336

Theatre

Dar es Salaam
Players
Little Theatre -
Oysterbay
PO Box 1845

Dar es Salaam
Tel: 34446

Bibliography

Africa Explored: Europeans in the Dark Continent 1769-1889 (1982), by Christopher Hibbert, published by Penguin, London.

African Wildlife Safaris, Spectrum Guide to (1989), published by Camerapix International, Nairobi.

Africa on a Shoestring (1989), by Geoff Crowther, published by Lonely Planet, Victoria.

Africa's Rift Valley (1974), by Colin Willock, published by Time-Life International, Netherlands.

An Ice Cream War (1983), by William Boyd, published by Penguin, London.

Arusha National Park (1987), published by the African Wildlife Foundation and Tanzania National Parks, Arusha.

East Africa (1986), published by Time-Life Books, Amsterdam.

East Africa, A Travel Survival Kit (1987), by Geoff Crowther, published by Lonely Planet Publications, Victoria.

East Africa International Mountain Guide (1986), by Andrew Wielochowski, published by West Col Productions.

East African Mountains and Lakes (1971), by Leslie Brown, published by East African Publishing House, Nairobi.

East African Wildlife, Insight Guide to (1989), by APA Publications, Hong Kong.

Eastern Africa — Handbook for the Traveller & Businessman (1983), published by Travintal, Hong Kong.

A Field Guide to the Birds of East Africa (1980), by J G Williams and N Arlott, published by Collins, London.

A Field Guide to The Larger Mammals of Africa, by Jean Dorst and Pierre Dandelor, published by Collins, London.

A Field Guide to the Mammals of Africa (1980), by Theodor Haltenorth and Helmut Diller, published by Collins, London.

A Field Guide to the National Parks of East Africa (1981), By J G Williams, published by Collins, London.

The Great Rift: Africa's Changing Valley (1988), by Anthony Smith, published by BBC Books, London.

Guide to East Africa (1985), by Nina Casimati, published by Travelaid Publishing, London.

A Guide to Kenya and Northern Tanzania (1971), by David F Horrobin, published by East African Publishing House, Nairobi.

Guide to Mount Kenya and Kilimanjaro (1981), published by the Mountain Club of Kenya, Nairobi.

A Guide to Tanzania National Parks (1988), by Lilla N Lyogello, published by Travel Promotion Services, Dar es Salaam.

A History of the Arab State of Zanzibar (1978), by Norman Bennet, published by Methuen, London.

A History of Zanzibar (1970), by S G Ayany, published by East Africa Literature Bureau, Nairobi.

Journey through Tanzania (1984), by Mohamed Amin, Duncan Willetts, and Peter Marshall, published by Camerapix Publishers International, Nairobi.

Kilimanjaro (1982), by John Reader, published by Elm Tree Books, London.

Kilimanjaro National Park (1987), by Jeannette Hanby, published by African Wildlife Foundation and Tanzania National Parks, Arusha.

Kilimanjaro, the White Roof of Africa (1985), by Harald Lange, published by The Mountaineers, Seattle.

The Lakes and Mountains of Eastern and Central Africa (1968), by J Elton, published by Frank Cass, London.

Lake Manyara National Park (1986), published by the African Wildlife Foundation and Tanzania National Parks, Arusha.

The Making of Tanganyika (1965), by Judith Listowel, published by Chatto and Windus, London.

Mikumi National Park (1987), published by the African Wildlife Foundation and Tanzania National Parks, Arusha.

National Development Corporation — 24th Annual Report 1988 (1988), compiled and published by the authors, Karatu.

National Investment Promotion Policy (1990), published by The President's Office — Planning Commission, Dar es Salaam.

Ngorongoro Conservation Area (1988), by Jeanette Hanby and David Bygott, published by Tanzania National Parks, Dar es Salaam.

Origins (1979), by Richard Leakey and Roger Lewin, published by Macdonald and Jane's, London.

Railway Across the Equator, the Story of the East African Line (1986), by Mohamed Amin, Duncan Willetts and Alastair Matheson, published by Bodley Head, London.

Sand Rivers (1981), by Peter Matthiessen, published by Aurum Press, London.

School Atlas for Zanzibar (1983), published by the Ministry of Education, Zanzibar.

Selous Game Reserve — A Guide to the Northern Sector, by Rolf D Baldus.

Serengeti, A Kingdom of Predators (1973), by George B Schaller, published by Collins, London.

Serengeti Home (1985), written and published by Kay Turner.

The Serengeti — Land of Endless Space (1989), by Lisa and Sven-Olof Lindblad, published by Elm Tree Books, London.

Swara: East African Wildlife Magazine, Vol11 No5 (1988), Vol12 No6 (1989), published by the East African Wildlife Society, Nairobi.

Tanzania: A Country Study (1978), published by American University, Washington, DC.

Tanzania at a Glance (1989), published by the Tanzanian Information Services, Dar es Salaam.

Tanzania Today (1968), written and published by University Press of Africa, Nairobi.

Tarangire National Park (1986), published by the African Wildlife Foundation and Tanzania National Parks, Arusha.

Traveller's Guide to Africa (1974), published by African Development and the African Contemporary Record, London.

Travellers' Guide to East Africa (1980), written and published by Thornton Cox, London.

The Tree Where Man Was Born (1972), by Peter Matthiessen, published by Collins, London.

Welcome to Zanzibar (1989), published by the Zanzibar Tourist Corporation, Zanzibar.

The White Nile (1983), by Alan Moorehead, published by Penguin, London.

Wild Lives (1989), by Doreen Wolfson McColaugh, published by the African Wildlife Foundation, Nairobi.

Zanzibar: Tradition and Revolution (1978), by Esmond Martin, published by Hamish Hamilton, London.